International Law in Asia

This series aims to provide the latest perspectives on international law in this ever changing region of Asia. Each book of this series will address specific aspect of highly contemporary global issues such as armed conflict, maritime disputes, human rights and refugee crises, sustainable development/climate change, outer space, finance and economy, trade (WTO and FTA), investment, development, technology, intellectual property, international crime, global health, regional questions, etc.

This book series invites leading international law scholars and practitioners in Asia to contribute their expertise in interpreting a wide range of legal questions that arise in relation to the above topics through an Asian lens. This series will serve as useful guide for international lawyers, diplomats, businessmen and students to understand current and future trends of international law in Asia.

Haifeng Deng

Green Energy Transition in China

Legal Challenges and Responses to the New Power System and Energy Internet

Springer

Haifeng Deng
School of Law
Tsinghua University
Beijing, China

ISSN 2731-8044 ISSN 2731-8052 (electronic)
International Law in Asia
ISBN 978-981-97-2933-3 ISBN 978-981-97-2934-0 (eBook)
https://doi.org/10.1007/978-981-97-2934-0

This Springer imprint is published by the registered company Springer Nature Singapore Pte Ltd.
The registered company address is: 152 Beach Road, #21-01/04 Gateway East, Singapore 189721, Singapore

Preface

After years of industrialization and economic growth at the expense of the environment, China has identified green energy transition as the essential path to achieving high-quality and low-carbon development in the future. In the process of green energy transition, the power system, serving as a fundamental carrier of secondary energy, plays a pivotal role. It is not only one of the core infrastructures of modern society but also a significant bottleneck in China's pursuit of achieving its "dual carbon" goals. Therefore, the green upgrade of the power system to a new energy system and the transition from traditional grid companies to Energy Internet companies have become key for China to fulfill its international commitments to climate change and to realize sustainable economic and social development. Based on this context, this book is intended to offer insights into the academic debates and legal issues that China may face in the process of green energy transition. It focuses on exploring the key legal challenges and potential solutions for the electricity sector, grid companies, and various stakeholders involved in the construction of new power systems and the development of the Energy Internet. The publication of this book is anticipated to positively contribute to the international discourse by presenting China's endeavors to tackle climate change and progress toward green energy transition through scholarly theoretical perspectives.

This book can be logically divided into theoretical and practical sections. The theoretical section focuses on macro-level fields such as the "Energy Internet" transition, "new power system" upgrades, and the "market-oriented regulation" of the electricity industry in the context of green energy transition. The Energy Internet is a new form of energy industry development that deeply integrates the Internet with energy production, transmission, storage, consumption, and the energy market. Built on electricity and prioritizing renewable energy sources, the Energy Internet optimizes the allocation of material, energy, information, business, and capital flows through multi-energy collaboration, supply and consumption collaboration, and centralized and distributed collaboration. In the development of the Energy Internet, the following legal risks need to be addressed: First, the development of Energy Internet companies relies on platforms, and in the process of transitioning to platform-based models, legal risks related to market access, unfair competition, and intellectual property protection must be considered. Second, in the era of information technology, the application of data as an empowering field for the development of the Energy Internet faces multiple challenges due to unclearly defined rules, necessitating the establishment of fundamental rules regarding data ownership, circulation, and transactions. Third, as grid companies are among the targets of mixed-ownership reform, it is necessary to clarify their functional positioning, that is, to define the industrial sectors that are wholly state-owned, the sectors where mixed ownership is implemented, and the scope for the entry of private capital.

The practical section aims to provide path selection and institutional support for the green and low-carbon transition of China's power system by identifying legal risks in the key operational aspects of new power systems and the Energy Internet, and through specific case studies. The construction of a new type of power system involves the construction and operation of new energy sources, the development and application of related technologies, the diversification of market trading varieties, the exploration of multiple trading rules, and the compliant operation of various market entities. The compliant operation of these scenarios requires a systematic and rigorous legal and regulatory framework for protection. To address this, the book selects three representative legal issues in the construction of new power systems for interpretation: legal issues related to long-term management of the new power system, electricity demand-side management, and energy storage construction.

As an emerging field, energy law research in China is still in its infancy. Therefore, there are relatively few legislative and academic research achievements related to power and energy transition, which poses a significant challenge for the writing of this book. The motivation for writing this book stems from the academic researches on the State Grid Corporation of China (SGCC) in 2019. I would like to extend my heartfelt gratitude to SGCC, State Grid Zhejiang Electric Power Co., Ltd., and the Konrad Adenauer Foundation of Germany for their generous support and the numerous conveniences they provided, which greatly facilitated the writing of this book. I would like to thank Konrad Adenauer Stiftung (KAS), Rule of Law Programme Asia for supporting the translation of the book and KAS will not receive any form of royalties out from the sale of the book. I would also like to express my heartfelt appreciation to Springer Nature for their selfless assistance in the publication of academic works. It is with the sincere help of institutions like yours, possessing a sense of social responsibility and academic dedication, that this work has been successfully published.

I look forward to my work providing some information and assistance to the academic and practical communities both in China and abroad in understanding the progress of China's green energy transition. I am eager to join colleagues from around the world in our joint efforts to contribute to the sustainable development of our planet.

Beijing, China
March 2024

Haifeng Deng

Acknowledgement Sincere thanks to the Social Science Special Project of Tsinghua University's Independent Research Program (2023THZWHQ02) for the support of this book.

Declaration of Competing Interests

The author declared no potential conflicts of interest or personal relationships that could have appeared to influence the research or publication of this book.

About This Book

As an advanced form of energy system development, the Energy Internet is crucial to promoting China's energy transition and building a clean, low-carbon, safe, and efficient energy system. In September 2020, President Xi Jinping proposed the goal of having CO_2 emissions peak before 2030 and achieving carbon neutrality before 2060 at the general debate of the United Nations General Assembly. See Xinhua News Agency (2020). In March 2021, General Secretary Xi Jinping reiterated the objective of carbon neutrality at the ninth meeting of the Central Financial and Economic Affairs Commission. The "3060 Goal" represents a broad and profound systemic transformation of the economic and social system, which is related to the sustainable development of the Chinese nation and the construction of a community with a shared future for humanity. The "14th Five-Year Plan" period is a critical time for achieving CO_2 emissions peak. During this crucial period, building a clean, low-carbon, safe, and efficient energy system, improving energy efficiency, accelerating energy transition, and constructing a new type of power system with new energy as the main body are both the development goals of the Energy Internet platform and a lofty historical mission. See Xinhua News Agency (2021).

References

Xinhua News Agency (2020) Statement by H. E. Xi Jinping President of the People's Republic of China at the General Debate of the 75th Session of the United Nations General Assembly. Retrieved January 5, 2024, from http://www.cppcc.gov.cn/zxww/2020/09/23/ARTI1600819264410115.shtml

Xinhua News Agency (2021) Xi Jinping Presides Over the Ninth Meeting of the Central Financial and Economic Affairs Commission. Retrieved January 5, 2024, from https://www.gov.cn/xinwen/2021-03/15/content_5593154.htm

Contents

Abbreviations

Administrative Compulsion Law	Administrative Compulsion Law of the People's Republic of China
AGC	Automatic Generation Control
Amendment (IX) to the Criminal Law	Amendment (IX) to the Criminal Law of the People's Republic of China
Anti-Monopoly Law	Anti-Monopoly Law of the People's Republic of China
Anti-Unfair Competition Law	Anti-Unfair Competition Law of the People's Republic of China
AVC	Automatic Voltage Control
BIS	Bank for International Settlements
CAISO	California Independent System Operator
CCCPC	Central Committee of the Communist Party of China
CCHP	Combined Cooling, Heat and Power
CCPA	US California Consumer Privacy Act
CFIUS	Committee on Foreign Investment in the United States
CHP	Combined Heat and Power
Civil Code	Civil Code of the People's Republic of China
CLOUD Act	Clarifying Lawful Overseas Use of Data Act
CNIL	Commission on Informatics and Liberty

Criminal Law	Criminal Law of the People's Republic of China
Cybersecurity Law	Cybersecurity Law of the People's Republic of China
Data Security Law	Data Security Law of the People's Republic of China
DSM	Demand-Side Management
EEA	European Economic Area
EGN	Energy Global Network
ELAN	Energy Local Area Network
Electric Power Law	Electric Power Law of the People's Republic of China
EMC	Energy Management Contracts
EMCA	ESCO Committee of China Energy Conservation Association
Energy Law (Draft for Comments)	Energy Law of the People's Republic of China (Draft for Comments)
Environment Impact Assessment Law	Law of the People's Republic of China on Environment Impact Assessment
EVs	Electric Vehicles
EWAN	Energy Wide Area Network
FERC	Federal Energy Regulatory Commission
Fire Protection Law	Fire Protection Law of the People's Republic of China
Flood Control Law (2016)	Flood Control Law of the People's Republic of China (Revised in 2016)
FREEDM	Future Renewable Electric Energy Delivery and Management
GAQSIQ	General Administration of Quality Supervision, Inspection, and Quarantine of the People's Republic of China
GDPR	General Data Protection Regulation
General Principles of the Civil Law	General Principles of the Civil Law of the People's Republic of China
GIS	Geographic Information System
ICANN	The Internet Corporation for Assigned Names and Numbers

ICO	Information Commissioner's Office
IES	Integrated Energy System
Insurance Law	Insurance Law of the People's Republic of China
IoT	Internet of Things
IoV	Internet of Vehicle
IPOs	Initial Public Offerings
IPPs	Independent Power Producers
IRENA	The International Renewable Energy Agency
ISO	The Independent System Operator
KAS	Konrad Adenauer Stiftung
LA	Load Aggregator
Labor Contract Law	Labor Contract Law of the People's Republic of China
LGPD	Brazil's General Data Protection Regulation
LNG	Liquefied Natural Gas
LPG	Liquefied Petroleum Gas
MEE	Ministry of Ecology and Environment
MEM	Ministry of Emergency Management
MHURD	Ministry of Housing and Urban-Rural Development of the People's Republic of China
MIIT	Ministry of Industry and Information Technology
MLPS 2.0	Multi-Level Protection Scheme 2.0
NCCPC	National Congress of the Communist Party of China
NDRC	National Development and Reform Commission of China
NEA	National Energy Administration of China
P2G	Power-to-Gas
PbD	Privacy by Design
Platform Economy Anti-Monopoly Guidelines	Guidelines of the Anti-monopoly Commission of the State Council for Anti-monopoly in the Field of Platform Economy
PPP	Public-Private Partnership

PV	Photovoltaic
QQIR	Quality, Quantity, Innovation, Risk
RAA	Registrar Authorization Agreement
Renewable Energy Law	Renewable Energy Law of the People's Republic of China
RTOs	Regional Transmission Organizations
SAMR	State Administration for Market Regulation
SASAC	State-owned Assets Supervision and Administration Commission of the State Council
Securities Law	Securities Law of the People's Republic of China
SERC	State Electricity Regulatory Commission
SGCC	State Grid Corporation of China
Shenzhen Data Regulations	Regulations of Shenzhen Special Economic Zone on Data
STA	State Taxation Administration of China
UHV	Ultra-High Voltage
V2G	Vehicle-to-Grid
VAT	Value-Added Tax
VPP	Virtual Power Plant
Water Law (2016)	Water Law of the People's Republic of China (Revised in 2016)
Work Safety Law	Work Safety Law of the People's Republic of China

Chapter 1
Overview of Energy Internet

Definitions of Energy Internet

Foreign Definitions of Energy Internet

In the 1970s, the concept of Energy Internet began to emerge. In 1986, Peter Meisen founded the Global Energy Network Institute, aiming to fully utilize renewable resources on a global scale through power transmission lines between countries. In 2004, The *Economist* first proposed the construction of an intelligent, automated, and self-healing Energy Internet based on the characteristics and technology of the Internet, marking the beginning of modern Energy Internet research.[1]

Countries began to put Energy Internet projects into practice. In 2008, Germany launched the E-Energy project to realize the intelligence of the entire chain of energy production, transmission, conversion, application, and storage through information and communication technology, becoming the first country to practice the Energy Internet. In 2008, the United States initiated the "Future Renewable Electric Energy Delivery and Management Systems" (hereinafter referred to as the "FREEDM Systems") project, researching efficient and intelligent distribution systems to support the integration of distributed renewable energy sources and the grid connection of distributed energy storage. In 2010, Japan implemented the "Digital Grid" plan, where various devices in the energy network would use IP to realize the transmission of information and energy.[2]

Perceptions of the Energy Internet vary in different countries/regions in their research and application of the Energy Internet, encompassing four variants: First, Energy Internet. This variant prioritizes the structure of the energy network, particularly the power grid. By drawing on the principles of openness and peer-to-peer of the Internet, it creates a new energy network through large-scale grids, microgrids,

[1] See Gao et al. (2018).

[2] Same as above.

H. Deng, *Green Energy Transition in China*, International Law in Asia,
https://doi.org/10.1007/978-981-97-2934-0_1

and other forms of interconnected networks, with a key emphasis on developing a distributed energy network architecture that integrates information and communication systems. Second, Internet of Energy. This variant prioritizes the information Internet and uses the Internet to collect, analyze, and make decisions to guide the operation of the energy network. Third, Intenergy. This variant emphasizes the deep integration of Internet technology and energy networks, facilitating two-way communication between energy and information, with the information support system guiding energy dispatch and energy flows directing user decisions to efficiently utilize renewable energy. Fourth, Multi-Energy Internet. This variant focuses on the joint transmission and optimized use of multiple energy sources.[3]

China's Definition of Energy Internet

"Built on a robust and intelligent power grid platform, Energy Internet is a smart power-centered energy system that deeply integrates and applies advanced communication technology, control technology and advanced energy technology to support the clean and low-carbon transition of energy and power, optimize the comprehensive utilization efficiency of energy, and facilitate flexible and convenient access for multiple entities. It is clean and low-carbon, safe and reliable, ubiquitously connected, efficient and interactive, and intelligent and open."[4] The Energy Internet is a developing concept with rich connotation and extension and strong inclusiveness. It represents a higher stage in the development of energy and power systems. Technically, the Energy Internet accelerates the realization of technological progress and integrated development. Advanced information and communication technologies such as "big data, cloud computing, the Internet of Things (IoT), mobile Internet, and blockchain" are widely and deeply applied in energy and power systems. Energy Internet technologies such as multi-energy conversion technology, coordinated operation technology, and user interaction technology are comprehensively upgraded, making the system characterized by digitalization, automation, and intelligence. Structurally, the Energy Internet has a strong and widespread network framework. Centralized energy systems, distributed energy systems, various energy storage facilities, and all types of users are interconnected in a user-friendly manner. Different energy systems are interconnected and support each other, and they develop in integration with social systems. Functionally, the Energy Internet has powerful resource allocation and service support capabilities. It effectively supports the large-scale development and utilization of renewable energy and the "plug and play" of various energy facilities. It achieves coordinated interaction between "source, grid, load, and storage," ensuring personalized, integrated, and intelligent service demands, and promotes the development of new energy business forms and models.[5]

[3] See Ma et al. (2015).

[4] Zhu and Zhi (2020, November 11).

[5] See Yang (2020, May 12).

The functional architecture of the Energy Internet has three layers, namely the physical foundation layer, the information application layer, and the market transaction layer. The physical foundation layer refers to a multi-energy collaborative energy network that integrates the power network with gas networks, heat networks, cooling networks, and other energy networks to facilitate the conversion and storage between various types of energy including electricity, gas, heat, and cooling, thereby improving the flexibility of user-side energy consumption. The information application layer refers to the cyber-physical energy system that utilizes massive information collection technology, energy information transmission technology, and the integration technology of information and physical energy systems to tap into the immense value of information data in the energy sector. The market transaction layer involves innovating energy operation models by leveraging the Internet and prioritizing user needs to enhance value creation. This layer fosters the development of various business models on commercial Internet platforms, including B2C, B2B, C2C, O2O, and P2P.[6]

The physical form of the Energy Internet is divided into three levels: Energy Local Area Network (ELAN), Energy Wide Area Network (EWAN), and Energy Global Network (EGN). ELAN is also known as the distributed integrated energy system (IES). Based on microgrids, ELAN integrates various networks such as heat, cooling, water, and gas to use local clean energy resources first while also considering purchased energy. EWAN utilizes ELANs as its foundational nodes, linking them through power grid, pipeline network, and transportation infrastructure to create a wide area interconnection across these nodes. EGN is achieved through the integration of multiple networks, including energy networks (transnational power grids, oil and gas pipelines), information networks (the Internet, private networks), and transportation networks (transnational highways, railways, waterways, etc.), to optimize the allocation of material, energy, information, business, and capital flows on a global scale.[7]

Characteristics of the Energy Internet

According to the "Guiding Opinions on Promoting Internet Plus Smart Energy Development" (Fa Gai Neng Yuan [2016] No. 392) issued by China in 2016, the Internet Plus smart energy, also known as the Energy Internet, is a new form of energy industry development that deeply integrates the Internet with energy production, transmission, storage, consumption, and the energy market. It is characterized by intelligent equipment, multi-energy coordination, information symmetry, decentralized supply and demand, a flat system structure, and open trading. Since electricity occupies an important position in the current energy system and China has formed a large-scale electric power transmission network, the power system has evolved to exhibit characteristics

[6] See Gao et al. (2018).

[7] Same as above.

akin to those of the Internet. Therefore, the Energy Internet is based on electricity and prioritizes renewable energy, aiming to optimize the allocation of material, energy, information, business, and capital flows through multi-energy collaboration, supply and consumption collaboration, and centralized and distributed collaboration. The power grid becomes the core platform for energy transition and utilization and serves as the key physical foundation for the Energy Internet.[8]

The Energy Internet is characterized by being clean and low-carbon, safe and reliable, ubiquitously connected, efficient and interactive, and intelligent and open. Clean and low-carbon: Green and environmentally friendly practices in all aspects of energy production, transmission, and consumption, adapting to a high proportion of clean energy integration, and achieving full absorption of clean energy. Safe and reliable: The energy grid structure is robust, with secure information networks and data operations, strong capabilities for accident risk prevention and self-healing, ensuring stable and reliable energy supply. Ubiquitous connected: Energy networks are widely distributed, with various centralized and distributed facilities and entities widely accessed. Cross-region and cross-energy systems are interconnected and support each other, and they develop in integration with information systems and social systems. Efficient and interactive: High efficiency in energy allocation and comprehensive utilization, good economic benefits, multi-energy complementation, source-grid-load-storage coordination, and friendly interaction among various entities. Intelligent and open: The Energy Internet possesses capabilities such as sensitive perception, intelligent decision-making, and precise control. It has a high level of digitalization and intelligence. Various facilities are "plug and play," serving the diverse needs of users, promoting market openness, and creating a win–win ecosystem.[9]

References

Gao F, Zeng R, Qu L, Zhang J (2018) Research on identification of concept and characteristics of energy internet. Electr Power 51(8):10–16. https://doi.org/10.11930/j.issn.1004-9649.201806095

Ma Z, Zhou X, Shang Y, Sheng W (2015) Exploring the concept, key technologies and development model of energy internet. Power Syst Technol 39(11):3014–3022. https://doi.org/10.13335/j.1000-3673.pst.2015.11.002

Yang S (2020, May 12) Interactive regulation of 'source-grid-load-storage'—the intelligent brain of the energy internet. State Grid News 3417:8

Zhu Y, Zhi T (2020, November 11) State grid's answer to energy transition—observations from the 2020 international forum on energy transition. China Electric Power News 7754:3

[8] Same as above.

[9] See Yang (2020, May 12).

Chapter 2
Business Models of Energy Internet Companies

Energy Internet companies typically use three business models: "IoT+", "Internet+" and "Energy+". The "IoT+" business model is often used in the new energy industry, energy storage industry, electric vehicle industry, power equipment industry, energy-saving products, and the research and development of intelligent devices. The "Internet+" business model combines energy development with Internet technology, resulting in new models that include electric power services, digital power, data services, information integration, and financial services. The "Energy+" business model mainly focuses on three modules: the power trading industry module, the intelligent microgrid industry module, and the Virtual Power Plant (VPP) module. The power trading industry module takes power trading as its core and adopts market competition for energy supply and demand. The intelligent microgrid industry module centers on energy management, with main business models including micro-grid planning and construction, operational management, energy services, value-added services, etc. The VPP module aims to smooth the load curve on the demand side, increase the load factor, and enhance energy utilization.[1]

The VPP Business Model

The VPP is a new generation of intelligent control technology and interactive business model that aggregates and optimizes the clean development of "source-grid-load-storage." Based on the traditional power grid physical structure, this technical model uses the Internet and modern information and communication technologies to aggregate various resources in the power grid, such as distributed power supplies, energy storage, and loads, for coordinated optimization of operational control and market transactions. It enables multi-energy complementarity on the supply side and

[1] Yu et al. (2019).

H. Deng, *Green Energy Transition in China*, International Law in Asia,
https://doi.org/10.1007/978-981-97-2934-0_2

flexible interaction on the load side and provides the grid with ancillary services such as peak shaving, frequency regulation, and standby, offering a viable solution for the efficient utilization of distributed clean energy sources.[2]

Grid companies carry out commercial operations of VPPs with a "one platform + multiple applications" architecture and aggregate a variety of adjustable resources, including thermal storage electric boilers, smart buildings, smart homes, user-side energy storage, adjustable industrial and commercial loads, and distributed PV in various pilot areas. Through this approach, grid companies establish a business model that involves multiple market participants, including integrated energy service providers, ancillary service suppliers, energy aggregators, and electricity sales companies and further create a VPP ecosystem. This unleashes new vitality in the energy economy on the user side, integrating a broad range of adjustable resources into the grid's optimized scheduling and real-time closed-loop control, thereby enhancing the grid's flexible adjustment capabilities, and promoting the consumption of new energy.

The Energy Big Data Business Model

"In the era of Energy Internet, energy systems are constantly generating, collecting, storing, and processing massive amounts of data. Big data follows the new Moore's Law and shows exponential explosive growth. People have begun to value data, and data-centric business models will play an important role in the Energy Internet, providing innovative services through the added value of information."[3] For example, a grid company carries out data value-added services based on energy big data to drive the digital transformation of the grid and the company, comprehensively improve the company's data management and value service capabilities, and build an integrated "source-grid-load-storage-use" energy data chain with the grid as the hub.[4]

The energy big data product and service models of Energy Internet companies can be roughly divided into five categories: basic data, decision support, platform application, solution, and win–win cooperation (ecological co-construction). Basic data services gather data such as company user energy consumption data, system operation data, and equipment and environmental monitoring data and use them to create basic data products through cleaning, clustering, desensitization, and other data analysis processing. These services also provide data APIs for users to directly query and download related basic data. Decision support services analyze data market demand and potential by taking into consideration the source channels and value segmentations of Energy Internet companies' power big data to form a series of non-targeted analytical reports and special reports. The analytical reports are mainly aimed at the general public, focusing on the patterns of energy and power development, analysis

---

[2] See State Grid Corporation of China (2018).

[3] Lv (2017).

[4] Wang et al. (2020), pp. 90–92.

of societal electricity consumption, analysis, and prediction of household electricity usage behaviors, etc. The special reports are mainly aimed at companies and government users, focusing on the analysis of energy consumption data of industries, fields, and regions that are of interest to the customers. Platform operation services identify the unique market value data (such as user product categories, behavioral characteristics, and product preferences) by analyzing companies' power big data and build service platforms to facilitate smooth connections between various product suppliers and between suppliers and consumers, creating value channels and providing users with precision marketing, information services, advertising services, and more. Solution services offer tailed solutions to cater specifically to the customized needs of government and company users based on companies' data asset value characteristics and generate revenue. Win–win cooperation services aim to deeply collaborate with data supply units, industrial Internet-related units, consumer Internet-related units, and public utilities to form a collection of datasets including energy consumption, geography, business, transportation, finance, and medical treatment. By deeply utilizing internal and external data, they accurately portray target users in multiple dimensions, and serve government and enterprise customers with desensitized data.[5]

New Energy and Energy Internet Energy-Saving Management Model

There are five major types of new energy sources: Firstly, wind power generation, for which China has introduced a range of supportive policies, with offshore wind power expected to become a future development trend. Secondly, solar PV power generation, which currently includes two main types of domestic PV power stations: ground-mounted stations and distributed PV stations. Thirdly, biomass power generation, where technology is continuously maturing and trends toward diversification, direct combustion, co-firing, and gasification are evident. Fourthly, nuclear energy, which mainly uses nuclear fission to release massive amounts of energy for power generation, with significant potential for future nuclear power development. Lastly, new energy for vehicles, referring to the power sources used in new energy vehicles, including power lithium batteries, nickel-metal hydride batteries, hydrogen fuel cells, and supercapacitors. New energy vehicles will become a crucial gateway for the integration of the Energy Internet with new energy sources. Firstly, during the charging process, electric vehicles need to exchange information with the charging station to control the charging current, which allows for the collection of data from the electric vehicles. Secondly, electric vehicles act both as a load on the power system and as an external device for energy storage and distributed power sources, connecting the power system with distributed energy storage devices or power sources.

Energy-saving management services for Energy Internet companies are part of the energy service industry. They involve the establishment of energy monitoring and

[5] See Wang et al. (2021).

control platforms and the use of sampling monitoring technology, communication technology, and computer software and hardware technology to monitor and manage the consumption of resources such as water, electricity, heat, and gas. Their service targets include industrial energy-saving systems and home energy-saving systems. The management of the industrial energy-saving systems involves real-time collection, computational analysis, and centralized dispatch of energy used in production, so as to meet the requirements of supply–demand balance and energy-saving and environmental protection. The management of home energy-saving systems involves real-time monitoring, data collection, statistical analysis, and other steps to achieve refined management of energy consumption and provide energy-saving solutions. Energy-saving management services will also provide data support for the development of industries such as equipment preparation and energy-saving renovation.[6]

Energy Storage Services

In 2017, the National Development and Reform Commission, the National Energy Administration, and three other authorities jointly issued the "Guiding Opinions on Promoting the Development of Energy Storage Technology and Industry," which calls for the exploration of several replicable business models, the cultivation of a number of competitive market entities, and the promotion of the energy storage industry to the initial commercialization stage.

Energy storage systems can participate in frequency regulation ancillary services by working with thermal power units. Power plants collaborate with energy storage companies in the business model of energy performance contracting, where the power plants provide the site, access for energy storage, and the qualifications for participating in the frequency regulation market, while the energy storage companies are responsible for investment, design, construction, operation, and maintenance. The incremental revenue from frequency regulation is shared between both parties.[7] Energy storage systems can also participate in peak-shaving ancillary services, which is particularly beneficial in the "Three North" regions of China—areas known for difficulties in integrating new energy sources and a lack of peak load regulation capabilities. Energy storage users can either partner with thermal, wind, or solar power plants for joint peak-shaving efforts or operate independently as market participants to offer peak-shaving services directly to the power grid. Energy storage users participating in peak shaving can bid for ancillary service transactions on the peak-shaving ancillary service platform. The compensation for peak-shaving is shared among thermal power plants, wind farms, PV power stations, and hydroelectric plants in accordance with policy requirements.[8]

[6] Hua (2015).

[7] See Zhang et al. (2018).

[8] See Peng (2018).

China is currently vigorously developing the new energy electric vehicle industry, which inevitably requires a significant enhancement of the charging service capabilities supporting electric vehicles. The large-scale construction of new charging piles will impose a heavy burden on conventional transformers and transmission and distribution lines. Therefore, it is necessary to build a certain amount of energy storage devices at charging stations to reduce the need for transformer capacity expansion and delay the need for upgrading transmission and distribution. Constructing energy storage stations at charging stations can also play a role in peak shaving and valley filling.

Power Trading Platforms

Energy-trading platforms offer wholesale and retail of electricity, VPPs, gas sales, heating services, purchasing and reselling of electricity for electric vehicles, etc. Energy-trading platforms provide not only spot trading but also forward contracts, futures contracts, and options contracts, creating a diversified financial trading environment. Over 30 power trading organizations have been set up throughout China at both the national and provincial levels. Among these, there are two national power trading organizations, one of which is the Beijing Power Trading Center established based on the State Grid.

In 2015, China issued the "Implementation Opinions on the Establishment and Standardized Operation of Power Trading Organizations," which clearly defines the functional positioning of power trading platforms: to provide standardized, open, and transparent power trading services for market entities under government regulation without the purpose of profit. The trading organizations are responsible for the construction, operation and management of the market trading platform, organization of market transactions, provision of settlement basis and related services, collection of bilateral contracts independently signed by power users and power generators, registration and management of market entities, disclosure, and release of market information, etc. Power generators, power sellers, and power users that are approved by competent governments register and trade on the platforms. Grid companies are shareholders of the trading platforms, but the operation of these platforms must be independent of the grid companies. Grid companies can also trade on the trading platforms.[9] The "Implementation Opinions on Promoting the Reform of the Power Selling Side" specify three types of power sellers, with the first type being grid companies. As the hubs of China's power transmission and distribution systems, grid companies shall ensure the security of power transactions. This includes

[9] National Development and Reform Commission, & National Energy Administration. Notice on Issuing Supporting Documents for the Power System Reform (Fa Gai Jing Ti [2015] No. 2752), Annex 3, Implementation Opinions on the Establishment and Standardized Operation of Power Trading Organizations.

providing non-discriminatory power supply services to market entities, offering guaranteed power supply services, ensuring the fair, non-discriminatory, and open grid, and shifting from provision of the fair, non-discriminatory, and open grid for power generators to provision of such a grid to power sellers and their proprietary users.[10]

Integrated Energy Services

Integrated energy services refer to both the integration of various types of energy (including electricity, gas, etc.) and the integration of services (including engineering services, investment services, operation services, etc.). The core of integrated energy services is network collaboration and data intelligence. Network collaboration requires an open, multilateral, complex market to form a multi-dimensional open ecosystem, while data intelligence needs to utilize big data technology to provide services with data collection and analysis. In 2019, China's first national integrated energy service online platform—Jiangsu Energy Cloud Network Platform—was officially launched. The platform gathers capital, technology, channels and talents from various fields, as well as energy users, energy suppliers and service providers, government agencies, universities and scientific research institutions, offering open and shared integrated energy services to all sectors of society.[11]

The integrated energy services platform includes Smart Energy Usage, Expert Services, Alliance Channel, Industry Information, Cloud Network Marketplace, and other sections. In the Smart Energy Usage section, energy customers can query real-time information on electricity load, consumption, and costs, receive customized power outage notifications, and access information on market-based electricity sales, demand response, distributed energy, energy storage, and more. This section also provides customized energy efficiency evaluation reports and improvement solutions for customers in different industries and regularly pushes energy efficiency diagnosis reports to these customers. The Expert Services section gathers energy service experts to provide instant and accurate professional consultation for the personalized issues of energy customers, helping them to analyze and solve problems. The Industry Information section provides the latest policies, technologies and other information in the integrated energy field as well as expert analysis, serving as a resource for various entities to learn advanced technologies and the latest policies.[12]

[10] National Development and Reform Commission, & National Energy Administration. Notice on Issuing Supporting Documents for the Power System Reform (Fa Gai Jing Ti [2015] No. 2752), Annex 5, Implementation Opinions on Promoting the Reform of the Power Selling Side.

[11] See Huang et al. (2019).

[12] Same as above.

References

Hua P (2015) Energy internet: business model is the key. Wind Energy 2015(3):22–28. https://doi.org/10.3969/j.issn.1674-9219.2015.03.006

Huang L, Zhang X (2019, September 24) Jiangsu energy cloud network platform officially launched—the 'energy efficiency check-up' expert arrives. State Grid News 3263:5

Lv M (2017) Re-examining the energy industry from the perspective of the internet. Energy 2017(4):32–35

Peng M (2018) Analysis of the application prospects of energy storage technology in power systems. Popular Utilization Electr 32(12):21

State Grid Corporation of China (2018) The proposal for IEC VPP international standards initiated by state grid corporation of china approved for project establishment. Telecom Power Technol 2018(1):160

Wang X, Wang Y (2020) Analysis report on domestic and international energy internet development. China Electric Power Press

Wang X, Chen A, Li J, Zheng C, Pan X, Yang Z (2021) Research on data business operation mode based on energy big data center. Distrib Utilization 38(4):37–42. https://doi.org/10.19421/j.cnki.1006-6357.2021.04.007

Yu X, Tan Z, Qu G (2019) Exploration for power business model and key technologies under condition of energy internet. Smart Power 47(2):9–14, 36. https://doi.org/10.3969/j.issn.1673-7598.2019.02.002

Zhang S, Jiao H (2018, April 10) Exploring the key to the three major application fields of energy storage. China Reform Daily 6532:5

Chapter 3
Researches on Legal Risks and Regulatory Policies for the Platform-Based Transformation of Energy Internet Companies

Regulatory Laws and Policies for the Transformation of Platform-Based Energy Internet Companies

The legal risks associated with the transformation of platform-based Energy Internet companies mainly pertain to the market access of such enterprises, energy-saving management for new and existing Energy Internet companies, regulation of energy storage, construction of power trading platforms, the establishment of integrated energy service platforms, etc. In order to sort out the legal risks associated with the platform-based transformation of Energy Internet companies, it is necessary to analyze and organize the current laws, regulations, and policies on the development of platform-based Energy Internet companies at home and abroad. In view of this, this section will first sort out China's regulatory laws and policies for Energy Internet companies, including the negative list system for market access, non-discriminatory access to the energy industry, the fair, non-discriminatory, open grid, etc. Secondly, this section will analyze the regulatory laws and policies for energy-saving management models of renewable energy and Energy Internet companies, including the regulatory laws and policies related to the grid-connected operation of renewable energy, energy-saving management business, energy storage services, power trading platforms, electric vehicle charging stations, integrated energy service platforms, as well as deepening the reform of the investment and financing system in the energy sector. Finally, this section will analyze the Energy Internet business models and regulatory laws and policies of Germany, the United States, and Japan from the perspective of comparative law.

H. Deng, *Green Energy Transition in China*, International Law in Asia,
https://doi.org/10.1007/978-981-97-2934-0_3

Regulatory Laws and Policies for the Transformation of China's Platform-Based Energy Internet Companies

Regulatory Laws and Policies for the Non-discriminatory Access Mechanism of the Energy Internet

(1) The Negative List System for Market Access

The implementation of a non-discriminatory access mechanism in the Energy Internet does not mean that the access restrictions for various energy entities are completely removed. Instead, all energy entities are still required to comply with the relevant access regulations of the energy market. These regulations are reflected in the negative list system for market access, which specifies prohibited items and permitted items.

In the document "Prohibitive Rules Related to Market Access" that accompanies the "Negative List for Market Access (2022 Edition)—Prohibited Category", specific provisions for energy access are made within the section on "Electricity, Heat, Gas and Water Production, and Supply Industries":

29. It is prohibited to construct new coal-fired power generation units, oil-fired power generation units, and coal-fired thermal power units that do not comply with national regulations.

31. In regions such as Beijing-Tianjin-Hebei, the Yangtze River Delta, and the Pearl River Delta, new projects are prohibited from constructing supporting self-supplied coal-fired power stations; it is also prohibited for public power plants to illegally convert to self-supplied power plants.

According to the "Negative List for Market Access (2022 Edition)—Permitted Category":

38. Do not Engage in Specific Businesses in the Fields of Electricity and Municipal Public Utilities Without a Permit.

101. Do not invest in or construct specific energy projects such as hydropower stations, thermal power stations, combined heat and power stations, and grid projects without a permit.

(2) Non-discriminatory Access to the Energy Industry

In addition to the energy market access regulations, China has also specifically established regulations for non-discriminatory energy access. The "Opinions on Further Deepening the Reform of the Power System" (Zhong Fa [2015] No. 9) stipulates that the key tasks for advancing the reform of the power system include "promoting the reform of the power trading system and improving the market-oriented trading mechanisms," and "steadily advancing the reform of the power selling side, and orderly opening up the distribution and sale of power business to social capital." The "Implementation Opinions on Orderly Opening Up of Power Generation and Consumption Plans" provides guidelines for establishing, regulating, and perfecting the direct trading mechanism and defines the scope of access for users and power generation.[1]

(3) Fair, Non-discriminatory, and Open Grid

According to the "Energy Law of the People's Republic of China (draft for comments)," the fair access mechanisms for energy transmission pipeline network facilities such as grids and oil and gas pipeline networks shall be perfected to allow qualified energy production and sales companies and other market entities to access in a fair and non-discriminatory manner. According to the "Implementation Opinions on Promoting the Reform of the Power Selling Side," grid companies shall provide various types of power supply services to market entities and their users without discrimination, ensuring a fair, non-discriminatory, and open grid. The "Guiding Opinions on Promoting Internet Plus Smart Energy Development" (Fa Gai Neng Yuan [2016] No. 392) states that the basic principles of the development of the Energy Internet are "making infrastructures available and allowing public participation."

In September 2021, the National Energy Administration issued the "Measures for the Supervision of a Fair and Open Grid," which stipulates that a fair, non-discriminatory, and open grid shall be provided in two ways: Firstly, grid companies shall provide fair and non-discriminatory grid access services to power generation projects; and secondly, grid companies shall provide fair and non-discriminatory grid-connection services, particularly integrated grid-connection services to local grids, incremental distribution networks, and microgrids.[2]

Regulatory Laws and Policies for Energy-Saving Management Models of Renewable Energy and Energy Internet Companies

(1) Regulatory Laws and Policies for the Grid-Connected Operation of Renewable Energy

The "Opinions on Further Deepening the Reform of the Power System" (Zhong Fa [2015] No. 9) specify in "improving grid-connected operation services" that efforts shall be actively made to promote the effective integration of power generation of new energy and renewable energy with other grids. In 2019, the National Energy Administration of China issued two notices: "Notice on Actively Promoting Subsidy-Free Grid Parity for Wind and Photovoltaic Power Generation" (Fa Gai Neng Yuan [2019] No. 19) and "Notice on Matters Related to the Construction of Wind and Photovoltaic Power Generation Projects in 2019" (Guo Neng Fa Xin Neng [2019] No. 49). These notices introduce bidding for subsidies as an innovation in the management

---

[1] National Development and Reform Commission, and National Energy Administration. Notice on Issuing Supporting Documents for the Power System Reform (Fa Gai Jing Ti [2015] No. 2752), Annex 4, Implementation Opinions on Orderly Opening Up of Power Generation and Consumption Plans.

[2] National Energy Administration. Measures for the Supervision of a Fair and Open Grid (Guo Neng Fa Jian Guan Gui [2021] No. 49), Articles 7 and 19.

policy for photovoltaic power generation construction, marking the beginning of the era of grid parity for the photovoltaic industry in China.[3]

To promote fair competition in the wind power and photovoltaic industries, the National Development and Reform Commission issued the "Notice on Improving the Feed-in Tariff Mechanism for Photovoltaic Power Generation" (Fa Gai Jia Ge [2019] No. 761) and the "Notice on Improving the Feed-in Tariff Policy for Wind Power Generation" (Fa Gai Jia Ge [2019] No. 882), aimed at advancing the development of new energy power generation. The National Energy Administration issued the "Notice on Improving the Power Trading Mechanism for Wind Power Heating to Expand the Application of Wind Power Heating" (Guo Neng Fa Xin Neng [2019] No. 35), which further expands the application scope and scale of wind power heating, creating new market demands for wind power.

In addition to wind power and solar power, biomass power was also included in the encouraged list. In the "Catalogue for the Guidance on Adjustment of Industrial Structure (2019 Version)," the National Development and Reform Commission has repeatedly emphasized the importance of biomass power generation and bio-natural gas. In 2019, the National Development and Reform Commission and other ministries and commissions issued the "Guiding Opinions on Promoting the Industrialization of Bio-Natural Gas" (Fa Gai Neng Yuan Gui [2019] No. 1895), which incorporates biomass-natural gas into the national energy development strategy.

(2) Regulatory Laws and Policies for Energy-Saving Management Businesses

The "Energy Conservation Law of the People's Republic of China" distinguishes and refines the general provisions on energy conservation and the specific provisions on energy conservation in various industries. According to Article 32 of the Energy Conservation Law, grid companies shall, according to the relevant provisions on the administration of energy conservation and power generation dispatching as set down by the department concerned under the State Council, arrange the incorporation of power generation units that are clean, efficient and complies with provisions into the grid.

In the "Guiding Opinions on Promoting Internet Plus Smart Energy Development" (Fa Gai Neng Yuan [2016] No. 392), the provisions for energy conservation are mainly reflected in "promoting business model innovation in the Energy Internet" and "expanding new models of value-added services for smart energy use."

Regulatory Laws and Policies for Energy Storage Services

In the context of the Energy Internet and with the vision of achieving carbon neutrality, renewable energy will occupy a larger share in the energy consumption structure. However, the intrinsic technical limitations of renewable energy technologies remain unresolved. New energy sources such as solar and wind power are characterized by their randomness, intermittency, and rapid variability in power

[3] Guo and Hu (2020).

generation. The direct grid integration of an extremely large number of these new energy generating units could potentially trigger safety incidents. Therefore, with increasing demand for new energy sources to be integrated into the grid, there is a growing necessity for adjusting energy storage devices in real time. The main role of energy storage is to mitigate the instability of renewable energy generation by shaving off peaks and filling valleys.

The Renewable Energy Law of the People's Republic of China (hereinafter referred to as the "Renewable Energy Law") clearly states the support for the development of the energy storage industry. As specified in paragraph 4 of Article 14, grid companies shall strengthen the construction of the grid, develop and apply smart grid and energy storage technologies, and improve the management of grid operation.

At the strategic level, the "Guiding Opinions on Accelerating the Construction and Transformation of Power Distribution Networks" (Fa Gai Neng Yuan [2015] No. 1899) require to advance pilot projects for the application of energy storage in power distribution networks. The "Energy Technology Revolution and Innovation Action Plan (2016–2030)" (Fa Gai Neng Yuan [2016] No. 513) lists key tasks such as "advanced energy storage technology innovation"; the "Measures for the Electricity Demand-side Management (revised)" (Fa Gai Yun Xing Gui [2017] No. 1690) requires the active development of key technologies such as energy storage and electric energy substitution and the promotion of large-scale friendly interaction between the supply side and the user side.[4]

In February 2016, the National Energy Administration issued the "Guiding Opinions on Promoting Internet Plus Smart Energy Development" (Fa Gai Neng Yuan [2016] No. 392), which states the need to promote the coordinated development of centralized and distributed energy storage. In June of the same year, the "Notice on Promoting the Participation of Electrical Energy Storage in the Compensation (Market) Mechanism Pilot Work for Electricity Ancillary Services in the 'Three North' Regions" (Guo Neng Jian Guan [2016] No. 164) stipulates that reasonable arrangement of electrical energy storage measures shall be made and that the participation of electrical energy storage facilities on both the power generation side and the user side in ancillary services including peak shaving and frequency regulation shall be promoted in the pilot regions. In December, the "Thirteenth Five-Year Plan for Renewable Energy Development" stipulates that combined with the development and construction of renewable energy power generation, distributed energy, new power microgrids and other projects, comprehensive energy storage technology application demonstrations shall be carried out.

In 2017, five ministries and commissions including the National Development and Reform Commission jointly issued the "Guiding Opinions on Promoting the Development of Energy Storage Technology and Industry" (Fa Gai Neng Yuan [2017]

[4] The National Development and Reform Commission, the Ministry of Industry and Information Technology, the Ministry of Finance, the Ministry of Housing and Urban–Rural Development, the State-owned Assets Supervision and Administration Commission of the State Council, & the National Energy Administration. Notice on Power Demand-side Management under the Supply-side Structural Reform (Fa Gai Yun Xing Gui [2017] No. 1690), Annex, Measures for the Electricity Demand-side Management (revised), Articles 16 and 22.

No. 1701), which identifies energy storage as an "important component and key supporting technology" of the Energy Internet. On June 25, 2019, the National Development and Reform Commission issued the "2019–2020 Action Plan for Implementing the Guiding Opinions on Promoting the Development of Energy Storage Technology and Industry," which further details specific measures.

Regulatory Laws and Policies for Power Trading Platforms

According to the "Opinions on Further Deepening the Reform of the Power System" (Zhong Fa [2015] No. 9), relatively independent power trading organizations shall be established to form a fair and standardized market trading platform. To implement the above opinions, the "Implementation Opinions on Promoting the Construction of the Power Market" stipulates that relatively independent power trading organizations shall be established to provide services for power trading. Based on the aforementioned document, the "Implementation Opinions on the Establishment and Standardized Operation of Power Trading Organizations" provide detailed regulations regarding the establishment of relatively independent trading organizations, the coordination between power trading organizations and dispatching organizations, the promotion of the formation of a standardized operating trading platform, and the strengthened supervision of trading organizations.

The "Implementation Opinions on Promoting the Independent and Standardized Operation of Power Trading Organizations" (Fa Gai Ti Gai [2020] No. 234) issued in February 2020 call for further clarification of the functional positioning of trading organizations, market management committees, and dispatching organizations, and promotion of the transformation of trading organizations into joint-stock companies.

Regulatory Policies for Electric Vehicle Charging Stations

(1) Construction of Electric Vehicle Charging Facilities and Land Approval and Utilization

Energy Internet companies shall fully utilize the relevant incentive policies issued by the state to carry out the construction of charging station facilities while coordinating with various stakeholders. According to the "Notice on Accelerating the Construction of Electric Vehicle Charging Infrastructure in Residential Areas" (Fa Gai Neng Yuan [2016] No. 1611), efforts shall be made to actively promote the electrification renovation of existing residential parking spaces to meet the power requirements of charging infrastructure in these areas, and the power supply facilities accompanying parking spaces in new residential areas shall be designed and constructed synchronously with main buildings. According to the "Guiding Opinions of the General Office of the State Council on Accelerating the Construction of Electric Vehicle Charging Infrastructure" (Guo Ban Fa [2015] No. 73), companies involved in charging services and property management are encouraged to participate in the construction, operation, and management of charging facilities in residential areas. According to the "Notice on Accelerating the Construction of Electric Vehicle Charging Infrastructure in Residential Areas" (Fa Gai Neng Yuan [2016] No. 1611), power supply companies shall actively advance the electrification of existing residential parking spaces to ensure they meet the power requirements of charging infrastructure in residential areas. According to the "Notice on Accelerating the Construction of Electric Vehicle Charging Infrastructure Within Organizations" (Guo Neng Dian Li [2017] No. 19), grid companies are responsible for the construction, operation, and maintenance of supporting grid-connection projects from property rights demarcation points to the grid and the provision of favorable conditions for charging infrastructure to be connected to the grid.

Regarding the acquisition and approval of land for the construction of electric vehicle charging facilities, the Civil Code of the People's Republic of China (hereinafter referred to as the "Civil Code") and the "Land Management Law of the People's Republic of China" stipulate related methods such as sale, donation, lease, and allocation, as well as the scope of the right to use land for construction purposes. According to the "Guiding Opinions of the General Office of the State Council on Accelerating the Construction of Electric Vehicle Charging Infrastructure" (Guo Ban Fa [2015] No. 73), in the planning of charging facilities for electric vehicles in public service sectors such as public transit, sanitation, and airport commuting that operate on fixed routes and locations, it shall be based on the operational needs of the routes, giving priority to the construction of charging facilities in conjunction with parking lot stations, and reasonably constructing stand-alone fast-charging stations and battery swap stations along the way; the construction of public charging facilities shall gradually progress from the city center to the outskirts and from priority development areas of the city to general areas.

(2) Safety Regulation of Electric Vehicle Charging Stations

"Urban Public Facilities—Specification for Operation Management and Service of Electric Vehicle Charging/Battery Swap Infrastructure" (GB/T 37293–2019) and "Urban Public Facilities—Requirements for Security and Protection System of Electric Vehicle Charging/Battery Swap Infrastructure" (GB/T 37295–2019) put forward relevant standards and requirements for the safe construction of electric vehicle charging stations, including safety control, fire safety, and safety technology precaution systems. The "Notice on Accelerating the Construction of Electric Vehicle Charging Infrastructure in Residential Areas" (Fa Gai Neng Yuan [2016] No. 1611) proposes the implementation of charging liability insurance, stating that manufacturers of charging infrastructure in residential areas shall purchase product liability insurance. The "Notice on Accelerating the Construction of Electric Vehicle Charging Infrastructure Within Organizations" (Guo Neng Dian Li [2017] No. 19) clarifies the safety responsibilities of units, charging facility construction contractors, charging facility operation service providers, and other parties, and actively promotes the adoption of product liability insurance and safety liability insurance for charging facilities.

(3) The Dominant Market Position of the Electric Vehicle Charging Station Business

The State Administration for Market Regulation has specified in Articles 7 to 11 of the "Provisions on Prohibiting Abuse of Dominant Market Positions" the factors for determining dominant market positions, which mainly include market share, the ability to control the sales market or the raw material procurement market, financial and technical conditions, the degree of reliance other operators have on the business operator in transactions, and the difficulty for other operators to enter the relevant market. According to the draft for comment, any actions excluding or restricting competition are deemed as an abuse of dominant market positions.

Operators of electric vehicle charging stations shall follow the "Notice on Issues Concerning the Feed-in Tariff Policy for Electric Vehicles" (Fa Gai Jia Ge [2014] No. 1668), which stipulates that "a supportive feed-in tariff policy shall be implemented for the power usage of electric vehicle charging and battery swapping facilities," "other charging facilities shall follow the classified catalog pricing applicable to their locations," "time-of-use electricity pricing policies shall be applied to the power usage of electric vehicle charging and battery swapping facilities during peak and off-peak hours," and "the costs of grid upgrades supporting electric vehicle charging and battery swapping facilities shall be included in the grid companies' transmission and distribution pricing."

Regulatory Laws and Policies for Integrated Energy Service Platforms

(1) Regulatory Laws and Policies for Integrated Energy Supply

The "Guiding Opinions of the State Council on Actively Propelling the Internet Plus Action Plan" (Guo Fa [2015] No. 40) stipulates the promotion of intelligent energy production and the widespread implementation of electricity demand-side management to enhance energy utilization efficiency. The "Guiding Opinions on Promoting Internet Plus Smart Energy Development" (Fa Gai Neng Yuan [2016] No. 392) encourages the construction of smart wind farms, smart photovoltaic power stations, and other facilities, as well as the development of Internet-based smart operational cloud platforms, to achieve intelligent production of renewable energy. The "Microgrid Management Measures (Draft for Comments)" (Guo Neng Zong Dian Li [2017] No. 107) encourages the development of microgrids as an important support for Internet + smart energy and a technical means for friendly interaction with the main power grid.[5]

The inability of electrical energy to fully meet diverse energy needs means that it will become increasingly common for power sellers to supply a combination of

[5] The General Administration Department of the National Energy Administration. Microgrid Management Measures (Draft for Comments) (Guo Neng Zong Dian Li [2017] No. 107), Preface.

energy resources, including electricity, heat, and gas.[6] The "Implementation Opinions on Promoting the Construction of Multi-energy Complementary Integration Optimization Demonstration Project" (Fa Gai Neng Yuan [2016] No. 1430) points out that in order to realize the multi-energy complementary integration optimization demonstration project, there are two main tasks: First, to establish an IES at the end-user level, and second, to establish a multi-energy complementary system including wind, solar, hydro, thermal, and energy storage.

According to the 2015 power reform plan, grid companies shall improve grid-connection services, support the grid connection of new energy, renewable energy, energy-saving and consumption-reducing, and integrated resource utilization units, and actively promote the effective integration of the power generation of new energy and renewable energy with other grids; accelerate the development and improvement of national technical standards for new energy and renewable energy research and development, manufacturing, assembly, grid connection, maintenance, retrofitting, and other aspects; and effectively guarantee the grid connection of new energy.[7]

(2) Regulatory Laws and Policies for Integrated Energy Services

Integrated energy services mainly include green energy-saving services, holistic demand response services, and tailored customization services.[8] The regulatory policies for green energy-saving services have been mentioned in the previous section. The following mainly introduce the regulatory policies for holistic demand response services and tailored customization services.

The "Opinions on Further Deepening the Reform of the Power System" (Zhong Fa [2015] No. 9) encourage power sellers to innovate services and provide users with value-added services including energy performance contracting, integrated energy saving, and energy usage consulting and encourage professional energy service companies to cooperate with users or build distributed power sources under the "energy performance contracting" model.

The "Guiding Opinions on Actively Propelling the Internet Plus Action Plan" (Guo Fa [2015] No. 40) stipulates the advancement of green energy network development that integrates a smart grid as the distribution platform and e-commerce as the trading platform, along with the integration of hardware such as energy storage facilities, IoT, intelligent electricity-using devices, and derivative services like carbon trading and Internet finance.

The "Guiding Opinions on Promoting Internet Plus Smart Energy Development" (Fa Gai Neng Yuan [2016] No. 392) stipulates the acceleration of intelligent energy consumption by encouraging the construction of smart homes, smart buildings, smart communities, and smart factories, characterized mainly by intelligent terminals and flexible energy trading, to support the development of smart cities.

---

[6] Guo and Hu (2020).

[7] Central Committee of China and State Council. Opinions on Further Deepening the Reform of the Power System (Zhong Fa [2015] No. 9).

[8] Guo and Hu (2020).

The "Implementation Opinions on Promoting the Construction of Multi-energy Complementary Integration Optimization Demonstration Project" (Fa Gai Neng Yuan [2016] No. 1430) stipulates that innovative integrated energy supply system business models for end-users should be developed, and that the construction of an Internet-based smart energy information service platform should be accelerated to provide users with open, shared, flexible, and intelligent integrated energy supply and value-added services.

Regulatory Policies for Deepening the Reform of the Investment and Financing System in the Energy Sector

The investment and financing operations of energy companies will involve the entry of multiple market participants, increasing the role of the market in resource allocation, and leading to the formation of some new business models. These will be reflected in energy retail competition, energy system operations, and energy trading operations. Consequently, in the process of deepening the reform of the investment and financing system in the energy sector, the government is paying increasing attention to the regulation and guidance of investment and financing activities of Energy Internet companies.

The "Implementation Opinions on Deepening the Reform of the Investment and Financing System in the Energy Sector" (Guo Neng Fa Gai [2017] No. 88) provides guidance and regulation on the investment and financing activities of energy companies. First, it stipulates that the status of energy companies as the main investors should be established when acquiring investment projects. Second, it requires in-process and post-event supervision of investment activities of energy companies. Third, it emphasizes strengthening planning guidance to ensure that energy planning plays a constraining and guiding role. Fourth, it calls for special regulatory requirements in investment areas with overcapacity or potential overcapacity risks, such as coal mines and thermal power. Fifth, it proposes to enhance the construction of a credit system for energy companies to achieve the openness and sharing of credit information. Sixth, in terms of energy system reform, it calls for advancing complementary reforms, implementing measures for power system reform, encouraging state-owned energy companies to carry out mixed-ownership reforms, and promoting institutional and mechanism innovation.

Regulatory Laws and Policies for International Platform-Based Energy Internet Companies

Since the twenty-first century, some developed countries have begun to implement Energy Internet projects. In 2008, Germany launched the E-Energy project to realize the intelligence of the entire chain of energy production, transmission, conversion, application, and storage through information and communication technology, becoming the first country to practice the Energy Internet. In 2008, the United States initiated the "FREEDM Systems" project, researching efficient and intelligent distribution systems to support the integration of distributed renewable energy sources and the grid connection of distributed energy storage. In 2010, Japan implemented the "Digital Grid" plan, where various devices in the energy network would use IP to realize the transmission of information and energy.[9] Developed countries started exploring and developing the field of Energy Internet earlier. The following attempts to systematically organize and summarize the business models of Energy Internet companies and the regulatory laws and policies in countries such as Germany, the United States, and Japan, in order to provide useful references for the transformation of China's platform-based Energy Internet companies.

Business Models and Regulatory Laws and Policies of German Platform-Based Energy Internet Companies

(1) Business Models

In 2000, Germany initiated an energy transition strategy aimed at making the country's energy use more "environmentally friendly, economical, and secure." In December 2008, the German Federal Ministry of Economics and Technology also began to put Energy Internet projects into practice in smart countries/regions. In 2008, Germany launched the E-Energy project to realize the intelligence of the entire chain of energy production, transmission, conversion, application, and storage through information and communication technology, becoming the first country to practice the Energy Internet. In 2008, the United States initiated the "FREEDM Systems" project, researching efficient and intelligent distribution systems to support the integration of distributed renewable energy sources and the grid connection of distributed energy storage. In 2010, Japan implemented the "Digital Grid" plan, where various devices in the energy network would use IP to realize the transmission of information and energy.[10] On the basis of the grid, the E-Energy technology innovation promotion plan was launched and six regions put typical Energy Internet business model into practice. For example, the core of the eTelligence demonstration project is to improve new energy consumption capabilities, use Internet technology to establish an energy regulation system, and introduce the concept of VPPs. The core of the Smart-Watts demonstration project is a community power trading platform for distributed energy, which uses information networks to inform users of real-time electricity prices, guides residents to use electricity during off-peak hours, and adjusts electricity consumption plans in real time. The core of the RegModHarz demonstration project is to achieve 100% clean energy supply within the regional electricity market.

[9] See Gao et al. (2018).

[10] Same as above.

It is worth mentioning that Germany has established business operation models for energy storage systems supporting new energy. Taking the PV plus storage industry as an example, the main business models include (1) ownership model of PV plus storage. After a user purchases the PV plus storage system, they can self-consume the electricity produced by the rooftop PV. The power company has control over the energy storage and charges it for free for the user in the "zero electricity price" scenario. In addition, the company can gain revenue by integrating user-side energy storage systems to provide system operators with ancillary services such as load balancing. (2) Community sharing model. Connect distributed PV, energy storage, and combined heat and power generation equipment into the system and create a current account system where energy revenue can offset expenditures by taking advantage of the complementarity between the community's power generation capacity and electricity demand. This approach enhances the operational efficiency of the system and leads to higher economic gains.[11]

(2) Regulatory Laws and Policies

In terms of renewable energy, Germany has been experimenting with methods such as "replacing gas with electricity" and "replacing oil with electricity" to gradually phase out traditional fossil fuels and replace them with renewable energy-generated power.[12] The German "Renewable Energy Act" of 2000 has ensured a long-term fixed electricity pricing system and explicitly stipulates that regional grid operators are obligated to purchase electricity generated from renewable sources, guaranteeing prioritized grid access for renewable energy. According to "Energy Concept" of 2010, Germany aims to complete "energy transition" by 2050 and realize an energy supply system predominantly powered by renewable energy sources.[13]

In terms of power infrastructure, Germany has issued the "Technical Requirements for the Connection to and Parallel Operation with Medium-Voltage Distribution Networks" and the "Technical Requirements for the Connection to and Parallel Operation with Low-Voltage Distribution Networks" in 2011, which strictly and explicitly stipulate the technical standards and indicators for distributed power sources that are connected to the medium- and low-voltage distribution networks.[14] Additionally, Germany has revised the "Energy Industry Act" and introduced the "Grid Expansion Acceleration Act" and the "Federal Demand Planning Act" aimed at streamlining the planning and approval processes to accelerate the construction of the power grid. This facilitates the transportation of the abundant wind power resources from the northern regions to the western and southern regions, where there is a higher demand for energy.[15]

In terms of new energy and integrated energy, Germany's "Act on Granting Priority to Renewable Energy Sources" of 1997 encourages and supports the development

[11] Li et al. (2020).

[12] Wang (2016a, b).

[13] See Li (2018), p. 7.

[14] Same as above.

[15] See Zhang (2014).

of integrated energy. The "Combined Heat and Power Act" of 2002 stipulates the priority grid connection for combined heat and power electricity, as well as the methods and proportions for sharing the grid-connection price and electricity price with users. The "Supplementary Provisions to the Combined Heat and Power Act" of 2011 increased the support for the construction of combined heat and power facilities, new thermal pipelines, and heat storage systems.[16]

In terms of energy storage, Germany implemented two rounds of energy storage incentive policies from 2013 to 2018, providing investment subsidies and low-wage loans for the installation of energy storage equipment supporting household PV power generation.[17] In 2017, Germany simplified the application procedures for new market participants to enter the secondary frequency control and minute reserve markets, paving the way for grid-level energy storage applications to transit from primary frequency control to operating in the two markets.

Business Models and Regulatory Laws and Policies of Platform-Based Energy Internet Companies in the United States

(1) Business Models

In 2008, the National Science Foundation of the United States established the "FREEDM System," introducing for the first time the concept of an "Energy Internet." Within this system, energy primarily comes from small-scale, modular distributed renewable sources, and users can control their own energy needs through a plug-and-play interface. The modular energy is coordinated and managed by energy routers to achieve rational allocation and utilization of energy.[18]

In market applications, Energy Internet projects in the United States utilize VPP services to aggregate flexible user loads, user-side energy storage, and distributed power generation, enabling direct participation in energy market transactions.[19] In terms of energy storage, the United States has adopted an energy storage application model used for ancillary services and a distributed PV plus storage power generation application model. Typical business models for energy storage supporting new energy established in the United States mainly include the following three categories: (1) Equipment purchase model. Users purchase PV plus storage equipment for self-production and consumption and maintain the system themselves. (2) PV leasing model. Users do not need to purchase the equipment; instead, they pay a certain equipment lease fee each month from the electricity savings. (3) Power purchase agreement model. The PV plus storage system provider signs a third-party agreement with the user and the power company. The system provider is responsible for the construction and maintenance of the system and sells the electricity to the power

[16] See Li (2018), pp. 9–10.

[17] Hu et al. (2019), p. 370.

[18] Liu et al. (2016), p. 26.

[19] Wang et al. (2020).

company; the power company resells it to the user; the user provides their rooftop for power generation and pays a lower electricity price.[20]

(2) Regulatory Laws and Policies

In terms of smart grids, the 2009 "American Recovery and Reinvestment Act" emphasizes the importance of investing in and constructing smart grids and calls for funding for projects related to smart grids. In 2011, the United States proposed the "Policy Framework for the 21st Century Grid," aimed at establishing a modernized electricity transmission infrastructure and facilitating the open deployment of smart grid technologies.

In terms of clean energy, the United States' 1978 "Public Utility Regulatory Policies Act" mandates that power companies must purchase power from qualifying clean energy producers, which provides favorable conditions for renewable energy projects to participate in the competitive energy market. The 1979 "Energy Tax Act" favors clean energy projects by offering policy incentives, including deductions on investment taxes and expedited depreciation. The 2005 "Energy Policy Act" addresses the fundraising difficulties for clean energy projects by introducing clean renewable energy bonds and providing loan guarantees for such projects. The 2009 "American Recovery and Reinvestment Act" stipulates funding and tax incentives for relevant industrial research and projects and includes wind and solar energy among the clean energy projects eligible for accelerated depreciation benefits. The 2009 "New Energy Policy" encourages the vigorous development of clean energy. The 2014 "Action Plan for Promoting the Development of New Energy Centered on Photovoltaic Power Generation" supports the development of clean energy including PV. In 2015, the "Clean Power Plan" officially took effect, aiming to curb greenhouse gas emissions through the decreased production of electricity via fossil fuels and the encouragement of renewable energy adoption. That same year, the "Comprehensive Budget Act" extended the period of applicability for clean energy tax incentives.[21]

In terms of comprehensive energy, "Combined Heat and Power (CHP): A Vision for the Future of CHP in the U.S." published in 1999 presented a development timeline for combined heat and power generation. The "Energy Policy Act of 2001" provides tax incentives for combined heat and power distributed energy projects and suggestions to streamline the approval process. The "Energy Independence and Security Act of 2007" stipulates that integrated energy planning must be carried out in major energy supply and consumption processes.[22]

In terms of energy storage, Order No. 890 of 2007 and Order No. 719 of 2008 allow energy storage to enter the power wholesale market. From 2009 to 2011, the United States issued a series of "Renewable and Green Energy Storage Technology Plans," which provide tax incentives for investments in grid-scale energy storage. In 2013, Order No. 784 stipulates that grid operators can directly purchase ancillary

[20] Li et al. (2020).

[21] Sun (2018), pp. 30–31.

[22] Li (2018), pp. 7–10.

services and energy storage services settlement mechanisms from third parties.[23] The 2017 "Energy Storage Tax Incentive and Deployment Act" provides a similar investment tax credit for energy storage systems.[24]

Business Models and Regulatory Laws and Policies of Japanese Platform-Based Energy Internet Companies

(1) Business Models

In 2010, Japan launched the "Smart Energy Community" plan and began research related to energy and smart grids. The following year, Japan implemented the "Digital Grid" plan based on digital grid routers.[25]

In the field of distributed energy, the distributed Energy Internet applies the concept of collaborative sharing from the Internet to the energy sector, aiming to resolve the imbalance between supply and demand in traditional distributed energy systems through interconnectedness, and to achieve deep emission reductions from a localized to a holistic approach. In addition, the reform of the power and energy system oriented toward integrated energy services provides effective support for the network application of distributed energy.[26]

(2) Regulatory Laws and Policies

In terms of grid infrastructure, the 1995 "Technical Guidelines on Grid Connection" clearly supports the development of distributed energy devices.

In terms of renewable energy, the 2011 Renewable Energy Act stipulates that the proportion of renewable energy in power supply must reach 20% by 2020. The revised "Renewable Energy Act" published in the following year sets the feed-in tariffs for solar, wind, and geothermal power generation at 2 to 4 times the price of thermal power generation, in order to promote renewable energy power generation.[27]

In terms of new energy, Japan enacted the "Act on Special Measures Concerning New Energy Use" in 1997 to encourage new energy technologies such as wind power generation, solar power generation, and energy vehicles.

In terms of distributed energy, after the release of the "Kyoto Protocol Target Achievement Plan" in 2005, Japan introduced a series of policies to build an urban energy area system, and the networked application of distributed energy is one of the important measures. The 2005 "Guidelines for Regional Energy Utilization" stipulates in detail the implementation process of regional energy utilization, relevant laws and regulations, etc. The 2007 "Guidelines for Promoting Heat Supply Based on the Utilization of Unused Regional Energy" discusses the construction of regional

23 Lv (2019), p. 14.

24 Hu et al. (2019), p. 370.

25 See Gao et al. (2018).

26 See Ren et al. (2017).

27 See Li (2018), page 8.

heating networks to effectively utilize the scattered low-grade unused thermal energy within cities. The 2010 "Basic Energy Plan" emphasizes the optimized utilization of energy at the urban block level, especially the effective utilization of renewable energy and unused energy within the region.[28]

In terms of energy storage, Japan mainly uses financial incentives to encourage the adoption of energy storage systems in residential areas, while the government requires grid companies to install batteries on the transmission grid to stabilize the power supply frequency. Alternatively, they can purchase ancillary services from suppliers. Additionally, there are rewards for using batteries in distribution grids or microgrids.[29]

Conclusion

By comparing the development and regulatory policies of Energy Internet-related industries in China and other countries, the author draws the following conclusions:

The analysis of the development models of Germany's "industry coupling" Energy Internet, the United States' "resilient" Energy Internet, and Japan's hydrogen Energy Internet reveals that there is a high level of agreement among these countries on the characteristics of the Energy Internet, such as multi-energy coupling, decentralized distribution, and the integration of a significant portion of renewable energy. At the same time, each country has also developed its unique development strategies tailored to its national circumstances. At the practical level, Energy Internet demonstration projects in these countries generally focus on the user side, showcasing cutting-edge concepts, key technologies, and important elements of regional energy interconnection in practice.[30]

Promote the Reform of the Power System to Create an Open Policy Space

While promoting the Energy Internet, the United States and Germany have also been driving reforms in their power markets. In the United States, most regional power markets have been reformed, creating competitive wholesale markets. In Germany, the transmission sector has been completely separated from the original nine major companies, striving toward a more flexible electricity pricing mechanism, more efficient supply and demand interaction, and a more secure guarantee system. The marketization reform of the power market has broken the relatively closed industry structure of the energy sector, creating a policy environment for the development of the Energy Internet, lowering the barriers to entry, and providing growth opportunities

---

[28] See Ren et al. (2017).

[29] Lv (2019), page 15.

[30] Wang and Wang (2020), p. 34.

for innovative companies. The booming emergence of Energy Internet technologies and business models in the two countries is closely related to electricity reform.[31]

Promote the Standardization and Unification of Energy Interfaces in the Construction of the Energy Internet Information Model

The German E-Energy demonstration projects are based on information technology, and each project result involves the conversion of communication protocol interfaces. By contrast, the development of information and communication systems in China's energy network has been relatively slow, and the standards are quite diverse. In the context of the current Internet Plus era, China needs to first break through the standardization and unification of internal interfaces within single energy systems and then expand to diversified energy systems.[32]

Pay Attention to the Establishment of a Standard System in the Energy Internet Development System

The Energy Internet not only involves the conversion, transmission, distribution and consumption of various energy sources, but is also directly related to the interface of the information model in the Energy Internet, including the establishment of multiple standard systems. The E-Energy project has initially established some standard systems. During the construction of Energy Internet demonstration projects, China should pay attention to the establishment of standard systems.[33]

Emphasize the Role of the User Side in the Development of Energy Internet

With the upgrading of interaction between energy supply and demand, the user side attracts more attention in the Energy Internet, and new business models based on user demands have emerged in the US and German markets. For example, in the United States, Tesla is committed to building a new distributed energy system and Opower combines psychology and big data to guide user demand response; in Germany, Sonnen builds a community solar energy trading platform. This gives users more options, makes energy use more intelligent, meets the requirements of green, low-carbon, and personalized energy use, and further promotes the development of the Energy Internet from the consumer side.[34]

---

[31] Zhang (2017).

[32] Yin et al. (2015).

[33] Same as above.

[34] Zhang (2017).

Legal and Policy Risks of the Transformation of Platform-Based Energy Internet Companies

Identification of Legal and Policy Risks of the Energy Grid System of the Energy Internet

Introduction to the Development of the Energy Network Framework of the Energy Internet Platform

The Energy Internet is an expansion of the smart grid. First, it extends from the power grid to a broader energy system domain, with the power grid being its core foundational network infrastructure. Second, it evolves from a purely physical electrical network to an information Internet that includes various types of users, meaning that all kinds of market entities are also active elements of the Energy Internet. Third, it expands from distributed power sources to distributed energy sources. Fourth, it extends from purely electric vehicles to new energy vehicles such as those powered by hydrogen energy. Fifth, it involves hydrogen energy or Power-to-Gas (P2G) technologies, expanding from simple power storage to energy storage, which enhances large-scale power storage capabilities and applications within smart cities or communities. Sixth, it moves from power trading to new interactive businesses such as new energy quota trading and virtual dispatch of user-side resources.[35] The energy network framework is the material foundation of the Energy Internet, serving as the infrastructure that carries energy flows and covers all aspects of energy production, conversion, transmission, storage, and consumption. Centered on electricity, it enables flexible conversion and mutual support among various types of energy such as electricity, gas, heat, and cooling.

Analysis on Legal and Policy Risks of Regulatory Businesses

(1) Regulatory Risks Associated with Achieving Carbon Neutrality by 2060

(a) Background Description

On September 22, 2020, President Xi Jinping stated at the General Debate of the 75th Session of the United Nations General Assembly that China will scale up its Intended Nationally Determined Contributions by adopting more vigorous policies and measures. We aim to have CO2 emissions peak before 2030 and achieve carbon neutrality before 2060.[36] The proposal of the carbon neutrality goal signifies acceleration in the transformation of the energy structure, which aligns with the original intention of constructing an Energy Internet. It especially calls for the power industry

---

[35] Tian et al. (2015).

[36] See Xinhua News Agency (2020).

to take the lead in rapidly advancing the leapfrog development of China's energy structure from coal-centric power generation to clean and low-carbon energy-centric power generation.[37] As the energy sector progresses toward the carbon neutrality goal, a flexible and efficient power grid is required for safeguarding its journey. With the integration of large-scale and unstable renewable energy sources into the grid, the Energy Internet platform is confronted with a range of regulatory risks.

(b) Identification of Legal Risks

Under the goal of carbon neutrality, Energy Internet platforms mainly face two types of regulatory risks: liability risks for renewable energy power consumption and regulatory risks caused by unstable renewable energy power generation. Despite that grid companies shall buy the entire quantity of the grid-connected power generated with renewable energy within the coverage of their power grids as stipulated in Article 14 of the "Renewable Energy Law," provinces with substantial renewable energy capacities are grappling with widespread problems of wasted hydroelectric, wind, and solar energy. In May 2019, the National Development and Reform Commission and the National Energy Administration jointly issued the "Notice on Establishing and Improving the Guarantee Mechanism for Renewable Power Consumption" (Fa Gai Neng Yuan [2019] No. 807), which formally establishes the renewable energy electricity quota system, clarifies the minimum proportion targets for the consumption of renewable power within the total power consumption as well as the incentive targets for each provincial region, and emphasizes that the responsibility for consumption should be jointly borne by the power supply and sale companies and the power users. As China continues to vigorously promote the development of renewable energy, Energy Internet platforms face both regulatory risks from energy authorities and legal risks of civil litigation. Specifically, the platforms may be investigated by regulatory authorities due to complaints from renewable energy power generators, and be named in regulatory reports, which could lead to negative social impacts. In severe cases, they may also face penalties such as fines. In addition, Energy Internet companies could be subject to environmental public interest litigation initiated by environmental protection organizations under the "Environmental Protection Law of the People's Republic of China" and the "Civil Procedure Law of the People's Republic of China," potentially resulting in the risk of high compensation costs.

In addition to the risks associated with the consumption of renewable energy power, the inherent technical flaws of renewable energy power also pose certain regulatory risks to Energy Internet platforms. Wind power, solar power, and other new energy sources are easily affected by the climate, and their power supply is random and volatile. As the proportion of coal-fired power generation decreases and the proportion of renewable energy generation increases, this poses greater challenges to the long-term safe and stable operation of the power grid.[38] On one hand, the energy transition demands a reduction in carbon emissions produced from energy generation and consumption, progressively establishing an energy system based on zero-carbon

[37] Guo and Tang. (2020).

[38] Same as above.

sources; on the other hand, the instability of renewable energy power supply also requires relatively stable thermal power for peak shaving, in order to ensure the safe and stable operation of the power grid. Energy Internet platforms also face legal risks caused by the instability of renewable energy power generation under the carbon neutrality goal. Specifically, if the platforms fail to effectively balance the power supply and demand during peak power consumption periods, causing peak power gaps and threatening the secure supply of power, such platforms may be subject to regulatory penalties.

(2) Legal Risks Arising from Energy Internet Platforms Violating the Principles of Fairness, Non-discrimination, and Openness

(a) Background Description

During the development of the Energy Internet, the traditional concept of the power sector as a natural monopoly is changing. To enhance the efficiency of energy use and ensure the healthy and safe development of the energy market, it is essential to encourage fair competition and fully utilize the market's role in resource allocation. Articles 53 and 65 of the "Energy Law of the People's Republic of China (Draft for Comments)" (hereinafter referred to as the "Energy Law (Draft for Comments)") and the "Measures for the Supervision of a Fair and Open Grid" respectively make crucial provisions for a fair, non-discriminatory, and open grid. In the course of developing Energy Internet platforms, it is particularly important to pay attention to legal risks that may arise from violating the principles of fairness, non-discrimination, and openness.

(b) Identification of Legal Risks

According to Articles 7 and 19 of the "Measures for the Supervision of a Fair and Open Grid," grid companies are required to provide fair, non-discriminatory, and open services in two aspects: grid access and grid interconnection. Firstly, regarding grid access services, grid companies must offer fair and non-discriminatory access services to power generation projects. This means that grid companies shall not refuse the access applications from power project owners without justified reasons, nor can they delay the access process without cause. Grid companies shall provide essential information to power project owners, such as the location for grid access, available capacity, actual usage capacity, transmission methods, the number of available intervals, and related technical parameters, for the purpose of grid access. For distributed generation facilities that meet national construction requirements, grid companies shall not impose technical requirements that are higher than national and industry standards, except for necessary technical requirements to ensure the safe operation of the grid and equipment. Additionally, grid companies shall charge service fees reasonably. Second, grid companies shall provide grid interconnection services fairly and without discrimination. Violation of the aforementioned provisions regarding grid access and grid interconnection may lead to legal risks.

Analysis on Legal Risks of Competitive Businesses

(1) Legal Risks Faced by Platform-Based Economic Entities in the Context of Diversified Market Entities in the Energy Internet

(a) Background Description

The release of the "Opinions on Further Deepening the Reform of the Power System" by the Central Committee of China and the State Council, six major supporting documents for power system reform by the National Development and Reform Commission and the National Energy Administration, including the "Implementation Opinions on Advancing the Reform of Prices of Power Transmission and Distribution," as well as targeted reform plans such as the "Implementation Opinions on Promoting the Reform of the Power Selling Side" in 2015 comes with a transformation in the traditional structure of the power industry, which was previously composed of power generators, grid companies, and power users. The establishment and relative independence of the electricity trading centers have led to a multi-buyer-multi-seller market trading model, with new market entities and transaction patterns emerging continuously. In the process of building the Energy Internet, the advent of new technologies and business models has also provided opportunities for new market participants to become strong competitors. The diversification of market entities and the complexity of transaction models have introduced new legal risks to the signing and execution of power trading contracts.

In addition, Energy Internet companies should pay attention to and adjust their role in the competitive market while building the Energy Internet and moving toward a platform-based and shared model to avoid legal risks arising from suspected abuse of market position to restrict and eliminate competition.

(b) Identification of Legal Risks

Firstly, there may be legal risks arising from power trading contracts. In the context of the development of the Energy Internet and the reform of the power system, the trading entities have changed from the original two parties including power suppliers and users to multiple parties including power generators, transmitters and distributors, sellers, and users, creating new legal relationships and rights and obligations. Therefore, it is necessary to pay attention to the potential risks associated with trading contracts in the following new trading scenarios. First, failure to timely adjust the signing mode and terms of power trading contracts for wholesale users such as power sales companies and large power users may pose legal risks to Energy Internet companies; second, independent power sales companies enter the power trading market, which may cause potential legal risks to Energy Internet companies in terms of power trading contracts; third, power distribution and sales companies fail to promptly adjust the signing mode and terms of power sales contracts according to changes in the contract parties after entering the power sales market; fourth, power sales companies sign power supply contracts with market users.

Secondly, there may be legal risks arising from the restriction of competition. New energy power generation, distributed energy storage, energy conservation, and other businesses have seen increasingly open market environment. It is expected that competition in these sectors will gradually intensify due to policy expectations, and the market order is also under strict regulation by laws such as antitrust legislation. On April 10, 2021, the State Administration for Market Regulation lawfully imposed administrative penalties on Alibaba Group for its monopolistic "choose one from two" practice, fining the company 4% of its 2019 domestic sales of CNY 455.712 billion, totaling CNY 18.228 billion.[39] This was the first antitrust fine issued in China's platform economy. It should be recognized that economic platforms, including the Energy Internet, are not only market entities but also serve as "infrastructure" that suppliers and demanders access and interact with. They are providers of trading facilities, and therefore possess the nature of quasi-public goods. Moreover, platforms benefit from economies of scale, economies of scope, and network externalities. They also have access to a wealth of information from market participants regarding transactions and settlements, which gives them an advantage in customer and data.[40] Energy Internet companies should maintain high sensitivity to the gradually changing market ecosystem, and be vigilant of legal risks arising from violating antitrust laws and policies due to restricting competition. This mainly includes the legal risks that may arise from actions in violation of the "Anti-Monopoly Law of the People's Republic of China" (hereinafter referred to as the "Anti-Monopoly Law") and the "Guidelines of the Anti-monopoly Commission of the State Council for Anti-monopoly in the Field of Platform Economy" (hereinafter referred to as the "Platform Economy Anti-Monopoly Guidelines") and other laws and regulations. Such actions include abusing the market dominant position in the platform economy to engage in unfair pricing practices, selling below cost without justifiable reasons, refusing to transact, imposing transaction restrictions, or implementing differential treatment toward transaction counterparts in the conduct of competitive business in relevant markets.

(2) Analysis on Legal Risks That May Be Caused by Technical Risks in Energy Management

(a) Background Description

The development of the Energy Internet will generate a multitude of new inventions and applications, such as the IES, which, as a fundamental component of the Energy Internet, can achieve effective scheduling and efficient utilization of different energy resources within a region (such as a city, community, or industrial park). Compared to the traditional energy supply systems that operate independently, such as power, heating, and natural gas systems, the main characteristics of IES can be summarized as unified energy dispatching, bidirectional energy flow, and free energy conversion. These three characteristics all focus on a central concern: the efficient utilization of regional energy resources.[41] IES incorporates a variety of energy forms including

---

[39] State Administration for Market Regulation. Administrative Penalty Decision of the State Administration for Market Regulation (Guo Shi Jian Chu [2021] No. 28).

[40] Sichuan Observation News (2021).

[41] Qu et al. (2019).

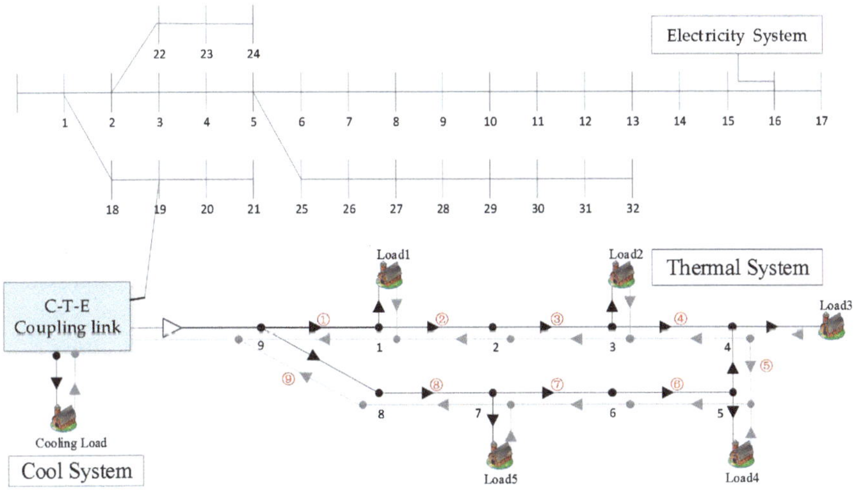

Fig. 3.1 Topology of cooling-thermal-electric IES (Qu et al. 2019)

electricity, natural gas, heat, and cooling. This system encompasses various energy operation modes, control devices, and coupling parts. Within the system, there are parts that are easy to control, such as conventional power plants, combined heat, power, and cooling systems, and energy storage devices, as well as parts with strong intermittency and greater control difficulty, such as wind and PV power generation. In addition, the types of energy within the system include electricity, which is difficult to store in large quantities, and energy forms that are easier to store and transfer, such as thermal energy, natural gas, and hydrogen. The IES involves dynamics at the component or equipment level, such as various electrical, gas, and heating devices, as well as at the unit level, including integrated building energy supply systems, microgrids, and combined heat, power, and cooling systems. This complexity makes the system's model highly intricate.[42]

In the article "Steady-State Power Flow Analysis of Cold-Thermal-Electric IES Based on Unified Power Flow Model" published by Qu, L et al. in *Energies*, an electric power subsystem, a thermal subsystem, and a cooling subsystem are modeled and coupled to establish a cold-thermal-electric IES (Fig. 3.1). Combined with the unified power flow model and the system's nonlinearity and strong coupling, the Newton–Raphson method is employed to facilitate the solution of the unified power flow. Moreover, to analyze the sensitivity of the system's characteristics under various input conditions, the article analyzes different values for parameters such as photovoltaic power output and bus electrical load power in the electrical system, as well as source-node supply water temperature and the pipeline length of the heat supply network in the thermal system, providing a scientific basis for system operation and power flow optimization. Additionally, the article reviews and analyzes the legal risks that may

[42] See Wang (2016a, b), p. 2.

arise from the technical uncertainties of IES based on the "Risk Society" theory and further proposes measures for risk prevention.[43]

(b) Identification of Legal Risks

Firstly, there may be legal risks arising from technology upgrades and system operation and maintenance. IES is significantly different from traditional power grids. Its energy flows are more complex, and optimized operations involve more stakeholders. As the load and network complexity increase, it is challenging to maintain table stable operation of IES. In addition, various extreme external natural disasters may exacerbate this challenge. Although the probability of such disasters is low, the resulting damage can be extremely severe. This includes safety risks due to flaws in the grid design, losses to users caused by not meeting national power supply quality standards and agreements, and significant accidents and serious consequences resulting from production safety facilities or conditions that do not comply with national regulations. Energy Internet companies shall be liable for damages to users due to infringement caused by the use of new technologies. In serious cases, they may be subject to administrative penalties and further face criminal responsibility.

(3) Risks Arising from the Restructuring of the Legal System for Energy Trading

(a) Background Description

With the popularization of distributed and renewable energy, traditional energy consumers may become "prosumers" (entities that both produce and consume energy). This gives rise to new energy consumption models. The power market reform and the construction of the Energy Internet will allow prosumers to more widely participate in shared energy storage transactions. The massive complex and interrelated multilateral transactions lead to intricate profit models and settlement rules. To address the real-time interaction needs of multiple participants in future shared energy storage transactions, blockchain technology might offer a solution. The four core technologies of blockchain—distributed storage, encryption algorithms, consensus mechanisms, and smart contracts—could effectively handle the demands of these complex transactions. However, relying on the underlying technology of blockchain and self-executing smart contracts to manage these complex models may also introduce potential legal risks.

(b) Identification of Legal Risks

Firstly, if there are design or operational errors in the running of energy blockchain and smart contracts that lead to property loss for users, and if the platform is found to have intentional or negligent fault, the platform could be deemed to have committed a civil tort and may face legal risks associated with the obligation to pay damages for the infringement. In the context of the Energy Internet, the roles of producers, sellers, transmitters, and storage operators in transactions may overlap and change

[43] Qu et al. (2019).

dynamically, which could further complicate the attribution of tort liability, leading to an increased legal risk.

Secondly, the underlying design of blockchain and smart contracts leads to a tendency for smart contracts to automatically execute without adequately considering the actual intentions of the parties involved, which could potentially conflict with the principle of respecting the autonomy of the parties' intentions, as emphasized in the Civil Code. In addition, if a platform defines the legal rights and obligations of both the platform and its users through a standard form of electronic contract in order to mitigate the legal barriers to the automatic execution of smart contracts, there is a risk that such an electronic contract could be considered a violation of consumer rights.

Identification of Legal and Policy Risks of the Information Support System of the Energy Internet

Introduction to the Development of the Information Support System of the Energy Internet Platform

"The global energy crisis and the continued growth in energy demand have highlighted the limitations and contradictions of the existing architecture for energy production and consumption. The rapid development of distributed renewable energy, the introduction of national "Internet+" action plans, and the emergence of new demands and concepts are both subjective and objective driving factors that have prompted the smart grid to expand its connectivity. This expansion is integrating deeply with other energy networks, such as natural gas, cooling/heating, and hydrogen energy networks, and is constructing a novel "Energy Internet" that merges information and energy based on the principles of the Internet."[44] Based on the wide-area multi-energy flow system and the information Internet, the Energy Internet will enable on-demand transmission and friendly interaction between energy producers and consumers, thereby closely integrating the energy network with the information support system.

The most significant difference between Energy Internet platforms and traditional energy companies is their focus on the application of information technology and the close connection of energy systems. Through the Internet, people can easily upload and download information, allowing for immediate and balanced exchanges of information. The combination of the Internet and energy trading enables every participant in the Energy Internet to become an equal and autonomous information center and energy center. This means that energy producers and consumers can quickly switch roles, directly interact with each other, and produce energy, connect to the grid, consume energy, or convert energy types at any time, thereby achieving the highest efficiency. From the perspective of Energy Internet platform companies,

[44] Zhang et al. (2016), p. 7.

the construction and operation of the Energy Internet require massive energy user data (personal data and non-personal data sources), including but not limited to user personal privacy information, power consumption information, thermal consumption information, user heating information, information of intelligent equipment (including new energy vehicles), and real-time dynamic power data information of the power grid. Internet platform companies should be concerned with user privacy protection, cross-border data governance, and the rights, attributes, and exercise of public data in the big data era. For Energy Internet platforms, the information support system involves the collection, storage, analysis, and utilization of massive amounts of data. In the context of increasingly strict data governance and frequent data breaches (for example, in July 2019, the American social media giant Facebook was fined $5 billion by the Federal Trade Commission for alleged user information leaks), these platforms should pay close attention to the legal risk analysis of the information support system and the construction of a data compliance system.

Information can be further divided into personal information and non-personal information depending on whether it can be used to identify a natural person. According to Article 1034 of the Civil Code, personal information is the information recorded electronically or in other ways that can be used, by itself or in combination with other information, to identify a natural person, including his name, date of birth, identification number, biometric information, residential address, telephone number, email address, health information, whereabouts, and the like. Non-personal information is not specially defined by any national regulation. The definition of "industrial data" made by the Ministry of Industry and Information Technology can be used as a reference. According to Article 2 of the "Guidelines for Classification and Grading of Industrial Data (Trial)" (Gong Xin Ting Xin Fa [2020] No. 6), industrial data refers to data generated and applied throughout the entire life cycle of products and services in the industrial field, including but not limited to, data generated and used by industrial companies during research and development, design, production manufacturing, business management, operation, and maintenance services, as well as data generated and used by industrial Internet platform companies during processes such as equipment connection, platform operation, and industrial APP applications. This section, building upon the analysis of legal risks associated with personal information within the Energy Internet platform's information support system, will focus on identifying the legal risks involved in the collection, storage, analysis, utilization, and sharing of non-personal information. It will also propose targeted measures for risk prevention.

Analysis on Legal Risks of Regulatory Businesses

(1) Analysis on Legal Risks of the Public Nature of Energy Data

(a) Background Description

Currently, there are no specific laws or administrative regulations dedicated to the supervision and regulation of industrial data, particularly energy-related data. The existing regulatory framework is primarily based on local laws and administrative rules established by the local governments and people's congresses, along with their standing committees, in provinces, autonomous regions, directly administered municipalities, and cities with districts. This study has reviewed the data supervision policies concerning industrial data, particularly public data, across different regions in China, and has specifically highlighted the legislative practices of Shenzhen Special Economic Zone, Beijing, Tianjin, and Chongqing.

The "Regulations of Shenzhen Special Economic Zone on Data" (hereinafter referred to as the "Shenzhen Data Regulations") is one of the few local regulations nationwide that clearly defines data rights and the first to make such definition. According to Articles 2 and 4 of "Shenzhen Data Regulations," natural persons shall enjoy the rights of personality with respect to personal data as provided for by law, administrative regulations, and these regulations. Natural persons, legal persons, and unincorporated organizations shall enjoy the property rights to the data products and services they have legally processed, as provided for by law, administrative regulations, and these regulations. However, they shall not endanger national security and public interests, nor shall they infringe upon the lawful rights and interests of others. The "Shenzhen Data Regulations" also clearly defines the public data. For example, in Article 2, public data refers to the data generated and processed by public management and service institutions in the course of performing their public management duties or providing public services in accordance with the law; public management and service institutions refer to state organs, public institutions, and other organizations managing public affairs according to law within this municipality, as well as organizations that provide education, health and wellness, social welfare, water supply, electricity supply, gas supply, environmental protection, public transportation, and other public services.

The "Beijing Public Data Management Measures" also includes the energy data collected and analyzed by Energy Internet companies in their production and operations into the scope of public data. In addition, according to the provisions of the draft opinion, companies with public service functions shall converge public data, including energy information, to the municipal and district-level big data management platforms.[45]

Unlike Shenzhen and Beijing, which include business data obtained by companies responsible for providing public services within the scope of public data for supervision, Chongqing and Tianjin have not classified legally obtained energy data by these companies as public data. Moreover, Tianjin has enacted the "Tianjin Regulations on Promoting the Development and Application of Big Data" to encourage energy companies to perform big data analysis and efficient utilization of legally collected and stored energy data.

(b) Identification of Legal Risks

[45] Beijing Big Data Work Promotion Group. Beijing Public Data Management Measures, Articles 3 and 13.

After sorting out the energy data regulatory policies in various places, it can be seen that the regulatory policies that pose a greater legal risk to the Energy Internet platforms mainly stem from those local policies that classify energy data as public data. Accordingly, the main risks that Energy Internet platforms may face include legal risks arising from the infringement of the national ownership of public data, as well as legal risks due to the failure to share public data in a timely and sufficient manner.

Firstly, there may be legal risks arising from the infringement of the national ownership of public data. Data, especially energy data as public data, has a strong public resource nature. Although the "Shenzhen Data Regulations" do not absolutely prohibit Energy Internet platforms from analyzing and utilizing energy data, the stipulation that the ownership of public data belongs to the state introduces legal uncertainties and regulatory risks for Energy Internet platforms when they collect, analyze, and seek to monetize the value of energy data.

Secondly, there may be legal risks arising from failure to share public data in a timely and sufficient manner. Both "Beijing Public Data Management Measures" and "Shenzhen Data Regulations" stipulate the sharing and opening of public data. However, due to the lack of clear standards for data sharing in current laws and policies, there is no accurate criterion for distinguishing between public data that "should be shared" and data that "need not be shared." In practice, this can easily lead to conflicts between the public data that "should be shared" and the legitimate commercial secrets of Energy Internet companies, as well as the privacy information of energy users which should be legally protected. If Energy Internet platforms fail to properly manage and classify public data that "should be shared" and data that "need not be shared," they may incur penalties from data regulatory agencies and legal risks arising from infringement of user privacy.

(2) Legal Risks Arising from Cross-border Data Flows

(a) Background Description

As one of the world's largest utility companies, grid company A operates in a region that covers 88% of the domestic land area, providing power to over 1.1 billion people. Internationally, the company has successfully invested in and operates 12 key energy network assets in nine countries and regions, including the Philippines, Brazil, Portugal, Australia, Hong Kong China, Italy, Greece, Oman, and Chile.[46] This giant state-owned grid company's business scope has expanded across multiple regions globally. As nations worldwide place greater emphasis on safeguarding their citizens' personal data, there is a parallel aspiration to establish an interconnected global energy network. In this context, the governance of cross-border data flows becomes a critical issue that must be addressed during the development of Energy Internet platforms.

(b) Identification of Legal Risks

[46] State Grid Corporation of China (2022).

Firstly, there may be risks of cross-border outflow of domestic data. In 2017, China made its first unified regulation on cross-border data flow, proposing typical requirements for Chinese data sovereignty, which attracted widespread attention from the international community. According to Article 37 of the "Cybersecurity Law of the People's Republic of China" (hereinafter referred to as the "Cybersecurity Law"), critical information infrastructure operators that gather or produce personal information or important data during operations within the mainland territory of the People's Republic of China, shall store it within the Chinese mainland. Unlike the "Cybersecurity Law," which focuses on storing data locally, the "Data Security Law of the People's Republic of China" (hereinafter referred to as the "Data Security Law") takes into account the reality that data needs to flow across borders. This law clearly states that China supports the free movement of data, but the precondition is that the security of data must be guaranteed during its international transfer. Based on the currently effective "Cybersecurity Law," "Data Security Law," and "Personal Information Protection Law of the People's Republic of China," the legal risks that Energy Internet platforms may face when transferring data overseas mainly include failing to store data collected within China as required, not conducting security assessments as required, not obtaining personal information protection certification from professional institutions, transferring data to overseas recipients without consent and permission according to legal procedures, and providing personal information to overseas law enforcement or judicial bodies without approval from the relevant authorities.

Secondly, there may be risks of cross-border inflow of data from outside the territory. As previously stated, if the operations of Energy Internet companies span across multiple regions around the world, their ultimate objective would be to facilitate a connected global energy network. In this context, the data regulatory policies of foreign countries play a significant role in the growth and development of these Energy Internet platforms. EU issued the "General Data Protection Regulation" (GDPR) in 2016 and the "Regulation on the Free Flow of Non-personal Data" in 2018, which stipulate different cross-border flow strategies for personal and non-personal data, respectively, and that the outflow of personal data from EU member states must meet the conditions required in applicable laws. In addition to promoting anti-data localization policies to the outside world, the United States enacted the "Clarifying Lawful Overseas Use of Data Act" (CLOUD Act) in February 2018. The CLOUD Act allows "qualified foreign governments" to issue data retrieval orders directly to organizations within the United States after signing an executive agreement with the U.S. government, and the United States can similarly retrieve data directly from organizations within the territory of the agreement country. In the process of signing bilateral agreements related to the CLOUD Act, one of the conditions set by the United States is to cancel data localization policies, which leads to countries that need to retrieve data from the United States allowing more data to flow toward the United States, ultimately resulting in a stronger dependence on the United States. While the United States promotes policies for the free flow of data, it has not relaxed controls over critical domestic data. The Committee on Foreign Investment (CFIUS) has extensive powers to prevent foreign companies from jeopardizing national security. Measures it can take include requiring foreign network operators and telecommunications groups to sign security agreements, demanding that communication infrastructure be located within U.S. territory, and insisting that communication data, transaction data, user information, and the like be stored exclusively within the United States.[47]

Legal Risks Arising from Unclear Ownership of Energy Data

(1) Background Description

Different holders and legal relationships are involved in each stage of energy data generation, collection, storage, processing, transmission, analysis, and utilization: The generation of energy data may involve the personal interests or business of the original data user; the collection, organization, and analysis of energy data may involve the intellectual achievements of those dedicated to the development and application of big energy data, and the transmission and trading of energy data may involve the property rights of those who control this data.[48] To clarify the aforementioned issues, it is necessary to analyze the legal nature of energy data and the ownership thereof.

(2) Identification of Legal Risks

Firstly, there may be legal risks arising from violating the general provisions of the "Anti-Unfair Competition Law of the People's Republic of China" (hereinafter referred to as the "Anti-Unfair Competition Law"). In the absence of a clear definition of property rights, the "Anti-Unfair Competition Law" provides financial remedies for data rights protection. The business of Energy Internet platforms covers the entire dynamic process of energy data generation, collection, storage, processing, transmission, analysis, and utilization. As the lifecycle of data is prolonged, and the process of its generation involves numerous rights holders, the rights and obligations relationships are relatively complex. Once a third party claims data ownership rights against the Energy Internet platforms or sues for the data they control infringing upon the third party's legitimate rights and interests, the Energy Internet platforms will face the risk of being penalized under the "Anti-Unfair Competition Law."

Secondly, the non-exclusive nature of energy data greatly increases the risk of illegal data acquisition. As can be seen in individual cases, courts have recognized that companies can claim certain property rights over "data assets" that they have obtained or held through effort within the framework of the "Anti-Unfair Competition Law." However, this recognition does not imply that companies can use the data assets they control at will. The legal and compliant processing of data throughout its lifecycle is a prerequisite for mining the value of data assets. Although the non-competitivity and non-exclusivity of data facilitate free data flow, they also increase the legal risks for companies to acquire and use data. If a company possesses data obtained

[47] See Liu (2020).

[48] See Fan (2021).

through illegal means, or if it infringes upon the legitimate rights and interests of others during the data collection and usage process, this will not only expose the company to legal risks but also severely diminish the potential value of its data assets. For example, recently, several big data companies have been embroiled in criminal investigations for allegedly collecting personal information illegally, leading to their potential seizure, suspension of operations, or even closure.[49]

Identification of Legal and Policy Risks of the Value Creation System of the Energy Internet

Introduction to the Development of the Value Creation System of the Energy Internet Platform

As the application layer for the Energy Internet, the value creation system helps maximize the energy value using innovative energy application models. For the purpose of developing new models and new business formats to explore the value of the Energy Internet industry by integrating energy with the Internet and adopting market-oriented operations, it is necessary to build a value creation system that can facilitate innovative applications, market operations, and value exploration in the ecological chain of the Energy Internet.

The Energy Internet creates value based on user needs, provides innovative information-based value-added services using a data-centric business model, performs business innovation driven by technology, and explores benefits by seizing the opportunities of reform. The Energy Internet will seamlessly integrate energy production, transmission, transformation, storage, and consumption and restore the intrinsic commodity attributes of energy. This will dismantle the existing monopoly in energy sales and promote the development of competitive retail market models in the energy sector. In addition, the Energy Internet will attract third-party capital to invest in and operate within the energy field, thereby breaking through the current administrative regulatory constraints on energy trading.[50]

In the Energy Internet ecosystem, participants are more diverse, and the traditional value stream has evolved into a value network based on multilateral cooperation. In the value creation system of the Energy Internet, in addition to the traditional power generation, transmission, distribution, sales, and dispatching, there are emerging new energy services, energy management, energy storage, hardware enabling, and so on. The traditional power value flow has derived new value creation, leading to the emergence of digital power generation optimization suppliers, distributed energy service providers, and energy aggregators.[51] The value creation system of Energy Internet companies is a mutually beneficial ecosystem. Typical business forms include

[49] See Ning et al. (2020).

[50] See Chen et al. (2015).

[51] See Nan (2020), pp. 20–21.

distributed PV service ecosystem, integrated energy efficiency service ecosystem, electric vehicle service ecosystem, energy e-commerce service ecosystem, data commercialization service ecosystem, online industrial chain financial ecosystem, electrical equipment service ecosystem, and so on.

Analysis on Legal Risks of Regulatory Businesses

(1) Legal risks arising from industry standards in the electric vehicle charging station business

(a) Background Description

The electric vehicle charging station business mainly involves two core areas: Firstly, the construction and operation of a charging station network, which is a fundamental service to ensure orderly charging for electric vehicles; secondly, the establishment of a smart Internet of Vehicle (IoV) using the information collected from the interaction between electric vehicles and charging stations, which provides information-based value-added services to relevant participants in the electric vehicle service chain.

(b) Identification of Legal Risks

Firstly, there may be regulatory risks in the construction of electric vehicle charging stations. The main regulatory risks faced during the construction of electric vehicle charging stations include the risk of land approval not being granted due to the lack of relevant land planning, as well as risks related to fire safety supervision. Due to the lack of land use planning, there is a risk that real estate developers will not cooperate with the State Grid in constructing supporting grids or even not allow the construction of charging stations in residential and commercial areas. Besides, the limited capacity of transformers in old residential and commercial areas requires the renovation of the supporting grids. In addition, the current government land planning lacks the provision of electric vehicle charging stations, which leads to difficulties in land approval and affects the large-scale networked construction of charging stations. The inherent fire risks associated with charging stations also hinder their construction.

Secondly, there may be regulatory risks arising from compulsory management of electric vehicle charging stations. According to the "Announcement on Adjusting the Catalog of Measuring Instruments Subject to Compulsory Management" (No. 42, 2020) issued by the State Administration for Market Regulation, electric vehicle charging stations have been included in the catalog and have been subject to compulsory management from January 1, 2023.

(2) Regulatory Challenges for Deepening the Reform of the Investment and Financing System in the Energy Sector

The power sector in China presents a vast landscape for construction and investment opportunities, with several Energy Internet companies boasting significant financial strength for investment.

In 2017, the National Energy Administration issued the "Implementation Opinions on Deepening the Reform of the Investment and Financing System in the Energy Sector" (Guo Neng Fa Gai [2017] No. 88), which not only provides a number of investment and financing benefits for the energy sector but also establishes the regulatory requirements for such activities.

Energy Internet companies, when vying for investment projects, will have to navigate the risks associated with open competition and project assessment. They will be subject to stringent regulation throughout the entire investment process. Their investment actions must align with national planning, subjecting them to compliance risks. In sectors like coal mining and thermal power, where there is existing or potential overcapacity, these companies will be subject to the state's rigorous specific regulatory measures. Furthermore, their investment credibility is at stake, as they could face regulatory repercussions for any breach of trust.

Analysis on Legal Risks of Competitive Businesses

(1) Market Risks of Electric Vehicle Charging Station Businesses Abusing Their Dominant Market Position

In 2015, the General Office of the State Council issued the "Guiding Opinions on Accelerating the Construction of Electric Vehicle Charging Infrastructure" (Guo Ban Fa [2015] No. 73), which stipulates that the government should foster innovative frameworks according to market conditions, give full play to the leading role of the market, and guide social capital to participate in the construction and operation of the charging infrastructure system by promoting the PPP model, increasing financial support, and establishing a reasonable price mechanism. These guiding opinions have attracted a large amount of state-owned and private companies to the market. Electric vehicle manufacturers, state-owned companies, and private companies are the key operators in China's charging station market. The leading companies include TELD, Star Charge, and SGCC.

Energy Internet companies that dominate the electric vehicle charging station market will face legal risks associated with the abuse of market dominance.

(2) Legal Risks of Energy Storage Businesses

(a) Background Description

The "Opinions on Further Deepening the Reform of the Power System" (Zhong Fa [2015] No. 9) redefines the functions of grid companies. These companies are now required to focus on investing in and operating grids, as well as on transmitting and distributing power. They are responsible for ensuring the safety of the grid system and for guaranteeing that the grid operates in a fair, non-discriminatory manner, while also fulfilling the duty to provide universal power services. This reform shifts the income source of grid companies from relying on the margin between the purchase and sale prices of electricity to earning income based on the transmission and distribution tariffs approved by the government. Due to the natural monopoly characteristics of the power transmission and distribution industry, it is necessary for the government to regulate the pricing of these services. The essence of transmission and distribution price regulation is that the government sets a ceiling on the permissible revenue for grid companies, which is conducive to achieving significant public policy objectives of the government departments. It also effectively incentivizes grid companies to reduce costs and enhance the efficiency of resource allocation. With government regulation of transmission and distribution pricing in place, grid companies must allocate the costs of the transmission and distribution network reasonably and establish specific pricing for these services. A scientific method of cost allocation for transmission and distribution is of great importance for the healthy and stable operation of grid companies and for providing high-quality power supply services.

(b) Identification of Legal Risks

In 2019, the National Development and Reform Commission officially issued the "Measures for Supervision and Review of Power Transmission and Distribution Pricing Costs," which clearly stipulates that costs unrelated to the power transmission and distribution business of grid companies, such as those for pumped-storage power stations and electrical energy storage facilities, should not be included in the cost of transmission and distribution pricing.[52] In the current domestic environment, investment is still primarily led by grid companies, with limited participation from social capital. The investment intensity in energy storage stations on the grid side will directly affect the innovative development of business models. In terms of profit models, energy storage facilities invested in by grid companies lack a mechanism to guide costs effectively and energy storage projects invested in by social capital lack predictable profit margins. Compared to the application of energy storage stations abroad, the characteristics of energy storage stations put into operation in China are as follows: They are all invested in and constructed by subsidiaries of the grid companies, which then lease them. Their function is to ensure the reliable supply of power and the safe and stable operation of the grid, and the related costs have not yet been clearly guided through any mechanism.[53]

(3) Legal Risks of Energy-Saving Services

(a) Background Description

Energy-saving services refer to services in which professional third-party organizations (energy management agencies) help their clients solve technical and implementation problems in energy-saving operation transformation.[54] Energy-saving services are often provided in the form of energy performance contracting. China's first national standard in the energy-saving service industry is the "Guidance on

---

[52] National Development and Reform Commission, and National Energy Administration. Measures for Supervision and Review of Power Transmission and Distribution Pricing Costs (Fa Gai Jia Ge Gui [2019] No. 897), Article 10.

[53] Shi (2019).

[54] Zhang (2012), p. 8.

Energy Performance Contracting" (GB/T 24915–2010), which was drafted by the China National Institute of Standardization, the ESCO Committee of China Energy Conservation Association (EMCA) and other authorities and was officially implemented on January 1, 2011. To adapt to the fast-changing economic landscape in China and the increasingly diversified energy performance contracting models, the revised "Guidance on Energy Performance Contracting" (GB/T 24915–2020) was officially implemented on October 1, 2020, which superseded the 2010 version. The above standards are intended to provide technical support for the rapid and orderly development of the energy-saving service industry and serve as the technical specifications for energy performance contracting projects and the basic operating guide for energy service companies.

(2) Identification of Legal Risks

According to the "Guidance on Energy Performance Contracting" (GB/T 24915–2020), common contract types include shared savings contracts, guaranteed savings contracts, energy cost management contracts, financing lease contracts, and contract types formed by any combination of the above four basic types.[55] The diversity of energy performance contract types leads to inconsistencies in judicial practice regarding the determination of the nature of contracts by courts. Different determinations of the nature of energy performance contracts may lead to legal risks associated with court jurisdiction, contract rescission, determination and assumption of breach of contract liability, and contract validity.

(4) Legal Risks Arising from the Integrated Development and Utilization of Distributed Energy

(a) Background Description

Distributed energy is a local distributed energy supply system that provides electricity, heat, and cooling. Based on the principles of thermodynamics and the concept of integrated energy cascade utilization, it generates and uses electricity, heat, and cooling by consuming primary energy sources.[56] Distributed energy, with its high-energy efficiency, flexible operation, and good economy, is gradually becoming an important source of power generation. The key to the development of distributed energy is "direct local electricity trading," and solving this issue is the most critical breakthrough in advancing the energy revolution. China's current policies on distributed energy are presented in the "Notice on Launching a Pilot Market-based Trading for Distributed Power Generation" (Fa Gai Neng Yuan [2017] No. 1901), the "Supplementary Notice on Launching a Pilot Market-based Trading for Distributed Power Generation" (Fa Gai Ban Neng Yuan [2017] No. 2150), the "Interim Measures for the Management of Development and Construction of Distributed Wind Power Projects" (Guo Neng Fa Xin Neng [2018] No. 30), etc.

[55] State Administration for Market Regulation and Standardization Administration of China. Guidance on Energy Performance Contracting (GB/T 24915–2020).

[56] See Huang (2018).

(b) Identification of Legal Risks

There may be legal risks arising from discrepancies in grid-connection fee standards. Grid-connection fees refer to the charges collected by grid companies to recover the investment in grid framework and the costs of operation and maintenance, in order to obtain a reasonable return on assets. In China's distributed power generation market, grid-connection fees are involved in the following two trading modes: a. the direct trading mode, in which distributed power generation project entities directly trade with power users, while grid companies charge the grid-connection fees; b. the entrusted trading mode, in which distributed power generation project entities entrust grid companies with the task of selling electricity on their behalf, with grid companies deducting the grid-connection fees (including electricity loss during transmission) from the comprehensive electricity tariffs and transferring the remaining revenue to the distributed power generation project entities.[57] The calculation of grid-connection fees in China is closely related to cross-subsidies. However, the current cross-subsidy lacks a unified calculation criterion, resulting in discrepancies in grid-connection fee standards.

There may be risks arising from "direct local electricity trading" contracts. In distributed power generation trading, contract parties must meet market access conditions; otherwise, it may lead to legal risks associated with contract validity and the like. For example, policy documents such as the "Notice on Launching a Pilot Market-Based Trading for Distributed Power Generation" (Fa Gai Neng Yuan [2017] No. 1901) and the "Jiangsu Province Market-Based Trading Rules for Distributed Power Generation (Trial)" have stipulated market access qualifications for power generators and power purchasers. Failure to meet the above qualifications could result in the legal consequence of the contract being invalid.

Summary of Legal Risks Associated with the Platform-Based Transformation of Energy Internet Companies

The energy network framework is the physical infrastructure that allows the grid connection, transmission, distribution, and dispatching of renewable energy within the Energy Internet platform. The introduction of the Energy Internet has shattered the traditional boundaries between supply and demand within the energy industry, significantly enhancing the interconnection, interoperability, and complementarity of primary and secondary energy such as coal, oil, natural gas, heat, and electricity.[58] To achieve China's "dual carbon" goals, which are to achieve peak carbon emissions by 2030 and carbon neutrality by 2060, the development and utilization of renewable energy are particularly crucial for China's energy transition. In this process, the

[57] National Development and Reform Commission, and National Energy Administration. Notice on Launching a Pilot Market-based Trading for Distributed Power Generation (Fa Gai Neng Yuan [2017] No. 1901).

[58] Ma et al. (2015).

Energy Internet plays a significant role. One of its core functions is to use the Internet information technology to dispatch and consume renewable power across different regions more efficiently. In addition, the Energy Internet also helps to optimize the storage of renewable energy and promote the development of distributed energy. However, during the effort to achieve peak carbon emissions and carbon neutrality, the State Grid's transformation into an Energy Internet platform also faces many regulatory risks associated with the energy transition process as well as legal risks stemming from market competition. These include regulatory risks associated with achieving the carbon neutrality goal by 2060, legal risks caused by the Energy Internet platform's failure to provide fair, non-discriminatory, and open services, regulatory risks arising from the platform's reform to separate primary and auxiliary businesses, legal risks of market competition faced by platform-based economic entities in a diversified market environment, legal risks due to energy management technological risks, risks arising from the restructuring of legal systems for energy trading, etc.

The section on the analysis of legal risks associated with the information support system of the Energy Internet platform and the prevention measures describes the legal risks that may arise from the information support system during the transition into the Energy Internet by analyzing the business characteristics of the information support system and with reference to the "Electricity Consumption-Based Environmental Monitoring" and "New Energy Cloud" services of the State Grid. These legal risks include the legal risks arising from the public nature of energy data, legal risks generated by the cross-border flow of data, legal risks that may arise from the "New Energy Cloud" service due to the infringement of personal information rights, legal risks caused by unclear ownership of energy data, legal risks associated with improper collection and application of non-personal information data by the "Electricity Consumption-Based Environmental Monitoring" service, etc. According to current laws, the legal nature of energy data is not yet clear. However, considering the trend of China's Internet platform supervision and the important role of the energy sector in national security, as it relates to the national economy and people's livelihoods, there is a high probability that energy data will be classified as public data. Therefore, the Energy Internet platform should follow the principle of prudence in the collection and utilization of energy data. In compliance with the national regulations on the management of public data collection, it should fully realize data sharing, break down data barriers, and reduce the cost of data acquisition.

The integration of the innovative Internet technologies will enhance the production, transmission, and utilization efficiency of the traditional energy sector. Under the framework of the Energy Internet, innovative business models are continuously emerging, reshaping the innovation ecosystem within the energy sector, thereby achieving the goal of creating value.[59] The value creation system of the Energy Internet platform serves as a vehicle for value realization, supporting the business processes of the State Grid. Based on relevant laws, regulations and regulatory policies, as well as the business characteristics of the value creation system, we have identified the following hidden legal risks in the value creation system: land use and

[59] See Chen et al. (2015).

fire safety risks during the construction and maintenance of electric vehicle charging stations, risks related to fair competition and mixed-ownership reform in energy finance businesses, risks of "price discrimination" using big data in integrated energy services, difficulties in allocating investment costs in energy storage businesses, and legal risks associated with cross-subsidization in the integrated development and utilization of distributed energy.

References

Chen Q, Liu D, Lin J, He J, Wang Y (2015) Business model and market mechanism of energy internet (I). Power Syst Technol 39(11):3050–3056. https://doi.org/10.13335/j.1000-3673.pst.2015.11.006

Fan J (2021) Research on the protection of big data rights and interests with the protection of personal data rights and interests as the core. J Inf Secur Res 7(12):1166–1177. https://doi.org/10.3969/j.issn.2096-1057.2021.12.009

Gao F, Zeng R, Qu L, Zhang J (2018) Research on identification of concept and characteristics of energy internet. Electric Power 51(8):10–16. https://doi.org/10.11930/j.issn.1004-9649.201806095

Guo H, Hu M (2020) A review of China's energy policy and the adjustment orientation in 2020. Int Petroleum Econom 28(2):45–54. https://doi.org/10.3969/j.issn.1004-7298.2020.02.007

Guo W, Tang R (2020) The power industry under the 2060 carbon neutrality goal. Energy 2020(11):19–26

Hu J, Li Q, Huang B, Feng K (2019) Business model research of energy storage on grid side adapted to application scenarios and policy environment in China. J Glob Energy Interconnect 2(4):367–375. https://doi.org/10.19705/j.cnki.issn2096-5125.2019.04.007

Huang Y (2018) Researches on distributed energy policy and industrial development. Gas & Heat 37(4):24–27. https://doi.org/10.13608/j.cnki.1000-4416.2018.04.007

Li D, Shi Y, Li Y (2020) Research on the business model of energy storage systems in the energy internet. Power Demand Side Manage 2020(2):77–82. https://doi.org/10.3969/j.issn.1009-1831.2020.02.014

Li M (2018) Researches on energy internet business model based on synthetic energy supply and demand service. Master's Dissertation, North China Electric Power University

Liu Y (2020) Comparative analysis of China, US, and EU policies on cross-border data flows and international trends. China Inf Secur 2020(11):75–78. https://doi.org/10.3969/j.issn.1674-7844.2020.11.018

Liu X, Niu X, Wang B, Lin J, Zhang J, Wang Y (2016) A review on the energy internet. Electric Power 49(3):24–33. https://doi.org/10.11930/j.issn.1004-9649.2016.03.024.10

Lv G (2019) Research of energy storage application mode under the background of energy internet. Master's Dissertation, North China Electric Power University. https://doi.org/10.27140/d.cnki.ghbbu.2019.000418

Ma Z, Zhou X, Shang Y, Sheng W (2015) Exploring the concept, key technologies and development model of energy internet. Power Syst Technol 39(11):3014–3022. https://doi.org/10.13335/j.1000-3673.pst.2015.11.002

Nan D (2020) The research on CR power transformation strategy based on internet+. Master's Dissertation, Shenzhen University. https://doi.org/10.27321/d.cnki.gszdu.2020.001160

Ning X, Wu H, Chen S, Lin Y (2020) Misunderstandings and compliance conditions of data assets. Shanghai Legal Studies 2020(13):235–242. https://doi.org/10.26914/c.cnkihy.2020.042028

Qu L, Ouyang B, Yuan Z, Zeng R (2019) Steady-state power flow analysis of cold-thermal-electric integrated energy system based on unified power flow model. Energies 12(23):4455–4471. https://doi.org/10.3390/en12234455

Ren H, Yang T, Wu Q, Gao W (2017) Current status of distributed energy internet in Japan and its enlightenment to China. Sino-Global Energy 22(12):15–23

Shi Z (2019) Analysis of foreign energy storage station applications and implications for China. Energy 2019(6):79–82

Sichuan Observation News (2021) Perspectives on the first anti-monopoly fine in the platform economy. Retrieved January 5, 2024, from https://new.qq.com/rain/a/20210412A02KLX00

State Grid Corporation of China (2022) Company Profile from the official website of State Grid Corporation of China, Retrieved January 5, 2024, from http://www.sgcc.com.cn/html/sgcc/col2022121208/column_2022121208_1.shtml

Sun S (2018) Researches on the role of government in the construction of energy internet in China. Master's Dissertation, North China Electric Power University

Tian S, Luan W, Zhang D, Liang C, Sun Y (2015) Technical forms and key technologies on energy internet. Proc CSEE, 35(14):3482–3494. https://doi.org/10.13334/j.0258-8013.pcsee.2015.14.002

Wang M, Wu H, Yang L, Qiao S, Hui H, Yang Y, Ding Y (2020) Development status and prospects of the Energy Internet in electricity markets. Power Demand Side Manage 22(2):1–7. https://doi.org/10.3969/j.issn.1009-1831.2020.02.001

Wang Z (2016) Germany's energy transition: policy and achievements. Int Forum 18(2):74–81. https://doi.org/10.13549/j.cnki.cn11-3959/d.2016.02.013

Wang Y (2016) Economic scheduling of integrated energy systems containing electricity, heat, and natural gas based on conditional value-at-risk. Master's Dissertation, North China Electric Power University

Wang X, Wang Y (2020) Analysis report on domestic and international energy internet development. China Electric Power Press

Xinhua News Agency (2020) Statement by H.E. Xi Jinping President of the People's Republic of China at the General Debate of the 75th Session of the United Nations General Assembly. Retrieved January 5, 2024, from http://www.cppcc.gov.cn/zxww/2020/09/23/ARTI1600819264410115.shtml

Yin C, Yang D, Geng G, Fan Z (2015) Summary of energy internet projects in Germany and its enlightenment to China. Power Syst Technol 39(11):3040–3049. https://doi.org/10.13335/j.1000-3673.pst.2015.11.005

Zhang B (2014) German energy transition strategy and its lessons. China Power Enterprise Manage 2014(8):50–53. https://doi.org/10.3969/j.issn.1007-3361.2014.08.012

Zhang Y, Chen Z, Cai Z, Li L, Song W (2016) New generation of cyber-energy system: energy Internet. Electr Power Automat Equipm 36(9):1–7 and 16. https://doi.org/10.16081/j.issn.1006-6047.2016.09.001

Zhang S (2012) Study on the continuous improvement mechanism of energy service quality. Master's Dissertation, Tianjin University of Technology

Zhang Y (2017) Promotion progress and enlightenment of international energy internet. Shanghai Energy Conservat 2017(6):333–338. https://doi.org/10.13770/j.cnki.issn2095-705x.2017.06.006

Chapter 4
Researches on Legal Risks of Data Use by Energy Internet Companies

Since 2020, Energy Internet companies have thrown their full weight behind the construction of new digital infrastructure. Capitalizing on the historic opportunities presented by the development of new digital infrastructures such as 5G networks, the industrial Internet, and IoT, these companies have been pooling resources and unlocking potential. They are strengthening the cultivation and expansion of emerging digital industries and are committed to innovating business models, including the operation of basic resources and platforms, as well as data monetization. However, despite the broad prospects and plans at the technological level, the legislative and judicial practices concerning corporate data rights have not been as satisfactory as desired. Data rights and data protection are not the same thing. In Europe and the United States, data protection usually refers to the protection of personal information. In China, based on the differences between personal information and data outlined in Articles 111 and 127 of the "General Principles of the Civil Law of the People's Republic of China" (hereinafter referred to as the "General Principles of the Civil Law"), personal information protection and data rights have no overlaps.[1] Despite the fervent attention and rapid progress in protecting personal information both domestically and internationally, Article 127 of the "General Principles of Civil Law" does acknowledge legal protection for data, yet it fails to clearly define what "data" is or establish its scope. Similarly, the Civil Code, which came into effect on January 1, 2021, does not address this issue either. Consequently, the question of who ultimately owns data remains unanswered.

China has repeatedly called for data rights confirmation. The "13th Five-Year Plan for National Informatization" has underscored the need to accelerate the legislation of data ownership and data management. At the 13th National People's Congress, the Financial and Economic Committee of the National People's Congress proposed to improve the rules on data ownership, rights, and transactions. At the 19th National Congress of the Communist Party of China, President Xi Jinping clearly demanded

[1] See Han (2020).

H. Deng, *Green Energy Transition in China*, International Law in Asia,
https://doi.org/10.1007/978-981-97-2934-0_4

the development of regulations for confirmation, openness, circulation, and trading of data resources, as well as the improvement of the data property rights protection system. Despite these high-level directives, actual judicial practice regarding the protection of data rights has lagged. The rights to data have not yet been directly recognized by the judiciary, and current cases are often resolved by applying the basic provisions of the "Anti-Unfair Competition Law."[2] As the legal proverb goes, "where there is no remedy, there is no right." In judicial practice, the ambiguous attitude toward data rights directly affects whether they can be fully protected as a new type of right. This ambiguity also has a negative impact on those entities eager to extensively explore and utilize data.

The massive corporate data of Energy Internet companies is both an untapped "digital gold mine" and a legal risk that cannot be ignored if not handled carefully. The purpose of this research is to establish a solid legal foundation to assist Energy Internet companies in utilizing and protecting data during their transition. For clarification, the rights and interests of data mentioned herein include the protection and utilization of both personal information and non-personal information, such as industrial data.

Types of Data Involved in the Operation of Energy Internet Companies

The Energy Internet extensively expands upon the smart grid, surpassing it in scope, structure, and complexity. In the Energy Internet, data is generated throughout the entire chain of energy production, transmission, conversion, control, trading, and consumption. In addition, a large amount of social, economic, and environmental data that impacts the Energy Internet will also be collected and used in the Energy Internet.[3] Specifically, the following types of data are involved in Energy Internet operations:

Non-personal Data

Energy Internet companies, as industrial companies that participate in energy production, transmission, and consumption, are gradually transforming into platform-based companies. The data generated in the operations of Energy Internet companies include the following:

---

[2] Same as above.

[3] Tan et al. (2019).

Equipment Status Monitoring Data, Which Includes the Data Collected by Sensors from Power Generation Equipment, Transmission and Distribution Equipment, Gas Pipelines, Electric Vehicles, and Electrical Equipment That Are Connected to the Energy Internet

Energy Conversion and Consumption Data, Which Includes a Large Amount of Customer Business Data and Energy Trading Records Resulting from the Participation of Hundreds of Millions of Energy Users, Smart Devices, and Electric Vehicles in the Energy Marketing Business Within the Energy Internet

Take the optimized operation of the IES as an example. In order to achieve optimal and coordinated operation of source-grid-load-storage for IES, optimal control of power flow is required. Based on the typical cold-thermal-electric IES, the system power purchase costs, energy station construction costs, thermal system pipeline laying costs, and pollutant gas treatment costs are taken as objective functions. In terms of constraints, power balance constraints and power flow balance constraints are considered for the power subsystem, the thermal subsystem, and the energy conversion process. During the control process, data such as the system control data, power generation data, operating data of multi-energy conversion equipment, energy storage data, and load energy use data are generated.[4] The optimization of power flow in an IES can enhance the accuracy of output data and safeguard the data integrity for Internet companies. This also serves as the technical foundation for analyzing the legal risks associated with the application of various types of data.

Data Generated from Internal Company Management, Which Includes Data Generated in the Process of Human Resources and Materials, Capital Operations, ERP Management, and Collaborative Office

External Data, Which Includes Geographical and Meteorological Data such as Geographic Information System (GIS), Temperature, Wind, Precipitation, and Environmental Data Like Earthquakes and Floods. Although These Data Are Not Directly Produced by the Energy Internet, They Have Short-Term or Long-Term Impacts on the Operation of the Energy Internet

Personal Data

In addition to industrial data, a large amount of personal data is used in the daily operations of Energy Internet companies. According to Article 1034 of the Civil Code (effective as of January 1, 2021), personal data is the information recorded electronically or in other ways that can be used, by itself or in combination with

[4] Oyang et al. (2020), (November).

other information, to identify a natural person, including his name, date of birth, identification number, biometric information, residential address, telephone number, email address, health information, whereabouts, and the like. Besides, the concept of sensitive personal data is frequently mentioned. Sensitive personal data refers to personal data that, once disclosed, illegally provided, or misused, could jeopardize personal and property safety, easily lead to damage to an individual's reputation, physical and mental health, or result in discriminatory treatment.[5]

Energy Internet Data Lifecycle

The data lifecycle refers to the different stages the above-mentioned non-personal data and personal data undergo in the business of Energy Internet companies, from data collection, data storage, data use, data transmission and exchange, to data destruction.

Data Collection

In the operation of Energy Internet companies, data collection mainly involves the following scenarios:

Automatic collection of system operation data by a network of sensors; collection of partner data in paper or electronic forms during transactions; collection of data related to the company and its employees during internal management; user data collection through technologies such as smart meters, IoV, and IoT; and collection of publicly available information either manually or through automated tools such as web crawlers.

Data Storage

Data storage refers to the stage where the collected data is stored in digital form on physical media. Common data storage methods include using traditional physical media (such as CDs, hard drives, etc.), storing on company-owned servers, and using servers provided by third-party cloud services.

Data Use

Data use includes both the direct use of raw data and the use of results obtained from data cleaning, analysis, and mining.

[5] State Administration for Market Regulation and Standardization Administration of China. Information Security Technology—Personal Information Security Specifications (GB/T 35273–2020).

Data Transmission and Exchange

Data transmission and exchange include data sharing, data transfer, and other forms. If an Energy Internet company comprises many subsidiaries and sub-subsidiaries with independent legal person status, data sharing and transfer may occur within the system during the application of big data. If an Energy Internet company undergoes acquisition, merger, restructuring, or even bankruptcy proceedings, data transfer may be involved.

Data Destruction

Data that serves no practical purpose or has outlived its storage duration should typically be disposed of. Methods of destruction include the erasure and anonymization of personal information.

Domestic and International Legislation and Practice of Data Use

Domestic Legislation

In recent years, the National People's Congress and its Standing Committee have attached great importance to legislation related to personal information protection. In 2012, the Standing Committee of the National People's Congress passed the "Decision on Strengthening Network Information Protection," which establishes basic norms for the collection and use of personal information, as well as the obligations of network service providers to protect the security of personal information. In 2013, the "Law of the People's Republic of China on the Protection of Consumer Rights and Interests" was amended to include special provisions for the protection of consumer personal information. In 2009 and 2015, the "Amendment (VII) to the Criminal Law of the People's Republic of China" and the "Amendment (IX) to the Criminal Law of the People's Republic of China" (hereinafter referred to as the "Amendment (IX) to the Criminal Law") were passed, which specifically added crimes and penalties for the sale or illegal provision, theft, or illegal acquisition of citizens' personal information. In 2016, the "Cybersecurity Law" was adopted, which enriches and perfects the rules for the collection and use of personal information, as well as the obligations and responsibilities of network operators to protect personal information. In March 2017, the "General Principles of Civil Law" were passed at the fifth session of the 12th National People's Congress, which stipulates the protection of personal information and data as an important civil right.[6] In May 2020, the Civil Code was passed at the

[6] Wang et al. (2019), (June 5).

third session of the 13th National People's Congress, which continues and refines the provisions on personal information and data protection that were outlined in the "General Principles of Civil Law." Beyond these foundational legislative efforts, specialized statutes such as the "Personal Information Protection Law of the People's Republic of China" and the "Data Security Law of the People's Republic of China" have been included in the legislative plan of the National People's Congress. As a result, a preliminary framework for data protection regulations in China has been created.

In addition to the fundamental laws, China also provides relevant administrative regulations, judicial interpretations, departmental rules, normative documents, and national standards to guide the behaviors of all parties involved in data application activities.

Fundamental Laws

Civil Code of the People's Republic of China.

"Cybersecurity Law of the People's Republic of China".

"Personal Information Protection Law of the People's Republic of China".

"Data Security Law of the People's Republic of China".

"Criminal Law of the People's Republic of China".

"Cryptography Law of the People's Republic of China".

Administrative Regulations

"Administrative Measures for Scientific Data".

Judicial Interpretations

"Interpretation of the Supreme People's Court and the Supreme People's Procuratorate on Several Issues concerning the Application of Law in the Handling of Criminal Cases of Infringing on Citizens' Personal Information".

"Guidelines for Procuratorial Organs on Handling of Criminal Cases Involving Infringement of Citizens' Personal Information",

Departmental Rules

"Administrative Measures for the Multi-level Protection of Information Security".

"Regulations on the Protection of Personal Information of Telecommunication and Internet Users".

"Measures for Cybersecurity Review".

"Methods for Identifying Collection and Use of Personal Information in Violation of Laws and Regulations by Apps".

"Guidelines for the Construction of the Online Data Security Standards System (Draft for Comment)".

Normative Documents

"Measures for Data Security Management" (Draft for Comment).

"Guidelines for Safeguarding Personal Information in Apps" (Draft for Comment).

"Guidelines for Classification and Grading of Industrial Data (Trial)".

National Standards

GB/T 35273–2020 "Information Security Technology—Personal Information Security Specifications".

GB/Z 28828–2012 "Information Security Technology—Guide for Personal Information Protection on Public and Commercial Service Information Systems".

GB/T 37964–2019 "Guide for De-identifying Personal Information".

GB/T 34978–2017 "Technical Requirements for the Protection of Personal Information on Mobile Smart Devices".

GB/T 37932–2019 "Information Security Technology—Security Requirements for Data Exchange Services".

GB/T 37138–2018 "Guide for the Implementation of Multi-level Protection of Information System Security".

GB/T 37973–2019 "Big Data Security Management Guide".

GB/T 35274–2017 "Security Capability Requirements for Big Data Services".

International Legislative Practices

The EU General Data Protection Regulation (GDPR)
The EU Regulation on Free Flow of Non-personal Data
The US California Consumer Privacy Act (CCPA)
Brazil's General Data Protection Regulation (LGPD)

Conclusion on Legislative Practices

Despite the establishment of key individual pieces of legislation such as the "Personal Information Protection Law" and the "Data Protection Law" in China, it is often the case that departmental rules, policy documents, and national standards are the ones that actually provide guidance in practice. These documents tend to address specific issues within the realm of data protection with clear and detailed provisions and guidelines. However, they carry a lower legal weight and are not strong enough to act as decisive references in legal disputes. To put it succinctly, the current practice of data protection in China still frequently encounters the dilemma of having no solid legal ground to stand on in many situations. This lack of legal clarity leaves entities uncertain about the legality of their actions, which in turn leads to unnecessary legal risks and potential vulnerabilities.

Domestic and International Law Enforcement and Judicial Practices on Data Protection

Domestic Law Enforcement and Judicial Practices

(1) Typical Administrative Cases

   (a) Administrative penalty decision on Jiang XX (anonymized) for illegally obtaining, selling, and providing personal information to others (Qing Gong (Jiang) Xing Fa Jue Zi [2020] No. 1753).
   (b) Administrative penalty decision for Xinyu Ruiwei Information Technology Co., Ltd. (Yu Gong (Wang) Jue Zi [2020] No. 0009).
   (c) Special rectification of apps infringing on user rights.
   (d) Other administrative enforcement cases.

(2) Typical Criminal Cases

In May 2017, the Supreme People's Court of China announced seven typical cases of crimes involving infringement of citizens' personal information, which specifically include:

(a) The case of Shao Baoming and others infringing on citizens' personal information (Dongyang City People's Court of Zhejiang Province (2016) Zhe 0783 Xing Chu No. 1171).
(b) The case of Han Shijie, Kuang Yuanhong, Han Wenhua, and others infringing on citizens' personal information (Badong County People's Court of Hubei Province (2016) E 2823 Xing Chu No. 132).
(c) The case of Zhou Bincheng and others infringing on citizens' personal information (Pinghu City People's Court of Zhejiang Province (2016) Zhe 0482 Xing Chu No. 1022).

(d) The case of Xia Fuxiao infringing on citizens' personal information (Keqiao District People's Court of Shaoxing City, Zhejiang Province (2017) Zhe 0603 Xing Chu No. 97).
(e) The case of Xiao Fan, Zhou Hao, and others infringing on citizens' personal information (Hongshan District People's Court of Chifeng City, Inner Mongolia Autonomous Region (2016) Nei 0402 Xing Chu No. 396).
(f) The case of Du Mingxing, Du Minglong infringing on citizens' personal information (Gulou District People's Court of Nanjing City, Jiangsu Province (2016) Su 0106 Xing Chu No. 943).
(g) The case of Ding Yaguang infringing on citizens' personal information (Yueqing City People's Court of Zhejiang Province (2016) Zhe 0382 Xing Chu No. 2332).

(3) Typical Civil Cases

(a) The case of infringement liability dispute between Shen XX (anonymized) and Alipay (China) Network Technology Co., Ltd. (Beijing Chaoyang District People's Court (2018) Jing 0105 Min Chu No. 36658).
(b) The case of network infringement liability dispute brought by Yu XX (anonymized) against Alipay (China) Network Technology Co., Ltd., Beijing Leyoudakang Technology Co., Ltd. Haidian Qinghe Maternity and Baby Products Store, Zhejiang Taobao Network Co., Ltd., and Zhejiang Tmall Network Co., Ltd. (Beijing Haidian District People's Court (2018) Jing 0108 Min Chu No. 13661).
(c) The case of network infringement liability dispute over privacy rights and personal information rights between Huang XX (anonymized) and Tencent Technology (Shenzhen) Co., Ltd. Guangzhou Branch, Tencent Technology (Beijing) Co., Ltd. (Beijing Internet Court (2019) Jing 0491 Min Chu No. 16142).
(d) The first-instance civil judgment on the network infringement liability dispute between Beijing Microlive Vision Technology Co., Ltd. and Xu XX (anonymized) ((2019) Jing 0491 Min Chu No. 6694)
(e) The case of commercial bribery and unfair competition dispute brought by Shenzhen Tencent Computer System Co., Ltd. and Tencent Technology (Shenzhen) Co., Ltd. (Tianjin Binhai New District People's Court (2019) Jin 0116 Min Chu No. 2091).
(f) The case of commercial bribery and unfair competition dispute between Anhui Meijing Information Technology Co., Ltd. and Taobao (China) Software Co., Ltd. (Hangzhou Intermediate People's Court of Zhejiang Province (2018) Zhe 01 Min Zhong No. 7312).

Conclusion on Domestic Law Enforcement and Judicial Practices

(1) Administrative Enforcement

Articles 41 to 44 of the "Cybersecurity Law" serve as the current and generally applicable legal rules for the protection of personal information, providing a legal basis for regulatory authorities to carry out enforcement work on personal information protection. According to statistics from publicly available administrative penalty decisions, nearly half of the administrative penalties are based on Article 41, which pertains to the legality, legitimacy, necessity, and the requirements to inform and obtain consent in the collection and use of personal information. In the field of administrative enforcement, it's clear that regulating apps is currently the top priority for data protection authorities. Looking ahead, we may see a shift from solely focusing on app governance to a broader approach that includes thorough compliance evaluations of not just apps, but also third-party SDKs, mini-programs, and app stores, among other areas. Since apps serve as a vital platform for Energy Internet companies to operate, the importance of managing compliance risks associated with apps is growing for these businesses. At the national level, app governance is primarily carried out by specialized task forces, the Ministry of Industry and Information Technology, and the Ministry of Public Security. Additionally, local regulatory authorities, such as the Communications Administrations in Beijing, Shanghai, Guizhou, Guangdong, and other regions, are conducting their own inspections and enforcement actions concerning the collection and use of personal information by apps within their jurisdictions. This indicates that the current governance of apps in China is characterized by overlapping enforcement by multiple authorities and at various levels, which poses a significant administrative liability risk for businesses that cannot be overlooked.

(2) Criminal Enforcement

In recent years, the trend in criminal enforcement in the field of data protection has been very pronounced, especially in the protection of personal information data. Since the implementation of the "Amendment (IX) to the Criminal Law," the number of criminal cases involving the infringement of citizens' personal information has been increasing year by year. As of January 25, 2021, China Judgments Online has published a total of 9,071 cases related to the infringement of citizens' personal information. Specifically, there were only 10 cases in 2015 and 287 cases in 2016, but the number soared to 1,209 cases in 2017. In the following years of 2018, 2019, and 2020, the number of published cases each year exceeded 2,000.

(3) Civil Enforcement

According to statistics on relevant civil judgments, the number of civil lawsuits triggered by the infringement of personal information rights has been increasing year by year since the implementation of the "General Principles of Civil Law." This year, influenced by the pandemic, the number of cases has slightly declined, but there are still cases that have attracted widespread social attention.

From a corporate compliance perspective, with the refinement of laws and regulations and the growing awareness of citizens' personal rights, Energy Internet companies, as collectors of vast amounts of personal information, are likely to face an inevitable increase in litigation related to personal information disputes in future. In order to prove their innocence during legal proceedings, it is not enough for Energy Internet companies to take necessary measures to protect personal information in accordance with laws, regulations, and supervisory requirements. They must also consider implementing data protection practices in a "verifiable" manner. This approach enables them to provide evidence of their compliant data handling activities during litigation, which is an essential requirement for building a data compliance system.

International Law Enforcement and Judicial Practices

Announcement time	Type	Regulatory authority	Companies/acts involved	Result
2018.5	Regulatory enforcement	CNIL	**Google LLC** In May 2018, two European non-profit privacy and digital rights organizations filed complaints with the French National Commission on Informatics and Liberty (CNIL) alleging that Google had adopted a "forced consent" policy in its handling of personal user data. The data collected included a vast amount of personal information about users, which was also used for commercial advertising purposes without the users' knowledge[7]	On January 21, 2019, the CNIL's restricted committee imposed a financial penalty of 50 million euros, approximately CNY 380 million, against the company Google LLC, in accordance with the GDPR, for lack of transparency, inadequate information, and lack of valid consent regarding the ads personalization

(continued)

[7] Kang (2019).

(continued)

Announcement time	Type	Regulatory authority	Companies/acts involved	Result
2018.6	Regulatory investigation	ICO	**Ticketmaster** Ticketmaster UK announced that malicious software was discovered on the Inbenta product hosted by one of their third-party suppliers, which may have allowed hackers to steal certain customer details, including names, addresses, email addresses, telephone numbers, payment details, and Ticketmaster login information	The Information Commissioner's Office (ICO) stated that it is collecting evidence and will determine whether GDPR penalties are applicable by assessing the incident and the timing of events
2018.6	Regulatory enforcement	ICO	**British Airways** British Airways' website experienced a data breach, which resulted in the personal information of approximately 500,000 passengers being compromised During the incident, user traffic was redirected to a fraudulent website, where attackers collected detailed customer information, including personal and banking details such as names, addresses, email addresses, as well as credit card numbers, expiration dates, and the security code (CVV) on the back	The ICO deemed that British Airways lacked the necessary technical and organizational measures to ensure information security. In early October 2019, the ICO issued a fine of 183 million pounds, approximately 200 million euros, against the airline. Additionally, British Airways is facing a collective lawsuit that could amount to 3 billion pounds

(continued)

(continued)

Announcement time	Type	Regulatory authority	Companies/acts involved	Result
2018.7	Litigation	Bonn State Court, Germany	**The Internet Corporation for Assigned Names and Numbers(ICANN) vs. EPAG** In early 2014, ICANN required German domain name registrars, including EPAG, to sign a new "2013 Registrar Authorization Agreement (RAA)," which mandated registrars to verify and validate certain WHOIS data. The agreement required the defendant EPAG to fulfill the obligation of collecting personal information of the registrants	After the implementation of the GDPR, the defendant refused to continue collecting personal information according to the contract and even intended to offer data deletion services. The defendant argued that the plaintiff's actions violated the principle of data minimization under Article 5(1)(c) of the GDPR and the requirement under Article 25 for services and products to be designed according to the principles of Privacy by Default and Privacy by Design (PbD). These reasons were recognized by the preliminary court
2018.7	Regulatory enforcement	Dutch Data Protection Authority	Sample inspections were conducted on 30 large companies in 10 private industries, including industrial and metals, catering, communications, financial services, etc	(No results found)
2018.9	Regulatory enforcement	ICO	**Aggregate (AIQ)** The company's retention of data on British citizens violates Articles 5 and 6 of the GDPR	The ICO released a GDPR enforcement notice to AIQ in July, demanding corrective actions within 30 days. Should AIQ fail to comply, they will incur a fine of up to 20 million euros. AIQ has lodged an appeal against the notice

(continued)

(continued)

Announcement time	Type	Regulatory authority	Companies/acts involved	Result
2018.10	Regulatory investigation	Irish Data Protection Commission	**Facebook** Approximately 3 million European users were affected by a security vulnerability in Facebook in September, with the risk of their personal information being stolen	The investigations into the data breach and into Facebook's adherence to GDPR regulations continued
2018.11	Regulatory enforcement	ICO	**Marriott International** Marriott International revealed that a breach of its Starwood guest reservation database exposed the personal information of 339 million hotel guests. The breach affected 30 million residents from 31 European Economic Area (EEA) countries, including 7 million UK residents. According to an investigation by the ICO, the vulnerability in the Starwood guest reservation database due to a cyberattack has been present since July 2014 and was only discovered in 2018	In response to this incident, the ICO has issued a fine of 124 million euros to Marriott International, while Marriott faces a class-action lawsuit claim of 12.5 billion dollars in the United States

(continued)

(continued)

Announcement time	Type	Regulatory authority	Companies/acts involved	Result
2018.11	Regulatory enforcement	ICO	**Facebook and Cambridge Analytica (banned)** Facebook users' personal information was collected without their consent, with data from at least one million UK users being collected and at risk of further misuse. Facebook failed to take effective remedial measures after discovering the API abuse and information leak	A fine of 500,000 pounds was imposed under the Data Protection Act 1998
2018.11	Regulatory enforcement	German Data Protection Agency	**Knuddels.de** The online chat platform Knuddels.de suffered a cyberattack exposing around 808,000 email addresses and more than 1.8 million usernames and passwords. The website was found to have just stored sensitive information in plain text without any other protection measures	Knuddels.de was fined €20,000 by the Data Protection Authority of Baden-Württemberg for failing to comply with the data security standards regarding pseudonymization and encryption of personal data of users as required by Article 32(a) of the GDPR

Conclusion on International Law Enforcement and Judicial Practices

Regulations with cross-border supervisory capabilities, such as the GDPR, have significant influence. Especially in cases of personal data breaches or inadequate protection, fines can amount to 1–4% of a company's annual revenue, which can have a major negative impact on business operations. Moreover, the loss of reputation is immeasurable. As of September 24, 2019, 22 European data regulatory agencies have imposed a total of 370 million euros in administrative fines on 87 cases.

Legal Risks of Data Use by Energy Internet Companies

.

Legal Risks Caused by Breach of Data Compliance Obligations

Legal Risks of Using Non-personal Data

(1) Legal Risks Arising from Unclear Data Ownership

Energy Internet companies will continue to grapple with the challenge of transaction pricing and rights protection due to unclear data ownership until there is a clearer definition of non-personal data rights and protection under Chinese laws and regulations.

(2) Legal Risks Arising from Improper Collection and Use of Non-personal Data

There may be legal risks in using non-personal data. Particularly, if such data includes trade secrets, Energy Internet companies may face civil, criminal, and administrative liabilities for improperly collecting and using this information, as this could constitute a violation of the "Anti-Unfair Competition Law" and the "Criminal Law."

Legal Risks of the Use of Data Generated from Company Operations

(1) Legal risks arising from the collection and use of employee personal information

Common risk points for companies in collecting and using employee personal information include:

- Improper use of personal data in job applicants' resumes;
- Risks caused by the leakage of sensitive information such as personal biometric information in medical examination reports upon employment;
- Lack of provisions related to the use of personal information in labor contracts;
- Risks associated with the collection of biometric information through attendance and access control systems;
- Risks arising from providing employee personal information to external service providers;
- Risks that may arise from internal investigations of employees;
- Risks related to monitoring employee movements in specific business operations;
- Risks due to changes in corporate control (divestiture, merger, or restructuring);
- Legal risks associated with the use of employee images for endorsements;
- Legal risks due to the cross-border transfer of employee personal information.

Legal Risks of Collecting User Data

(1) Typical risks arising from the collection and use of personal user information include:

(a) Risks arising from the historical collection of personal information in residential power supply contracts

Energy Internet companies, during the power provision process, are able to gather personal data from residents through the power supply contracts they enter into. However, given historical limitations, these contracts may not include detailed clauses on the handling of personal information. As a result, when dealing with residents' private data, these companies must exercise heightened caution to ensure they do not overstep legal boundaries due to the absence of explicit consent, thereby avoiding potential legal risks.

(b) Risks Arising from Websites and Apps Collecting Personal Information

To facilitate users in purchasing electricity and to offer diversified services, Energy Internet companies are utilizing multiple channels to conduct online electricity sales and are developing dedicated apps and websites. However, these platforms typically require users to provide personal information during the registration process. As Energy Internet companies continue to evolve, we can expect a surge in new websites and apps that collect personal data. Additionally, an increasing number of these services are integrating third-party applications and plugins, which introduces risks that should not be underestimated.

(c) Risks Arising from Smart Meters Collecting Personal Information

Smart meters are capable of logging a user's electricity usage history. Energy Internet companies, by analyzing this data, can deduce insights into a user's spending habits and status. When combined with the user information gathered at the time of the smart meter's installation, this information can expose the user's daily routines, which constitutes sensitive personal data. In addition, some smart meter technologies used abroad can identify which appliances and devices are being used, thereby gaining access to even more personal information about the user. Furthermore, the installation of smart meters is mostly carried out by Energy Internet companies, and the associated power supply contracts typically lack specific provisions on the collection of personal information. This kind of information collection without the user's authorization may lead to serious legal issues.

(d) Legal Risks Arising from the Use of IoT (including IoV)

Energy Internet companies plan to extensively promote the use of IoT and consider it an important step in their transformation. Common risk points for companies in using IoT are as follows:

- Collecting personal information directly without obtaining user informed consent in an appropriate form;

- Excessive collection of information caused by the "one-click" collection of information by IoT apps;
- Failure to provide additional notification for the collection of sensitive information such as biometric information;
- Cross-border data transmission risks caused by the widespread distribution of IoT devices;
- Risks caused by unclear division of responsibilities between Energy Internet companies and third parties due to the numerous systems, platforms, and participants designed in IoT applications.
- Legal Risks Arising from User Profiling

Common risk points under user profiling scenarios include:

- Direct user profiling without the explicit consent of the user;
- Adverse effects caused by the combination of direct user profiling and automated decision-making systems;
- Issues arising from the combination of indirect user profiling and personalized display, including significant identification issues, opt-out choices and the right to anonymity, and discriminatory pricing issues.
- Legal Risks Arising from the Violation of Personal Information Cross-border Transfer Regulations.

Energy Internet companies, as owners, managers, and network service providers of the Energy Internet, collect and generate personal information domestically which clearly falls under the types of information restricted by the "Cybersecurity Law." Violating the regulations by transferring personal information across borders will also incur compliance risks.

(g) Risks Arising from Violation of Overseas Personal Information Protection Regulations

In recent years, countries around the world have been actively developing legislation to protect data, with the EU's GDPR being one of the most notable examples. These regulations have a wide scope and impose severe penalties for violations. Therefore, Energy Internet companies must strictly comply with the data protection laws of the countries or regions where they operate overseas to avoid significant compliance risks.

(2) Legal Liabilities for Illegal Collection and Use of User Data.

(a) Illegally Collecting and Using Personal User Information May Incur Civil Liability for Infringement.

If an Energy Internet company improperly discloses users' personal information during its operations, it may face civil litigation related to the issue. In practice, a court tends to shift the burden of proof to the company, requiring it to assume the responsibility of reverse onus, which means proving that it has taken reasonable protective measures and that the personal information breach was not caused by their actions. The burden of proof on the company is thus heavy.

(b) Improper Acquisition of a Competitor's User Information May Constitute Unfair Competition.

Judicial protection against unfair competition may become a "double-edged sword." On the one hand, for Energy Internet companies, judicial protection can help them safeguard valuable information such as personal user data (including user portraits), ensuring the company's legal rights are upheld. On the other hand, if a company improperly acquires information during market competition, it could also incur legal liabilities for itself. Therefore, companies must be cautious when handling such information.

(c) Companies May Face Administrative Liabilities for Infringement of Personal Information.

According to Article 64 of the "Cybersecurity Law," companies that violate personal information protection regulations may be subject to administrative penalties by the "relevant competent authorities." However, it is currently unclear which level and which administrative entity is responsible for imposing such penalties. Likewise, the extent of the infringement of personal information and the consequences of the harm caused are not clearly defined in terms of their impact on the final penalty results. Faced with these uncertainties, companies must remain vigilant and strictly comply with the laws and regulations on personal information protection to avoid any administrative penalties that may be imposed by the "relevant competent authorities."

(d) Companies' Failure to Establish Compliance Measures May Increase the Risk of Corporate Criminal Activity.

Even if the infringement of personal information is committed by an individual employee, the company could also be deemed to have committed a crime if there is evidence that the company had the subjective intent to commit the crime. When courts evaluate whether an employee's actions reflect the company's will, an important factor is whether the company has implemented policies and measures to prevent employees from engaging in criminal behavior. In other words, whether the company's compliance measures regarding the handling of personal information are effectively implemented will directly affect whether the company will be held criminally liable. Therefore, companies must pay close attention to the establishment of compliance measures.

(e) Companies May Face Liabilities for Violation of Foreign Personal Information Protection Regulations (Taking GDPR as an Example).

The GDPR requires companies to review the way they process data and establish procedures to protect data, including reporting data breaches, while ensuring compliance with relevant legal requirements in the protection of personal data. If a company is found by the EU to be in violation of GDPR, the maximum penalty can be up to 20 million euros or 4% of the company's global annual turnover, whichever is higher. After the formal implementation of the GDPR, regulatory authorities in various countries have issued a large number of hefty fines. For example, IAG was fined 183.4

million pounds for a theft incident involving customer data from its website and app, and Marriott International was fined 99.2 million pounds due to the leakage of personal user information. If an Energy Internet company breaches regulations, it may incur hefty fines that can significantly disrupt its normal business activities, not only within EU but also beyond, leading to severe consequences.

Legal Risks Caused by Violation of Cybersecurity Compliance Obligations

Legal Liabilities Caused by Violation of Relevant Requirements in MLPS 2.0

Energy Internet companies that fail to comply with the Multi-Level Protection Scheme 2.0 (MLPS 2.0) may face significant legal liabilities on two fronts: firstly, according to Article 59 of the "Cybersecurity Law," where network operators do not perform cybersecurity protection duties, the competent authorities will order corrections and give warnings; where corrections are refused or it leads to harm to cybersecurity or other such consequences, a fine of between CNY 10,000 and 100,000 shall be levied; and the directly responsible management personnel shall be fined between CNY 5000 and 50,000. Secondly, the potential for criminal liability should not be underestimated. The "Amendment (IX) to the Criminal Law" has introduced the crime of refusal to fulfill cybersecurity management duties, specifying that network service providers who, after being ordered by supervisory authorities to take corrective measures, continue to neglect the cybersecurity management duties required by law and administrative regulations, shall be sentenced to imprisonment of not more than three years, criminal detention, or surveillance, with the possibility of additional fines or standalone fines.

Legal Risks Caused by Violation of Relevant Regulations and Requirements on Critical Information Infrastructure

The Energy Internet is considered a part of the critical information infrastructure. According to Article 59 of the "Cybersecurity Law," where critical information infrastructure operators do not perform cybersecurity protection duties as provided for in Articles 33, 34, 36, and 38 of this Law, the competent departments will order corrections and give warnings; where corrections are refused or it leads to harm to cybersecurity or other such consequences, a fine of between CNY 100,000 and 1,000,000 shall be levied; and the directly responsible management personnel shall be fined between CNY 10,000 and 100,000.

Conclusion on Legal Risks of Data Use by Energy Internet Companies

Energy Internet companies have accumulated huge amounts of historical data in their long-term operations, and they continue to encounter an ever-growing variety of new data types. Despite that data use is vital to the transformation of grid companies, improper use of data may incur civil, administrative, or even criminal liabilities. As such, data use must be carried out within the framework of data compliance. Based on the previous discussion, Energy Internet companies are grappling with some practical challenges in implementing data compliance measures. These challenges are outlined below:

Firstly, the legal systems related to data compliance both domestically and internationally are far from robust, leading to uncertainty in what should be compliant regulations. Despite the establishment of key individual pieces of legislation such as the "Personal Information Protection Law" and the "Data Protection Law" in China, it is often the case that departmental rules, policy documents, and national standards are the ones that actually provide guidance in practice. These documents tend to address specific issues within the realm of data protection with clear and detailed provisions and guidelines. However, they carry a lower legal weight and are not strong enough to act as decisive references in legal disputes. To put it succinctly, the current practice of data protection in China still frequently encounters the dilemma of having no solid legal ground to stand on in many situations. This lack of legal clarity leaves entities uncertain about the legality of their actions, which in turn leads to unnecessary legal risks and potential vulnerabilities. At the international level, the legislative model exemplified by the EU's GDPR is overly biased toward the protection of data subjects, with a significantly greater emphasis on the empowerment of personal rights over property rights. The excessive emphasis on the protection of personal rights is bound to become an impediment to the development of the data industry. This can result in entities lacking data resources struggling to legitimately acquire data, while those in possession of data resources find it difficult to realize the inherent value of the data.[8] Regarding non-personal data, the legislative practices in both the European Union and China recognize the value of such data. However, instead of granting exclusive rights to data subjects over this type of data, these practices tend to promote the openness and sharing of such data from the perspective of public interest. In summary, under these empowerment frameworks, companies like the State Grid that hold substantial data assets are subject to significant constraints. A primary risk for these Energy Internet companies is the ambiguity around data ownership and the lack of clarity on how the data can be used.

Secondly, the enforcement of protection laws and judicial practices domestically and internationally has outpaced the development of the legislative system, with legal risks becoming extremely urgent and apparent. In terms of administrative enforcement, the special governance of apps is a case in point, while in the criminal

[8] See Wang (2019).

enforcement, the number of cases and severity of sentences for crimes involving the infringement of citizens' personal information are increasing. The recognition of data rights in the Civil Code also highlights the significant risk of civil liability for the protection of personal information. Regulations with cross-border supervisory capabilities, such as the GDPR, have significant influence. Especially in cases of personal data breaches or inadequate protection, fines can amount to 1% to 4% of a company's annual revenue, which can have a major negative impact on business operations. Moreover, the loss of reputation is immeasurable. Unlike the domestic situation where the enforcement of protection laws often falters due to a lack of high-level legal support, regions outside of China such as the EU demonstrate a clearly stronger resolve and intensity when enforcing relevant laws. The regulatory risks implied by this disparity are evident for Energy Internet companies operating on the international stage.

Lastly, the legal risks associated with data use by Energy Internet companies can be divided into two main categories: those related to data compliance obligations and those related to cybersecurity compliance obligations. In terms of data compliance, the legal risks include potential legal issues when using non-personal data, risks associated with the use of data generated during the company's daily operations, and challenges encountered in the collection and use of user data. These risks may lead to civil liabilities, such as those for unfair competition, administrative liabilities as stipulated by Article 64 of the "Cybersecurity Law," and even criminal liabilities, such as the crime of infringing upon citizens' personal information. Furthermore, if the company violates regulations on the protection of personal information abroad, it may also face transnational legal liabilities, including but not limited to hefty fines under extraterritorial jurisdiction. In terms of cybersecurity compliance, the legal risks include violations of requirements in MLPS 2.0, as well as violations concerning critical information infrastructure. Currently, there are relatively few typical enforcement cases in China, but the associated legal risks should not be underestimated

References

Han X (2020) The dilemma and solutions of data rights confirmation. Oriental Law 2020(1):97–107. https://doi.org/10.3969/j.issn.1007-1466.2020.01.009

Kang D (2019) Google fined 50 million euros by French authorities for violating GDPR. China Internet 2019(1):59

Oyang B, Qu L, Yuan Z, Lu C, Tian B (2020) Study on steady-state power flow optimization of cold-heat-electricity integrated energy system. Paper presented at the meeting of the 2020 IEEE sustainable power and energy conference (iSPEC), Chengdu, China

Tan Z, Cheng L, Shi S, Wang W, Xu W, Hua J, Lan C, Yu T (2019) Discussion on key technologies of Energy Internet access equipment. Power Syst Prot Cont 47(14):140–152. https://doi.org/10.19783/j.cnki.pspc.181151

Wang B, Ni Y, Yu J (2019) Personal information protection law included in the legislative plan. People's Daily, p 04

Wang L (2019) Research on legal issues of commercialization of personal data. Doctor's Dissertation, Central University of Finance and Economics. https://doi.org/10.27665/d.cnki.gzcju.2019.000076

Chapter 5
Researches on Legal Risks of Capital Operations in Energy Internet Companies

As the reform of the power system continues and the level of marketization increases, the commodity nature of energy will become increasingly apparent. This means that the various links in the energy industry, including production, transmission, conversion, storage, and consumption, will be interconnected. In this process, the involvement of third-party capital in the operations of energy companies is expected, and the role of the market in resource allocation will become more significant. Consequently, new business models are anticipated to emerge, which will be reflected in the competition of energy retail, the operational management of energy systems, and the operations of energy trading. In terms of energy retail competition, the power system reform has promoted the opening of the power sales market, which allows five different types of market participants to act as power sellers, creating a new "multi-buyer-multi-seller" market trading model. Under this model, power sellers can attract user resources by offering stable and cost-effective electricity, personalized service packages, and additional value-added information services and represent users to purchase power in the power market. In terms of system operation, the power system reform has introduced a significant change by opening up the operational rights of incremental distribution assets to third-party social capital. This move has paved the way for the emergence of new business models for operators of distribution networks and microgrids, effectively challenging the longstanding monopoly held by traditional grid companies. These new business models can achieve vertical integration of different stages such as power generation, distribution, and sales. They operate by managing the physical network and charge logistics and management fees for energy delivery. At the same time, the new models can also meet the diverse electricity needs of users. In terms of energy trading operations, the proposal to establish a power trading center as part of the power system reform will promote the creation of an independent and competitive trading platform, leading to the emergence of

H. Deng, *Green Energy Transition in China*, International Law in Asia,
https://doi.org/10.1007/978-981-97-2934-0_5

new business models.[1] As a result of these developments, the capital operations of Energy Internet companies will become more complex.

Analysis of Capital Operations in Energy Internet Companies

Mixed-Ownership Reform of Energy Internet Companies

The Third Plenary Session of the 18th Central Committee of the Communist Party of China and the Report of the 19th National Congress of the Communist Party of China clearly proposed to promote the mixed-ownership reform of state-owned enterprises. "A mixed economy with cross holding by and mutual fusion between state-owned capital, collective capital, and non-public capital is an important way to materialize the basic economic system of China."[2] Developing a mixed-ownership economy is a key approach to deepening the reform of state-owned enterprises. In response to the growing international competition and challenges, it is necessary to deepen the reform of the mixed-ownership system in state-owned enterprises, to improve the modern corporate system and the corporate governance structure. This will enhance the efficiency in the allocation and operation of state-owned capital, optimize the layout of the state-owned economy, and strengthen the vitality, control, influence, and risk resistance of the state economy. We should actively adapt to and lead the new normal of economic development, promote the transformation of the operating mechanisms in state-owned enterprises, amplify the function of state-owned capital, and ensure the preservation and appreciation of state-owned assets.[3] Through the mixed-ownership reform of state-owned enterprises, we aim to achieve comprehensive reforms in corporate structure, management methods, company decision-making, employee incentives, and profit distribution.

Based on the practices of mixed-ownership reform in state-owned energy enterprises at both central and local levels from 2018 to 2019, we can identify three types of business models that are propelling the reform process[4]: The first type focuses on fundamental businesses of state-owned energy enterprises, with individual projects (such as power plants, mines, and new energy projects) as the "concurrent" energy production and supply of the underlying business units. These projects require significant investments, often exceeding hundreds of millions or even tens of billions of CNY. Given such high investment amounts, enterprises must consider their capital

[1] See Chen et al. (2015).

[2] The Third Plenary Session of the 18th Central Committee of the Communist Party of China. (2013). Decision of the CCCPC on Some Major Issues Concerning Comprehensively Deepening the Reform.

[3] State Council. Opinions of the State Council on the Development of Mixed-Ownership Economy by State-owned Enterprises (Guo Fa [2015] No. 54).

[4] Liu (2020).

structure and sources of funding. In 2019, there were at least dozens of equity transfer projects in the fields of electricity, coal, and new energy, all aimed at optimizing financial structures and investment models. The second type involves businesses with a relatively high degree of marketization, such as design and consulting services that support energy production and supply, as well as the production and supply of energy equipment, trade, and supply chain management. These businesses not only support and serve the main energy industry but also operate in a highly competitive market environment. The third type includes new businesses, new models, and new resources. The incubation and growth of these new businesses require market mechanisms and professionals who possess new knowledge. To transform these potential opportunities into future supportive businesses, energy companies recognize it is necessary to adopt market-oriented reform measures, including mixed-ownership reform, in order to push them to the market from the outset and promote the formation and enhancement of competitiveness.

Driven by these three types of business models, state-owned energy enterprises, whether to optimize investment patterns and financial structures or to promote the development of new energy businesses and models, all face significant financing needs. To meet these needs, companies can choose from a variety of financing methods, each with its own advantages. The financing channels available to power companies can be mainly divided into two types: equity financing and debt financing.[5] Equity financing typically includes attracting strategic investors, raising funds through stock financing, and employee stock ownership plans. Debt financing mainly refers to raising funds through commercial bank loans or bond issuance.

Investment Landscape of Energy Internet Companies

"During the 13th Five-Year Plan, China's power industry is shifting from focusing on expansion in scale to pursuing quality and efficiency. The quality of development has been significantly improved, the structure has been greatly optimized, and the technological content has been significantly enhanced. There is huge space for power construction and investment."[6] Chinese Energy Internet companies attach great importance to their investment operations. For example, a grid company pointed out in its notice that "Affected by the macroeconomic downturn and China-US trade tensions, the growth rate of electricity demand continues to decline, and the profitability of the grid business has dropped significantly… The extent of losses across the company's various levels continues to expand, with investment capacity gradually weakening… Strict control over grid investment is necessary to ensure the sustainable development of the company and the grid." Therefore, in the first half of 2020, the grid company reduced investment, and the basic investment in grid construction was completed at CNY 165.7 billion, a year-on-year increase of 0.79%,

[5] See Peng (2009), p. 272.

[6] CIPIE (2017).

and a substantial increase of 46.12% from the previous period, accounting for less than 40% of the annual investment.[7] In the second half of 2020, to mitigate the impact of the pandemic on the national economy, the grid company, leveraging the advantage of the power grid as a major national infrastructure, initiated and resumed work on key projects worth over CNY one hundred billion. Through active and prudent investment, it effectively stimulated the development of upstream and downstream companies in the industrial chain, promoted the low-carbon transition of energy development, supported the effective implementation of national strategies, and aided in the high-quality development of the national economy.[8]

With the continuous development of Internet technology, "intelligentization" and "Energy Internet" have become key directions for the future development of the energy industry. For example, a grid company introduced the concept of "Ubiquitous Electric Internet of Things" at the beginning of 2019, which involves the extensive use of mobile Internet, artificial intelligence, and other modern information and advanced communication technologies throughout the various segments of the power system. This concept aims to achieve comprehensive connectivity of all things and human–machine interaction within the power system, and offer an intelligent service system comprised of a perception layer, a network layer, a platform layer, and an application layer, and capable of comprehensive status monitoring, efficient information processing, and convenient and flexible application. This means that the investment landscape of grid companies is undergoing fundamental changes, shifting from a stage dominated by ultra-high voltage and strong smart grid construction to a focus on investments in information and communication technology. With the basic formation of China's main grid infrastructure, a structural shift in investment by grid companies is expected in future. In particular, the proportion of investment in the fields of intelligence and informatization associated with the construction of the ubiquitous power IoT will significantly increase.[9]

Generally speaking, although Energy Internet companies have been cautious about investment due to the impact of the international economic situation, under the general trend of China's energy reform, the investment of Energy Internet companies is expected to continue to expand. Projects related to the Energy Internet, new energy technology, renewable energy, and integrated energy services will become important sectors for domestic investment by Energy Internet companies. Opportunities are accompanied by challenges. The emergence of new investment sectors has increased the investment risks of Energy Internet companies. In the investment process, from a macro perspective, it is necessary to comprehensively control the domestic investment risks of Energy Internet companies; from a micro perspective, grid companies may encounter different risks during the transformation to Energy Internet companies based on different investment methods used. These risks include the following: risks in equity mergers and acquisitions, risks in asset acquisitions,

---

[7] Wa (2020).

[8] Zhu and Mo (2020).

[9] See Jiexitz (2019).

risks under the PPP model, and some conventional management risks that may be encountered in all three of the aforementioned investment methods.

Cross-Border Mergers and Acquisitions of Energy Internet Companies

In recent years, Energy Internet companies have been progressively expanding their global footprint with an increasing variety of asset types and investment approaches, establishing themselves as a key driver in the advancement of international capacity collaboration. In terms of regional layout, Energy Internet companies focus their investments primarily in Asia, Europe, the Americas, and Oceania, with countries along the "Belt and Road" route being key targets for their overseas investments. Regarding the type of assets, these companies' overseas mergers and acquisitions predominantly concentrate on clean energy, with hydroelectric projects having the largest share, followed by wind power, power grids, and thermal power projects. This also indirectly indicates that the cross-border mergers and acquisitions by Energy Internet companies are contributing to energy transition.

In the process of cross-border mergers and acquisitions of Energy Internet companies, the following major challenges may arise. Firstly, there is an increasing stringency in international investment reviews concerning key sectors such as energy and power, particularly regarding market access and national security risks. The following will elaborate on the tightening of national security reviews by the Committee on Foreign Investment in the United States (CFIUS) on Chinese investments. In recent years, China has become the most scrutinized country by CFIUS. The U.S. is continuously expanding the powers of CFIUS, especially with regulations that mandate declarations for transactions involving foreign government-affiliated investors, which clearly target Chinese companies. Additionally, the EU enacted the Regulation on Foreign Direct Investment Screening in 2019, which imposes strict interventions and reviews on foreign acquisitions in critical industries such as energy and power, aimed at restricting foreign investors. Secondly, Energy Internet companies may also encounter antitrust risks during cross-border M & A activities. For example, the EU often regards Chinese state-owned enterprises as a collective entity, leading to increasingly stringent antitrust and sectoral reviews for Chinese state-owned companies. According to the EU's Third Energy Package, any company with direct or indirect control over transmission systems is not permitted to control power generators or sellers. Thirdly, Energy Internet companies must comply with regulatory oversight and approvals from administrative authorities when engaging in cross-border M and A. Although the policy of streamlining administration and delegating powers has simplified the approval process for overseas investment projects in recent years, the procedures remain complex and should not be overlooked. This is particularly true for state-owned grid companies, which need to submit approval or filing materials to various departments such as the State-owned Assets Supervision and Administration

Commission, the National Development and Reform Commission, and the Ministry of Commerce. Each department has different requirements, placing higher demands on the communication, coordination, and material preparation capabilities of these companies.

At present, Chinese companies hold a significant share of cross-border investments in the global power industry and have become the leading source of capital for international investments in this sector. In future, under the new trend of comprehensive development of the Energy Internet, grid companies are expected to increase their investments and acquisitions in new technologies and new business models, such as energy storage, electric vehicle charging, artificial intelligence, and demand-side response. The trend of cross-sector competition in the power industry is set to become even more pronounced.

Legal Risks of Mixed-Ownership Reform of Energy Internet Companies

Analysis of Financing Models of Energy Internet Companies

As mentioned above, the financing channels available to power companies can be mainly divided into two types: equity financing and debt financing. Equity financing typically includes attracting strategic investors, raising funds through stock financing, and employee stock ownership plans. Debt financing mainly refers to raising funds through commercial bank loans or bond issuance.

Attracting Strategic Investors

In the process of energy companies transitioning into Energy Internet companies, attracting strategic investors offers significant benefits. Firstly, it helps the integration of resources from all sides, allowing for the mutual complementation of strengths between the company and the strategic investors. Secondly, it can facilitate the optimization of shareholder structure and enhance the company's governance system. It is common for energy companies to bring in strategic investors. They have various options to do this, such as mergers, acquisitions, capital increases, and share expansion. In the reform of mixed-ownership systems in state-owned companies, private equity investment is a relatively common option.[10] When companies seek to attract

[10] For example, in 2019, Sinochem Energy released 20% of its shares and successfully attracted five strategic investors who collectively invested CNY 11.555 billion. These five strategic investors include: Agricultural Bank Financial Asset Investment Co., Ltd., ICBC Financial Asset Investment Co., Ltd., Beijing Chengtong ICBC Equity Investment Fund (Limited Partnership), Qingdao Zhongxindinghui Equity Investment Partnership (Limited Partnership), and CITIC Securities Investment Co., Ltd. For another example, Tianjin Jinran Public Utilities issued an announcement on

strategic investors, they need to be clear about the amount of investment they plan to attract and decide accordingly on the proportion of equity they are willing to release.

Stock Financing

Equity financing refers to the process where existing shareholders of a company are willing to relinquish a portion of their ownership in order to introduce new investors through capital increase. Compared to debt financing, the advantages of equity financing include less pressure on the return of capital and dividend payouts, as well as an enhanced ability to withstand risks. Moreover, if the company can attract strategic investors with specific resources, it can achieve synergistic benefits and rapidly expand its own strength.[11] One of the disadvantages of listed financing is that more open and transparent company management is required.

Employee Stock Ownership

Employee stock ownership plays a crucial role in the mixed-ownership reform, serving both as a means to generate capital and to offer equity-based incentives to key management and technical personnel. This approach will foster a profound connection between the growth of innovative ventures, such as grid Internet platforms, and employees.

Loans

The power industry is a typical industry that intensively utilizes long-term and short-term bank credit. Given that other financing channels in China are not yet mature and fully developed, credit from commercial banks stands as the most important source of financing for China's power companies.[12] Long-term loans refer to loans borrowed from banks or other non-bank financial institutions with a term of more than one year. Long-term loans are mainly used to purchase fixed assets and to fulfill the working

September 27, 2020 stating that Tianjin State-owned Capital Investment Corporation had informed them of its ongoing public listing process to seek strategic investors. The goal is to allow strategic investors to acquire a portion of the equity in Tianjin Energy Investment Group through the transfer of shares and the issuance of new shares. Specifically, if the strategic investor is a wholly state-owned or state-controlled company, they could obtain up to 51% of the equity in Tianjin Energy Investment Group through this process; if the strategic investor is not wholly state-owned or state-controlled, they could acquire 34% of the equity. The announcement also pointed out that Tianjin State-owned Capital Investment is the direct wholly-owned owner of Tianjin Energy, which in turn is the direct wholly-owned owner of Tianjin Gas. Tianjin Gas holds approximately 1.2975 billion domestic shares, accounting for about 70.54% of the company's total issued shares.

[11] See Peng (2009), pp. 324–325.

[12] Same as above, p. 286.

capital requirements of a business. Their advantages include quick financing, lower financing costs, greater flexibility, and the benefit of financial leverage. However, the downsides are higher financial risk, numerous restrictive covenants, and a limited amount of financing available.[13] For power companies, the primary cost of bank loans is the interest expense, which is determined by the loan interest rate. When selecting a bank, it is necessary to choose the appropriate loan product, incur the minimum borrowing costs, and secure the most favorable loan terms. The financing of China's power construction relies heavily on long-term loans, and the situation varies for different power projects. Hydropower and thermal power primarily use domestic loans, while nuclear power was predominantly financed by foreign capital before 2006.

Issuance of Corporate Bonds

China began to issue power construction bonds as early as the 1980s. In addition to state-owned power corporations issuing corporate bonds, local power enterprises also issued their own.[14] The advantage of issuing corporate bonds is that they offer a lower cost of financing compared to equity financing, allowing for the rapid collection of substantial funds. However, there are drawbacks to this approach: Firstly, there is a higher financial risk. Bonds typically have fixed maturity dates, necessitating regular principal and interest repayments, which constantly puts financial pressure on the issuer. During times of economic downturn, these repayments can become a severe financial burden, potentially leading to bankruptcy. Secondly, there are numerous restrictions. The conditions for issuing bonds are often more numerous and stricter than those for long-term loans or finance leases, thereby limiting the company's use of bond financing and potentially affecting its future fundraising capabilities. Thirdly, the scale of financing is constrained. Generally, the amount a company can raise through bond issuance is subject to certain limits.[15]

The traditional financing methods of power companies are characterized by two features: first, they are capital-intensive with long investment return cycles; second, the investment returns are relatively stable with low investment risks.[16] This round of mixed-ownership reform is market-oriented, allowing state-owned energy companies to integrate more into the market and adopt market-based approaches for financing. Additionally, the energy regulatory authorities have implemented a series of laws and regulations, primarily focusing on the efficient use of energy, diversification of energy sources, and establishing a strategic energy reserve system.[17] In this context, state-controlled Energy Internet companies involved in the mixed-ownership reform

---

[13] Same as above, pp. 299–300.

[14] Same as above.

[15] Same as above.

[16] Same as above, pp. 271–272.

[17] See Deng and Farah (2020).

process must also pay attention to the relevant regulatory provisions and fulfill the important functions of state-owned companies.

Legal Risks in Routine Operations

Legal Risks in Power Supply Business

In the process of conducting power supply operations and related activities, Energy Internet companies may face legal risks such as overdue settlement of electricity purchases, underpayment, and improper implementation of electricity pricing, all of which could violate the Civil Code and settlement agreements.

Legal Risks of Occupational Injury Insurance

If an Energy Internet company fails to strictly comply with the provisions of the Civil Code and the "Insurance Law of the People's Republic of China" (hereinafter referred to as the "Insurance Law") in a construction project by not securing insurance coverage for the project in a timely manner, by inadequately reviewing clauses on the insured's rights and exemption in the project insurance contract, or by submitting incomplete or incorrect documentation for insurance claims, it may face a claim denial by the insurance company and thus suffer financial losses.

Legal Risks of External Guarantees

Energy Internet companies may face legal risks of economic loss during the process of providing external guarantees, potentially due to violations of regulations such as the Civil Code.

Legal Risks of Fixed Asset Management

During the mixed-ownership reform, Energy Internet companies may encounter issues related to the transfer of fixed assets. Special attention should be paid to asset valuation, regulatory approval, and general procedural issues.

Personnel Reallocation

The mixed-ownership reform process also involves the issue of personnel reallocation. According to the "Regulations on the Placement of Redundant Staff in State-owned Companies," a state-owned company may initiate early termination of labor contracts if substantial shifts in production and business operations necessitate workforce downsizing. This action must be taken with the approval of the workers' representative assembly following a thorough discussion. Nonetheless, the company is obligated to honor the terms of the contract. Should the contract lack specific terms regarding termination, the company is required to provide the employee with severance pay proportional to their tenure at the company.[18] Courts have ruled that when managing the early retirement of employees within a company, both the employer and the employee must establish explicit agreements concerning wages and associated benefits. The living allowance provided by the company for retirees must meet or exceed the level mandated by policies or the agreed-upon terms. Jiaozuo City Sports Hotel did not pay the agreed-upon retirement living expenses to an employee named Xue. As a result, the court ordered the hotel to compensate Xue for the shortfall.[19] Therefore, companies involved in personnel reallocation need to ensure the following: (1) establish standardized labor contract relations in accordance with the "Labor Contract Law of the People's Republic of China" (hereinafter referred to as the "Labor Contract Law"); (2) clearly stipulate the liabilities for breach of contract to ensure enforceability; (3) strictly adhere to the procedures required by the "Labor Contract Law" and internal company regulations during the personnel reallocation process.

Attracting Strategic Investors

In the process of attracting strategic investments, there are certain legal risks that need to be mitigated. Key legal norms and bases include the following: the "Guiding Opinions on Deepening the Reform of State-owned Enterprises," the "Guiding Opinions on Encouraging and Regulating the Introduction of Non-state-owned Capital into State-owned Enterprise Investment Projects," the "Opinions of the State Council on Encouraging, Supporting and Guiding the Development of Individual and Private Economy and Other Non-Public Sectors of the Economy," the "Interim Administrative Measures for the Assessment of State-owned Assets of Enterprises," the "Negative List for Market Access (2022 Edition)," the "Special Administrative Measures for Foreign Investment Access (Negative List) (2021 Edition)," the "Implementation Opinions on Orderly Opening Up of Power Generation and Consumption Plans," the "Implementation Opinions on Promoting the Reform of the Power Selling Side," the "Notice on Strengthening the Management of Equity Participation by State-owned Enterprises," and others.

---

[18] Regulations on the Placement of Redundant Staff in State-owned Companies (State Council Order No. 111), Article 12.

[19] See Judicial case. The first-instance civil judgment on the labor dispute between Xue XX (anonymized) and Jiaozuo Sports Hotel, civil judgment from Shanyang District People's Court of Jiaozuo City Henan Province (2014 Shan Min Lao Chu Zi No. 00131), February 4, 2015.

Improper Valuation

In the process of mixed-ownership reform of state-owned enterprises, valuation is a key step and also the foundation for attracting strategic investors. The most common improper valuation is the valuation of tangible assets such as land and real estate at their original purchase prices, without considering the appreciation these assets may have experienced in the market. Some companies even convert state-allocated land into state-owned shares at zero value and incorporate them into their own company's shares. In addition, intangible assets in state-owned assets, such as patents, trademarks, goodwill, and brands, that often hold significant value and potential for appreciation are overlooked or undervalued far below their actual worth. This practice undoubtedly constitutes the misappropriation of state-owned assets, whether intentional or not.[20]

Unqualified Strategic Investors

(1) Market Participant Qualifications

The "Implementation Opinions on Promoting the Reform of the Power Selling Side" clarifies the access conditions for market participants on the power selling side, including the following: A. Access conditions for power sellers. (a) Must have independent legal person status. (b) Must meet Asset requirements. (c) Must possess equipment and business premises appropriate for the scale of electricity sales and business scope being applied for, as well as have dedicated professionals who understand the basic technical and economic characteristics of the power system. (d) Power sellers that have the right to operate distribution networks must obtain a power business license (for the supply category). B. Access conditions for direct trading users. (a) Must comply with national industrial policies, with both unit energy consumption and environmental emissions meeting national standards. (b) Users with their own power generation facilities must undertake government funds established in accordance with the law, as well as policy-based cross-subsidies and system reserve charges that align with industrial policies. (c) Microgrid users must meet the conditions for connecting to the microgrid system.[21]

(2) Market Access Conditions

According to the "Negative List for Market Access (2022 Edition)," entities are prohibited from engaging in power businesses and from undertaking the installation (including repair and testing) of power facilities without permission from the National Energy Administration. Entities are not allowed to handle the resettlement tasks for large and medium-sized water conservancy and hydropower projects

[20] Zhou (1996).

[21] National Development and Reform Commission, & National Energy Administration. Notice on Issuing Supporting Documents for the Power System Reform (Fa Gai Jing Ti [2015] No. 2752), Annex 5, Implementation Opinions on Promoting the Reform of the Power Selling Side.

without obtaining the necessary permits from the Ministry of Water Resources and the Energy Administration, or without following the legal procedures. In addition, certain energy projects require approval before investment and construction can commence. These projects include hydroelectric stations, pumped-storage power stations, thermal power stations (including captive power plants), combined heat and power plants (including captive power plants), wind farms, nuclear power plants, and grid projects.[22] According to the "Special Administrative Measures for Foreign Investment Access (Negative List) (2021 Edition)," the construction and operation of nuclear power stations must be under Chinese control. Public air transport companies must be under Chinese control, and a foreign investor, along with its affiliated companies, is limited to a maximum investment of 25%. Moreover, the legal representative of the company must be a Chinese citizen.[23]

(3) Special Requirements of State-Owned Enterprises

According to the "Notice on Strengthening the Management of Equity Participation by State-owned Enterprises," state-controlled Energy Internet companies shall strictly screen potential partners when introducing strategic investors. Thorough due diligence shall be conducted by assessing their qualifications and reliability using different credit information sources and third-party investigations to ensure that only those with excellent management practices and strong reputations are selected. Prospective partners with records of dishonesty, administrative penalties, criminal offenses, or other regulatory or legal violations shall be considered cautiously or prohibited depending on the severity of the issues. Potential partners that have close personal connections (such as spouses, children and their spouses, or other relatives) or shared financial interests with the leaders of the equity investment entity or its main shareholders at any level shall not be selected.[24]

Improper Shareholding Ratio of Strategic Investors

The shareholding ratio determines each shareholder's decision-making power over the company. A strategic investor holding a disproportionately large stake can lead to the risk of state-owned capital losing control of an enterprise, which is particularly hazardous for state-owned enterprises in critical sectors that are vital to the national economy and people's livelihoods. On the other hand, too small a stake is

[22] National Development and Reform Commission, & Ministry of Commerce. Special Administrative Measures for Foreign Investment Access (Negative List) (2021 Edition) (No. 47 order by NDRC and MOC), Items 38–39, Item 101.

[23] National Development and Reform Commission, & Ministry of Commerce. Special Administrative Measures for Foreign Investment Access (Negative List) (2021 Edition) (No. 47 order by NDRC and MOC), Items 8 and 11.

[24] State-owned Assets Supervision and Administration Commission. Notice on Strengthening the Management of Equity Participation by State-owned Enterprises (Guo Zi Fa Gai Ge Gui [2019] No. 126).

not conducive to stimulating the enthusiasm of strategic investors to participate in reforms, nor does it allow for the adoption of their corporate governance models.[25]

Issuance of Securities

Legal Risks Arising from the Ineligibility of Bond Issuers

If an Energy Internet company fails to adhere strictly to the regulations of the "Securities Law of the People's Republic of China" (hereinafter referred to as the "Securities Law") during the process of issuing bonds and disclosing information, and is found to have fabricated false documents and materials to fraudulently obtain bond issuance approval, then the company will be exposed to legal risks arising from the bond issuer not meeting the eligibility criteria.

Legal Risks of Failing to Report Important Issues

If Energy Internet companies fail to adhere strictly to the reporting and disclosure requirements mandated by the "Securities Law," and if they are found to be fabricating false information, issuing misleading statements, or omitting significant details in their reports and disclosures, they could be at risk of not meeting the obligation to report important issues as demanded by the law.

Legal Risks of Failing to Apply the Funds Raised to the Predetermined Purposes

Energy Internet companies must define the exact purposes for the funds raised through their Initial Public Offerings (IPOs) in their internal decision-making procedures during the planning phase and adhere strictly to these stated objectives. Unauthorized reallocation of funds raised through bonds could lead to legal consequences for failing to apply the capital to the predetermined purposes.

Risks of State-Owned Equity Dilution and Loss of Control

Listing a state-owned Energy Internet company may result in dilution of state-owned equity and loss of control. The Energy Internet company shall retain control of the company as appropriate and provide an evaluation report proving that the dilution of state-owned shares will not harm the interests of state-owned assets.

---

[25] Same as above.

Legal Risks of Data Business Listing

When Energy Internet companies develop Internet platform-based businesses, there may be special legal risks associated with raising funds and developing a mixed-ownership economy. The listing of data businesses has its particularities. There have already been several cases where failure to comply with legal regulations regarding data collection and use has easily led to the failure of going public.

Employee Stock Ownership

Employees Participating in Equity Incentives Not in the Allow List

The "Opinions on State-controlled Mixed-Ownership Enterprises' Implementation of the Pilot Employee Stock Ownership Program" explicitly stipulate that certain individuals may not be included in the employee stock ownership program as shareholder employees.

Legal Risks Associated with Procedural Approval, Publicity, and Accounting

To mitigate these risks, strictly follow the procedures for equity transfer in accordance with the "Company Law of the People's Republic of China" and the "Opinions on State-controlled Mixed-Ownership Enterprises' Implementation of the Pilot Employee Stock Ownership Program."

Legal Risks of Domestic Investment by Energy Internet Companies

Macro Legal Risks

Investment refers to the act of investing capital, either domestically or abroad, with the aim of earning profits. This act typically involves directly managing businesses by founding or buying them, acquiring shares or bonds issued by companies, as well as engaging in the lending of funds and purchasing real estate, among other activities.[26] Domestic investment refers to investment activities within China. For Energy Internet companies, common domestic investment activities include equity M & A, asset M & A, and PPP models. Equity M & A refers to the investment

[26] Liu (1995), p. 283.

activity where an Energy Internet company, acting as the acquirer, engages in equity transactions with the shareholders of a target company, thereby becoming a shareholder of that company.[27] Typically, equity M & A include three methods: equity swaps, capital increase and share expansion, and the transfer of equity. The transaction process primarily consists of stages such as decision-making, financing, the transfer of management rights, and integration. During the equity M & A process, the eventual change in the target company's equity structure, that is, the transformation of its management, will inevitably lead to influential changes in the overall operation of the target company. Therefore, the damages that could arise from the risks incurred during this process are also likely to be substantial. Since the Energy Internet company will be responsible for the management actions of the target enterprise after the M & A, the risks involved in the equity M & A process pose a substantial threat to the Energy Internet company. Asset M & A involves investors acquiring a target company's key operational assets, which can include real estate, intangible property, and machinery, to tap into the target company's earning potential.[28] When conducting asset M & A, investors achieve control over the target company by purchasing its core assets and businesses. As can be seen, the goal of this approach is consistent with that of equity M & A.[29] To minimize the risks associated with asset M & A, Energy Internet companies shall ensure the legality of their asset purchases. Unlike equity M & A and asset M & A, investments under the PPP model are not aimed at acquiring a company, but rather at selecting projects to invest in based on the main business of the Energy Internet. Taking a grid company as an example, grid construction is one of the company's primary businesses. Therefore, projects such as microgrid construction and power transmission and distribution network upgrades become potential investment options for the company. The "Notice of the National Energy Administration on Actively Promoting the PPP Model in the Energy Sector" issued in 2016 calls for the promotion of PPP construction in three key types of energy projects. One of these types is the power and new energy category, which includes the following: the construction and renovation of power supply and urban distribution networks, the transformation and upgrading of rural grids, transmission projects with clear asset boundaries, the construction and operation of charging infrastructure, distributed power generation projects, microgrid construction and renovation, smart grid projects, energy storage projects, PV poverty alleviation projects, hydropower station projects, combined heat and power projects, and electricity substitution projects, among others.[30] In PPP models, the government and private companies jointly invest in a project, where both parties share the profits and bear the responsibilities together. Typically, the government invests by injecting capital into Energy Internet companies and providing subsidies to bridge feasibility gaps.[31] Nevertheless, compared to private companies, the government's

[27] See Huang (2018), p. 139.

[28] Xu et al. (2016), p. 24.

[29] See Cheng et al. (2015), p. 72.

[30] See China Energy News (2016).

[31] See Wang (2018).

share in project investment is relatively small; hence, private companies remain the main bearers of project risks.

By observing the investment market environment for domestic Energy Internet companies, we can see that these companies are facing certain uncertainties in the market and management aspects, which could lead to legal risks. These risks include frequent policy changes, information asymmetry, unstable fundraising, and imperfect operational management, among others. Firstly, regarding policy changes, since energy is a vital material for national economic development and social stability, its macro utilization must comply with the country's energy planning and relevant policy regulations. This means that changes in policy have a critical impact on the adjustment of the energy structure, which directly affects the investment decisions of Energy Internet companies. For example, since China set forth its goals for peaking carbon emissions and achieving carbon neutrality, large-scale development and utilization of renewable energy, improvement of energy efficiency, and deep emission reduction have become the basic directions for the development of the energy industry. In particular, renewable energies, primarily wind and solar power, along with integrated development models that combine photovoltaic, energy storage, and charging, are set to be the focal points in the power industry's development.[32] Renewable energy sources have received substantial support from the government, while traditional energy sources are often not encouraged. Nevertheless, due to the stability of traditional energy supplies, they continue to play a crucial role in ensuring China's energy security and still have a presence in the investment realm of Energy Internet companies. Therefore, whenever new energy policies (especially those related to environmental protection) are introduced, some investment projects in traditional energy may face the risk of becoming non-compliant with regulations.

In real life, information is often incomplete. When one party has more information than the other, this asymmetry can lead to the better-informed party exploiting their advantage in ways that are detrimental to the interests of the less-informed party. Once the party at an informational disadvantage becomes aware of the potential exploitation, they will take steps to protect their own interests.[33] For Energy Internet companies, having an informational edge in investment processes means they hold a wealth of market information; however, this advantage can exacerbate their monopolistic tendencies and increase the risk of violating antitrust laws and other relevant regulations. Conversely, if they find themselves on the less-informed side, they may suffer losses due to illegal activities of the other party, resulting from the informational imbalance.

Unstable fundraising refers to a situation where Energy Internet companies exhibit insufficient financing capacity during the investment process, or where the expected amount of funds calculated for an investment falls short of the actual amount required. For investment activities, whether it's equity M & A or capital M & A, a corresponding price must be paid to complete the takeover of the target company. In the case of project investments under the PPP model, adequate capital is required to

[32] See Zhang and Ran (2021).

[33] See Yu (2019), p. 190.

support the operation of the project. In any of these scenarios, a shortfall in funding can lead to default actions by Energy Internet companies, triggering legal risks associated with default. Imperfect operational management refers to a situation where Energy Internet companies, after completing mergers and acquisitions or initiating project construction, fail to manage the target company or the project effectively due to managers' lack of understanding, insufficient experience, or susceptibility to economic incentives, among other subjective and objective factors. This inadequate management can lead to various operational legal risks for the Energy Internet companies.

It can be seen that domestic investments by Energy Internet companies are mainly threatened by legal risks that may arise during equity M & A, asset M & A, and project investments under the PPP model. Overall, these three types of investment activities jointly face legal risks arising from frequent policy changes, information asymmetry, unstable fundraising, and imperfect operational management.

Equity M & A

During equity M & A, Energy Internet companies face different risks in stages such as decision-making, financing, the transfer of management rights, and integration.

Decision-Making Risks

In the investment and mergers and acquisitions of energy companies, market demands are shifting due to the industry's transition from traditional to new energies. During this process, various market factors contribute to market volatility, introducing decision-making uncertainties for companies engaging in mergers and acquisitions. Consequently, investing companies should exercise caution when selecting M & A partners. This risk is evident during the preparatory and decision-making stages of M & A. The presence of multiple uncertain market factors can increase the unpredictability of decision-making. The risk is mainly associated with the selection of the target company and the assessment of the acquiring company's own capabilities.[34]

(1) Information Risks

From an objective perspective, many risks in M & A stem from the internal risks present before the acquisition, due to the limitations that acquiring companies face in obtaining information about their targets. For instance, there are often restrictions on information acquisition between the acquirer and the target company, leading to information asymmetry. Information asymmetry can impede the effective functioning of market economies, preventing markets from achieving optimal outcomes. Therefore, when private equity firms engage in financing and acquisitions, a lack of transparency

[34] See Wu (2012).

can severely affect the operational efficiency of the entire market economy.[35] From a subjective standpoint, acquiring companies may lack a clear understanding of their own M & A capabilities and motivations. During the operation of a business, owners can sometimes overestimate their financial strength and have overly optimistic forecasts for future growth, which can result in reckless expansion. This issue often arises during the M & A pricing process, where overconfidence in one's financing and debt repayment abilities can inflate the acquisition price. This overvaluation may lead to acquisition failure due to insufficient funds and, in extreme cases, even bankruptcy of the company.[36] Selecting a promising target market is crucial for the future development of a company. The vitality of the market economy can drive the growth of a company. Conversely, if a market with a bleak outlook is chosen, not only is it difficult for the company to achieve good development, but it may also harm investment returns. Therefore, selecting M & A targets and markets with good development potential is critical.[37] The case described below regarding credit assessment is a classic example of this risk.

Company A, introduced by natural person B, expressed an interest in acquiring equity in Company C, an environmentally-friendly manufacturing company. Upon review, Company A found that Company C was qualified to produce eco-friendly products and held corresponding invention patents, as well as an independent brand. During the feasibility study, Company A recognized the company's significant research potential and alignment with national industrial policies, suggesting a promising development outlook. The acquisition of equity in Company C promised to yield substantial market benefits post-acquisition. Consequently, after a standard credit review, Company A completed the equity acquisition of Company C, becoming its largest shareholder and gaining control of the company. However, following the acquisition, the company received a court summons for failing to repay a small business loan of 20 million and the associated interest, resulting in legal action. This case exemplifies the challenges of equity investment due to information asymmetry. Investors cannot fully grasp all the information about the target company, making the credit review of the target company a critical factor in the success or failure of equity investments. In this instance, Company C concealed the fact that it had substantial external debts it could not repay, and Company A failed to uncover this significant debt during the investment review process. This indicates that Company A did not fulfill its due diligence obligations, thereby exposing the investment to considerable risk.

(2) Policy Risks

Policy changes are a significant risk factor for companies engaging in M & A, as they can affect the value of the company being acquired and the potential synergies after M & A. For instance, the rapid growth of China's renewable energy sector in recent

---

[35] Ding (2013).

[36] Xing (2018).

[37] Sun (2018).

years is largely attributed to the support from national policies, regulations, and incentive measures. The government has introduced policies and regulations such as the "Renewable Energy Law" and the "Medium- and Long-Term Program for Development of Renewable Energy" to promote the development of renewable energy sources. Take Shenzhen Expressway Company Limited as an example. On March 15, 2019, its subsidiary Shenzhen Expressway Environmental Co., Ltd. signed an equity acquisition agreement with Nanjing Anbeixin Investment Management Co., Ltd and Nanjing Wind Power Technology Co., Ltd., acquiring a 30% stake in Nanjing Wind Power. After the transaction was completed, they further invested in Nanjing Wind Power, ultimately holding a 51% stake.[38] Nanjing Wind Power primarily engages in the utilization of wind resources and wind power generation. Recent national policies, such as the "Notice on Improving the Feed-in Tariff Policy for Wind Power" and the " Interim Administrative Measures for Additional Subsidy Funds for Price of Renewable Energy Power," have provided tax incentives for wind power project construction, greatly enhancing the economic viability of projects. However, if future national support policies for the wind power industry are adjusted, such as reducing tax incentives, then the operational profits of Shenzhen Expressway's acquisition and additional investment in Nanjing Wind Power could be significantly affected.[39]

With the establishment of the "14th Five-Year Plan" and the goal of achieving carbon neutrality, the investment direction of Energy Internet companies has also changed accordingly. The proposals for formulating the 14th Five-Year Plan for National Economic and Social Development and the Long-Range Objectives Through the Year 2035, adopted at the Fifth Plenary Session of the 19th Central Committee of the Communist Party of China, cover multiple aspects including carbon emissions, power infrastructure construction, and the development of new energy sources.[40] The energy planning during the 14th Five-Year Plan period brings new momentum to the energy industry. In 2019, China resolutely implemented the new energy security strategy of "Four Revolutions and One Cooperation," focusing on the green and low-carbon transformation and deepening the structural reform of the energy supply side. This not only maintained a reasonable growth of energy production but also promoted a steady improvement in energy quality.[41] The 14th Five-Year Plan emphasizes the need to put into practice the new energy security strategy of "Four Revolutions and One Cooperation," especially by strengthening the construction of "smart energy systems" and the development of "new energy technologies."[42] China has announced its goal to achieve carbon neutrality by 2060, signifying that the profound transformation toward the 2.0 version of China's energy system has already commenced. Further reforms in the power sector will greatly influence the development of renewable energy, the application of energy storage technologies,

---

[38] Jia (2019).

[39] State-owned Assets Supervision and Management Commission of Shenzhen Municipal People's Government (2019).

[40] Xinhua News Agency (2020).

[41] Liu (2020).

[42] China Commercial Industry Research Institute (2020).

the use of digital technologies, and the construction of an Energy Internet. The International Energy Agency, in its report "Power Systems in Transition: Challenges and Opportunities Ahead for Electricity Security" published in October 2019, warned of the new challenges to electricity supply security that could arise from the widespread application of digital technology and system interconnectivity.[43] These put forward requirements for the investment direction of Energy Internet companies. Investment projects should contribute to the rapid reshaping of the power system, especially in the field of distribution networks. Besides, the establishment of the goal of achieving carbon neutrality will inevitably impact future carbon pricing. The level of internal carbon prices will directly determine the feasibility of energy projects, which will significantly disrupt the investment rules in the energy sector.[44]

(3) Procedural Risks

In their equity investments, energy companies may face risks such as violations of the Company Law and other relevant legal provisions. These risks can stem from a failure to perform decision-making procedures, procedural deficiencies in equity investment decisions, or a failure to perform reasonable review obligations. For example, an engineering technology research center decided to invest CNY 799,000 (the investment was reviewed and approved during an office meeting jointly held by a national engineering technology research center and a chemical research institute, where specific arrangements for the amount, price, and proportion of the investment were made). However, during this investment process, no approval document from the supervisory authority of the engineering technology research center was found. According to the provisions of the "Company Law," the investing entity of state-owned assets, when making investments, has the rights to obtain investment returns, make major decisions, and select managers. Therefore, the engineering technology research center should follow its charter and implement internal decision-making procedures when making external investments. However, there were deficiencies in the procedures of this investment made by the engineering technology research center, especially in making relevant decisions, as it did not report to its supervisory authority in a timely manner and obtain approval.

Financing Risks

Mergers require substantial financial support from businesses, as only with sufficient funding can the smooth completion of a merger be ensured. While mergers and acquisitions have the potential to create new economic value and may be reasonably priced, inappropriate financing methods can ultimately harm shareholder interests[45] and even increase the operational capital pressure on the company. Therefore, it is essential to raise adequate funds to ensure that merger and acquisition activities

---

[43] Chen (2021).

[44] Same as above.

[45] Nie and Luo (2010).

can proceed smoothly. Different companies adopt various fundraising strategies. Typically, energy companies raise funds through long-term loans. For example, at the end of the third quarter of 2012, China Guodian Corporation's long-term borrowing increased from CNY 58.7 billion at the beginning of the year to CNY 68.5 billion, an increase of CNY 9.8 billion.[46] It is noteworthy that traditional credit institutions and banks usually do not offer loan services specifically designed for corporate mergers and acquisitions, making it challenging for companies to secure commercial bank support when financing through debt. Debt financing refers to the process where acquiring companies raise funds by issuing corporate bonds. This method has lower financing costs but takes longer and has limited fundraising capacity. Equity financing is another approach, with issuing common stock being a primary method for fundraising. Common stock eliminates the burden of mandatory principal and interest payments, thereby lowering the financial risk for the company.[47]

Risks of Transfer of Management Rights

In the process of corporate mergers, companies that contribute more capital not only need to obtain the financial control of the merged company but also need to acquire the business management rights of the company. For example, although PipeChina was officially established as a state-owned enterprise in the energy industry on December 9, 2019, it had already signed an agreement with China National Offshore Oil Corporation in Beijing on April 1, 2020, regarding the transfer of management rights of oil and gas infrastructure projects.[48] If the merger is completed and the business management rights are not transferred to the new management in a timely manner, this will bring potential risks to the investors. The main problems with the unsuccessful transfer of management rights include: First, the merged company may not have the conditions to transfer the main operating rights to the investors due to the current corporate management standards. Since general corporate management standards do not stipulate the provisions related to the investors having the main operating rights, investors do not have the authority to manage and operate the company after the merger. Second, during the process of corporate mergers, both parties may not reach an agreement on the issue of business management rights. In the process of transferring operating rights, the exit of the original management may have an adverse effect on the operating rights of the investors. Third, the acquired company may use the relationships of internal employees to influence the company. Specifically, minority shareholders may join forces with company employees to form a situation that opposes the investors. Since the investors are external forces and lack an understanding of the internal situation of the company, this may lead to confusion and helplessness for the investors in management. In summary, these problems may all lead to restrictions encountered by the investors in the process of business

[46] Yuan (2012).

[47] See Bei (2020).

[48] 21st Century Business Herald (2020).

management, which is not conducive to the smooth progress of future corporate management work.

Integration Risks

One of the main goals of a company's merger and acquisition is to maximize shareholder wealth. In order to achieve this goal, after completing the merger and acquisition, the investing company needs to make effective synergy and cooperation in operation and management with the target company. Obtaining the operational control of the target company in the merger and acquisition is just the starting point. After that, the merged and acquired company must be integrated and developed, which is a relatively risky step.[49] Due to differences in business methods, philosophies, and regulations between different companies, it is challenging to effectively integrate the management, operations, human resources, and other aspects of the target company with the investing company. In addition, special attention needs to be paid to the integration of confidentiality management systems. Especially for those Energy Internet companies whose main business involves public interest and national security, the confidentiality management system of the acquired company must be consistent with the Energy Internet companies. Business activities must adhere strictly to relevant confidentiality regulations and be conducted with a strong emphasis on safety. Failure to do so could result in the risk of national secrets being compromised. For example, there was a case involving a cadre named Zheng, who was assigned by his superiors to another department for training and was allowed to copy a large number of classified documents, including seven top-secret files and one confidential file, on a top-secret computer. Later, Zheng was transferred to grassroots work, carrying a USB flash drive with a large amount of classified information. Since the grassroots unit was located in a remote area and only had a local area network connected to the Internet, this classified USB flash drive was subsequently frequently used on the Internet and was eventually discovered during a network inspection. Zheng was given an administrative warning for serious violations, and the leaders of the two departments were also criticized in a notification.[50] Although this case was not caused by equity mergers and acquisitions, it suggests that improper integration after mergers and acquisitions can also lead to classified information leakage. According to the regulations of the confidentiality system, classified files should be stored separately from non-classified files and use specialized storage rooms and storage equipment to ensure the security of classified files.[51]

[49] Bei (2020).

[50] Song (2012).

[51] See Sun (2018).

Asset M & A

Asset M & A and equity M & A are two different concepts. Equity M & A involves acquiring shares from existing shareholders of a target company or participating in a capital increase to obtain a stake in the company's equity. Asset M & A refers to investors acquiring assets of a target company with development potential (such as the company's working capital, real estate, and machinery). By managing and operating these assets, investors aim to obtain a portion of the company's economic benefits and capabilities, similar to what is achieved through equity M & A. Asset M & A and equity M & A have several key differences: Firstly, the method of change is different. When conducting an equity M & A, it is necessary to complete the relevant change procedures with the administrative department for industry and commerce. In contrast, some asset M & A may not require change procedures with the administrative department for industry and commerce, but if real estate is involved, it is mandatory to go through the property transfer procedures with the real estate department. If the entire assets of a company are being acquired, the acquired company will also need to go through the cancellation procedures with the administrative department for industry and commerce. Secondly, there is a difference in the assumption of debt. In an equity M & A, shareholders will assume the corresponding debt according to their shareholding ratio. In an asset M & A, however, the original debts of the target company remain the responsibility of the acquired company. Third, taxes are different. After the equity transfer, shareholders are required to pay personal income tax on the capital gains. Following the asset transfer, the target company is liable for taxes such as Value Added Tax (VAT) and business tax. When engaging in asset M & A, Energy Internet companies may encounter asset evaluation risks, payment risks, and operational risks.

Asset Evaluation Risks

In the process of asset M & A, the acquirer needs to have a clear understanding of their acquisition targets. An unclear objective or an inaccurate evaluation of the assets can lead to an insufficient understanding of the investment risks involved. Asset M & A represents the transfer of ownership of assets in the market, which is fundamentally different from the ordinary buying and selling of goods. The process is typically complex and can be influenced by a variety of objective and subjective factors that may cause fluctuations in the evaluation of assets. When evaluating the value of assets, it is crucial to first ensure that the ownership of the assets being evaluated is clear and undisputed. Furthermore, when economic activities within various departments of a company necessitate asset evaluation, it is important to select an appropriate asset evaluation agency to carry out the evaluation based on the specific circumstances.

Payment Risks

Payment risks in corporate mergers and acquisitions refer to the potential risks that may arise from the chosen method of payment.[52] If a non-compliant payment method is used in an asset acquisition, it can not only lead to financial risk but also potentially affect the process of asset transfer. For example, a company's contract templates usually include a clause with details of a designated bank account for receiving payments. When entering into agreements with external partners, the company specifies a particular receiving account for the partners to make payments via wire transfer. Should there be any changes to the receiving account, the contract stipulates that the company must notify the paying party in writing within three days of the account change, or else the receiving party bears the legal consequences. In a specific case, the company experienced a change in its receiving account and notified the contact person of the paying party by phone. However, the paying party failed to fulfill the payment obligation by the payment deadline. Subsequently, the company issued a written demand for payment, but the paying party deferred on the grounds of an incorrect receiving account, directly affecting the company's normal cash flow. In a mature M & A market, common methods of payment include equity, cash, or a combination of both. Based on past experience, using a combination of these payment methods can effectively mitigate payment risks, thereby reducing financial risks that may threaten the company's development.

Operational Risks

Upon completing the signing of the asset acquisition agreement, the acquirer will be able to participate in the production and operational activities of the acquired company. From that point forward, the acquirer is responsible for assuming and addressing the various risks that may arise during the course of business operations. These include, but are not limited to, risks associated with procurement, product sales, fundraising for operations, product transportation, decision-making, foreign investments, and tax obligations of the company. There are many unpredictable factors in the entire merger process. From an external production standpoint, the merged entity is primarily influenced by national policies, which can affect the company's production cycles, loan interest rates, etc. On a more granular level, the merger can also impact the acquirer's financial situation, including aspects such as fundraising capabilities, fluctuations in the valuation of the acquired company, proprietary technology, financial structure, and staff turnover. All these factors can have an impact on the M & A activity, potentially leading to a final outcome that significantly deviates from the anticipated results.

[52] Xiang (2020).

PPP Mode

PPP is a new financing model for projects. Unlike traditional financing methods, PPP financing is not arranged based on the creditworthiness of the project investors or sponsors, but rather primarily on the anticipated returns from the project, the project assets, and the extent of government support. Within PPP projects, the income generated from project operations, along with the benefits derived from government support, constitute the primary sources for loan repayment. Additionally, assets held by the project company and limited guarantees provided by the government serve as security to ensure the safety of the loans.[53] On November 28, 2017, the National Development and Reform Commission issued the "Guiding Opinions on Encouraging Private Capital Participation in Government and Social Capital Cooperation (PPP) projects" (Fa Gai Tou Zi [2017] No. 2059). This document clearly indicates that for projects with large investment scales, long cooperation periods, and complex technical requirements, the state encourages cooperation among private companies, or between private companies and state-owned companies, foreign-funded companies, and other types of companies. Such collaborations can take the form of joint bidding consortia or the establishment of mixed-ownership companies, thereby fully leveraging the strengths of different companies. This demonstrates the state's supportive and encouraging stance toward collaborations between private and state-owned enterprises through the PPP model. Taking the example of a Chinese grid company's recent years' practice in PPP projects, this company has been involved in PPP projects that usually entail substantial investment amounts and encompass a variety of project types. For example, in July 2018, State Grid Information & Telecommunication Group, as the lead entity of a consortium that included Shenzhen Yingda Capital Management Co., Ltd. and Fanglue Inland Port Group, successfully won the bid for the "Linfen City Big Data Industrial Park PPP Project." In the first year alone, the operational subsidy for this project reached CNY 135.3 million.[54] On April 24, 2019, the Prime Minister of Ethiopia met with the directors of this grid company in Beijing, where both parties witnessed the signing of the execution agreement for the Ethiopian PPP Transmission and Distribution Project between China Electric Power Equipment and Technology Co., Ltd. and the Ministry of Finance of Ethiopia. Since the inception of the "Belt and Road" initiative, the grid company has undertaken numerous projects in Ethiopia, including the GDHA 500 kV Transmission and Substation Project, Light Rail Support Transmission and Substation Project, Ethiopia-Kenya $\pm$ 500 kV DC Transmission Line Project, and Medium and Low Voltage Distribution Network Upgrade and Transformation Project, with the contract value totaling approximately USD 1.8 billion.[55]

Scholars have selected microgrid construction projects as case studies, employing the QQIR (Quality, Quantity, Innovation, Risk) approach to analyze the potential risks faced by investors in the power sector under PPP financing schemes. The findings

[53] See Wu (2004).

[54] China Government Procurement (2018).

[55] See State Grid Corporation of China (2019).

indicate that investors in the power industry are subject to relatively high risks under the PPP model. These risks are categorized into financial, operational, market, political, construction, environmental, cooperative, and legal risks.[56] Given the substantial amount and variety of projects, Energy Internet companies face significant and complex risks when engaging in financial activities through PPP projects. However, due to the consistent adherence to the PPP model across all these projects, there is a high degree of uniformity in their operational processes. Based on this uniformity, we can analyze the risks that Energy Internet companies might encounter according to the operational flow of PPP projects. Specifically, these risks include decision-making, budgeting, financing, authorization, and withdrawal risks.

Decision-Making Risks

Energy Internet companies have come to realize that developing integrated energy services is a key strategic direction for them. Take a grid company as an example. Since 2017, it has been offering integrated energy services within its power supply region. At the beginning of 2019, the company formulated the "2019–2020 Action Plan for Advancing Integrated Energy Service Development," where they identified four main areas of business development and planned to capitalize on the new wave of energy technology and information and communication technology revolutions, as well as the opportunities presented by industry integration, focusing on promoting the Energy Internet and smart energy use. Their goal is to establish an open, cooperative, and mutually beneficial energy service platform, striving to position the company as a major practitioner, deep participant, key driver, and exemplar in the field of integrated energy services.[57] Integrated energy services refer to both the integration of various types of energy (such as electricity, gas, heat, and cooling) and the integration of services (including engineering services, investment services, operation services, etc.).[58] As the integrated energy industry develops, Energy Internet companies are encountering new challenges when making investment decisions. Firstly, exceptional integrated energy service projects are rare. Secondly, only those projects that truly center customer value in their service offerings can be considered genuine integrated energy services. In this context, the profit models for Energy Internet companies need to be adjusted. They do not only rely on traditional investment returns, such as profit-sharing models from Energy Management Contracts (EMC). Instead, these companies must earn customer recognition by providing high-quality services and have customers cover operational costs, rather than merely seeking straightforward investment returns.[59] This shift in profit models implies that, in the process of advancing integrated energy services, Energy Internet companies will face new decision-making risks when selecting PPP projects—risks that did not exist before.

[56] Wang and Li (2019).

[57] Meng R (2020).

[58] Feng (2017).

[59] Yu (2021).

Budgeting Risks

Firstly, in the implementation of PPP projects, many companies face the issue of incomplete budget management, which directly leads to the improper execution of the projects. Specifically, when competing for PPP projects, companies often lack a thorough practical analysis in budget preparation and overlook the budgeting for potential additional costs, such as expenses incurred from construction delays due to unforeseen factors.[60]

Moreover, in an effort to expedite construction progress, companies may not adhere strictly to budgetary constraints when procuring materials. Should the purchasing costs exceed the budget, it can have a detrimental impact on the entire lifecycle of the project and may also impede its smooth progression.[61]

Furthermore, many companies exhibit shortcomings in their management of financial budgets. A number of businesses continue to rely on traditional contract project management approaches that fail to meet the stringent demands of PPP projects, leading to inefficiencies in financial budgeting. This not only increases the construction costs of the project but also significantly affects the operational profits during the management phase. Therefore, strengthening corporate cost control and improving the budget management system under PPP projects plays a very important role in preventing corporate financing risks.[62]

Lastly, it is difficult for contracts to cover all possible scenarios and risks. Taking PPP contracts as an example, their contract terms typically range from 10 to 30 years. During this time, factors such as market demand, currency value, tax rates, and others may change, posing challenges to long-term budget planning. The project's financing methods, construction schedule and quality, implementation of operational plans, and the rate of return on investment can all impact the project's ultimate profitability. For instance, in the "Shandong Zhonghua Power Project," the total investment reached CNY 16.8 billion, with an installed capacity of 3 million kw. This project was undertaken by Zhonghua Power Company Limited, jointly initiated by Shandong Electric Power, Shandong International Trust, CLP Power Hong Kong, and Électricité de France, with a cooperation term of 20 years. After this term, the power plant assets would be wholly owned by the Chinese side. This project not only boasted the largest installed capacity and the highest loan amount among China's BOT power projects to date, but it was also acclaimed as China's top PPP project in 1998. To ensure smooth cooperation, the project company signed an "Operation and Electricity Purchase Agreement" with the Shandong Power Grid, which stipulates a minimum annual electricity sales volume. According to the Memorandum of Understanding signed by the former State Planning Commission in 1998, the completed Shiheng Phase I and Phase II power plants were allowed a relatively high feed-in tariff of CNY 0.41/kWh, which basically guaranteed the project revenue. However, in October 2002, when the new unit of Heze Power Plant was put into operation, the electricity

[60] Hou (2020).

[61] Same as above.

[62] Same as above.

price approved by the Shandong Provincial Price Bureau had dropped to CNY 0.32/ kWh. The price was too low to cover the project's normal operating costs. More seriously, starting from 2003, the Shandong Provincial Development and Reform Commission reduced the minimum purchase volume of electricity from Zhonghua Power by Shandong Electric Power from 5500 h per year to 5100 h. According to the contract, Shandong Electric Power was still obligated to buy at least 5500 h of electricity at the planned price and had to bear the cost difference itself. Ultimately, the cooperation was unsustainable, resulting in a significant decrease in the project revenue.[63]

Financing Risks

In PPP projects, infrastructure development is the primary investment focus. To attract private capital, local governments often offer varying degrees of revenue guarantees and risk compensation for certain projects. For instance, in the PPP project of the Linfen City Big Data Industrial Park, the fees collected from users were insufficient to cover the cost and reasonable profits of social capital or the project company. Consequently, the government adopted a "feasibility gap subsidy" approach,[64] providing economic support to social capital or the project company through fiscal subsidies, capital injections, preferential loans, and other policies.[65] Under this model, companies may overlook financial risks in contract management. To gain a competitive edge in the market, companies might be at a disadvantage when signing PPP project contracts, leading to a lack of risk awareness and unprofessional risk assessments during the contract management process. Should the government default or engage in similar actions, companies could suffer significant losses, triggering financing risks. Therefore, when undertaking large-scale PPP projects, enterprises should pay close attention to financing risk assessment to reduce their debt risks. This is especially true for PPP projects that are highly dependent on government involvement. Companies should conduct thorough investigations and accurate assessments before deciding whether to participate in bidding.[66]

Authorization Risks

Energy Internet companies may encounter administrative regulatory risks when it comes to the authorization of PPP projects. Specifically, the proposed investment project may fail to launch if it does not satisfy the criteria set forth in the project review process. Passing relevant verification procedures is a prerequisite for Energy Internet companies to launch a PPP project. The construction of PPP projects involves

---

[63] Beijing Mingdingren Education Consulting Co., Ltd. (2015).

[64] China Government Procurement (2018).

[65] PPP-ol (2023)

[66] Hou (2020).

the allocation of public resources and the fulfillment of public interests. In order to strengthen the supervision of PPP projects, the "Notice on Strengthening Management of the Investment and Construction of PPP Projects in Accordance with Laws and Regulations" issued by the National Development and Reform Commission in 2019 underscores the importance of conducting a thorough and detailed feasibility analysis and review of PPP projects. First of all, the feasibility of PPP projects must be assessed from multiple perspectives, including economic and social development needs, planning requirements, technical and economic feasibility, environmental impact, investment and financing plans, resource utilization efficiency, and the contribution to enhancing the quality of life for the public. Judging from the characteristics of grid projects, power resources, as an important energy source, play a supporting role in economic and social development, and rational planning of grid projects is crucial to national power security. When investing in grid projects, special attention should be paid to whether they can meet the demands of social-economic development and align with existing plans. In May 2020, the National Development and Reform Commission and the National Energy Administration issued the "Notice on Strengthening and Regulating Investment Management of Power Grid Planning," which mandates that the investment plans of grid companies must closely connect with grid planning to ensure that planned projects can be implemented smoothly. It can be seen that misalignment with planning has become a significant regulatory risk for grid projects. For instance, the grid planning of a power supply company did not comply with the overall urban and rural planning, leading to restrictions in the routing corridors during implementation. As a result, the plan had to be amended and re-submitted for approval. In addition, the use of power resources is closely related to environmental protection. Faced with global climate change and newly established national emission reduction targets, grid companies must determine their investment direction under the guidance of the new emission reduction goals when making investment decisions on PPP projects.[67]

Secondly, in the review of PPP projects, the government's scrutiny of proposed corporate investment projects represents a form of intervention in the market economy. As China's market-oriented reforms deepen, the government's direct control over the economy is gradually diminishing. In 2004, the State Council issued the "Decision of the State Council on Reforming the Investment System," which clarifies that government approval will no longer be required for projects not funded by the government. Instead, the systems of "Authorization" and "Record-filing" will be used where appropriate. The "Regulations on the Administration of Corporate Investment Projects by Authorization and Record-filing "issued in 2016 details clear regulations for the authorization and record-filing systems for corporate investment projects. According to Article 3 of the "Regulations on the Administration of Corporate Investment Projects by Authorization and Record-filing," projects involving national security, significant production layout, strategic resource development, or major public interest shall be subject to authorization administration. Projects other than those prescribed in the preceding paragraph shall be subject

[67] Zhang (2020).

to record-filing administration. This indicates that the government is relaxing its scrutiny over corporate investment projects. However, considering the public interest nature of grid projects, the State Council specified the authorization and record-filing requirements for grid projects in the "Catalogue of Investment Projects Subject to Government Authorization (2016 Edition)." In May 2020, the National Development and Reform Commission and the National Energy Administration issued the "Notice on Strengthening and Regulating Investment Management of Power Grid Planning," which emphasizes the need to promote a graded and categorized management of power investment projects. Power grid projects within the scope of the planning should follow the relevant procedures in accordance with the "Regulations on Government Investment" and the "Regulations on the Administration of Corporate Investment Projects by Authorization and Record-filing."

Thirdly, investment projects also face the risk of failing to obtain approval due to errors in early-stage planning, such as issues with site selection or problems with environmental impact assessments. For example, a company planned to construct a 10-kilovolt power line without undergoing formal approval for the route planning. During construction, the line had to cross over residential houses, fields, and graveyards in rural areas, which led to resistance and complaints from local residents. They demanded to see government documents authorizing the legal construction of the line. Lacking such documentation, the project's construction was questioned even when coordinated with local township governments, preventing its completion and subsequent operation as planned.

This case illustrates that grid companies may still encounter the risk of failing to get project authorizations when undertaking investment projects. According to the provisions of the "Notice on Strengthening Management of the Investment and Construction of PPP Projects in Accordance with Laws and Regulations" and the "Regulations on the Administration of Corporate Investment Projects by Authorization and Record-filing," PPP projects that have not completed formal approvals, authentications, record-filings, as well as feasibility studies and review procedures are considered non-compliant projects and are strictly prohibited from commencing construction. For projects that require authorization administration, if construction starts without the necessary authorization procedures, or if the location, scale, or content of the construction deviates from the authorization documents, they may face administrative penalties such as work stoppages, production halts, or fines. If a company obtains authorization documents through deceit, bribery, or other improper means, depending on the severity of the case, the company may be subject to administrative or even criminal responsibility.

Withdrawal Risks

Domestic PPP projects have seen rapid growth over time. As the relevant application systems continue to be updated, the market entry barriers for these types of projects are gradually being lowered, leading to a sharp increase in the number of PPP projects. To address the widespread misuse of PPP, the Ministry of Finance issued the "Notice on Regulating the Management of the Comprehensive Database for PPP Projects" (hereinafter referred to as the "Notice"), which introduces the national comprehensive PPP project database. According to the "Notice," newly added PPP projects must be suitable for the PPP model, with thorough preliminary preparation, and incorporate a pay-for-performance mechanism. As for projects that are already in the database, those that exhibit specified issues such as not undergoing the mandatory two evaluations, unsuitability for continued use of the PPP model, irregular operations, legal or regulatory violations, or lack of transparency will be subject to withdrawal. The Ministry of Finance has disclosed that, as of July 2019, 90 PPP projects across various regions have opted out of the database. Some of these projects were even initiated by state-owned enterprises and subsidiaries of listed companies. An instance of this is the PPP project for the Shanxi Linfen City Big Data Industrial Park, which was led by the State Grid Information & Telecommunication Group.[68]

Conventional Management Risks

In the capital operation process, Energy Internet companies primarily face the conventional management risk of executive negligence of duty. This risk is manifested when the company's operational managers fail to fulfill or improperly execute their duties in accordance with relevant laws and regulations, leading to the potential loss of corporate assets, state-owned assets, or other severe consequences. In the process of investment activities, the decisions and actions of executives are the fundamental basis for the initiation and execution of investment activities. Market risks, political risks, and legal risks are objective risks inherent in the investment process, whereas the risk of executive negligence of duty is a subjective risk. Subjective risks are more challenging to identify and regulate compared to objective risks, and they persist throughout the entire investment activity. Item 3 of Article 15 of the "Supervision Law of the People's Republic of China" clearly stipulates that oversight authorities shall conduct oversight of executives of state-owned enterprises. The "Implementation Measures for the Accountability for Illegal Operations and Investments by Central Enterprises" (Trial) provides more detailed provisions for the negligence of duty of state-owned enterprise executives. As leaders, organizers, and decision-makers of their enterprises, the executives of state-owned enterprises play a critical role in areas such as selecting financing parties and making investment decisions. Whether they fully perform their duties directly influences the final results of investment and financing decisions. In practice, executives differ in experience, ability, understanding of investment and financing laws and regulations, and ethical standards. Executives lacking experience and ability are prone to overlook risk information in the investment and financing process and make incorrect judgments about market demand, thereby increasing the risks associated with the investment and financing activities of state-owned enterprises. Those with low ethical standards

---

68 China Business News (2019).

may engage in actions detrimental to the enterprise's capital operations in order to gain improper benefits, such as using related-party transactions to channel benefits or illegally siphoning off funds. Based on the presence of ethical issues, the risks of executive negligence of duty can be divided into general negligence of duty risks and integrity risks.

General Negligence of Duty Risks

General negligence of duty risks for executives in state-owned enterprises refer to the risks of inaction or improper performance of duties that are not induced by moral factors such as corruption. They often manifest as risks arising from non-compliance with procedures. In the context of investment activities, these risks primarily include dereliction in investment risk management, fixed asset investments, and investments in mergers and acquisitions.

Investment risk management is the process of predicting, assessing, and controlling potential risks associated with investments, which encompasses risk identification, risk analysis, risk assessment, risk decision-making, and risk monitoring. Typically, companies will develop specialized risk management systems tailored to their own investment characteristics. When making investment decisions, executives who fail to implement these systems or do so without sufficient rigor are prone to overlooking critical risk information and struggling to respond to risks in a timely manner. For instance, a company once invested several hundred million CNY in the construction of a project without conducting adequate feasibility studies. Consequently, the project's economic performance post-launch was poor, resulting in a cumulative loss of CNY 252 million over four years and causing a significant loss of state-owned assets. According to the "Three Major and One Large" decision-making (that is, decision-making on major issues, major appointments and removals, major projects, and the use of large amounts of money) regulations, major decisions require feasibility studies and demonstrations prior to implementation. The company's failure to conduct proper assessments for the investment project as required constituted a violation of the "Three Major and One Large" decision-making procedures, exemplifying a classic case of the risk of executive negligence of duty. In addition to neglecting system compliance, there is also a risk that executives of state-owned enterprises will fail to conduct legal reviews of economic contracts and critical decisions during the investment process as required. This failure could lead to violations of state-owned asset supervision regulations and result in severe liabilities. Fixed asset investment is one of the key forms of investment for state-owned enterprises. For power grid companies, this often manifests as investment in the power grid and related infrastructure projects. Executives face risks of negligence of duty when making fixed asset investments, often due to neglecting proper investment procedures. These risks can include making illegal investments in projects on the negative list, failing to modify project plans as required, and experiencing project delays and cost overruns due to managerial disarray. For state-owned enterprises, mergers, and acquisitions are not only a significant mode of investment but also a crucial means of engaging in the marketplace. During investment processes, as well as mergers and acquisitions, executives may make serious decision-making errors due to a lack of experience and capability, failing to consider significant risks adequately. There may also be cases where they have not fulfilled their duties, either by neglecting to conduct thorough risk assessments or by not adhering to established decision-making and approval procedures. Furthermore, issues can arise if post-acquisition integration is not carried out according to relevant plans, or if shareholders do not exercise their rightful powers. These problems may result in losses for the company.

Integrity Risks

The integrity risk for state-owned enterprise executives refers to the possibility for these individuals to engage in corrupt behaviors, such as seeking personal gain through their public power, either in the performance of official duties or in their daily lives.[69] It is also a manifestation of managerial failure. From the purpose perspective, the primary cause of integrity risks is the drive for economic benefits, especially in the field of investment, where the funds involved are often substantial. Consequently, this makes the management of these funds highly susceptible to issues of integrity. From the perspective of fund management, executives may maliciously acquire state-owned assets through the following methods: violating decision-making and approval procedures or exceeding their authority to raise and use funds; retaining funds, settling income and expenses, or opening bank accounts in their own names in violation of regulations; creating slush funds; raising funds, issuing stocks or bonds, making donations, providing guarantees, entrusting financial management, borrowing funds, or opening letters of credit, as well as handling bank bills in violation of regulations; falsifying expenditures to obtain funds; over-issuing or indiscriminately issuing employee salaries and benefits in violation of regulations; misappropriating, embezzling, or stealing funds, or committing fraud due to a lack of financial internal control or failure to implement financial internal control systems. From the operation perspective, managerial corruption may occur in the processes of procurement and sales management, fixed asset investments, and investments in mergers and acquisitions. In terms of procurement and sales management, executives may seek undue benefits in several ways: engaging in financing trade activities in violation of regulations or conducting fictitious trade activities such as "round-tripping" or "fake transactions"; improperly transferring benefits through related-party transactions against regulations; providing credit sales, qualifications, guarantees, or advance payments against regulations, thereby indirectly financing or investing through business prepayments or material transactions; engaging in commodity futures, options, or other derivative transactions against the rules. In terms of fixed asset investments, there is a risk that executives may not adhere to the required tendering procedures for purchases and construction projects, potentially interfering with or manipulating the bidding process. For instance, in the bribery

[69] See Baike (2023)

case of Guan XX (anonymized), the former Deputy General Manager (at the vice-ministerial level) of a certain grid company, the court found that Guan had facilitated bidding and project contracting for related entities in projects that included the power communication backbone network, substation renovation, and the decoration of a production dispatch building. He illegally accepted bribes totaling CNY 4.545 million, 40,000 US dollars, 10,000 euros, and shopping cards valued at CNY 50,000, which constituted the crime of bribery. Consequently, he was sentenced to twelve years in prison and had CNY 400,000 of his personal property confiscated.[70] For another instance, Linyang Energy Company has made multiple large-scale acquisitions of its controlling shareholders and its subsidiaries since its listing. Statistics show that Linyang Energy spent as much as CNY 732 million in cash for these related-party transactions.[71] In terms of investments in mergers and acquisitions, executives face two main types of integrity risks. The first involves providing advances in various forms to other joint venture partners in violation of regulations. The second entails channeling benefits to related parties through methods such as acquiring entities at a high premium.

Compared with general negligence of duty risks, integrity risks are more challenging to identify promptly because they focus on the intentional actions of executives, which often involve deliberate concealment. Correspondingly, the losses caused by integrity risks will be more serious. For instance, in the case of Wei Qinghai accepting bribes and holding huge amounts of property from unidentified sources, from the second half of 2007 to February 2015, the defendant Wei Qinghai exploited his various high-ranking positions—including Deputy General Manager and Party Secretary of Heilongjiang Electric Power Company, General Manager of China Electric Equipment Company, Deputy Head of the State Grid Smart Grid Research Institute's Preparatory Group, Deputy Director of the State Grid Corporation's Central China Division, and Deputy General Manager of Central China Power Grid Co., Ltd.—to grant favors in exchange for personal gain. During this period, he received bribes totaling CNY 10.33 million, and his personal wealth included over CNY 40 million that could not be accounted for.[72] Wei Qinghai's corrupt dealings went undetected for eight years, beginning in 2007. The resulting loss to state-owned assets exceeded CNY 50 million, highlighting the significant impact of integrity risks among executives on the operation and capital management of state-owned companies. To mitigate this risk, regulatory bodies within the state have intensified oversight of the integrity of management personnel in state-owned enterprises, imposing stricter penalties. When the threshold for criminal legal responsibility is met, offending managers are expected to bear the corresponding criminal liabilities. In this particular case, despite the defendant's confession and restitution, he was

[70] See Zhou (2015).

[71] See Tian (2021).

[72] See Judicial case. The second-instance criminal judgment for Wei Qinghai accepting bribes and holding huge amounts of property from unidentified sources, criminal judgment from the Intermediate People's Court of Sanmenxia City Henan Province. 2019 Yu 12 Xing Zhong No. 6, February 25, 2019.

still sentenced to ten years and six months in prison for bribery, along with a fine of CNY 2 million, in accordance with the principle of leniency. Additionally, for the crime of possessing a large amount of property with no explained origin, the defendant received a six-year prison sentence. Given the concurrent sentences for multiple crimes, the court determined a total imprisonment of thirteen years and a fine of CNY 2 million.

Legal Risks of Cross-Border Mergers and Acquisitions by Energy Internet Companies

In recent years, despite a reduction in cross-border mergers and acquisitions by Chinese companies, state-owned energy companies have remained actively involved in such transactions to acquire advanced technologies and resources and increase their market competitiveness and production scale. At the end of 2016, China introduced a series of regulatory policies related to overseas investment, strengthening control over Chinese companies' expansion abroad. In August 2017, the General Office of the State Council forwarded the "Guidance on Further Directing and Regulating Overseas Investment Direction" developed by four departments. The "Guidance" emphasizes the principles of maintaining the status of enterprises as the mainstay, commitment to deepening reforms, pursuit of mutual benefit and win–win outcomes, and focus on risk prevention. It categorizes overseas investments by Chinese enterprises into three classifications: encouraged, restricted, and prohibited. Additionally, it provides four guarantees: guidance based on classification, improvement of management mechanisms, enhancement of service levels, and strengthening of security measures. From this, it can be seen that China's current approach to cross-border mergers and acquisitions is "keeping a right balance between delegation and the exercise of control with strengthened guidance." As of October 2017, Chinese companies' overseas mergers and acquisitions have totaled 86.3 billion US dollars, indicating a continued high level of activity. Currently, the "Belt and Road" initiative aims to diversify China's energy supply channels. International trade in energy products has increased opportunities for energy import and export. China encourages domestic companies to export and invest to participate in global competition and trade.[73] For example, a grid company participating in and serving the "Belt and Road" initiative has expanded its global reach from Europe to the Middle East and further to South America. Since the start of the 13th Five-Year Plan, the company has made new overseas investments totaling 13.2 billion US dollars, with its equity assets increasing from 38 billion US dollars at the end of 2015 to 65 billion US dollars. The company has successfully invested in and operates 12 key energy network asset projects across nine countries and regions, including the Philippines, Brazil, Portugal,

[73] See Deng and Farah (2020).

Australia, Hong Kong (China), Italy, Greece, Oman, and Chile. These operations are stable and have yielded substantial returns.[74]

Cross-border mergers and acquisitions are economic activities riddled with complex legal issues, presenting a multitude of legal risks. In the case of a certain grid company's negotiation to acquire the American wind power assets of AES, the American company uploaded information concerning significant defects in the wind turbines to their database only the night before the contract signing. To mitigate substantial risks, the Chinese party included a termination clause in the share purchase agreement. If the two parties cannot agree on a compensation mechanism for the major turbine defects, the agreement would be terminated.[75] Before engaging in cross-border mergers and acquisitions, Energy Internet companies must carefully consider several key issues, including market access risks, antitrust concerns, national security issues, political factors, exchange rates, and labor-related matters. The following sections will elaborate on these risks in detail.

Market Access

Market access initially arose within the framework of tariff and trade negotiations. It refers to the conditions a member provides to the services and associated service providers of other members. These conditions should meet or exceed the commitments outlined in their respective schedules, including duration, restrictions, and terms. The concept of market access in the energy investment sector is based on the principle of national economic sovereignty.[76] Market access is a critical issue for energy companies, including grid companies, when engaging in cross-border mergers and acquisitions, often being perceived as a form of political risk. This risk is present from the initiation of investment and acquisition projects to the long-term operation after project completion. Due to differences in political systems, even Chinese-listed grid companies may sometimes struggle to gain recognition in foreign markets.[77] Cross-border mergers and acquisitions can have a significant impact on capital flows between countries and may even affect the industrial structure and trends of the host country. Consequently, host country governments usually regulate and intervene in cross-border mergers and acquisitions to safeguard their economic security. Host country governments typically subject mergers and acquisitions involving national defense, energy, and other sectors to complex and stringent review processes.[78] Political resistance has increased the risk of cross-border mergers and acquisitions by state-owned companies, with many such projects ultimately failing due to political reasons. Therefore, Energy Internet companies must fully understand the policies and

[74] State Grid Corporation of China (2021).

[75] Economic Information (2012).

[76] Yiu (2011).

[77] Yu (2016), p. 26.

[78] See Li (2014), p. 20.

laws of the target country's government before embarking on mergers and acquisitions, and try to align their objectives with the intentions of the target country's government to avoid losses.[79]

Political Risks from Host Countries

In the process of investing in overseas projects, grid companies must first confront market access risks. These risks are primarily reflected in whether the investment transactions can obtain approval from the host country's government, which is often influenced by the host government's policies and its citizens' attitudes towards foreign investors.[80] There are various methods of market access, including negative lists, licensing, authorization, registration, approval, and record-filing. These methods typically involve restrictions on the sectors in which foreign investors can invest, stipulated rights and obligations, as well as permitted investment proportions.[81] For example, the United States stipulates that foreign companies or individuals cannot acquire more than 25% of the shares in American companies in the aviation and maritime sectors, with similar market access regulations in place for the telecommunications and financial industries.[82] In addition, during the operation of a project, grid companies also face political risks. These risks mainly relate to the stability of the host country's political landscape, laws, and policies, which directly affect the operational security of overseas assets and the level of investment returns.[83] For example, companies may encounter the risk of nationalization by the host country's government. In 2012, in the Latin American region, the Spanish electricity grid company experienced such nationalization of its transmission company in Bolivia.[84]

Among Chinese energy companies, state-owned enterprises are the primary players in overseas M & A, which in turn leads host countries to perceive acquisitions involving companies with government connections as attempts to conceal national interests. This suspicion can make it a political concern. Many countries today are highly sensitive to the overseas M & A of state-owned enterprises. When energy M & A projects involve national strategic interests, they often encounter interference and restrictions from the host country's government. This interference often manifests in the form of political, economic, legal, and public opinion guidance to control M & A activities, making it highly concealed. Some energy-rich countries have revised their regulations and policies on foreign M & A, addressing issues such as qualifications, targets, and industries for M & A, the proportion of investment equity, and employment. In particular, they have conducted strict reviews

[79] See Yu (2016), p. 26.
[80] See Yu (2016), p. 14.
[81] Jia (2017).
[82] Chen and Chen (2006).
[83] See Yu (2016), p. 26.
[84] Yu et al. (2012).

of M & A entities with state-owned backgrounds, namely state-owned enterprises.[85] Here is one example: "The Philippine government has issued a 'negative list' that outlines the restricted and prohibited areas for overseas investment in the country. The Philippine government has specified 11 areas where foreign investment is prohibited from entering the country. Those related to the energy industry include small-scale mining, the exploration of marine resources in archipelago waters, territorial waters, and exclusive economic zones, and the small-scale development and utilization of resources from rivers, lakes, bays, and lagoons, among others. The government strictly controls the equity ratio of foreign investors in restricted industries. In industries related to the exploration and development of natural resources, while the Philippine government allows foreign investment, it restricts the foreign equity ratio to no more than 40%."[86] More examples: "Indonesia announced the imposition of punitive tariffs on the export of energy resources such as thermal coal. The M & A projects of Wuhan Iron & Steel Group and Minmetals Corporation were rejected by the Australian Department of Defense, citing concerns about their potential threat to national security-related actions. Following the rejection by the Libyan government, China National Petroleum Corporation abandoned their pursuit to acquire Verenex Energy, a Canadian oil company in which 86.3% of shares are owned by the Libyan government."[87] "The U.S. government intervened in CNOOC's proposed acquisition of Unocal due to concerns that it could pose a risk to the country's economic and national security."[88]

Policy Risks from Host Countries

Host countries may adjust their policies and regulations about M & A in the energy sector due to political and economic considerations. These policies and regulations may involve investment restrictions, taxation measures, and the nationalization of foreign enterprises, aimed at restricting the M & A of local energy enterprises by foreign enterprises or enhancing the benefits of domestic enterprises. For example, in 2008, Zambia unexpectedly abolished the Development Agreements signed between the government and major mines and implemented a new "Mines and Minerals Development Act."[89] The implementation of this Act not only raised mining taxes, but also reclaimed small-scale exploration and mining rights from foreign-invested enterprises. Another example is Australia, which boasts a favorable political, economic, legal, and natural resource environment, making it a highly sought-after investment destination for many countries. As such, numerous Chinese energy enterprises have already established their presence in Australia. However, the Australian government made an abrupt announcement that starting from July 1, 2012, a resource rent tax

[85] See Qiu (2018), p. 92.
[86] Chao and Jing (2017).
[87] Qiu (2018), p. 93.
[88] Yang (2019).
[89] Zhou (2017).

would be imposed on resource and energy enterprises registered in Australia at a rate of 40%. As a result, the effective tax rate for these enterprises increased from 43 to 57%.[90] Besides higher taxes for Chinese energy enterprises operating overseas, the implementation of this policy could potentially result in an increased risk of nationalization of these enterprises in Australia due to the unique nature of energy reserves. This could cause significant losses of overseas assets for these Chinese enterprises. In energy-rich countries in Africa and Latin America, not only do they lack comprehensive legislation to protect the rights and interests of foreign investors, but the judicial system is often out of step with laws and regulations. This makes it difficult for foreign investors to rely on international laws or agreements to safeguard their investment interests.[91] As a result, the evolving policies and regulations in host countries have heightened the risks associated with overseas M & A for Chinese energy enterprises.[92]

For instance, a cross-border project in Romania and the Ausgrid project in Australia both failed due to legal and policy risks in the host countries. During the implementation of the REN project, the Portuguese government announced to levy the "Energy Sector Extraordinary Contribution" on all energy enterprises, with a higher proportion applicable to those with foreign investments. This increased the tax burden for overseas enterprises, which hurt on their profits and dividends. Specifically, changes in the legal framework that governs investments in host countries make it difficult to accurately predict long-term returns. Such changes will introduce uncertainty into the investment return mechanism, making it impossible to guarantee the expected return on investment. Additionally, changes in the investment environment of host countries may cause potential investment projects to be banned or suspended by the government. Finally, political and policy changes in host countries, such as economic sanctions, export controls, and "double counter" investigations, can have a negative impact on companies and executives.

Compliance Risks

When engaging in overseas investment, besides considering the legal regulations of the host country, grid companies must also be aware of the risk of facing investment prohibition or administrative penalties due to non-compliance with the requirements for investments to be made by state-owned enterprises in the country. According to the "Measures for the Supervision and Administration of Overseas Investments by Central Enterprises," the State-owned Assets Supervision and Administration Commission of the State Council (SASAC), on behalf of the State Council, performs its responsibilities as an investor for state-owned enterprises. These involve guiding state-owned enterprises in establishing and refining their overseas investment

[90] Wang et al. (2017).

[91] Gu (2018).

[92] Qiu (2018), p. 92.

management systems and carrying out supervision from three perspectives: ex-ante, in-process, and ex-post.

Ex-ante Risks

From the ex-ante perspective, grid companies may face the risk of being disallowed from making investments due to not fulfilling China's classified supervision requirements on overseas investments. First of all, in terms of the scope of investment, Article 14 of the "Measures for the Supervision and Administration of Overseas Investments by Central Enterprises" stipulates that "In principle, central enterprises are not allowed to engage in overseas investments unrelated to their dominant area of business. If there is a specific need to invest in non-dominant business areas, it should be submitted to the SASAC for review and approval, and implemented in cooperation with central enterprises that have advantages in relevant dominant business areas." Secondly, when it comes to the types of investments, the "Interim Measures for the Reporting of Outbound Investments Subject to Record-filing or Approval" specify that foreign investment projects must be approved and filed using the "encouraged development + negative list" approach. The "Guidance on Further Directing and Regulating Overseas Investment Direction" provides detailed instructions on the types of investments that are encouraged, restricted, and prohibited. For overseas investments that are encouraged, they enjoy more favorable conditions in terms of taxation, foreign exchange, insurance, customs, and information, and can easily obtain approval and complete the filing procedures. On the other hand, for overseas investments that are restricted or prohibited, grid companies will face more scrutiny during the review process, which may require more thorough investigations before investing.

In-process Risks

As for in-process risks, major overseas investment projects are subject to random supervision and inspection by the SASAC. Grid companies are required to adhere to the "report all filings (approvals)" principle and provide quarterly updates on their overseas investment status to SASAC before the 10th day of the month following the end of the first, second, and third quarters of each year, as per the SASAC's requirements.[93] Embarking on overseas investments presents grid companies with a range of hurdles. Firstly, due to geographic limitations, the monitoring of critical information such as project completion, personnel management, and risk changes proves to be more challenging overseas than domestic investments in China. Failure to address this challenge properly can lead to a loss of control over such investments, increasing the risk of untruthful or false investments and failure to fulfill reporting

[93] The SASAC. Measures for the Supervision and Administration of Overseas Investments by Central Enterprises (Order of the SASAC of the State Council No. 35), Article 19.

obligations. Secondly, investments abroad are subject to risk information such as changes in national policies and market conditions that may be hard to come by, hindering companies from making timely adjustments to investment decisions and fulfilling reporting obligations.

Ex-post Risks

Regarding ex-post risks, the project evaluation should primarily consider the operation and income performance of the investment project after its completion. Given their status as significant state-owned enterprises, the profits and losses generated by grid companies through their investments have a direct impact on the growth or decline of state-owned assets. This makes them a key target of supervision by the SASAC. Article 21 of the "Measures for the Supervision and Administration of Overseas Investments by Central Enterprises" states that "The SASAC oversees and guides the post-evaluation of overseas investment projects by central enterprises. This involves selecting significant projects for evaluation, communicating the results to the respective companies, and endorsing successful experiences drawn from project operation." In general, grid projects are characterized by their long-term nature. During the operation process, grid companies' overseas investments are exposed to the risk of long-term regulatory failure. For instance, the integrity of managers may decline over time and as regulations are relaxed.

Foreign Exchange Financing Control Risks

The report "The Green Swan: Central banking and financial stability in the age of climate change" released by the Bank for International Settlements (BIS) in early 2020 pointed out that climate change brings financial risks and currency risks to the financial industry.[94] Exchange rate risk is a significant component of market system risks, with foreign exchange financing control being the primary area of concern. Foreign exchange financing control encompasses a set of strict regulatory measures imposed by applicable laws on cross-border M & A in terms of foreign exchange inflows and outflows, financing and lending activities, among others. Most of China's cross-border M & A transactions encounter the challenge of managing significant capital requirements. Regardless of the financial model employed, the conversion of multiple currencies can introduce exchange rate issues. For example, debt swaps, stock swaps, cash acquisitions, or any combination of these methods can also contribute to exchange rate risk. Changes in global interest rates can cause fluctuations in the value of the securities of the targeted company for acquisition. The foreign exchange rate issues that arise during the M & A process can have a

[94] Wang et al. (2020).

direct impact on the payment price of the acquisition, the cost of financing, the cost of raising funds, and the cost of management.[95]

In 2012, the International Telecommunications Union in Queensland, Australia announced that a Chinese grid company had won a bidding process to obtain partial equity in a southern Australian company. The project was scheduled to be delivered before the end of the year. China and Australia have strong complementarity in the field of electricity. The regulatory policies for the Australian electricity industry are stable, well-established, transparent, and the corresponding market is well-managed and orderly. There is significant potential for long-term cooperation between Chinese and Australian enterprises in terms of technology, capital, and other areas. This transaction marks a significant overseas investment project for Chinese grid companies and is the first successful M & A transaction for a Chinese company in Australia, following prior projects in Brazil, Portugal, and the Philippines. The primary risk associated with this transaction is the volatile exchange rate of the Australian dollar, i.e., exchange rate risk. Due to the recent decline in primary product prices, the Australian dollar has become significantly weaker against the US dollar, posing increased exchange rate risks for the RMB.[96]

Security Review Risks from Host Countries

Chinese enterprises investing overseas may face situations where the host country may block any Chinese investments or acquisitions of their local companies citing reasons such as a potential impact on their national economy and military security. The majority of countries have not provided a precise definition of "security review" in their security review legislation. Instead, the criteria for security review are typically outlined through enumeration, which include the identity of the investor, the industry in which the investment is made, control rights, and potential harm caused by the investment. Additionally, countries continue to adapt the standards and scope of security review in response to evolving circumstances.[97] In general, national security review refers to the thorough examination conducted by a government, based on legal provisions, of foreign investors, particularly those controlled by foreign governments, that aim to acquire control of local companies through M & A and enter industries such as military defense that could potentially impact national security. The earliest national security review legislation in the U.S., known as the "Exon-Florio Amendment," used the concept of national security. China's "Anti-Monopoly Law" and related regulations both use the term "security review" instead of specifically mentioning "national security review." However, both the "Anti-Monopoly Law" and the "Circular of the General Office of the State Council on the Establishment of Security Review System Regarding Merger and Acquisition

[95] See Li (2014), p. 21.

[96] Same as above, p. 31.

[97] He (2012).

of Domestic Enterprises by Foreign Investors" emphasize that the purpose of this legislation is to safeguard national security. Many countries have passed laws that require national security reviews of foreign investments. For example, in July 2007, the U.S. announced the "Foreign Investment and National Security Act of 2007." This Act, along with the "Exon-Florio Amendment," the "Byrd Amendment," and the "Foreign Investment Risk Review Modernization Act of 2018," has established a comprehensive legal framework for cross-border M & A in the field of national security in the U.S.[98] "Between 2004 and 2006, France introduced measures to provide exceptional safeguards to 11 vital industries and 20 major companies in order to restrict foreign M & A activities. Canada implemented limitations on foreign investments in several key, sensitive industries through the 'Foreign Investment Review Act' and the 'Canada Investment Act' to protect national security."[99] "Germany, Japan, the United Kingdom, Australia, and other countries have established laws addressing the impact of foreign investments on national security from perspectives such as industrial law, foreign exchange, foreign investment and trade, and other related legal areas.[100] Other countries within the EU have also been promoting special legislation related to national security." Most of the aforementioned legislation underscores the importance of establishing specialized agencies that aim to review and restrict foreign investments for merging and acquiring key enterprises in certain industries and conduct national security reviews on some foreign investments to safeguard national security.[101] This reveals that countries attach great importance to national security.

Antitrust Risks

The review of concentration of undertakings, as stipulated in the antitrust laws or competition laws of different countries, encompasses not only the types of concentration of undertakings, reporting thresholds, and reporting obligations, but also lays down the review process. If the review proceeds to a substantive examination phase, it will encompass specific standards for such examination. When it comes to conducting the antitrust review of cross-border M & A by multinational companies in one particular country, there are typically clear and specific substantive and procedural laws to adhere to, well-defined agencies for antitrust law enforcement, and established and transparent review standards and processes. However, conflicts of law would arise when the review is to be conducted simultaneously in different countries.[102]

---

98 Shao and Wang (2008).

99 Mu and Xiao (2009).

100 Zhang and Liu (2012).

101 See Zhang (2008).

102 See Wang (2012), p. 252.

Antitrust Regulations of the U.S. On Foreign Investments

The U.S. antitrust legal system consists primarily of three fundamental legislations: the "Sherman Act," the "Clayton Act," and the "Federal Trade Commission Act."[103] The earliest antitrust law passed by the U.S. Congress was called the "Sherman Act," which does not explicitly regard M & A as an anti-competitive practice.[104] Australia does not have a standalone anti-monopoly law, and its anti-monopoly review of foreign M & A is primarily addressed through the prohibition and exemption of M & A as outlined in the "Trade Practices Act." This is also a primary focus of this section. This act combines antitrust law, anti-unfair competition law, and consumer rights protection law, creating an antitrust law model unique to Australia. Officials from the Australian Competition and Consumer Commission maintain that the country's competition law model is distinguished by: for antitrust, a comprehensive ban on all anti-competitive practices, complemented by appropriate public interest exemptions; and for anti-unfair competition and consumer protection, a complete prohibition of practices such as misleading consumers and frauds.[105] Chinese enterprises seeking M & A in Australia should have a thorough understanding of Australia's anti-monopoly review system for M & A, and make strategic use of the relevant provisions of the "Trade Practices Act" to safeguard their rights and interests.

Antitrust Regulations of Australia on Foreign Investments

The antitrust provisions of the "Trade Practices Act" center on four key aspects. The first is prohibiting anti-competitive agreements. There are three forms of anti-competitive agreements under this Act. "First, fixing prices: this occurs when uniform prices are established through an agreement, often taking the form of recommended prices. Second, direct restrictions: operators agree to restrict specific suppliers or customers through an agreement. Third, indirect restrictions: one party conspires with another to restrict the commercial activities of a third party, whether in providing goods or services to others, acquiring goods or services from others, or engaging in import and export trade." The second is "prohibiting abusing a dominant market position. Abusing a dominant market position refers to the engagement of operators in the following practices: excluding or causing substantive damage to competitors, preventing others from entering a specific market, and preventing or impeding others from competing in a specific market. The prerequisite for an operator to abuse a dominant market position is that it holds a dominant position in a specific market. Dominant market positions are determined by the court on a case-by-case basis."[106] Generally, a dominant market position is determined against three criteria: "First,

[103] Yu (2008), p. 126.

[104] Wang and He (2008).

[105] Zhang and Xiao (2006).

[106] Li and Wu (2013).

market share; second, ease of market entry; and third, under the given market conditions, the scope and extent of the operator's ability to engage in business activities freely without being affected by competitors or potential competitors. This Act does not prohibit operators from obtaining and possessing a dominant market position, but it prohibits those with a dominant market position from abusing their dominant position to restrict market competition." The third is prohibiting exclusive dealing and restricting resale prices. "Exclusive dealing refers to the practice where operators force their trading partners to accept unreasonable trading conditions and restrict their freedom of choice, which causes substantive damage to competition in a specific market. Unreasonable trading conditions include requiring trading partners to refrain from procuring goods or services from competitors of the operator and restricting them from reselling goods or services to specific third parties in designated markets. The "Trade Practices Act" prohibits exclusive dealing, but allows operators who have engaged in such practice to report to the Competition and Consumer Commission and apply for exemption.[107] Restricting resale prices refers to the practice where manufacturers, suppliers, and wholesalers establish a minimum resale price for their products, and resellers are prohibited from selling the products at a price lower than this minimum. The main methods of restricting resale prices include: reaching agreements with resellers to agree on a minimum resale price, setting a minimum resale price for resellers, providing resellers with special discounts to induce them not to sell at a discount, and threatening to discontinue supply to force resellers to accept the minimum resale price." The last one is prohibiting M & A activities that restrict competition. The direct or indirect acquisition of property belonging to another legal or natural person by a legal or natural person shall not result in a reduction or potential reduction of market competition; otherwise, such practice shall be prohibited. To evaluate whether M & A activities result in a reduction or potential reduction of market competition, it is important to consider the following factors: "actual and potential international competition in a specific market; the difficulty of entering a specific market; market concentration in a specific market; the counterbalances between enterprises in a specific market; the possibility of surviving enterprises to raise prices after M & A; the difficulty of obtaining substitute products in a specific market; the vitality of a specific market, including growth capabilities, innovation capabilities and product diversification; possible weakening of market vitality and competition effect caused by M & A; the nature and extent of vertical integration in a given market. Under the 'Trade Practices Act', enterprises have the option to voluntarily submit M & A reports. If the parties involved in the M & A have concerns that the transaction may violate the 'Trade Practices Act', they can submit a report to the Competition and Consumer Commission for approval."[108]

---

[107] Ji (2019).

[108] See The Department of Economic Regulations of the State Economic and Trade Commission (2002).

Labor Risks

Personal Risk

"Due to the unique nature of grid-related jobs, the employees of grid companies face greater personal safety risks during production, construction, operation, and maintenance compared to those working in other types of companies. Therefore, the labor risks associated with overseas M & A of grid companies are more pronounced compared to those of other companies. Many countries have stringent protections for their own workers, and their labor policies often impose restrictions on the number of foreign employees in companies.[109] Consequently, after Chinese grid companies complete overseas M & A, they are subject to various restrictions imposed by the host country's laws and labor unions. As a result, the hiring of employees tends to prioritize local individuals. In case of a personal safety accident, this may lead to dissatisfaction from the local government and public opinion, ultimately worsening the business environment for these companies."[110]

Takeover Risk

In addition to personal safety risks, the majority of labor disputes center on the employees of the host country, who may encounter disputes with the resulting company regarding issues such as recruitment, dismissal, salary, social welfare, and employee pension. Chinese companies typically do not prioritize resolving labor disputes. When not confronted with concurrent large-scale labor disputes, they tend to brush them under the carpet, a practice influenced by the overall social environment in China. Nevertheless, this situation has the potential to spread and have a negative impact on the resulting company overseas.

The unemployment problem has emerged as a sensitive issue on a national scale in numerous countries. The practice of Chinese companies bringing in their own employees and arbitrarily laying off workers has increasingly sparked discontent among local governments and people. What is particularly noteworthy is that Chinese companies fail to appreciate the influence of trade unions in Western countries. Instead, they assume that Western trade unions, like their Chinese counterparts, lack genuine power and can be appeased with superficial measures.[111] The trade unions are mass organizations of the working class that emerged and developed amidst the rivalry between the proletariat and the bourgeoisie.[112] "In countries with well-established trade unions, particularly Western capitalist countries, legislation is generally adopted to protect trade union rights. Guided by their fundamental mission of protecting labor interests, trade unions wield significant influence in preventing

---

[109] Yu (2018).
[110] Yu (2016), p. 27.
[111] See Ai (2011), p. 37.
[112] Wang and Jiang (2018).

companies from violating workers' rights and facilitating the resolution of conflicts between employers and workers. In overseas M & A transactions, the trade unions of many host country enterprises hold substantive 'veto power'. Their attitude is a critical factor in determining the success or failure of the M & A."[113]

Summary of Legal Risks of Capital Operations in Energy Internet Companies

First and foremost, the mixed-ownership reform is predicated on the ongoing normal operation of the company. Apart from the conventional risks encountered by most enterprises, including contractual risks, intellectual property risks, corporate infringement disputes, and tax payment risks, Energy Internet companies are also exposed to unique legal risks such as those related to power supply operations, grid construction, external guarantees, fixed asset management, and personnel reallocation.

The mixed-ownership reform of Energy Internet companies involves the following types of risks. First, it is important to prevent the risk of state-owned asset loss due to inadequate supervision and incomplete reform implementation. The key lies in leveraging the function of the multi-level capital market to "discover and fairly determine prices." This necessitates selecting professional appraisal agencies to carry out asset evaluations and submitting the evaluation plan to regulatory authorities. Second, national laws and regulations impose strict thresholds for market entry. It is essential to ensure that qualification criteria are met in order to avoid the potential failure of the mixed-ownership reform in the power and related industries. Third, the mixed-ownership reform must be firmly grounded in national energy safety and economic development. The Energy Internet enterprises engaged in this reform function as a provider of basic public services, which are critical sectors where the controlling position of state capital must be guaranteed. Fourth, in the process of evolving the mixed-ownership economy within emerging industries, particularly data services, it is essential to determine the appropriate scope of data and other associated rights. This includes determining if these rights can be utilized by mixed-ownership enterprises and, if so, within what limits. Not only is this a concern for companies in their day-to-day operations, but it is also a consideration in the broader context of mixed-ownership reform. Fifth, it is necessary to comply with relevant regulatory norms and procedural requirements.

Secondly, the domestic investment process of Energy Internet companies is complex. From an analysis of investment methods, it can be found that Energy Internet companies primarily utilize three capital operation methods for domestic investments: equity M & A, asset M & A, and PPP models. To ensure the security of domestic investment activities conducted by Energy Internet companies, it is essential to analyze the potential risks they may encounter under these capital operation

[113] Wang (2018), p. 21.

methods, as well as the conventional management risks that commonly arise during the capital operation process. Through a risk analysis conducted from the operation process perspective, the following findings emerge: In terms of equity M & A, Energy Internet companies face risks in decision-making, financing, management rights transfer, and integration. When engaging in asset M & A, Energy Internet companies encounter asset evaluation risks, payment risks, and operational risks. When it comes to PPP models, Energy Internet companies are affected by changes in the investment environment of the energy industry and face risks across various stages of decision-making, budgeting, financing, approval, and more. Even after approval, there remains the risk of projects being withdrawn due to non-compliance. In terms of conventional management risks, the investment projects of Energy Internet companies often involve high values. On one hand, the negligence of duty by company managers may result in significant losses of state-owned assets. On the other hand, such circumstances can also facilitate corruption among managers, posing an additional challenge.

Lastly, with the advancement of the Belt and Road Initiative, the overseas M & A transactions conducted by Chinese energy companies continue to expand. Energy Internet companies face a wide variety of risks in implementing overseas M & A. Grid companies are often viewed as enterprises that possess national strategic assets. Destination countries tend to place greater emphasis on the political background of the acquirer and conduct rigorous reviews. There is even a growing trend of politicization in certain countries, such as erecting barriers to transactions on the pretext of national security concerns. Furthermore, before any cross-border M & A project is initiated, it is important to consider various factors such as compliance risks, antitrust issues, exchange rate fluctuations, and labor issues.

References

21st Century Business Herald (2020) CNOOC officially transfers infrastructure management rights to pipe China. Retrieved 29 Nov 2023, from http://www.chinapower.com.cn/xw/cycj/20200403/13866.html

Ai L (2011) Study on China's enterprise of the legal risk of transnational mergers and acquisitions and countermeasures keeping it away. Master's Dissertation, Nanjing University of Finance and Economics

Baike B (2023) Government integrity risks. Retrieved 29 Nov 2023, from https://baike.baidu.com/item/%E5%BB%89%E6%94%BF%E9%A3%8E%E9%99%A9/8707761?fr=ge_ala

Bei L (2020) Legal risks and their prevention in corporate equity mergers and acquisitions. Legal Vis 2020(2):139–140

Beijing Mingdingren Education Consulting Co., Ltd. (2015) Evaluation of nine failed PPP projects at home and abroad. Water Indus Market 2015(10):50–52

Chao L, Jing W (2017) Legal risks for energy investment access in the '21st century maritime silk road' and countermeasures". J China Univ Min Technol (Soc Sci) 5(2017):59–65

Chen X (2021) Vision for 2060: embracing the new era of energy. Retrieved 29 Nov 2023, from https://mp.weixin.qq.com/s/nUE7JVdj5fW870FOfOIomQ

Chen Q, Liu D, Lin J, He J, Wang Y (2015) Business model and market mechanism of energy internet (I). Power Syst Technol 39(11):3050–3056. https://doi.org/10.13335/j.1000-3673.pst.2015.11.006
Cheng F, Li Y, Tang J (2015) Corporate growth through M & A: ten classic examples from china's listed companies. Guangdong Economy Publishing House
Chen Y, Chen W (2006) Host Nations' governing system of M & A by Foreign Capital & Home Nations' legal countermeasures. Wuhan Univ J (Philos Soc Sci) 59(6):852–856. https://doi.org/10.3969/j.issn.1672-7320.2006.06.022
China Business News (2019) Financial department withdraws 90 PPP projects in July, involving many state-owned enterprises and listed companies. Retrieved 29 Nov 2023, from https://www.sohu.com/a/338849494_120157453
China Commercial Industry Research Institute (2020) Spotlight on the '14th Five-Year Plan' for energy: seven highlights to observe the future development of the energy sector (illustrated). Retrieved 5 Jan 2024, from http://finance.eastmoney.com/a/202003101413012710.html
China Energy News (2016) National development and reform commission promotes PPP construction in three key types of energy projects. Retrieved November 29, 2023, from http://www.cpnn.com.cn/zdyw/201609/t20160901_920986.html
China Government Procurement (2018) Announcement of preliminary winning bid for the Linfen City big data industry park PPP project by the Linfen economic and information committee. Retrieved 29 Nov 2023, from http://www.ccgp.gov.cn/cggg/dfgg/cjgg/201807/t20180710_10250828.htm
CIPIE (2017) SGCC Invests CNY 1.4 Trillion in Grid Upgrades During the 13th Five-Year Plan, Smart Grids Emerge as Future Trend. Retrieved November 29, 2023, from http://www.cnwep.com/bencandy.php?fid=4&id=443920
Deng H, Farah PD (2020) China's energy policies and strategies for climate change and energy security. Soc Sci Electron Publ 13(2):141–156. https://doi.org/10.1093/jwelb/jwaa018
Ding J (2013) Legal risks of private equity financing and acquisitions. J Xinjiang Univ (Phil, Hum Soc Sci) 41(5):16. https://doi.org/10.13568/j.cnki.issn1000-2820.2013.05.025
Economic Information (2012) State grid negotiates to purchase AES's wind power assets in the U.S.. Retrieved 29 Nov 2023, from http://www.jjckb.cn/2012-02/29/content_360833.htm
Feng H (2017) An investigation into the current state and business models of integrated energy services internationally and domestically. China Electr Equip Indus 2017(6):34
Gu L (2018) The practice and enlightenment from cross-border M & A of listed companies in Shangyu. Financ Minds 3(1):82–92. https://doi.org/10.20032/j.cnki.cn10-1359/f.2018.01.007
He D (2012) National security review risks and legal countermeasures of the Chinese enterprises' overseas acquisition. Legal Forum 27(2):48–55
Hou F (2020) PPP project financing risk management and solutions. Bus News 2020(8):78–79
Huang C (2018) A complete guide to equity financing from start-up to IPO. Economic Press China
Ji P (2019) Discussion of legislation for abuse of market dominance in Australia. J Heilongjiang Univ Technol 19(3):103–107. https://doi.org/10.3969/j.issn.1672-6758.2019.03.021
Jia P (2017) Study on the development trend of Chinese enterprises' involvement in cross-border mergers and acquisitions-based on the practice of China's 'going out' strategy. Econ Relat Trade 2017(7):77–80. https://doi.org/10.3969/j.issn.1003-5559.2017.07.020
Jia J (2019, March 20) Shenzhen expressway acquires Nanjing wind power—environmental protection industry becomes second main business. Shenzhen Economic Daily, p 04
Jiexitz (2019) SGCC's investment in information technology poised to surge. Retrieved November 29, 2023, from http://www.ocn.com.cn/touzi/chanye/201909/ehnjz10090829.shtml
Li S (2014) State-owned energy enterprises cross-border M & A risk and countermeasure research: the state grid merger cases analysis. Master's Dissertation, Southwestern University of Finance and Economics
Li X, Wu Q (2013) Comparison study of abuse of dominant position between Australia and China. Theor Pract Finan Econ 34(183):251. https://doi.org/10.3969/j.issn.1003-7217.2013.03.025
Liu X (1995) Handbook of business conduct and ethics. China Statistics Press

Liu B (2020) The progress and insights from the mixed-ownership reform in China's Energy Sector in 2019. Retrieved November 29, 2023, from https://baijiahao.baidu.com/s?id=166447075231 6290694&wfr=spider&for=pc

Liu W (2020, January 20) Stable total energy supply and demand with ongoing energy structure optimization. China Information News, p 03

Meng R (2020). State grid corporation vigorously develops integrated energy services to meet diverse energy needs of users. Retrieved 29 Nov 2023, from http://shupeidian.bjx.com.cn/html/20201014/1109733.shtml

Mu Y, Xiao X (2009) China's national security review system of foreign capital M & A. Chin J Law 2009(5):54–61

Nie Z, Luo M (2010) An analysis of financing risks in weaker firms acquiring stronger ones. Commun Finan Account 2010(9):10. https://doi.org/10.16144/j.cnki.issn1002-8072.2010.26.021

Peng W (2009) Power development and financing: insights from new energy investment. Shanghai University of Finance and Economics Press

PPP-ol (2023) Subsidies to bridge feasibility gaps. Retrieved 29 Nov 2023, from http://www.PPP-ol.com/PPPSchool/show-861.html

Qiu M (2018) Overseas mergers and acquisitions in energy enterprise value evaluation research. Doctor's Dissertation, Central University of Finance and Economics

Shao S, Wang X (2008) National security review and investigation measures of foreign mergers and acquisitions in U.S.A.: an overview of constructing China's counterpart mechanism. Jurist 2008(3):154–160. https://doi.org/10.3969/j.issn.1005-0221.2008.03.022

Song J (2012) Understanding the risks of data breaches: a three-case study on preventing policy violations. Confidentiality Work 2012(9):54–55. https://doi.org/10.19407/j.cnki.cn11-2785/d.2012.09.025

State Grid Corporation of China (2019) State grid corporation of china signs PPP implementation agreement for transmission and distribution project with Ethiopia. Retrieved 29 Nov 2023, from http://www.chinasmartgrid.com.cn/news/20190425/632566.shtml

State Grid Corporation of China (2021) The final year of the 13th Five-Year Plan! overview of state grid's high-quality reform and development. Retrieved 29 Nov 2023, from https://new.qq.com/rain/a/20210106a0dmcf00

State-Owned Assets Supervision and Management Commission of Shenzhen Municipal People's Government (2019) Shenzhen expressway's strategic acquisition of 51% shares in Nanjing wind power marks its foray into the environmental and wind energy industry. Retrieved November 29, 2023, from http://gzw.sz.gov.cn/zwgk/qt/pcgz/content/post_4789777.html

Sun W (2018) Risk factors and preventive measures in corporate equity mergers and acquisitions. Enterp Reform Manage 2018(20):7. https://doi.org/10.13768/j.cnki.cn11-3793/f.2018.2702

Sun W (2018) Security measures for confidential archival information. Econ Vis 2018(10):149

The Department of Economic Regulations of the State Economic and Trade Commission (2002) Examination of the anti-monopoly legislation of Australia and New Zealand (Part 1). China Econ Trade Herald 2002(13):49–50. https://doi.org/10.3969/j.issn.1007-9777.2002.13.033

Tian T (2021) Chairman of Linyang energy placed under investigation due to suspected involvement in illegal capital operations and subsidy arrears. Retrieved 29 Nov 2023, from https://mp.weixin.qq.com/s/QmsHu4tCseEY3tE7ejQEiQ

Wa U (2020) Decoding state grid's mid-year work conference: grid investment set to accelerate in second half. Retrieved November 29, 2023, from https://new.qq.com/omn/20200722/20200722A0GO3I00.html

Wang R (2012) Study on legal issues in cross-border mergers and acquisitions by multinational companies. Doctor's Dissertation, Fudan University

Wang X (2018) Insights into PPP investment control post-PPP reforms. Retrieved November 29, 2023, from https://www.sohu.com/a/249428836_480400

Wang Q (2018)@@ Research on legal risks prevention of labor M & A by Chinese enterprises. Master's Dissertation, Southwest University of Political Science and Law

Wang X, He Y (2008) The new development on the national security examination system in American foreign capital merger and its enlightenments—also on the Implementation of the Article 31 of anti-monopoly law of P.R.C. Stud Law Bus 2008(6):11–21. https://doi.org/10.16390/j.cnki.issn1672-0393.2008.06.011

Wang B, Jiang L (2018) Labor legal risks and precautions against Chinese enterprise overseas M & A under the background of "the belt and road." J Shandong Univ Finan Econ 30(6):5–12. https://doi.org/10.3969/j.issn.1008-2670.2018.06.002

Wang T, Li Y (2019) Analysis of project financing risks for PPP microgrids projects in China. Sci Technol Indus 19(8):93–97. https://doi.org/10.3969/j.issn.1671-1807.2019.08.017

Wang Y, Shi Y, Wu Z (2020) Financial risk management under "green swan" events. Modern Bank 2020(7):64–66

Wang W, Chu F, Liu L (2017) Tax risk analyses and suggestions for enterprises' cross-border mergers and acquisitions: taking Chinese "going-out" enterprises investing in Kazakhstan as a case study. Int Taxation China 2017(9):47–51. https://doi.org/10.19376/j.cnki.cn10-1142/f.2017.09.009

Wu Y (2004) PPP, a new project financing method. Shanghai Bus 2004(3):46

Wu C (2012) A brief discussion on several legal risks in corporate mergers and acquisitions and their prevention. Railway Purchase Logist 2012(5):59–60. https://doi.org/10.3969/j.issn.1673-7121.2012.05.015

Xiang T (2020) A brief discussion on the risks of corporate mergers and acquisitions. Finan Account Monthly 2020(10):86

Xing Z (2018) A brief analysis of financial risk prevention and control in corporate mergers and acquisitions. Finan Account 2018(4):77. https://doi.org/10.3969/j.issn.1003-286X.2018.04.038

Xinhua News Agency (2020) Recommendations of the 14th five-year plan: promote the energy revolution and enhance new energy consumption and storage capabilities. Retrieved 29 Nov 2023, from https://www.sohu.com/a/429981051_771862

Xu Z, Zha Y, Zhao T (2016) Key points, difficulties, and case analysis of corporate mergers and acquisitions taxation. Lixin Accounting Publishing House

Yang Y (2019) Analysis of the legal risk management of cross-border mergers and acquisitions by Chinese enterprises. Modern Bus 2019(19):114–115. https://doi.org/10.14097/j.cnki.5392/2019.19.051

Yiu DW (2011) Multinational advantages of Chinese business groups. A theoretical exploration. Manag Organ Rev 7(2):249–277. https://doi.org/10.1111/j.1740-8784.2010.00210.x

Yu J (2008) A monograph on legal issues facing multinational companies. Law Press

Yu R (2016) Research on overseas M & A risk management of Chinese power grid enterprises. Master's Dissertation, North China Electric Power University

Yu K (2018) Labor risks and preventive measures in cross-border mergers and acquisitions by Chinese enterprises. Hebei Enterp 2018(6):74–75. https://doi.org/10.3969/j.issn.1008-1968.2018.06.035

Yu S (2019) Principles of economics. China Railway Publishing House

Yu Q (2021) What does "integrated" mean in integrated energy services? Retrieved 5 Jan 2024, from https://m.bjx.com.cn/mnews/20210111/1128562.shtml

Yu R, Yu B, Dong L (2012) Beware of the 'nationalization' of overseas energy and power assets. State Grid News 2012(11):64–66

Yuan P (2012) China Guodian corporation financing completes financing, total long-term loans reach 68.5 billion. Retrieved 29 Nov 2023, from https://finance.ifeng.com/a/20121217/7440372_0.shtml

Zhang G (2008) Study on the legal issues on the state security in foreign capital M & A—based on analysis of challenges facing Chinese enterprises in overseas investments and mergers and acquisitions in resources, energy, and high technology. Inter Trade 2008(9):62–66. https://doi.org/10.14114/j.cnki.itrade.2008.09.005

Zhang K (2020) Ministry of environment warning: industries such as investment and financing should pay attention to national emission reduction targets to avoid investment risks. Retrieved 5 Jan 2024, from https://m.yicai.com/news/100786450.html

Zhang X, Xiao M (2006) Improvement of the anti-monopoly legal system in foreign mergers and acquisitions. Cult Hist Vis 2006(16):66–68

Zhang Q, Liu Y (2012) New developments in Australia's national security review system for foreign mergers and acquisitions. Law Rev 2012(4):62–69. https://doi.org/10.13415/j.cnki.fxpl.2012.04.008

Zhang X, Ran Z (2021) In pursuit of carbon neutrality, new energy sees boundless opportunities with the rise of integrated PV-storage-charging systems. Retrieved 5 Jan 2024, from https://mp.weixin.qq.com/s/MpS8iEKHEUlfKFsfP1XJGA

Zhou Y (1996) An analysis of the current state of state-owned asset loss and legal countermeasures. Soc Sci 5:75–76. https://doi.org/10.19863/j.cnki.issn.1002---3240.1996.05.014

Zhou R (2015) Senior power official arrested: unlocking the shady story of corruption in power-related bidding. Retrieved 5 Jan 2024, from https://www.chinacourt.org/article/detail/2015/09/id/1705429.shtml

Zhou S (2017) Study on external risks and countermeasures for cross-border mergers and acquisitions by Chinese enterprises. World Econ Stud 2017(5):78–84. https://doi.org/10.13516/j.cnki.wes.2017.05.007

Zhu Y, Mo F (2020) State grid: enhancing the national economy's high-quality growth through grid investment. Retrieved January 5, 2024, from http://shupeidian.bjx.com.cn/html/20200313/1053873.shtml

Chapter 6
Legal Issues on Long-Term Management of New Power Systems

The construction of a new type of power system is a significant and era-defining topic in the energy sector. It serves as a vital pillar supporting the green and low-carbon energy transition. The construction of a new type of power system involves the construction and operation of new energy sources, the development and application of related technologies, the diversification of market trading varieties, the exploration of multiple trading rules, and the compliant operation of various market entities. These scenarios require professional legal services. Among the different mechanisms facilitating the construction of new power systems, the energy performance contracting model stands out as a market-oriented approach. One of the areas where this model is applied is rooftop photovoltaic (PV) projects. These projects involve multiple stakeholders such as rooftop lessors, project owners, energy-saving service companies, and users. The distinct characteristics of these projects, including the involvement of multiple stakeholders and a long operational lifespan of up to 25 years, give rise to potential legal risks in rooftop leasing and energy performance contracts, and it becomes essential to adopt appropriate legal measures to address these risks. Specifically, in terms of rooftop leasing contracts, there are legal risks associated with building and rooftop property defects, as well as lease agreement terms. In the context of energy performance contracts, there are legal risks related to the standardization of grid-connection fees for market transactions in distributed generation.

H. Deng, *Green Energy Transition in China*, International Law in Asia,
https://doi.org/10.1007/978-981-97-2934-0_6

Stakeholders Involved in Rooftop PV Projects Under the Energy Performance Contracting Model and Their Legal Relationships

China's "dual carbon" goals have presented new requirements for emission reduction in the power industry and greatly facilitated the construction of new power systems. The "Central Committee of the Communist Party of China (CCCPC) and the State Council's Opinions on Fully, Accurately, and Comprehensively Implementing the New Development Concept and Achieving Carbon Peak and Carbon Neutrality" issued on September 22, 2021, states that we should "build new power systems with new energy as the main energy source and enhance the grid's capacity to accommodate and regulate a high proportion of renewable energy." The "Action Plan for Carbon Dioxide Peaking before 2030" (Guo Fa [2021] No. 23) issued by the State Council on October 24 of the same year sets the goals of speeding up the development of new power systems during the "14th Five-Year Plan" period. The goals include "building a new electric power system that the share of new energy resources keep increasing, and working toward an optimized distribution of clean electricity generation on a broad scale." The report of the 20th National Congress of the Communist Party of China (NCCPC) held on October 16, 2022, also proposes in the green development section to "thoroughly advance the energy revolution. Coal will be used in a cleaner and more efficient way. We will speed up the planning and development of a system for new energy sources and get actively involved in global governance in response to climate change."[1]

In the process of building new power systems, the energy performance contracting model plays an important role as a market-oriented mechanism.[2] On April 2, 2010, the General Office of the State Council forwarded the "Notice on the Opinions on Accelerating the Implementation of Energy Performance Contracting and Promoting the Development of the Energy Conservation Service Industry" (Guo Ban Fa [2010] No. 25) issued by the National Development and Reform Commission of China (NDRC) and other departments. The "Notice" puts forward the concept of "energy performance contracting," defining it as a service mechanism where "the energy-saving service company signs energy performance contracts with users to provide users with energy-saving diagnosis, financing, transformation and other services, and recovers investment and obtains reasonable profits by means of energy-saving benefit sharing, which can greatly reduce the capital and technical risks of energy-saving renovation of energy-using units. It is an effective energy-saving measure." The "Notice" also requires to promote the development of energy-saving service industry by improving policy measures such as increasing funding support, implementing tax support policies, improving relevant accounting systems, further improving financial services, and strengthening the guidance and services for the development of

[1] Xi (2022).

[2] See Chongqing Blue Jay Electronic (2011).

energy-saving service industries.[3] On August 9, 2010, the General Administration of Quality Supervision, Inspection and Quarantine of the People's Republic of China (GAQSIQ) and the Standardization Administration of the People's Republic of China issued the "General Technical Rules for Energy Performance Contracting" (GB/T 24915–2010). The rules were replaced by the "Guidance on Energy Performance Contracting" (GB/T 24915–2020) issued by the State Administration for Market Regulation (SAMR) and Standardization Administration of China on March 31, 2020. Both of them provide contract samples for energy performance contracting projects in the attachments as a reference. The latter categorizes projects into different types such as shared savings projects, guaranteed savings projects, and energy cost management projects.[4]

In addition to the definition of energy performance contracting projects and contract samples, China's normative documents also provide sufficient financial policy support for energy performance contracting projects. On June 3, 2010, the Ministry of Finance of China and NDRC issued the "Interim Management Regulations on Financial Incentives of Energy Performance Contracting Projects" (Cai Jian [2010] No. 249) and stated "to standardize and strengthen the management of financial incentive funds and improve the efficiency of fund use"; on October 19, 2010, the General Office of NDRC and the General Office of the Ministry of Finance issued the "Supplementary Notice on Matters Related to Financial Incentives of Energy Performance Contracting Projects" (Fa Gai Ban Huan Zi [2010] No. 2528), which provides supplementary provisions on the applicable projects of financial incentives and other contents.[5] On December 30, 2010, the Ministry of Finance and the State Taxation Administration of China (STA) issued the "Notice on Value-Added Tax, Business Tax and Corporate Income Tax Policies to Promote the Development of the Energy-Saving Service Industry" (Cai Shui [2010] No. 110), which provides tax incentive policies for the development of the energy-saving service industry.[6] On December 17, 2013, STA and NDRC issued the "Notice on Collection and Management Issues Concerning the Implementation of Corporate Income Tax Incentive Policies for Energy Performance Contracting Projects of Energy-Saving Service Companies" (STA and NDRC 2013 No. 77), which supplements and completes the tax incentive policies for energy-saving service companies.[7] On July 20, 2011, the

---

[3] See General Office of the State Council. Opinions on Accelerating the Implementation of Energy Performance Contracting and Promoting the Development of the Energy Conservation Service Industry (Guo Ban Fa [2010] No. 25).

[4] See State Administration for Market Regulation, and Standardization Administration of China: Guidance on Energy Performance Contracting (GB/T 24915–2020).

[5] See General Office of NDRC, and the General Office of the Ministry of Finance. Supplementary Notice on Matters Related to Financial Incentives of Energy Performance Contracting Projects (Fa Gai Ban Huan Zi [2010] No. 2528).

[6] See Ministry of Finance, and State Taxation Administration of China. Notice on Value-Added Tax, Business Tax and Corporate Income Tax Policies to Promote the Development of the Energy-Saving Service Industry (Cai Shui [2010] No. 110).

[7] See State Taxation Administration of China, and National Development and Reform commission. Notice on Collection and Management Issues Concerning the Implementation of Corporate Income

General Office of NDRC and the General Office of the Ministry of Finance issued the "Notice on Further Strengthening the Supervision and Inspection of Energy Performance Contracting Projects" (Fa Gai Ban Huan Zi [2011] No. 1755), which points out the main problems in the financial incentives of energy performance contracting projects, and puts forward the requirements for supervision and inspection based on the problems.[8]

The energy performance contracting model can be applied to various areas for new power systems, and it is difficult to list them all in the report.[9] Distributed rooftop PV is selected as an example for analysis based on factors such as widespread applicability and representativeness. On September 2, 2014, the National Energy Administration of China (NEA) issued the "Notice on Further Implementing Distributed Photovoltaic Power Generation Policies" (Guo Neng Xin Neng [2014] No. 406). On September 24, 2014, eight departments including the Zhejiang Provincial Development and Reform Commission jointly issued the "Notice from the National Energy Administration on Further Implementing Distributed Photovoltaic Power Generation Policies" (Zhe Fa Gai Neng Yuan [2014] No. 827). The notices require the overall coordination of rooftop resources, improvement of the development model, grid connection, and operation services of distributed photovoltaic power generation, supporting power grid technology and management system construction, electricity bill settlement, and subsidy allocation[10]; The "Notice of the People's Government of Zhejiang Province on Issuing the Comprehensive Work Plan for Energy Conservation and Emission Reduction in Zhejiang Province During the 13th Five-Year Plan" (Zhe Zheng Fa [2017] No. 19) issued on May 3, 2017, proposes to "focus on promoting the development of distributed photovoltaic power generation." On May 3, 2018, the Economy and Information Technology Commission of Zhejiang issued the "Notice on Issuing the Implementation Plan for the Construction of Green Manufacturing System in Zhejiang Province (2018–2020)" (Zhe Jing Xin Zi Yuan [2018] No. 98), which proposes the construction of green parks and promoting engineering projects such as distributed photovoltaic power generation in industrial parks.[11] On June 20, 2021, the General Administration Department of NEA issued the "Notice on Issuing the Pilot Program for the Development of Rooftop Distributed Photovoltaics in the Whole County (City, District)" (Guo Neng Zong Tong Xin Neng [2021] No. 84), which states the plan to organize nationwide pilot projects for the development of distributed rooftop photovoltaics across counties (cities, districts) for the rapid

---

Tax Incentive Policies for Energy Performance Contracting Projects of Energy-Saving Service Companies (STA and NDRC [2013] No. 77).

[8] See General Office of NDRC, and the General Office of the Ministry of Finance. Notice on Further Strengthening the Supervision and Inspection of Energy Performance Contracting Projects (Fa Gai Ban Huan Zi [2011] No. 1755).

[9] See IEA (2019).

[10] See National Energy Administration of China. Notice on Further Implementing Distributed Photovoltaic Power Generation Policies (Guo Neng Xin Neng [2014] No. 406).

[11] See Economy and Information Technology Commission of Zhejiang. Implementation Plan for the Construction of Green Manufacturing System in Zhejiang Province (2018–2020) (Zhej Jing Xin Zi Yuan [2018] No. 98).

development of the distributed rooftop photovoltaic industry; on May 6, 2022, the General Office of the Central Committee of the Communist Party of China and the General Office of the State Council issued the "Opinions on Promoting Urbanization Construction with Counties as an Important Carrier," which states that we should "promote clean, low-carbon, and safe energy sources and efficient energy use, encourage non-fossil energy consumption and the development of distributed energy, and facilitate rooftop distributed photovoltaic power generation in areas where conditions permit." On July 1, 2022, the Economy and Information Technology Department of Zhejiang issued the "Notice on Issuing the Technology Transformation Action Plan for Industrial Energy Saving and Carbon Reduction in Zhejiang Province (2022–2024)" (Zhe Jing Xin Lv Se [2022] No. 134), which also promotes new energy application as a key area of the transformation action plan, stating that we should "support parks and companies to build green and low-carbon microgrid, promote industrial parks and companies to build distributed photovoltaic and user-side energy storage projects, and explore new models of photovoltaic and storage integration."

From the perspective of legal risks, rooftop distributed PV power generation requires the use of rooftop PV power generation equipment to generate power. To build PV power generation equipment on the rooftop, rooftop leasing is required in most cases. The rooftop lessor and lessee have a legal relationship through a leasing contract.[12] To use equipment to generate power, legal relationships are often formed between project owners (investors), energy service companies, and users through energy performance contracts.[13] However, investing in rooftop distributed PV power stations is a long-term commitment, with an operating period of up to 25 years. During this period, any legal issues arising from the rooftop lessor, project owners, energy service companies, users, or any other stakeholders involved can become significant risks to the operation of rooftop distributed PV stations. It is crucial to promptly identify and mitigate potential legal risks.

Legal Risks of Rooftop Leasing Contracts

According to the "Interim Measures for the Management of Distributed PV Power Generation Projects" (Guo Neng Xin Neng [2013] No. 433) issued on November 18, 2013, distributed PV power generation projects should meet the following conditions in terms of construction requirements: "buildings and facilities used should be legal; if the project entity and the owner of the building, site, or facilities on which the project is built are different entities, the project entity should sign a usage or leasing agreement for the building, site, or facilities with the owner and, depending on the operating mode, sign an energy service agreement with the power user." Based on this technical specification, the process of installing PV equipment on rooftops involves legal risks associated with rooftop leasing. The following three risks are involved:

[12] See Hao (2017).

[13] See Yan and Yan (2012).

Legal Risks Arising from Incomplete Construction Documents and Licenses for the Building of the Leased Rooftop

Buildings Without a Permit for a Planned Construction Project or Planned Rural Construction

If the building of the leased rooftop does not have a permit for a planned construction project in accordance with the law within urban or town planning areas, or the building is not constructed in accordance with the provisions of the permit for a planned construction project, or if the building does not have a permit for planned rural construction in accordance with the law within rural planning areas, or the building is not constructed in accordance with the provisions of the permit for planned rural construction, administrative penalties may arise such as to stop construction, rectify within a specified period, demolish within a specified period, confiscation of assets or illegal income, and fines.[14] It may also result in the invalidation of the rooftop leasing contract,[15] thereby affecting the possession and use of the leased rooftop.

At the normative level, laws, regulations, and other normative documents impose requirements on the aforementioned planning permits. According to paragraph 1 of Article 40 of the "Law of the People's Republic of China on Urban and Rural Planning," "for the construction of buildings, structures, roads, pipelines, and other projects in an area covered by the plan of a city or town, the developing unit or individual shall apply for a permit for a planned construction project to the department in charge of urban and rural planning under the people's government of the city or county concerned or to the township people's government designated by the people's government of the province, autonomous region, or municipality directly under the Central Government." Paragraph 1 of Article 41 states that "for construction of township enterprises, rural public facilities and public welfare undertakings in areas covered by the plan of a township or village, the developing unit or individual shall make an application to the people's government of the town or township concerned, which shall report the matter to the department in charge of urban and rural planning under the people's government of the city or county concerned for issue of a permit for planned rural construction."[16] Articles 36–38 of the "Urban and Rural Planning Regulations of Zhejiang Province" also specify the requirements for the permit for planned construction for the construction of urban and rural buildings. A permit for a planned construction project or planned rural construction is required for urban and rural buildings.[17]

---

[14] See Administrative penalty case. Administrative penalties for construction without a construction project planning permit (Zhou Gao Zong Zhi Fa Jue Zi [2022] No. 0009).

[15] See Li (2012).

[16] Law of the People's Republic of China on Urban and Rural Planning, Paragraph 1 of Article 40 and paragraph 1 of Article 41.

[17] See Committee of the People's Congress of Zhejiang Province. Urban and Rural Planning Regulations of Zhejiang Province, Articles 36–38.

If the aforementioned planning permit is not obtained or construction is not carried out in accordance with the provisions of the aforementioned permit, laws, regulations, and other normative documents also specify the administrative penalties. According to Article 64 of the "Law of the People's Republic of China on Urban and Rural Planning," where a unit engages in construction without obtaining the permit for a planned construction project or without complying with the provisions in the said permit, it shall be ordered to discontinue construction by the department in charge of urban and rural planning under the local people's government at or above the county level; if measures for rectification can be adopted to eliminate the impact on the implementation of the plan, it shall be ordered to make rectification within a time limit and be fined not less than five percent but not more than ten percent the cost of the construction project; otherwise, it shall be ordered to demolish the project within a time limit; if the project cannot be demolished, the project itself or the unit's unlawful income shall be confiscated, and it may, in addition, be fined not more than ten percent the cost of the construction project. Article 65 states that "where a unit engages in construction in an area covered by the plan of a town or village without obtaining the permit for planned rural construction or without complying with the provisions in the said permit, it shall be ordered by the people's government of the township or town concerned to discontinue construction and to make rectification within a time limit; if it fails to rectify on the expiration of the prescribed time limit, the construction project may be demolished."[18] Articles 59–60 of the "Urban and Rural Planning Regulations of Zhejiang Province" also specify the administrative penalties for failure to obtain the aforementioned planning permit or failure to carry out construction in accordance with the provisions of the aforementioned permit.[19] For disputes regarding lease contracts for buildings within an area covered by the plan of a town or village, the "Interpretation of the Supreme People's Court on Several Issues Concerning Specific Application of Law in the Trial of Cases on Disputes over Contracts for Lease of Urban Houses" (amended in 2020) can be used as a reference, unless otherwise stipulated by law. According to Article 2 of the interpretation, "if the lessor leases a building that does not have a permit for a planned construction project or has not been constructed in accordance with the provisions of the permit for a planned construction project, the lease contract signed with the lessee is invalid. However, if the permit is obtained or the construction is approved by the competent authority before the conclusion of the first-instance court debate, the People's Court should consider the contract valid."[20]

If the building of the leased rooftop does not have a permit for a planned construction project or planned rural construction, or if it is not constructed in accordance with the provisions of the permit, there may be inconveniences in the usufruct of the

[18] Law of the People's Republic of China on Urban and Rural Planning, Articles 64–65.

[19] See Committee of the People's Congress of Zhejiang Province. Urban and Rural Planning Regulations of Zhejiang Province, Articles 59–60.

[20] Interpretation of the Supreme People's Court on Several Issues Concerning Specific Application of Law in the Trial of Cases on Disputes over Contracts for Lease of Urban Houses (Fa Shi [2020] No. 17), Article 2.

rooftop and the installation of photovoltaic equipment due to administrative penalties. This situation may lead to disputes between the lessor and the lessee due to the invalidity of the lease contract.

Temporary Buildings Without Approval

If the building of the leased rooftop is a temporary building that is not approved or not constructed in accordance with the approved content, administrative penalties may arise such as to demolish within a specified period or fines.[21] It may also result in the invalidation of the rooftop leasing contract.[22] In addition, the limited duration of temporary buildings can lead to uncertainty regarding the occupancy and use of the rooftop.

In terms of the required documents for temporary buildings, temporarily constructed buildings in an area covered by the plan of a city or town need to be approved by the competent authority and demolished before the expiration of use period. According to paragraphs 1–2 of Article 44 of the "Law of the People's Republic of China on Urban and Rural Planning," "temporary construction carried out in the area covered by the plan of a city or town shall be subject to approval by the department in charge of urban and rural planning under the people's government of the city or county concerned. If temporary construction affects the implementation of the short-term construction plan or the detailed control plan, traffic, the appearance or safety of a city, etc., no approval may be granted. Temporary buildings shall be demolished by the building unit itself before the expiration of the approved time limit on use."[23] The "Urban and Rural Planning Regulations of Zhejiang Province" also provide corresponding provisions for the approval and demolition of temporary buildings. For example, Article 46 stipulates that "for buildings, structures, and related temporary facilities that are determined to be demolished according to the planning permit, the construction unit or individual shall demolish them before applying for the verification of completion planning for the construction project." Paragraph 1 of Article 48 stipulates, "for land users conducting temporary construction in the area covered by the plan of a city or town, they should obtain a permit for a planned temporary construction project issued by the urban or county government's urban and rural planning authority. Temporary constructions carried out within the construction project site area for construction purposes and temporary constructions that have obtained a permit for planned use of land for temporary construction according to this regulation are exempted. If temporary construction affects the implementation

[21] See Administrative penalty case. Administrative penalties for failure to demolish temporary buildings and structures beyond the approved period (Yu Yao Zong Zhi Fa Jue Zi [2022] No. 09–0051), October 17, 2022.

[22] See Zhang (2022).

[23] Law of the People's Republic of China on Urban and Rural Planning, Paragraphs 1 and 2 of Article 44.

of the short-term construction plan or the detailed control plan, traffic, the appearance or safety of a city, etc., no approval may be granted by the urban or county government's urban and rural planning authority."[24]

In terms of legal consequences, if a temporary building is not constructed with approval or in accordance with the approved content or is not demolished beyond the approved period, the construction unit or individual may be subject to administrative penalties. According to Article 66 of the "Law of the People's Republic of China on Urban and Rural Planning," if a construction unit or an individual engages in temporary construction without approval, engages in temporary construction without complying with what is approved of, or fails to demolish the temporary building or structure at the expiration of the approved time limit, they shall be ordered to demolish the temporary construction project by the department in charge of urban and rural planning under the people's government of the city or county where they are located and may, in addition, be fined not more than one time the cost of the temporary construction project.[25] According to Article 3 of the "Interpretation of the Supreme People's Court on Several Issues Concerning Specific Application of Law in the Trial of Cases on Disputes over Contracts for Lease of Urban Houses" (amended in 2020), "if the lessor leases a temporary building that is not approved or not constructed in accordance with the approved content, the lease contract signed with the lessee is invalid. However, if the construction is approved by the competent authority before the conclusion of the first-instance court debate, the People's Court should consider the contract valid. If the lease period exceeds the use period of the temporary building, the portion of the lease term beyond the approved period is considered invalid. However, if the competent authority approves an extension of the use period before the conclusion of the first-instance court debate, the People's Court should recognize the validity of the lease during the extended use period."[26]

If the building of the leased rooftop is a temporary building that is not approved or not constructed in accordance with the approved content, or the building has not been removed beyond the approved period, there may be inconveniences in the usufruct of the rooftop and the installation of photovoltaic equipment due to administrative penalties. This situation may lead to disputes between the lessor and the lessee due to the invalidity of the lease contract. In addition, temporary buildings need to be demolished before the approved use period expires, and PV equipment cannot be used continuously.

---

[24] Committee of the People's Congress of Zhejiang Province. Urban and Rural Planning Regulations of Zhejiang Province, Article 46 and paragraph 1 of Article 48.

[25] Law of the People's Republic of China on Urban and Rural Planning, Article 66.

[26] Interpretation of the Supreme People's Court on Several Issues Concerning Specific Application of Law in the Trial of Cases on Disputes over Contracts for Lease of Urban Houses (Fa Shi [2020] No. 17), Article 2.

Building Land Without Land Use Right Certificate for Land for Construction or Collectively Owned Land

If the building of the leased rooftop does not have a land use right certificate for land for construction or collectively owned land and does not have other ownership basis, and the lessor is not the land use right holder of the land for construction or collectively owned land, risks such as inability to perform the lease contract or disputes with third parties regarding ownership outside the contract may arise.[27]

Based on existing laws, regulations, and other normative documents, the creation, alteration, alienation, or extinguishment of a land use right shall become effective upon registration in accordance with law. A title certificate shall be issued to the person entitled to the use right, and the content recorded in the register of immovable property shall prevail. According to Article 209 of the Civil Code of the People's Republic of China (Civil Code), "the creation, alteration, alienation, or extinguishment of a real right in immovable property shall become effective upon registration in accordance with law and shall not take effect without registration, unless otherwise provided by law." Article 214 states that "the creation, alteration, alienation, or extinguishment of a real right of the immovable property that is required by law to be registered becomes effective at the time when it is recorded in the register of immovable property." Article 217 states that "the real right certificate for immovable property is a proof of a right holder's entitlement to the real right in the immovable property. The items recorded in the real right certificate for immovable property shall be consistent with what are recorded in the register of immovable property; in case of inconsistency between the two, what is recorded in the register of immovable property shall prevail, unless there is evidence establishing a clear error in the register of immovable property." For the use right certificate for the land for construction, Article 349 of the *Civil Code* states that "to create a right to use the land for construction purposes, application shall be filed with the registration authority for the registration of the right. The right to use the land for construction purposes is created upon registration. The registration authority shall issue a title certificate to the person entitled to the right." According to Article 355 of the *Civil Code*, "where a right to use the land for construction purposes is transferred, exchanged, offered as capital contribution, or given away as a gift, an application for registration of the change shall be filed with the registration authority."[28] For the use right certificate for collectively owned land, paragraph 2 of Article 4 of the 2014 "Regulations on the Implementation of the Land Administration Law" states that "land owned by peasant collectives to be lawfully used for non-agricultural construction shall be registered with and recorded by people's governments at the county level, which shall, upon verification, issue certificates to confirm the right to the use of the land for such construction."[29] For the validity of the lease contract, Article 215 of the *Civil Code* states that "a contract

[27] See Hao (2018).

[28] Civil Code of the People's Republic of China, Articles 209, 214, 217, 349 and 355.

[29] Regulations on the Implementation of the Land Administration Law (2014), Paragraph 2 of Article 4.

concluded by the parties on the creation, alteration, alienation, or extinguishment of a real right becomes effective upon its formation, unless it is otherwise provided by law or agreed upon by the parties, and the validity of the contract is not affected by the fact that the real right is not registered."[30]

If no land use right certificate is obtained for the building of the leased rooftop, the lessor does not have the right to use the land for construction or rural land. On the one hand, this may fundamentally hinder the performance of the lease contract. On the other hand, it poses risks of disputes with third parties outside the contract regarding ownership rights.

Buildings Without a House Ownership Certificate or Other Property Ownership Certificates

If the building of the leased rooftop does not have a house ownership certificate or other property ownership certificates and does not have other ownership basis, the lessor is not the owner of the building, and risks such as inability to perform the lease contract or disputes with third parties regarding ownership outside the contract may arise.[31]

Based on existing laws, regulations, and other normative documents, the creation, alteration, alienation, or extinguishment of a house ownership shall become effective upon registration in accordance with law. An ownership certificate shall be issued to the person entitled to the ownership, and the content recorded in the register of immovable property shall prevail. According to Article 209 of the *Civil Code*, "the creation, alteration, alienation, or extinguishment of a real right in immovable property shall become effective upon registration in accordance with law and shall not take effect without registration, unless otherwise provided by law." Article 214 states that "the creation, alteration, alienation, or extinguishment of a real right of the immovable property that is required by law to be registered becomes effective at the time when it is recorded in the register of immovable property." Article 217 states that "the real right certificate for immovable property is a proof of a right holder's entitlement to the real right in the immovable property. The items recorded in the real right certificate for immovable property shall be consistent with what are recorded in the register of immovable property; in case of inconsistency between the two, what is recorded in the register of immovable property shall prevail, unless there is evidence establishing a clear error in the register of immovable property."[32] According to paragraphs 1–2 of Article 20 of the "Implementing Rules of the Interim Regulations on Real Estate Registration," "the immovable property registration authority shall fill in and issue the immovable property ownership certificate or immovable property registration certificate based on the register of immovable property. Except for mortgage registration, easement registration, prior notice registration, and demurrer registration, the

[30] Civil Code of the People's Republic of China, Article 215.

[31] See Hao (2018).

[32] Civil Code of the People's Republic of China, Articles 209, 214 and 217.

immovable property registration authority shall issue property ownership certificates to the right holders in accordance with the law in addition to the immovable property registration certificates."[33] According to Article 21 of the "Interim Regulation on Real Estate Registration," "registration is completed when the registration item is recorded in the register of immovable property. After the registration is completed, the immovable property registration authority shall issue an immovable property ownership certificate or registration certificate to the applicant in accordance with the law."[34]

Specifically, for urban house ownership certificates, paragraphs 2–3 of Article 61 of the "Administration Law of Urban Real Estate" states that "where a house has been built on the land for real estate development obtained pursuant to the law, an application for registration shall, on the strength of the certificate of land use right, be submitted to the department of housing administration under the local people's government at or above the county level. The department of housing administration under the local people's government at or above the country level shall issue a certificate of the ownership of the house after verification. Where transfer or modification of real estate is to be made, an application for registration of the modification of house property shall be submitted to the department of housing administration under the local people's government at or above the county level and on the strength of the certificate of the modified ownership of the house, an application for registration of the modification of the land use right shall be submitted to the department of land administration under the people's government at the corresponding level. Upon verification by the department of land administration under the people's government at the corresponding level, a new or a modified certificate of the land use right shall be issued by the people's government at the corresponding level."[35] For property ownership certificates for rural houses, paragraph 2 of Article 40 of the "Implementing Rules of the Interim Regulations on Real Estate Registration" states that "individuals who use house sites to build dwelling and auxiliary facilities in accordance with the law may apply for house site use rights and house ownership registration." Paragraph 2 of Article 44 states that "individuals who use collectively owned land for construction to establish enterprises, build public facilities, or engage in public welfare undertakings in accordance with the law may apply for the use right of collectively owned land for construction and register the ownership of buildings and structures on the land."[36]

If no property ownership certificate is obtained for the building of the leased rooftop, the lessor does not have the ownership of the building. On the one hand, this may fundamentally hinder the performance of the lease contract. On the other hand,

[33] Implementing Rules of the Interim Regulations on Real Estate Registration (2019), Paragraphs 1 and 2 of Article 20.

[34] Interim Regulation on Real Estate Registration, Article 21.

[35] Administration Law of Urban Real Estate, Paragraphs 2 and 3 of Article 61.

[36] Implementing Rules of the Interim Regulations on Real Estate Registration, Paragraph 2 of Article 40 and paragraph 2 of Article 44.

it poses risks of disputes with third parties outside the contract regarding ownership rights.

Buildings not Checked for Fire Protection Acceptance or Without Sufficient Rooftop Load

If the building of the leased rooftop is not checked for fire protection acceptance or the rooftop load is insufficient, administrative penalties may arise, such as fines, or orders to stop construction, use, production, or operation.[37]

To adhere to the requirements of existing laws, regulations, and other normative documents, fire protection acceptance should be a significant aspect to consider for construction projects. In terms of fire protection acceptance obligations, Article 13 of the "Fire Protection Law of the People's Republic of China" (Fire Protection Law) states that "when a construction project which needs fire protection acceptance according to the regulations of the State Council's housing and urban–rural development authority is completed, the construction unit shall submit an application for fire protection acceptance to the housing and urban–rural development authority. For construction projects not covered by the previous provision, the construction unit shall file a record with the housing and urban–rural development authority after acceptance, and the authority should conduct spot checks. Where a construction project, which, according to law, is subject to acceptance check in terms of fire protection, fails to undergo such check or fails to pass the check, it shall not be put to use; if other construction projects fail to pass the spot checks in accordance with law, their use shall be discontinued."[38] The "Interim Provisions on the Administration of Fire Protection Design Review and Final Inspection of Construction Projects" (Order No. 58 of the Ministry of Housing and Urban–Rural Development of the People's Republic of China (MHURD)) issued on August 21, 2023, stipulates the types of special construction projects. According to Article 15 of the interim provisions, "a fire protection design review system shall be implemented for special construction projects. The construction unit of special construction projects shall apply for a fire protection design review to the fire protection design review and acceptance authority. The fire protection design review and acceptance authority is responsible for the results of the review in accordance with law. The construction unit shall not carry out special construction projects that fail to undergo such review or fail to pass the review." Article 27 states that "a fire protection acceptance system shall be implemented for special construction projects. When a special construction project is completed, the construction unit shall submit an application for fire protection acceptance to the fire protection design review and acceptance authority. Where

[37] See Administrative penalty case. Administrative penalties for failing to apply for fire protection acceptance and filing after the completion acceptance of other construction projects (Hang Lin Ping Zong Zhi Fa Jue Zi [2022] No. 08-0190), October 14, 2022; The Preventing Roof Collapse (2018).

[38] Fire Protection Law, Article 13.

a construction project fails to undergo such acceptance check or fails to pass the acceptance check, it shall not be put to use."[39]

In terms of legal consequences, laws, regulations, and other normative documents stipulate administrative penalties for construction projects that violate fire protection design review, fire protection acceptance, acceptance filing, and other procedures. For construction projects that violate fire protection design review and fire protection acceptance procedures, paragraph 1 of Article 58 of the "Fire Protection Law" states that "in violation of the provisions of this Law, any unit that commits one of the following acts shall be ordered by the housing and urban–rural development authority and fire rescue agencies to suspend construction, stop using the project, or suspend production or business operation, and shall, in addition, be fined not less than CNY 30,000 but not more than CNY 300,000: (1) without authorization, starting construction of a project of which the design for fire protection, according to law, is subject to review, but fails to undergo such review according to law or fails to pass the review; (2) without authorization, putting to use a construction project which, according to law, is subject to acceptance check in respect of fire protection but fails to undergo such acceptance check or fails to pass the check; (3) failing to discontinue the use of a special construction project stipulated in Article 13 after it fails to pass the spot checks in accordance with law; (4) without authorization, putting a public place for large numbers of people to use or into business operation without the permission of fire rescue agencies, or when verification proves that the use and business conditions of the venue are inconsistent with the promised content." For construction projects that violate the acceptance and filing procedures, paragraph 3 of Article 58 of the "Fire Protection Law" states that "if the construction unit fails to submit the documents for fire protection to the housing and urban–rural development authority for filing after acceptance, as required by this Law, the housing and urban–rural development authority shall order it to rectify with a fine of less than CNY 5000."[40]

Work safety conditions should also be in place during the production and operation process. In terms of work safety obligations, Article 20 of the "Work Safety Law of the People's Republic of China" (Work Safety Law) states that "business entities shall meet the work safety conditions prescribed by this Law and other relevant laws, administrative regulations, and national or industry standards. Business entities not meeting such conditions shall not engage in production and other business activities."[41] According to the social organization standard "Acceptance Specifications for Rooftop Distributed Photovoltaic Power Generation Projects" issued by the Hangzhou Photovoltaic Association on January 14, 2019, rooftop load safety is crucial to photovoltaic equipment, so it is necessary to ensure that the rooftop meets

[39] Interim Provisions on the Administration of Fire Protection Design Review and Final Inspection of Construction Projects, Articles 15 and 26.

[40] Fire Protection Law, Paragraphs 1 and 3 of Article 58.

[41] Work Safety Law, Article 20.

the basic conditions for photovoltaic equipment and its operation.[42] According to the "Design Guideline for Installation of Solar Photovoltaic System on Existing Civil Buildings" (chief editor: Zhejiang Province Institute of Architectural Design and Research), the structural design, structural materials, durability, construction and strength of installation positions of buildings should meet the requirements of building structures and other safety aspects. At the same time, the brackets, supporting metal components, and connection points of photovoltaic systems should have the ability to withstand the system's weight, wind load, snow load, maintenance load, and seismic effects.[43]

For entities that fail to fulfill their management responsibilities for rooftop load production safety, Article 94 of the "Work Safety Law" states that "where the main responsible person of a business entity fails to perform the duty of work safety management specified by this Law, an order for corrective action within a specified period shall be made, with a fine of not less than CNY 20,000 nor more than CNY 50,000 imposed; or if corrective action fails to be taken within the specified period, a fine of not less than CNY 50,000 nor more than CNY 100,000 shall be imposed, and the production and operation entity shall be ordered to suspend production and business for rectification. Where a violation of law committed by the main responsible person of a business entity as mentioned in the preceding paragraph leads to the occurrence of any work safety accident, the person shall be removed from office as a disciplinary action; and if the violation constitutes any crime, the person shall be subject to criminal liability in accordance with the relevant provisions of the Criminal Law. Where the main responsible person of a business entity has received any criminal punishment or the disciplinary action of removal from office under the preceding paragraph, the person shall not serve as the main responsible person of any business entity within five years from the date of completion of serving the criminal punishment or the date when the disciplinary action is taken; or, if the person is liable for any serious or especially serious work safety accident, the person shall not serve as the main responsible person of any business entity in the same industry for life. "Article 95 states that where the main responsible person of a business entity causes a work safety accident by failing to perform the duty of work safety management specified by this Law, the emergency management authority shall impose a fine. In the event of an ordinary accident, a fine of 40% of annual income of the preceding year shall be imposed; In the event of a relatively big accident, a fine of 60% of annual income of the preceding year shall be imposed. In the event of a major accident, a fine of 80% of annual income of the preceding year shall be imposed. In the event of a particularly major accident, a fine of 100% of annual income of the preceding year shall be imposed.[44]

---

[42] See Hangzhou Photovoltaic Association. Acceptance Specifications for Rooftop Distributed Photovoltaic Power Generation Projects (T/HZPVA 001-2019).

[43] See Zhejiang Province Institute of Architectural Design and Research. Design Guideline for Installation of Solar Photovoltaic System on Existing Civil Buildings, Articles 4.0.3 and 4.0.4.

[44] Work Safety Law, Articles 94–95.

If the building of the leased rooftop is not checked for fire protection acceptance or the rooftop load is insufficient, there may be inconveniences in the usufruct of the rooftop and the installation of photovoltaic equipment due to administrative penalties, thus affecting the smooth progress of the project.

Legal Risks Arising from Defects in the Ownership or Other Rights of the Leased Rooftop

Rooftops Leased by a Person Without the Right of Disposal or Authority

If the rooftop lessor is not the owner, is not authorized by the owner, and is not ratified afterward, risks such as inability to perform the lease contract or disputes with third parties outside the contract regarding ownership may arise.[45] Existing laws, regulations, and other normative documents stipulate the legal consequences for lessors without the right of disposal and authority.

For the lack of right of disposal, paragraph 1 of Article 597 of the *Civil Code* states that "if the ownership of a subject matter is unable to be transferred owing to the fact that the seller fails to obtain the right of disposal, the buyer may rescind the contract and request the seller to bear default liability." For the lack of authority, paragraph 1 of Article 171 of the *Civil Code* states that "an act performed by a person without authority, beyond the authority, or after the authority is terminated is not effective against the principal who has not ratified it." For the lessee, Item 2 of Article 724 of the *Civil Code* states that if there are disputes over the attribution of rights of the leased object and the leased object cannot be used due to a reason not attributable to the lessee, the lessee may rescind the contract.[46] In this case, although the building of the leased rooftop has an immovable property ownership certificate and the building construction documents or licenses are complete, the lessor is neither the owner of the rooftop nor has the authority to act as an agent and is leasing the rooftop without the right of disposal or authority. This will result in the lessor being unable to perform their obligation to deliver the rooftop to the lessee for use. The lessee can only terminate the contract and claim compensation. The owner of the rooftop may also exercise their rights, thereby affecting the usufruct of the rooftop and the installation of photovoltaic equipment.

In addition, the combined disposal of buildings and land use rights can lead to an increase in the risks associated with the lack of the right of disposal.[47] For buildings on land for construction, Article 356 of the *Civil Code* states that "where a right to use the land for construction purposes is transferred, exchanged, offered as capital contribution, or given away as a gift, the buildings, structures, and auxiliary facilities

[45] See First Civil Division of the People's Court (2021).

[46] Civil Code of the People's Republic of China, Paragraph 1 of Article 171, paragraph 1 of Article 597 and Item (2) of Article 724.

[47] See Supreme Court (2022).

thereof attached to the land shall be disposed of concomitantly." Article 357 states that "where a building or structure, and auxiliary facilities thereof are transferred, exchanged, offered as capital contribution, or given away as a gift, the right to use the land for construction purposes in the land occupied by the building, structure, and auxiliary facilities thereof shall be disposed of concomitantly."[48] For buildings on collectively owned land, paragraph 1 of Article 6 of the 2014 "Regulations on the Implementation of the Land Administration Law" states that "if the ownership or use rights of land are legally changed and the transfer of the buildings, structures, and other fixtures on the land results in the transfer of the land use right, an application for land change registration must be submitted to the land administration authority at or above the county level where the land is located. The original land registration authority shall carry out the registration of changes in land ownership and use rights in accordance with the law. The change in land ownership or use rights shall take effect from the date of registration."[49] According to Article 2 of the "Interpretation of the Supreme People's Court on the Application of the Real Rights of the Civil Code of the People's Republic of China (I)," "if a party has evidence to prove that the records in the register of immovable property do not match the true rights status and that they are the true owner of the immovable property rights, and they request confirmation of their property rights, such a request shall be supported."[50] This indicates that the combined disposal of buildings and land use rights when they are transferred, exchanged, offered as capital contribution, or given away as a gift may increase the risk of lack of the right of disposal, because the buildings may not undergo timely registration changes.

Even if the immovable property ownership certificate for the building of the leased rooftop is examined, situations such as lack of right of disposal or authority may still exist. This can fundamentally hinder the performance of the lease contract or give rise to ownership disputes with third parties outside the contract, thereby affecting the usufruct of the rooftop and the installation of photovoltaic equipment.

Co-owned Rooftops Leased Without the Consent of the Required Proportion of Owners as Stipulated by Law

For a leased rooftop that is co-owned by multiple owners, risks such as inability to perform the lease contract or disputes with third parties outside the contract regarding ownership may arise due to lack of right of disposal in the following scenarios: A rooftop that is a common part of a building is leased without the decision being made by owners who collectively represent at least two-thirds of the total proportional area of the common property and also represent at least two-thirds of the voting

---

[48] Civil Code of the People's Republic of China, Articles 356–357.

[49] Regulations on the Implementation of the Land Administration Law (2014), Paragraph 1 of Article 6.

[50] Interpretation of the Supreme People's Court on the Application of the Real Rights of the Civil Code of the People's Republic of China (I) (Fa Shi [2020] No. 24), Article 2.

population, or without the consent of the owners who collectively own at least three-fourths of the total proportional area and at least three-fourths of the voting owners; a jointly owned rooftop is leased without the unanimous consent of all co-owners; or a rooftop with shared ownership by shares is leased without the consent of the owners holding more than two-thirds of the shares.[51]

First, for a rooftop that is a co-owned part of a building, Article 271 of the *Civil Code* states that "a unit owner has the ownership over an exclusive unit of a building, such as a dwelling space or a space used for operating businesses, and has the right to co-own and jointly manage the common space other than the unit." Article 278 states that other major matters relating to co-ownership and the right to joint management shall be jointly decided by the unit owners. The quorum for matters subject to the unit owners' joint decision shall be two-thirds or more of the exclusive units both by area and by number of unit owners. Decisions of matters provided in items 6–8 of the preceding Paragraph, including "changing the intended use of the co-owned space or making use of the co-owned space to engage in business activities," shall be subject to the consent of the unit owners representing three-quarters or more of the participating exclusive units both by area and by number of unit owners. Decisions of other matters provided in the preceding Paragraph shall be subject to the consent of the unit owners representing more than half of the participating exclusive units both by area and by number of unit owners.[52] According to item 1 of paragraph 1 of Article 3 of the "Interpretations of the Supreme People's Court on Several Issues Concerning the Application of Law in the Trial of Disputes over Ownership of Building Units" (amended in 2020), in addition to the co-owned parts defined by laws and administrative regulations, the following parts within the construction zone, including "basic structures such as the foundation, load-bearing structures, exterior walls, rooftop, public circulation areas such as passages, stairs, and lobbies, auxiliary facilities and equipment such as fire protection and public lighting, and structural components such as refuge floors, equipment floors, and equipment rooms," should also be recognized as co-owned parts specified in Chapter VI of the "Property Law of the People's Republic of China." Article 7 states that "the disposal of co-owned parts and matters that are decided by the owners' assembly in accordance with the law or should be decided jointly by owners as determined by the administrative regulations in accordance with the law shall be recognized as 'other major matters' as provided in Item (9) of paragraph 1 of Article 278 of the *Civil Code* regarding the rights of co-ownership and joint management."[53] For the difference between "changing the intended use of the co-owned space or making use of the co-owned space to engage in business activities" and "disposal of co-owned parts," the former is more similar to the rights of use and benefit, while the latter specifically refers to legal disposals such

[51] See Songming County People's Court of Yunnan Province (2024)

[52] Civil Code of the People's Republic of China, Articles 271 and 278.

[53] Interpretations of the Supreme People's Court on Several Issues Concerning the Application of Law in the Trial of Disputes over Ownership of Building Units (Fa Shi [2020] No. 17), Item (1) of Paragraph 1 of Article 3 and Article 7.

as transfer, abandonment, or encumbrance.[54] The act of leasing a rooftop, which is a co-owned part of a building, as a "change in the intended use of the co-owned space or making use of the co-owned space to engage in business activities" should be subject to voting by owners who own two-thirds or more of the area of the exclusive parts and two-thirds or more of the number of owners. Additionally, the consent of owners representing three-quarters or more of the area of the exclusive parts and three-quarters or more of the number of owners who participated in the vote is required.

Second, for a jointly co-owned rooftop or a rooftop co-owned by shares, Article 301 of the *Civil Code* states that "unless otherwise agreed by the co-owners, any disposition of the co-owned immovable or movable property, or any major repair or change of the nature or intended use of the co-owned immovable or movable property shall be subject to the consent of the co-owners by shares whose shares account for two-thirds or more of the total shares, or to the consent of all joint co-owners."[55] Accordingly, the lease of a rooftop of a jointly co-owned building shall be subject to the unanimous consent of the co-owners. The lease of a rooftop of a building co-owned by shares shall be subject to the consent of the co-owners whose shares account for two-thirds or more of the total shares.[56] According to paragraph 1 of Article 597 of the *Civil Code*, "if the ownership of a subject matter is unable to be transferred owing to the fact that the seller fails to obtain the right of disposal, the buyer may rescind the contract and request the seller to bear default liability."[57] If a co-owned rooftop is leased without the consent of the required proportion of owners as stipulated by law, the lease agreement will not be effective for some co-owners. As a result, the lease contract may be terminated, subsequently affecting the usufruct of the rooftop and the installation of photovoltaic equipment.

Rooftops Leased by the Sublessor Without Consent of the Original Lessor or with Sublease Terms Exceeding the Original Lease Term

If a rooftop is leased by a sublessor without the consent of the original lessor, or if the sublease term of the sublease contract exceeds the remaining lease term, risks such as inability to perform the contract or disputes with third parties outside the contract regarding ownership may arise due to lack of right of disposal.[58]

The current laws and regulations have provisions for subleasing activities and their legal effectiveness. According to Article 716 of the *Civil Code*, "a lessee may, upon the lessor's consent, sublease the leased object to a third person. The lease contract between the lessee and the lessor shall continue to be valid despite the sublease by the lessee, and if the third person causes loss to the leased object, the lessee shall bear

[54] See Qi (2009).

[55] Civil Code of the People's Republic of China, Article 301.

[56] See Li (2016).

[57] Civil Code of the People's Republic of China, Paragraph 1 of Article 597.

[58] See Fan (2021).

the liability for compensation." Article 717 states that "where a lessee, upon consent of the lessor, subleases the leased object to a third person, if the term of the sublease exceeds the remaining term of the lessee, the sublease in the period in excess of the original term shall not be legally binding on the lessor unless otherwise agreed by the lessor and the lessee."[59] Accordingly, the consent of the original lessor is required for rooftop subleasing, and the agreed sublease term should be within the remaining lease term of the sublessor. Subleasing that does not meet the above provisions will result in legal consequences. According to paragraph 1 of Article 597 of the *Civil Code*, if the ownership of a subject matter is unable to be transferred owing to the fact that the seller fails to obtain the right of disposal, the buyer may rescind the contract and request the seller to bear default liability.[60,61]

If a sublessor subleases a rooftop without the consent of the original lessor, or the sublease term exceeds the remaining lease term of the sublessor, the sublease will not be effective for the original lessor. The lease contract may be terminated, which affects the usufruct of the rooftop and installation of photovoltaic equipment.

Rooftops Leased Multiple Times

If the lessor enters into several lease contracts for the same roof, the lease contracts are all valid and the lessees each claim their right to perform their respective contract, risks such as inability to perform some contracts or disputes with third parties outside the contract regarding ownership may arise.[62]

For a rooftop that is leased multiple times, Article 5 of the "Interpretation of the Supreme People's Court on Several Issues Concerning Specific Application of Law in the Trial of Cases on Disputes over Contracts for Lease of Urban Houses" (amended in 2020) states that "If the lessor enters into multiple lease contracts for the same property, and all the contracts are valid, when lessees each claim their right to perform their respective contract, the people's court shall determine the lessees performing the contracts in the following order: (1) those who are already in lawful possession of the leased property; (2) those who have completed registration documents for records; (3) the lessee whose contract was concluded first. If a lessee who cannot obtain the leased property requests contract termination and compensation for losses, it shall be handled in accordance with the relevant regulations of the *Civil Code*."[63] This indicates that when multiple lease contracts are valid, the lessor cannot perform all the contracts simultaneously. After a lease contract for a rooftop is concluded, if there are other lease contracts concerning the same rooftop and the lessee has already

---

59 Civil Code of the People's Republic of China, Paragraph 1 of Article 716 and Article 717.

60 Civil Code of the People's Republic of China, Paragraph 1 of Article 597.

61 See Wu (2021).

62 See Hao (2017).

63 Interpretation of the Supreme People's Court on Several Issues Concerning Specific Application of Law in the Trial of Cases on Disputes over Contracts for Lease of Urban Houses (Fa Shi [2020] No. 17), Article 5.

lawfully occupied the rooftop or completed registration documents for records, the rights of use for that rooftop will change. According to paragraph 1 of Article 597 of the *Civil Code*, "if the ownership of a subject matter is unable to be transferred owing to the fact that the seller fails to obtain the right of disposal, the buyer may rescind the contract and request the seller to bear default liability."[64] Lessees who do not have performance priority can only request contract termination and compensation for losses.

Lessees who do not have performance priority cannot request the performance of the lease contract. The lease contract cannot be fundamentally performed and may be terminated, subsequently affecting the usufruct of the rooftop and the installation of photovoltaic equipment.

Rooftops Whose Building is Mortgaged or Seized

If the building of a rooftop is mortgaged before the rooftop is leased or before the possession is transferred after leasing, or if the rooftop is unlawfully leased by the debtor without the court's permission after the building has been seized, it will result in the inability to perform the rooftop lease contract or disputes over ownership with third parties outside the contract.

For the mortgage of a building, Item 1 of Article 14 of the "Interpretation of the Supreme People's Court on Several Issues Concerning Specific Application of Law in the Trial of Cases on Disputes over Contracts for Lease of Urban Houses" (amended in 2020) states that where there is any change in the ownership of the leased house during the term of the lease, if the lessee requests the transferee of the property to continue performing the original lease contract, the People's Court shall uphold such request. However, if a mortgage is created on the leased property before it is leased and a change in ownership occurs due to the mortgage holder exercising their mortgage rights, this situation is considered a statutory exception.[65] Furthermore, according to Article 405 of the *Civil Code*, "where a mortgaged property has been let to and possessed by another person prior to creation of the mortgage, the lease relationship shall not be affected by the mortgage."[66] If a mortgage is created before the transfer of possession after the rooftop is leased, it may affect the leasing relationship.[67] This indicates that if the building of the leased rooftop belongs is mortgaged during the aforementioned period, it may result in the inability to perform the rooftop lease contract and disputes over ownership with third parties outside the contract due to the exercise of mortgage rights.

64 Civil Code of the People's Republic of China, Paragraph 1 of Article 597.

65 Interpretation of the Supreme People's Court on Several Issues Concerning Specific Application of Law in the Trial of Cases on Disputes over Contracts for Lease of Urban Houses (Fa Shi [2020] No. 17), Item (1) of Article 14.

66 Civil Code of the People's Republic of China, Article 405.

67 See Shao (2020).

For the seizure of a building, Item 2 of Article 14 of the "Interpretation of the Supreme People's Court on Several Issues Concerning Specific Application of Law in the Trial of Cases on Disputes over Contracts for Lease of Urban Houses" (amended in 2020) states that where there is any change in the ownership of the leased house during the term of the lease, if the lessee requests the transferee of the property to continue performing the original lease contract, the People's Court shall uphold such request. However, as a statutory exception, if a leased property has been lawfully seized by a People's Court before the lease, the request for the transferee of the property to continue performing the original lease contract shall not be upheld.[68] After the property is seized, the property can still be used with the permission of the court. However, according to Article 24 of the Supreme People's Court's "Regulations on Seizing, Detaining, and Freezing Property in Civil Enforcement by People's Courts" (amended in 2020), when the debtor unlawfully leases the property, the lease contract remains valid but cannot be used to resist the claims of the executing party.[69] According to Item 1 of Article 724 of the *Civil Code*, if the leased object is seized or detained by the judicial authority or administrative authority in accordance with law and cannot be used due to a reason not attributable to the lessee, the lessee may rescind the contract.[70] This indicates that when a property is seized as a judicial or administrative enforcement measure, it can lead to a change in ownership of the leased property. Unless otherwise agreed, the lessee cannot request the transferee to continue performing the original lease contract. The lessee can only seek relief by terminating the contract.

The exercise of mortgage rights and property seizure will result in the inability to perform the lease contract. The former may also lead to ownership disputes with third parties outside the contract. These can affect the usufruct of the rooftop and the installation of photovoltaic equipment.

Rooftops Whose Building is Expropriated or Requisitioned

If the building of a rooftop is expropriated or requisitioned after the rooftop is leased, the lease contract cannot be performed.

"The State may, in the interest of the public, lawfully expropriate or requisition land and give compensation accordingly."[71] According to Article 327 of the *Civil Code*, "where a right to usufruct is extinguished or adversely affected due to expropriation or requisition of the immovable or movable property, the usufructuary has the right to compensation according to the provisions of Articles 243 and 245 of this

[68] Interpretation of the Supreme People's Court on Several Issues Concerning Specific Application of Law in the Trial of Cases on Disputes over Contracts for Lease of Urban Houses (Fa Shi [2020] No. 17), Item (2) of Article 14.

[69] See Regulations on Seizing, Detaining, and Freezing Property in Civil Enforcement by People's Courts (Fa Shi [2020] No. 21), Article 24.

[70] Civil Code of the People's Republic of China, Item (1) of Article 724.

[71] Constitution of the People's Republic of China, Paragraph 3 of Article 10.

Code." Paragraph 3 of Article 243 states, "in the case of expropriation of houses or other immovable property of organizations or individuals, compensation for the expropriation shall be made in accordance with law in order to safeguard the lawful rights and interests of the person whose immovable property has been expropriated. In the case of expropriation of individuals' dwelling houses, the housing conditions of such individuals shall also be guaranteed." Article 245 states, "an immovable or movable property of an organization or individual may, in response to an emergency such as providing disaster relief and preventing and controlling pandemics, be requisitioned within the scope of authority and pursuant to the procedures provided by law. The requisitioned immovable or movable property shall be returned to the aforementioned organization or individual after use. Where the immovable or movable property of an organization or individual is requisitioned, or where it is destructed, damaged, or lost after being requisitioned, compensation shall be made."[72] Consequently, the lessee will be unable to continue using and enjoying the rooftop and can only seek compensation or other means to protect their legitimate rights and interests.[73]

If the building of the leased rooftop is requisitioned or expropriated, although the lessee will receive compensation, it will still affect the usufruct of the rooftop and the installation of photovoltaic equipment.

Legal Risks Associated with Limited Lease Contract Term

The operation period of a rooftop distributed photovoltaic project is 25 years, which requires a corresponding lease term for the rooftop.[74] However, the required duration for project operation exceeds the maximum legal lease term, posing a risk of invalidity for the excess duration.

The maximum legal term of a lease contract is 20 years. According to Article 705 of the *Civil Code*, "the term of a lease may not exceed twenty years. If a lease exceeds twenty years, the part beyond twenty years is invalid. Upon expiration of the lease term, the parties may renew the lease contract, provided that the agreed term of lease may not exceed twenty years from the date of renewal."[75] If the operation period of a rooftop distributed photovoltaic project exceeds 20 years, the lease term for the rooftop would also be expected to exceed 20 years. However, lease agreements exceeding 20 years are deemed invalid. According to the "Questions and Answers on Civil Trial Practice" of the First Civil Division of the People's Court, if the parties agree to a lease contract term of 20 years with an automatic renewal for another 20 years upon expiration, the automatic renewal provision shall be deemed invalid

[72] Civil Code of the People's Republic of China, Paragraph 3 of Article 243, Article 245 and Article 327.

[73] See Jingzhou District People's Court of Jingzhou City (2020).

[74] See Juro (2024).

[75] Civil Code of the People's Republic of China, Article 705.

due to considerations such as the consumption period of the leased property, the need for adjustments of transaction conditions, and the possibility of renewing the lease contract before or upon its expiration.[76] According to Article 734 of the *Civil Code*, "where a lessee continues to use the leased object after the expiration of the term of the lease and the lessor has not raised any objection, the original lease contract shall continue to be valid, except that the lease term shall become unfixed."[77] When the maximum lease term of 20 years expires, if the lessee continues to use the leased property without any objection from the lessor, the original lease contract becomes a lease without a fixed term. According to Article 563 of the *Civil Code*, "for a contract under which the debtor is required to continuously perform an obligation for an indefinite period of time, the parties thereto may rescind the contract at any time, provided that the other party shall be notified within a reasonable period of time."[78] For rooftop lease contracts that exceed the valid lease term, if the term expires without renewal, it will affect the usufruct of the rooftop and installation of photovoltaic equipment. If the contract becomes a lease without a fixed term, it may be terminated at any time, which poses a significant risk to the usufruct of the rooftop and installation of photovoltaic equipment.

The aforementioned analysis of legal risks is based on the premise of defining the usufruct of the rooftop as a rooftop lease contract. However, there are different opinions regarding the nature of the usufruct of rooftops. In contrast to the viewpoint that defines the usufruct of the rooftop as a rooftop lease contract, another viewpoint defines it as an agreement within an energy performance agreement. According to the latter viewpoint, when the lease relationship is incorporated into an energy performance agreement, the lease contract is considered a non-gratuitous bilateral contract. Its typical characteristics involve the lessor delivering the leased property, and the lessee paying rent. On the other hand, the energy performance agreement focuses on energy savings, electricity payment, and settlement after the project is completed. It often includes provisions exempting the project owner (lessee) from paying rent. The contract content, purpose, and other elements differ from those of a lease contract. From the perspective of the rights and obligations related to the two types of rooftop usufruct, the rooftop usufruct provisions in an energy performance agreement and a rooftop lease contract are different fundamentally. The term of the rooftop usufruct provisions in an energy performance agreement is not subject to the maximum lease term limitation of the lease contract.[79] However, according to the "Interim Measures for the Management of Distributed PV Power Generation Projects" (Guo Neng Xin Neng [2013] No. 433) issued on November 18, 2013, if the project entity is not the owner of the building, site or facilities, the project entity should sign a usage or leasing agreement. This indicates that the normative document

[76] See First Civil Division of the People's Court (2021).

[77] Civil Code of the People's Republic of China, Paragraph 1 of Article 734.

[78] Civil Code of the People's Republic of China, Paragraph 2 of Article 563.

[79] See Jiang and Lin (2021).

identifies the usufruct of rooftops as use or lease.[80] Based on existing judicial cases,[81] rooftop distributed PV projects usually involve lease contracts, and courts evaluate and make judgments based on lease legal relationships in such cases. As a result, it is currently challenging for the practical departments to adopt the second viewpoint to define rooftop usufruct solely as provisions in energy performance agreements.

If the project period of 25 years is used as the leasing term of the lease contract, the duration of the lease contract that exceeds the maximum legal leasing period may be invalid.

Risks Associated with the Term of Energy Performance Contracts

According to the "Interim Measures for the Management of Distributed PV Power Generation Projects" (Guo Neng Xin Neng [2013] No. 433) issued on November 18, 2013, distributed PV power generation projects should meet the following conditions in terms of construction requirements: "buildings and facilities used should be legal; if the project entity and the owner of the building, site, or facilities on which the project is built are different entities, the project entity should sign a usage or leasing agreement for the building, site, or facilities with the owner and, depending on the operating mode, sign an energy service agreement with the power user."[82] For rooftop distributed PV projects, legal risks such as long contract periods and changes in objective factors may arise during the energy performance contracting process. In terms of the contract term, the following seven legal risks may arise.

Legal Risks Associated with Unclear Technical Standards or Non-compliance with Technical Standards

During the energy performance contracting process of rooftop distributed PV projects,[83] clear technical standards are critical because these projects have long operation periods and involve multiple technical aspects. However, rooftop distributed PV

---

[80] See the National Energy Administration of China. Interim Measures for the Management of Distributed PV Power Generation Projects (Guo Neng Xin Neng [2013] No. 433), Article 16.

[81] See Judicial cases. The second-instance civil judgment of contract dispute between Shaoxing Shangyu Wan Household Products Co., Ltd. and Shaoxing Shangyu Yongyang New Energy Co., Ltd. (2020 Zhejiang 06 Min Zhong No. 1883), July 6, 2020; the first-instance civil judgment of property rights protection dispute between Hangzhou Fucen Industrial Co., Ltd. and State Power Investment Corporation Sangniailuo (Hangzhou Fuyang) Photovoltaic Power Generation Co., Ltd. (2020 Zhejiang 0111 Min Chu No. 2451), July 27, 2020.

[82] The National Energy Administration of China. Interim Measures for the Management of Distributed PV Power Generation Projects (Guo Neng Xin Neng [2013] No. 433), Article 16.

[83] See United States Agency for International Development (2020).

projects are one of the applications of the new power system, and the technical standards for these projects may not be issued or updated in a timely manner, which could result in administrative penalties during project operation due to unclear standards. Furthermore, as time progresses and technology advances, the technical standards of the projects will change, and the projects need to be updated accordingly.

Normative documents have been established to provide the technical requirements for the construction of rooftop distributed PV projects. According to the "Interim Measures for the Management of Distributed PV Power Generation Projects" (Guo Neng Xin Neng [2013] No. 433) issued on November 18, 2013, in terms of construction technology, "the design and installation of distributed photovoltaic power generation projects shall comply with relevant administrative regulations, equipment standards, construction engineering specifications, and safety requirements. Entities responsible for project design, consultation, installation, and supervision shall possess the corresponding qualifications as stipulated by national regulations"; and "the photovoltaic cell modules, inverters, and other equipment used in distributed photovoltaic power generation projects shall undergo testing and certification by certification organizations accredited according to national regulations. The equipment shall meet the technical requirements for grid connection as specified by the relevant regulations." The "Notice on Revising the Implementation Rules for Grid Connection Service Management of Distributed Photovoltaic Power Generation Projects of State Grid Zhejiang Electric Power Company" (Zhe Dian Ying [2020] No. 52) issued on January 21, 2020, also requires that the power quality of distributed PV power generation projects connected to the grid should comply with national standards, and the engineering design and construction should meet national standards such as the "Code for design of photovoltaic power station" and "Code for construction of PV power station"; The implementation rules also stipulate that the project design, acceptance and testing should comply with documents such as the "Technical requirements for connecting photovoltaic power station to power system" (GB/T 19964), "Technical requirements for connecting photovoltaic power system to distribution network" (GB/T 29319), "Specification for operation and controlling for distributed resources connected to power grid" (GB/T 33592), "Technical requirements for grid connection of distributed resources" (GB/T 33593), and "Notice from the East China Regional Electricity Safety Production Committee Regarding the Special Inspection and Rectification of Frequency-Related Issues in Distributed Photovoltaic Projects in the East China Region" (Hua Dong Jian Neng An Quan [2019] Document No. 70).[84] According to the "Guidance on energy performance contracting" (GB/T 24915–2020) issued on March 31, 2020, in energy performance contracting projects, technical requirements related to elements such as energy condition diagnosis, energy baseline determination, energy-saving measures, quantified energy-saving indicators, savings sharing methods, savings measurement, and

---

[84] See Implementation Rules for Grid Connection Service Management of Distributed Photovoltaic Power Generation Projects of State Grid Zhejiang Electric Power Company (Zhe Dian Ying [2020] No. 52).

verification need to be confirmed. Specifically, this guidance references other technical documents, including the "General principles for energy balance of equipment using energy" (GB/T 2587), "General rules for calculation of the comprehensive energy consumption" (GB/T 2589), "General principles for energy balance of enterprise" (GB/T 3484), "Determination of energy savings in organizations" (GB/T 13234), "General principles for monitoring and testing of energy saving" (GB/T 15316), "General principle of energy audit" (GB/T 17166), "Energy management system requirements" (GB/T 23331), "General technical rules for measurement and verification of energy savings" (GB/T 28750), and "Guidance on implementation of measurement and verification of energy savings" (GB/T 32045).[85]

Technical standards for the grid connection and operation and maintenance safety of photovoltaic power generation are also established. For example, the Zhejiang Provincial Energy Bureau issued the "Notice on the Issuance of the Guidelines for Home Rooftop Distributed PV Power Generation Projects" (Zhe Dian Fa [2018] No. 21), stating that distributed PV enterprises engaged in sales services, installation services, and operation and maintenance services for home rooftop PV systems shall comply with relevant requirements, adhere to strict quality standards, and ensure the quality and long-term operation of the PV systems.[86] The appendix of the aforementioned implementation rules also presents typical schemes for distributed photovoltaic grid-connection systems, providing detailed connection specifications for full feed-in and self-consumption with surplus electricity fed into the grid.[87] According to the "Notice on Issuing the Guidelines for Promoting Rooftop Distributed Photovoltaic Project Development in Counties (Cities, Districts) in Zhejiang Province" (Zhe Neng Yuan [2021] No. 17) issued by Zhejiang Provincial Energy Bureau on November 26, 2021, the guidelines apply to newly built, expanded or renovated rooftop distributed PV projects in pilot counties (cities, districts) in Zhejiang. The guidelines can be used as a reference for projects in areas not included in the pilot. "On the Issuance of the 'Technical guideline for distribution network bearing capability of connected distributed photovoltaic stations by State Grid Zhejiang Electric Power Co., Ltd.' and 'Implementation Guidelines for Technical Specifications of Distributed Photovoltaic Systems by State Grid Zhejiang Electric Power Co., Ltd.'" is also aimed at strengthening the technical specifications for photovoltaic connection and conducting photovoltaic bearing capacity assessments. According to paragraph 1 of Article 28 of the "Zhejiang Province Electric Power Regulations" issued on September 29, 2022, "if power supply, energy storage and other projects meet the national grid-connection conditions and standards, the power supply enterprises shall provide grid-connection services within the specified time limit and shall not, without authorization, change the grid-connection standards." Paragraph 3 of Article

[85] See State Administration for Market Regulation, Standardization Administration of China. Guidance on Energy Performance Contracting (GB/T 24915–2020).

[86] See Zhejiang Provincial Energy Bureau. Guidelines for Home Rooftop Distributed PV Power Generation Projects (Zhe Dian Fa Zhan [2018] No. 21).

[87] See Implementation Rules for Grid Connection Service Management of Distributed Photovoltaic Power Generation Projects of State Grid Zhejiang Electric Power Company (Zhe Dian Ying [2020] No. 52).

28 of the regulations stipulates, "project owners of power supply, energy storage, and other projects shall ensure the security of the power grid in accordance with relevant national technical standards and specifications and shall not, without authorization, connect to the grid."[88]

Even if existing technical specifications have provided general guidance for the projects, contract disputes or administrative penalties may still arise due to unspecific agreements, indeterminate legal provisions, or non-compliance with applicable technical standards throughout the construction and progression of energy performance contracting projects.

Firstly, concerning the aforementioned technical requirements, the parties involved in the energy performance contracting projects shall make specific agreements to avoid potential disputes. However, in the event that such agreements are not pre-established, notwithstanding statutory guidance on the ex-post determination of pertinent contractual elements, additional costs may still arise.[89] According to Article 510 of the *Civil Code*, "After a contract becomes effective, where the parties have not agreed on such contents as the quality, price or remuneration, or the place of performance, and the like, or the relevant agreement is unclear, the parties may make a supplementary agreement; where the parties fail to reach a supplementary agreement, such contents shall be determined according to the relevant clauses of the contract or transaction practices." According to Item (1) of Article 511, where the quality requirements are not clearly stipulated and such content cannot be determined according to the supplementary agreement, relevant clauses of the contract, or the course of dealing, "the contract shall be performed in accordance with a mandatory national standard, or a recommendatory national standard in the absence of a mandatory national standard, or the standard of the industry in the absence of a recommendatory national standard. In the absence of any national or industrial standard, the contract shall be performed in accordance with the general standard or a specific standard conforming to the purpose of the contract."[90] Therefore, unclear provisions in the contract may be supplemented by agreement or determined by statutory means. Where the quality requirements are not clearly stipulated, the contract shall be performed in accordance with a mandatory national standard, recommendatory national standard, industrial standard, general standard, or a specific standard conforming to the purpose of the contract. However, reaching a supplementary agreement or resorting to statutory means may incur additional time and resource consumption. Should the parties fail to reach a consensus, the efficiency of the energy performance contracting projects may be hindered due to impeded performance.

---

[88] Zhejiang Province Electric Power Regulations, Paragraphs 1 and 3 of Article 28.

[89] See Liu (2020).

[90] Civil Code of the People's Republic of China, Article 510 and Item (1) of Article 511.

Secondly, regarding the technical standards for rooftop distributed PV, the existing specifications are ambiguous and not comprehensive, thereby leading to administrative and legal risks.[91] Illustratively, the prevailing standards for the elevated design are not specific. The "Design Guideline for Installation of Solar Photovoltaic System on Existing Civil Buildings" proposes that "appropriate enclosures should be installed around protruding parts of solar PV components that affect the sensory perception, using architectural components such as parapets." However, specific standards and the legal consequences of non-compliance are not clearly defined.[92] For example, in some regions, regulations stipulate that the elevated design for rooftop building-integrated PV (BIPV) shall not exceed 2.5 m in height, yet there are no clear guidelines for equipment or project acceptance. This deficiency may engender the classification of the structure as illicit, rendering it susceptible to demolition during its use. Regarding project filing, according to Article 14 of the "Interim Measures for the Management of PV Power Station Projects" (Guo Neng Xin Neng [2013] No. 329) on August 29, 2013, "provincial energy authorities shall implement filing management for PV power station projects in accordance with the provisions of the State Council on investment project management. Registered projects shall comply with the national solar power development plan, the annual indicative scale indicators, and annual implementation plans set forth by the energy authorities of the State Council for the region, ensuring grid-connection conditions are met." Based on these regulatory requirements, only project filing is required before construction, without the need for a permit. Regarding project acceptance, according to Article 23 of the "Interim Measures for the Management of PV Power Station Projects" (Guo Neng Xin Neng [2013] No. 329), "grid companies shall, within 45 working days after receiving the project unit's application for grid connection and commissioning, cooperate in carrying out grid connection commissioning and completion acceptance for the PV power station's grid-connected equipment and power output project in accordance with relevant national technical standards and management regulations. Grid companies shall sign grid connection dispatch agreements and power purchase contracts with the project unit. The grid-connected dispatch agreements and power purchase contracts signed by both parties must comply with the provisions of the 'Renewable Energy Law of the People's Republic of China' regarding full guaranteed purchase." Therefore, grid companies are responsible solely for the acceptance of grid-connected PV equipment and projects, not the main building. As for the acceptance of the main building, according to Article 45 of the "Law of the People's Republic of China on Urban and Rural Planning," "the urban and rural planning authority of the local people's government at or above the county level shall verify whether the construction project complies with the planning conditions in accordance with the provisions of the State Council. If it is not verified or does not

[91] See Administrative penalty case: Administrative penalty for construction without obtaining a construction project planning permit (Hang Shang Zong Zhi Fa Jue Zi [2022] No. 09–0117), October 31, 2022.

[92] See Zhejiang Province Institute of Architectural Design and Research. Design Guideline for Installation of Solar Photovoltaic System on Existing Civil Buildings, Articles 4.0.3 and 4.0.4.

comply with the planning conditions, the construction unit shall not proceed with the completion acceptance. The construction unit shall submit relevant completion acceptance materials to the urban and rural planning authority within six months after completion acceptance."[93] Consequently, it is imperative to clarify that the grid-connection commissioning and completion acceptance for the equipment and projects does not imply the acceptance of the main building by the government's planning and construction authorities. At this stage, the potential risk of incurring administrative penalties persists, which may hinder the progress of the project.

Thirdly, the differences resulting from changes in versions of technical standards for rooftop distributed PV[94] may also give rise to administrative and legal risks. Taking the changes in rooftop load standards as an example, it primarily involves the impact on bearing capacity and building structure safety due to factors such as height elevation and concrete construction after the installation of PV systems. Pursuant to the "Announcement on Promulgating the National Standard 'General Code for Engineering Structures' (GB 55001–2021)" (Announcement of the Ministry of Housing and Urban–Rural Development of the People's Republic of China [2021] No. 70) issued by the MHURD on April 9, 2021, this general code is a mandatory national engineering construction standard. Effective from January 1, 2022, this general code supersedes any mandatory provisions of other engineering construction standards. In the event of any discrepancies between relevant provisions and the stipulations of this general code, the latter shall prevail. In the case of changes in the building standards for rooftop loads or other relevant standards, notwithstanding the prior confirmation of load safety or the acceptance of equipment and projects, inspection and modification work should still be carried out to ensure safe production and operation. According to Article 20 of the "Work Safety Law," "Business entities shall meet the work safety conditions prescribed by this Law and other relevant laws, administrative regulations, and national or industry standards. Business entities not meeting such conditions shall not be engaged in production and other business activities."[95] As mentioned above, failure to fulfill the safety production management responsibilities stipulated by the "Work Safety Law" may subject the principal person in charge of the business entity to administrative penalties such as corrective orders within a prescribed timeframe, fines, production and business suspension for rectification, or even criminal liabilities. Therefore, modifications due to changes in rooftop load building standards or other related standards to meet safety production conditions may incur additional costs. Failure to promptly eliminate safety production risks during project operation may result in administrative and criminal liabilities, leading to the temporary or permanent suspension of the project due to the absence of necessary safety production conditions.

---

93 Law of the People's Republic of China on Urban and Rural Planning, Article 45.

94 See Lu (2015).

95 Work Safety Law, Article 20.

Fourthly, in terms of environmental impact assessment, failure to comply with relevant environmental impact assessment requirements may also result in administrative penalties.[96] According to Article 11 of the "Notice on the Issuance of Interim Measures for the Management of Distributed PV Power Generation Projects" (Guo Neng Xin Neng [2013] No. 433), "the project filing process for distributed PV power generation projects should be simplified as much as possible, exempting the need for supporting documents such as power generation permits, siting planning, land pre-review, soil and water conservation plans, environmental impact assessment, energy conservation evaluation, and social risk assessment." The "Management Catalogue for the Classification of the Environmental Impact Assessment of Construction Projects (2021 Edition)" (Ministry of Ecology and Environment (MEE) Order No. 16) stipulates that for projects with ground-based centralized PV power stations (with a total capacity greater than 6000 kW and a grid-connected voltage level not lower than 10 kV), an environmental impact assessment report is required. For other PV power generation projects, an environmental impact assessment registration form shall be submitted.[97] According to Paragraph 3 of *Article 31* of the "*Law of the People's Republic of China on Environment Impact Assessment*" (Environment Impact Assessment Law), "If a construction unit fails to file the environmental impact registration form for the construction project as required by law, the competent ecological environment department at or above the county level shall order the filing and impose a fine of not more than CNY 50,000."[98] Therefore, for commercial and industrial rooftop distributed PV projects, it is necessary to complete the environmental impact assessment registration and filing procedures. Failure to do so may subject the project company to administrative penalties, which could hinder the project's construction and operation.[99]

Legal Risks of Entity Changes

Due to the extended operational lifespan of rooftop distributed PV projects, significant costs are accumulated throughout the stages of cooperative investment, project construction, daily operation and maintenance, project settlement, and revenue sharing, as well as power transmission and distribution services.[100] These costs necessitate a certain period for recovery. If the real estate associated with the project

---

[96] See Administrative penalty case. Shaoxing City Keqiao District Keqiao Haifu Textile Co., Ltd. is suspected of failing to file an environmental impact registration form as required by law (Shao Shi Huan Fa Zi [2022] No. 10 [Ke]), April 28, 2022.

[97] See the Ministry of Ecology and Environment. Management Catalogue for the Classification of the Environmental Impact Assessment of Construction Projects (2021 Edition) (Ministry of Ecology and Environment Order No. 16), Item 90.

[98] Law of the People's Republic of China on Environment Impact Assessment, Paragraph 3 of Article 31.

[99] See Zhu et al. (2022).

[100] See National Renewable Energy Laboratory (2021).

undergoes asset transfers or bankruptcy liquidation involving the property owner or right holder, it is highly likely that energy performance contracts will be terminated, thereby introducing a higher risk of unrealized returns and difficulties in cost recovery.

On one hand, changes in ownership of real estate due to asset transfer pose certain risks. The advantage lies in the legal principle of "sales not devastating lease," which to some extent safeguards the stability of rooftop lease contracts.[101] For the interests of the lessee, the original rooftop lease contract can be continued by the transferee of the property. However, certain drawbacks remain. Firstly, the adaptation costs related to the new contracting party persist, and secondly, there is a lack of guarantee for the continued performance of other energy performance contracts within the project.

Regarding "sales not devastating lease," according to Article 725 of the *Civil Code*, "a change in the ownership of a leased object during the period that a lessee possesses the leased object in accordance with the lease contract does not affect the validity of the lease."[102] Furthermore, according to Article 14 of the "Interpretation of the Supreme People's Court on Several Issues Concerning Specific Application of Law in the Trial of Cases on Disputes over Contracts for Lease of Urban Houses" (revised in 2020), "where there is any change in the ownership of the leased house during the term of the lease, if the lessee requests the transferee of the property to continue performing the original lease contract, the People's Court shall uphold such request." However, there are exceptions to this rule. The exceptions include situations where "a mortgage has been set on the house before the lease, and the ownership changes due to the realization of the mortgage by the mortgagee" and "the house has been seized by the People's Court before the lease, and the lessee is unable to request the transferee of the property to continue performing the original lease contract."[103] Consequently, when the property owner changes, the validity of the house lease contract will not be affected. Except for the realization of the mortgage right and the court seizure, the lessee can also request the transferee of the property to continue performing the original lease contract.

Although the principle of "sales not devastating lease" applies to rooftop lease contracts, it is insufficient by itself to ensure the operation of the energy performance contracting projects. In practice, some courts require that the application of this principle is contingent upon the buyer's awareness of the lease agreement. Specifically, Article 30 of the "Answers of the Shanghai High People's Court to Questions about the Law Application in the Settlement of House Leasing Dispute (3)" stipulates that "for unregistered lease contracts, when the ownership of the property changes, the lessee cannot demand the continuation of the lease agreement from the

[101] See Chen (2020).

[102] Civil Code of the People's Republic of China, Article 725.

[103] Interpretation of the Supreme People's Court on Several Issues Concerning Specific Application of Law in the Trial of Cases on Disputes over Contracts for Lease of Urban Houses (Fa Shi [2020] No. 17), Article 14.

new property right owner based on the principle of 'sales not devastating lease'."[104] This legal provision introduces a potential impediment to the enforcement of rooftop lease contracts in certain regions, particularly where the absence of registration may preclude the enforceability of the lease, thereby affecting the use of the rooftop and its consequent revenue. Moreover, even in scenarios where the lease may persist post-transfer, new adaptation costs may arise due to changes in real estate ownership. Furthermore, except for the property lease contract, there is no legal basis for the enforcement of other energy performance contracts in the project. The non-performance of such contracts may result in the inability to realize anticipated power generation and consumption and its consequent revenue. After the transfer of property ownership, even if the contracts are not terminated, project owners may find themselves in a less favorable position during contract negotiations.

Notwithstanding the foregoing, if the owner or right holder of the real estate associated with the project undergoes bankruptcy liquidation, the rooftop lease contract or other energy performance contracts in the project may be terminated by the bankruptcy administrator.[105] Such a contingency is markedly pronounced in energy performance contracting projects where the enterprise acts as the owner or right holder of real estate. Especially for small- and medium-sized enterprises with shorter duration in China, the risk of enterprise bankruptcy liquidation during the project period is elevated. Moreover, the probability of enterprise bankruptcy is further increased when the enterprise, acting as the owner or right holder of the real estate, is involved in significant litigation or enforcement cases, or when they are listed as a debtor with a record of untrustworthiness in matters related to the credibility of the lessor.[106]

According to Article 18 of the "Enterprise Bankruptcy Law," "upon acceptance by the People's Court of the application for bankruptcy, the administrator is entitled to rescind or continue the performance of the contracts that have been concluded before the acceptance of the application for bankruptcy but the performance of which has not been completed, and notify the counterpart concerned of the same. When the administrator fails to give a notice to the counterparts concerned within 2 months of the acceptance of the application for bankruptcy or fails to reply to the counterparts concerned within 30 days of the demand of the counterpart concerned, it shall be deemed to have rescinded the relevant contracts. Where the administrator decides to continue the performance of the contracts, the counterparts concerned shall keep the performance of the contracts; provided that they are entitled to request the administrator to provide the guarantee for such performance, and when the administrator has not provided such guarantee, it shall be deemed to have rescinded the contracts."[107] When a bankruptcy application of the owner or right holder of the

[104] Answers of the Shanghai High People's Court to Questions about the Law Application in the Settlement of House Leasing Dispute (3) (Hu Gao Fa Min Yi [2005] No. 16), Article 30.

[105] See Xu (2009).

[106] See Anli Law Firm (2022).

[107] Enterprise Bankruptcy Law, Article 18.

real estate associated with the project is accepted by the People's Court, the administrator may terminate the executory rooftop lease contract or other energy performance contracts in the project. Additionally, the administrator's failure to notify, respond, or provide guarantees within a specified period shall also be deemed as contract termination. Furthermore, according to Article 22 of the "Enterprise Bankruptcy Law," "the administrator shall be appointed by the People's Court. Where the creditors' meeting finds that the administrator fails to fairly perform its functions legally or is otherwise not competent at the task, the People's Court may replace such administrator. The measures for appointment of an administrator and for determination of payment of an administrator shall be provided for by the People's Court."[108] In accordance with the "Provisions of the Supreme People's Court on Designating the Administrator during the Trial of Enterprise Bankruptcy Cases" (Fa Shi [2007] No. 8) passed on April 4, 2007, the administrator is designated or replaced by the People's Court, making it difficult to prevent contract termination by the administrator through prior agreements.

Furthermore, there are implications for the return of prepaid rent and compensation for damages after the administrator terminates the contracts related to the energy performance contracting projects. According to the reply letter of the Supreme People's Court (Zui Gao Fa Min Ta [2016] No. 93) in response to the "Request for Clarification on the Application of Law Regarding the Disputes Arising from Executory Lease Contracts Concluded by Bankrupt Enterprises" from the High People's Court of Hunan Province, if a lease contract is deemed terminated, the prepaid rent constitutes unjust enrichment, which should be refunded as required by law. According to *Item 3 of Article 42* of the "*Enterprise Bankruptcy Law,*" debts incurred as a result of the debtor's unjust enrichment shall be regarded as debts of common benefit and shall be returned at any time from the property of the bankrupt enterprise.[109] Moreover, regarding the related damages, as stipulated in Article 53 of the "Enterprise Bankruptcy Law," "where an administrator or debtor revokes a contract according to the provisions of this Law, the other party may declare his claims on the basis of his right to compensation for the damages caused by the revocation."[110] If the contracts in the project are terminated by the administrator, the right of the project owner and other contracting parties to claim compensation for damages will only be treated as common claims. As per Article 113 of the "Enterprise Bankruptcy Law," these claims will be ranked at the very end of all claims, posing a significant risk of non-repayment.[111]

---

[108] Enterprise Bankruptcy Law, Article 22.

[109] See Lou (2021).

[110] Enterprise Bankruptcy Law, Article 53.

[111] See Enterprise Bankruptcy Law, Article 113.

Legal Risks in Power Consumption

Failure to Fulfill Consumption Responsibility Weight

Regarding the national-level obligations and responsibilities for power consumption, if market entities such as grid companies, power sellers, project owners, and users fail to fulfill the minimum consumption responsibility weight and related obligations for renewable power, they face certain legal risks as entities responsible for power consumption.

In order to further promote the high-quality development of new energy power generation and achieve CO_2 emissions peak and carbon neutrality, China has introduced a suite of policy measures aimed at improving the consumption of power, especially new energy power.[112] On May 10, 2019, NDRC and NEA promulgated the "Notice on Establishing and Improving the Guarantee Mechanism for Renewable Power Consumption" (Fa Gai Neng Yuan [2019] No. 807). This notice "decided to set the responsibility weights of renewable power consumption for each provincial administrative region and establish a sound guarantee mechanism for the consumption of renewable power." In addition, the first category of entities responsible for consumption includes "various types of grid companies that directly supply/sell power to users, independent power sellers, and power sellers with the right to operate power distribution networks." These entities are responsible for "consuming an amount in proportion to their annual power sales." The second category includes "uses who purchase power through the power wholesale market and companies with self-supplied power plants." These entities are responsible for "consuming an amount in proportion to their annual power consumption." Additionally, "the State Grid and China Southern Power Grid guide the affiliated provincial grid companies to coordinate the fulfillment of renewable power consumption obligations by market entities within their service areas based on the approved consumption implementation plans of the respective provincial governments." Specifically, market entities can fulfill their consumption obligations not only by actually consuming renewable power but also through methods such as "purchasing excess renewable power from market entities that have exceeded their annual consumption targets (referred to as 'excess consumption') at a mutually agreed transfer (or trading) price"[113] or "voluntarily purchasing renewable energy certificates (referred to as 'green certificates'), with the renewable power associated with these certificates as the power consumption.[114] In terms of technical standards, the notice presents the technical calculation methods in the "Methods for Determining the Responsibility Weights of Renewable Power Consumption and Power Consumption Calculation (Trial)" and also sets forth the responsibility weights of renewable energy and non-hydropower renewable power

[112] See Qiu and Pan (2020).

[113] See Beijing Power Exchange Center (2021).

[114] See Notice of the National Development and Reform Commission and the National Energy Administration on Establishing and Improving the Guarantee Mechanism for Renewable Power Consumption (Fa Gai Neng Yuan [2019] No. 807), Articles 4, 5, and 7.

consumption for each province (including autonomous regions and municipalities directly under the central government) in 2018, 2019, and 2020.[115]

On May 11, 2021, NEA issued the "Notice on Matters Concerning the Development and Construction of Wind and Photovoltaic Power Generation in 2021" (Guo Neng Fa Xin Neng [2021] No. 25). This notice emphasizes the strengthening of the guidance mechanism for the responsibility weights of renewable power consumption. Simultaneously, it calls for the establishment of multiple guarantee mechanisms for grid connection, including guaranteed grid connection and market-based grid connection. According to the notice, "for newly connected projects necessary to meet the minimum consumption responsibility weight for non-hydropower in each province (region or city), guaranteed grid connection shall be implemented by grid companies. In 2021, the scale of guaranteed grid connection should not be less than 90 million kW. The scale of guaranteed grid connection can be exchanged between provinces. If the consumption responsibility weight for non-hydropower is fulfilled through cross-provincial power trading, following negotiations between the sending and receiving provinces, a long-term agreement shall be concluded with the grid companies. Subsequently, the guaranteed grid-connection scale in the sending province shall be reduced for the receiving province and increased for the sending province based on the new energy power transmitted (traded). Guaranteed grid-connection projects shall be organized by the provincial energy authorities through competitive allocation. For grid companies that fall outside the scope of guaranteed grid connection but still wish to be connected to the grid, grid connection can be realized by grid companies through market-based means such as self-construction, joint construction and shared ownership, or purchasing services. Grid-connection conditions mainly include supporting new flexible adjustment capabilities such as pumped hydro storage, storage-type solar thermal power generation, peak shaving of thermal power, new energy storage, and adjustable loads." In Zhejiang Province, the "Implementation Opinions on Further Strengthening the Work Related to Grid Connection Management of Photovoltaic Power Generation" (Zhe Dian Fa Zhan [2015] No. 489) promulgated on June 26, 2015, proposes that it is necessary to maintain sound grid-connection services and expedite the construction of grid-connection projects for PV power generation. The "Zhejiang Province Electric Power Regulations" also proposes specific provisions regarding grid-connection services. Paragraph 1 of Article 28 stipulates that "if power supply, energy storage, and other projects meet the national grid-connection conditions and standards, the power supply enterprises shall provide grid-connection services within the specified time limit and shall not, without authorization, change the grid-connection standards."[116] Essentially, the primary objective of these multiple guarantee mechanisms for grid connection is to ensure the effective fulfillment of responsibility weights of renewable power consumption.

---

[115] See Notice of the National Development and Reform Commission and the National Energy Administration on Establishing and Improving the Guarantee Mechanism for Renewable Power Consumption (Fa Gai Neng Yuan [2019] No. 807), Annexes 1, 2, and 3.

[116] Zhejiang Province Electric Power Regulations, Paragraph 1 of Article 28.

In terms of consumption responsibility weights for each province (city or district),[117] NDRC and NEA issued the "Notice on the Responsibility Weights of Renewable Power Consumption for Provincial Administrative Regions in 2020" (Fa Gai Neng Yuan [2020] No. 767) on May 18, 2020. This notice determines the responsibility weights of renewable power consumption for each province (city or district) in 2020. For Zhejiang Province, the minimum requirement for the overall consumption responsibility weight is 17.5%, with an incentive value of 19.6%. Regarding the non-hydropower consumption responsibility weight, the minimum requirement is 7.5%, with an incentive value of 8.3%.[118] On May 21, 2021, NDRC and NEA issued the "Notice on the Responsibility Weights of Renewable Power Consumption and Related Matters in 2021" (Fa Gai Neng Yuan [2021] No. 704). This notice determines the responsibility weights of renewable power consumption for each province (city or district) in 2021. For Zhejiang Province, the minimum standard for the overall consumption responsibility weight is 18.5%, with an incentive value of 20.5%. Regarding the non-hydropower consumption responsibility weight, the minimum standard is 8.5%, with an incentive value of 9.4%. These values represented an increase compared to the previous year. The notice also proposes the expected targets for the responsibility weight of renewable power consumption in each province (autonomous region, city) in 2022. For Zhejiang Province, the lowest expected value for the overall consumption responsibility weight is 19.46%, while for the non-hydropower consumption responsibility weight, it is 9.75%. These targets indicated an overall upward trend.[119] On April 21, 2022, NEA released the "Notice on the Completion of the Responsibility Weights of Renewable Power Consumption in 2021" (Guo Neng Fa Xin Neng [2022] No. 47). This notice provides an official review and disclosure of the completion of the aforementioned consumption responsibility weight. In both the overall consumption responsibility weight and the non-hydropower consumption responsibility weight, Zhejiang Province has surpassed the minimum standards.[120]

The clear delineation of rights and responsibilities for each entity within regulatory provisions is essential in directing the behavior of each entity. On August 11, 2021, the Zhejiang Provincial Development and Reform Commission issued the "Notice on Soliciting Public Opinions on the 'Implementation Plan of Renewable Power Consumption Guarantee in Zhejiang Province (Draft for Comment)' ." The implementation plan outlines the mechanisms for power consumption guarantee, allocation

---

[117] See Liu (2019).

[118] See National Development and Reform Commission and the National Energy Administration on the Responsibility Weights of Renewable Power Consumption for Provincial Administrative Regions in 2020 (Fa Gai Neng Yuan [2020] No. 767), Annex.

[119] See Notice of the National Development and Reform Commission and the National Energy Administration on the Responsibility Weights of Renewable Power Consumption and Related Matters in 2021 (Fa Gai Neng Yuan [2021] No. 704), Annexes 1 and 2.

[120] See Notice of the National Energy Administration on the Completion of the Responsibility Weights of Renewable Power Consumption in 2021 (Guo Neng Fa Xin Neng [2022] No. 47), Annex.

of consumption responsibility weights, management mechanisms for entities, fulfillment of consumption responsibility weights, division of work, relevant measures, and organizational implementation for renewable power consumption in Zhejiang Province. Regarding the market entities responsible for power consumption, the first category of entities includes power sales companies, that is, "various types of grid companies that directly supply/sell power to users, independent power sellers, and power sellers with the right to operate power distribution networks." Additionally, "the provincial power company assumes the assessment responsibilities for non-market users, except the third category of entities, including residents, agricultural and important public utilities, public services, and other users who do not purchase power through the power market. The second category includes power users, "who purchase power through the power wholesale market (excluding power users who sell power through power sales companies as agents) and companies with self-supplied power plants." Regarding the fulfillment of consumption responsibility weights, the entities can either "purchase or generate renewable power, and their actual utilization of renewable power (referred to as 'consumption') is the metric for fulfilling their assigned consumption responsibility weights. Alternatively, entities may "voluntarily purchase renewable energy certificates (referred to as 'green certificates') and Zhejiang Province's green power credits. The renewable power equivalent represented by these green certificates and green power credits shall be accounted for as consumption, with each green certificate and green power credit equating to 1000 and 100 kWh of renewable energy consumption, respectively. Moreover, entities are permitted to engage in "excess consumption trading across provinces." In terms of measures related to consumption responsibility weights, the implementation plan proposes an assessment mechanism for the renewable power consumption responsibilities and a reward and punishment mechanism. For example, in the assessment, consideration will be given to the renewable energy consumption that companies have already undertaken in carbon emission assessment. Regarding the reward and punishment mechanism, entities providing false data, failing to rectify within the specified timeframe, and refusing to fulfill consumption responsibility weight obligations may face penalties. The provincial development and reform commission (provincial energy administration) will establish a punishment mechanism, including the withdrawal of special funds for renewable energy and inclusion in joint disciplinary records for adverse credit.[121]

Therefore, fulfilling consumption responsibility weights is a regulatory obligation for power companies, power distribution companies, power sellers, and energy performance contracting users. Failure to fulfill the minimum consumption responsibility weights may result in negative consequences such as the imposition of accountability assessments and penalties on these market entities.

[121] See Zhejiang Provincial Development and Reform Commission. Notice on Soliciting Public Opinions on the "Implementation Plan of Renewable Power Consumption Guarantee in Zhejiang Province (Draft for Comment)", released on August 11, 2021.

Limitations on Safe Grid Operation

Regarding the utilization of rooftop distributed PV power generation, due to the inherent issues of frequency instability, voltage instability, and difficulties in maintaining balance and peak-load regulation, its grid connection may impact the safety and stability of the power system, thereby exposing grid companies to significant legal risks.[122]

Concerning the utilization of renewable energy sources, self-consumption alone may not fully accommodate the generated power capacity. Therefore, it's often necessary to connect to the grid to manage the excess capacity.[123] In this regard, grid companies are obliged to provide grid-connection services for distributed PV power generation. Concerning the improvement of grid connection and operation services for PV power generation, the "Several Opinions on Promoting the Healthy Development of the Photovoltaic Industry" (Guo Fa [2013] No. 24) issued by the State Council on July 4, 2013, proposes that "grid companies shall provide grid-connection services for PV power generation by optimizing system dispatch and operation and prioritizing the operation of PV power generation to ensure timely grid connection of PV projects and full purchase of the generated power. Grid companies shall also simplify the grid-connection methods and management procedure for distributed PV power generation, making the grid-connection service process publicly available. This initiative aims to create a simple and efficient grid-connection service system. Moreover, distributed PV power generation projects shall be exempted from system reserve capacity charges and other related service fees. Additionally, grid companies shall strengthen the supervision of grid connection and operation for PV power generation." Pursuant to the "Interim Measures for the Management of Distributed PV Power Generation Projects" (Guo Neng Xin Neng [2013] No. 433) issued by the National Energy Administration on November 18, 2013, grid companies shall provide services such as grid connection and operation, metering, and settlement for distributed PV power generation projects.[124] In accordance with the "Opinions on Facilitating Grid Connection Services for Distributed PV Power Generation (Interim)" issued on October 26, 2012, grid companies shall "actively foster conditions that ease the grid connection of distributed PV power generation projects, and create a 'green channel' to facilitate the construction of connection system projects." Additionally, grid companies shall offer a suite of services such as application acceptance based on the grid-connection procedure, formulation and consultation of grid-connection system plans, and management of grid-connection acceptance and grid-connection testing.[125] On January 28, 2022, the National Energy Administration held a press conference to release the grid connection and operation of renewable energy in 2021 and answer related questions. In terms of PV power

---

[122] See The Economic Daily (2022).

[123] See Energy Saver (2023).

[124] See National Energy Administration. Interim Measures for the Management of Distributed PV Power Generation Projects (Guo Neng Xin Neng [2013] No. 433).

[125] See Zhao (2014).

generation construction and operation, distributed PV accounted for over 50% of the total increase in national PV capacity in 2021. Regarding the utilization rate of PV power generation, the national utilization rate reached 98% in 2021, with a significant improvement in PV consumption in some regions.[126] According to the "China's Policies and Actions for Addressing Climate Change (2022)" released by MEE on October 27, 2022, by the end of 2021, the installed capacity of solar PV power generation in buildings reached 18.16 million kW. By 2030, the total installed capacity of wind power and solar power generation will exceed 12 kW. This data underscores the rapid development in distributed PV installations and grid connection and operation. Consequently, the utilization rate of PV power generation has also witnessed a rise.[127]

However, as the proportion of distributed PV systems grows, they become increasingly connected to the grid, and PV consumption is on the rise, market entities shall fulfill their assigned minimum consumption responsibility weights, while also considering the potential negative impact on grid operations that may arise from connecting distributed PV systems.[128]

The PV and other renewable energy sources exhibit a lack of stability, primarily characterized by strong intermittency, volatility, and randomness. The control technology for renewable energy generation also presents significant difficulties, posing a huge obstacle to the capacity of power grids to accommodate these sources. Specifically, new energy sources such as wind and solar power present strong randomness and large fluctuations in their power generation, leading to instability and intermittency. When this unstable and intermittent power is fed into the grid, it introduces uncontrollable fluctuating power into the traditional grid. This can result in significant electrical surges within the grid, causing voltage fluctuations or deviations in power frequency. Such occurrences present novel challenges to the safe and stable operation of the power system.[129] On July 4, 2013, the State Council issued the "Several Opinions on Promoting the Healthy Development of the Photovoltaic Industry" (Guo Fa [2013] No. 24), which calls for the improvement of grid-connection management and services. It states that there should be an "enhancement in the construction of supporting power grids. Grid companies shall strengthen the construction and transformation of power grids compatible with PV power generation to ensure that supporting power grids and PV projects are completed and put into operation simultaneously. There is also a push for the active development of microgrids and smart grids that integrate advanced energy storage and information technologies to increase the grid system's capacity to accommodate PV power generation. For PV power generation projects connected to the public grid, the connection works and the public grid transformation for the connection shall be invested in and constructed by the grid companies. For distributed PV power generation connected to the user

[126] See National Energy Administration (2022).

[127] See Ministry of Ecology and Environment. China's Policies and Actions for Addressing Climate Change (2022 Annual Report).

[128] See Luoqima (2021).

[129] See Kang and Qu (2014)

side, the public grid transformation caused by the connection shall be invested in and constructed by the grid companies." The specific entities responsible for construction include both power companies and project owners. In terms of grid transformation, the "Opinions on Facilitating Grid Connection Services for Distributed PV Power Generation (Interim)" issued on October 26, 2012, states that the connection works and the public grid transformation for distributed PV projects connected to the public grid shall be invested in and constructed by the grid companies. For distributed PV power generation projects connected to the user side, the connection works shall be invested in and constructed by the project owners, while the public grid transformation for the connection shall be invested in and constructed by the grid companies (in western regions, the grid-connection works are governed by the national current investment policies).[130]

National policies concerning power grid construction also closely align with the development of new energy and distributed power sources.[131] For example, the "Notice on Soliciting Public Opinions on the 'Implementation Plan of Renewable Power Consumption Guarantee in Zhejiang Province (Draft for Comment)'" issued on August 11, 2021, also emphasizes the importance of grid construction, demanding the guaranteed connection and full consumption of renewable power. Power companies shall implement a system of full guaranteed purchase for renewable energy power generation, accelerate the construction of an integrated and highly resilient power grid, and actively advance the planning and construction of ultra-high-voltage (UHV) AC ring networks. These measures create favorable conditions for the connection of renewable energy sources to the grid. There is also a push to expedite the construction of facilities such as small- and medium-sized pumped-storage power stations and electrochemical energy storage stations to enhance the grid's peak- real-timeshaving capabilities. This not only ensures the safe and stable operation of the power grid, but also fosters the prioritized consumption of renewable power.[132] According to Paragraphs 1–2 of Article 29 of the "Zhejiang Province Electric Power Regulations," "power supply companies shall enhance the grid intelligence to increase their capacity to accommodate renewable power. They shall give priority to dispatching renewable energy for power generation, fully purchasing the grid-connected power from renewable energy projects that meet the grid-connection standards within their coverage area, and settling payments in a timely and full manner in accordance with relevant national and provincial regulations." According to Article 56, "power supply companies shall conduct routine inspections and tests on power facilities for which they are responsible, to identify and rectify any potential safety hazards in power operation and power quality issues, thereby guaranteeing a safe and stable power supply. Additionally, users shall ensure the safety of their power facilities and equipment and shall take measures to prevent safety accidents. If their power

130 See Guo (2013).

131 See State Grid Corporation of China (2018).

132 Zhejiang Provincial Development and Reform Commission. Notice on Soliciting Public Opinions on the "Implementation Plan of Renewable Power Consumption Guarantee in Zhejiang Province (Draft for Comment)", released on August 11, 2021.

facilities and equipment present a risk to personal safety or the safety of power operation, immediate actions shall be taken immediately, including inspection, repair, or decommissioning to mitigate risks."[133] Within the grid companies, measures need to be taken to address the massive connection of distributed PV into the distribution grid. For example, the "Notice on Strictly Implementing National Standards to Further Strengthen the Regulation and Management of Distributed Photovoltaics" (Zhe Dian Tiao Zi [2022] No. 25) issued on March 29, 2022, highlights issues such as significant voltage fluctuations, voltage over-limit, and frequent tap changer operations on the main transformer in localized power grids. These issues not only disrupt power usage for users but also diminish the reliability of power equipment, thereby constraining the consumption of distributed PV power. The notice also stipulates that distributed PV systems connected at different voltage levels must possess specific adjustable capabilities. There is a drive to advance the implementation of on-premise reactive voltage control, automatic voltage control (AVC), automatic generation control (AGC), and information reporting functionalities for distributed PV systems connected at 380 V and 10 kV. These measures are crucial to ensure the safe and stable operation of an active distribution grid within the new power system and to facilitate the consumption of distributed PV power. In addition to considering their consumption obligations, various entities such as power companies, power distribution companies, power sellers, and energy performance contracting users must also navigate the operational safety and regulatory limits of the power grids. Moreover, they shall assume responsibilities related to the grid construction.

To mitigate the impact of power factor fluctuations, regulatory guidelines have been put in place to adjust electricity tariffs according to varying power factors. These adjustments aim to optimize the utilization of generation, power, and electrical equipment, thereby enhancing power efficiency and voltage quality. According to the "Notice on Issuing the 'Measures for Adjusting Electricity Tariffs Based on Power Factors'" ((83) Shui Dian Cai Zi No. 215) issued by the Ministry of Water Resources and Electric Power and the State Administration for Commodity Prices on December 2, 1983, "electricity tariffs for the month are calculated based on the determined power factor. If the power factor is above or below the specified standard, the monthly electricity tariffs, as calculated according to the stipulated electricity tariffs, will then be increased or decreased according to the percentages set out in the 'Power-factor-based Electricity Tariff Adjustment Tables' (Tables 1, 2, and 3). If a user's power factor falls between two numbers listed in the 'Power-factor-based Electricity Tariff Adjustment Tables', it will be calculated by rounding to the nearest value."[134] The tables use different numerical values as standard benchmarks. If the actual power factor is below the standard value, the user shall bear the additional electricity tariff. The power factor-based electricity tariff adjustment mechanism is designed to encourage users and other entities to make rational use of electricity

---

[133] Zhejiang Province Electric Power Regulations, Paragraphs 1–2 of Article 29 and Article 56.

[134] The Ministry of Water Resources and Electric Power, and the State Administration for Commodity Prices. Measures for Adjusting Electricity Tariffs Based on Power Factors (83 Shui Dian Cai Zi No. 215).

according to the established standard benchmarks. Otherwise, they may incur the risk of an increase in electricity bills.

Storage Challenges or Power Wastage

Given the variability and randomness of PV power generation, its output does not always align with users' peak and off-peak power demand. This mismatch can result in excess power that poses storage challenges or power wastage, ultimately detracting from the economic benefits of energy performance contracting projects.

In energy performance contracting projects, there are three operational models for distributed PV power generation: "full feed-in," "full self-consumption," and "self-consumption with surplus electricity fed into the grid." Regardless of the operational model employed, if the project owner cannot fully utilize the generated power either through self-consumption or feed-in, they may face challenges with power storage or wastage. This, in turn, may affect the economic viability of the project. As per the "Notice on Issuing the 'Clean Energy Consumption Action Plan (2018–2020)'" (Fa Gai Neng Yuan Gui [2018] No. 1575) issued by the National Development and Reform Commission and the National Energy Administration on October 30, 2018, by 2020, clean energy consumption issues should be largely resolved, with a PV power utilization rate exceeding 95% and a curtailment rate below 5%.[135] As per the "Notice on Matters Concerning the Development and Construction of Wind and Photovoltaic Power Generation in 2021" (Guo Neng Fa Xin Neng [2021] No. 25)" issued by the National Energy Administration on May 11, 2021, "targets for the consumption responsibility weight of renewable power and the reasonable utilization rate of new energy for each provincial administrative region shall be established and released. This is intended to guide the energy regulatory departments at the provincial level to adhere to their respective targets for non-hydropower renewable power consumption and reasonable utilization rates of new energy." In addition, the "Notice on Issuing the 'Management Measures for PV Power Station Consumption Monitoring and Statistics'" (Guo Neng Fa Xin Neng Gui [2021] No. 57) issued by the National Energy Administration on December 3, 2021, establishes a monitoring system and information release mechanism for PV power station consumption, as well as centralized methods for calculating the utilization rate of PV power stations.[136] The specific targets for the reasonable utilization rate of PV power and the centralized calculation methods are conducive to maximizing the use of generated power. However, despite these measures, the curtailment resulting from the existing instability in PV power generation can still lead to decreased overall economic efficiency.

---

[135] See Notice of the National Development and Reform Commission and the National Energy Administration on Issuing the "Clean Energy Consumption Action Plan (2018–2020)" (Fa Gai Neng Yuan Gui [2018] No. 1575).

[136] See Notice on Issuing the "Management Measures for PV Power Station Consumption Monitoring and Statistics" (Guo Neng Fa Xin Neng Gui [2021] No. 57).

Firstly, in practice, the method of commercial discounts plays a foundational role, and there is a lack of clear agreements regarding the obligation to consume power. In response to concerns about the curtailment of wind and solar power, research results indicate that for energy performance contracting projects, users' power consumption levels are often tied to commercial discounts. This approach can mitigate the issue of power curtailment to some extent. As mentioned earlier, the consumption of renewable energy sources such as PV power is limited by the operational safety of the power grid and its regulatory capacity. Power that is not consumed promptly and cannot be stored will be wasted. In practice, however, energy performance contracting projects typically follow the model of "self-consumption with surplus electricity fed into the grid." The public grid is generally capable of managing the feed-in of excess power. As a result, although there are many special provisions as commercial terms in energy performance contracts, explicit clauses that define users' obligations to consume power are less common. Instead, these contracts often include provisions that offer commercial discounts when users achieve a certain level of power consumption. This lessens the challenges associated with power storage and the potential power wastage.

Secondly, deviation settlement can significantly impact various entities such as power users and power sellers. For trading of power connected to the grid, a deviation settlement mechanism is adopted during the power trading process to encourage the maximized utilization of generated power by imposing charges for settling negative deviations. As per Item 4 of Article 12 of the "Notice on the Issuance of the 'Basic Rules for Medium- and Long-term Electricity Trading (Interim)'" (Fa Gai Neng Yuan [2016] No. 2784) issued by the National Development and Reform Commission and the National Energy Administration on December 29, 2016, it is required to "properly manage the grid's operation to guarantee the execution of power trading results (When deviations arise between actual execution and the agreed trading results due to the power dispatching organization's reasons, the grid company to which the dispatching organization belongs shall be responsible for the resulting economic liabilities) ."[137] Similarly, on December 17, 2021, the Zhejiang Provincial Development and Reform Commission, the National Energy Administration Zhejiang Regulatory Office, and the Zhejiang Provincial Energy Bureau jointly issued the "Notice on the Issuance of the 'Zhejiang Province Medium- to Long-term Electricity Trading Rules (Revision 2021)' ." This notice further specifies that all entities involved in the power market, including power users, power sellers, grid companies purchasing power on behalf of users, power generators, and grid companies, shall take into account any deviation charges stipulated in the trading contracts when settling electricity tariffs.[138]

[137] Notice of the National Development and Reform Commission, and National Energy Administration on Issuance of the "Basic Rules for Medium- and Long-term Electricity Trading (Interim)" (Fa Gai Neng Yuan [2016] No. 2784).

[138] See Notice of the Zhejiang Provincial Development and Reform Commission, National Energy Administration Zhejiang Regulatory Office, and Zhejiang Provincial Energy Bureau on the Issuance of the "Zhejiang Province Medium- to Long-term Electricity Trading Rules (Revision 2021)" (Zhe Fa Gai Neng Yuan [2021] No. 427).

With respect to the deviation adjustment settlement for wholesale market users, as per Article 98 of "Zhejiang Province Medium- to Long-term Electricity Trading Rules (Revision 2021)" (hereinafter referred to as the Rules), "wholesale market consumers can minimize the electricity consumption deviation using methods such as monthly bilateral negotiation, monthly centralized bidding, monthly listing for quotation, and monthly adjustment to annual contracts. Any electricity consumption deviation from the contracted monthly volume is incorporated into their transaction contracts as a deviation charge. If the consumers' actual electricity consumption during peak, mid-peak, and off-peak periods deviates from the monthly contracted volumes for these periods, the deviation for each period will be calculated separately and settled accordingly. Specifically, according to Item 1 of Article 100 of the Rules, any electricity consumption of wholesale market consumers during peak, mid-peak, or off-peak periods that exceeds the monthly contracted volume for the corresponding period shall be settled separately based on the deviation ratio. For actual electricity consumption during peak, mid-peak, and off-peak periods that fall between 105 and 120% or above 120% of the monthly contracted volume for the corresponding period, the part that exceeds the contracted volume for the corresponding period will be settled at the clearing price from the most recent and shortest cycle of centralized bidding in the market. The deviated electricity volume will incur a transaction contract deviation charge based on a specific percentage of the current benchmark price for regulated coal-fired power units in Zhejiang Province. Specifically, according to Item 2 of Article 100 of the Rules, any electricity consumption of wholesale market consumers during peak, mid-peak, or off-peak periods that is less than the monthly contracted volume for the corresponding period shall be settled separately based on the deviation ratio. For actual electricity consumption during peak, mid-peak, and off-peak periods that fall between 80 and 95% or below 80% of the monthly contracted volume for the corresponding period, the actual electricity consumption during these periods will be settled at agreed prices following the sequence of monthly bilateral negotiation trading, monthly centralized bidding, monthly listing for quotation, annual bilateral negotiation, and annual listing for quotation. The deviated electricity volume will incur a transaction contract deviation charge based on a specific percentage of the current benchmark price for regulated coal-fired power units in Zhejiang Province.[139]

With respect to the deviation adjustment settlement for power sellers, as per Article 102 of the Rules, "power sellers can minimize the electricity consumption deviation using methods such as monthly bilateral negotiation, monthly centralized bidding, monthly listing for quotation, and monthly adjustment to annual contracts. Any electricity consumption deviation from the contracted monthly volume is incorporated

[139] Notice of the Zhejiang Provincial Development and Reform Commission, National Energy Administration Zhejiang Regulatory Office, and Zhejiang Provincial Energy Bureau on the Issuance of the "Zhejiang Province Medium- to Long-term Electricity Trading Rules (Revision 2021)" (Zhe Fa Gai Neng Yuan [2021] No. 427), Article 98, and Items (1) and (2) of Article 100.

into their transaction contracts as a deviation charge. If the power sellers' actual electricity consumption deviates from the monthly contracted volumes during peak, mid-peak, and off-peak periods, the deviation for each period will be calculated separately and settled accordingly. Specifically, according to Item 1 of Article 104 of the Rules, any electricity consumption of power sellers during peak, mid-peak, or off-peak periods that exceeds the monthly contracted volume for the corresponding period shall be settled separately based on the deviation ratio. For actual electricity consumption during peak, mid-peak, and off-peak periods that fall between 105 and 120% or above 120% of the monthly contracted volume for the corresponding period, the part that exceeds the contracted volume for the corresponding period will be settled at the clearing price from the most recent and shortest cycle of centralized bidding in the market. The deviated electricity volume will incur a transaction contract deviation charge based on a specific percentage of the current benchmark price for regulated coal-fired power units in Zhejiang Province. Specifically, according to Item 2 of Article 104 of the Rules, any electricity consumption of power sellers during peak, mid-peak, or off-peak periods that is less than the monthly contracted volume for the corresponding period shall be settled separately based on the deviation ratio. For actual electricity consumption during peak, mid-peak, and off-peak periods that fall between 80 and 95% or below 80% of the monthly contracted volume for the corresponding period, the actual electricity consumption during these periods will be settled at agreed prices following the sequence of monthly bilateral negotiation trading, monthly centralized bidding, monthly listing for quotation, annual bilateral negotiation, and annual listing for quotation. The deviated electricity volume will incur a transaction contract deviation charge based on a specific percentage of the current benchmark price for regulated coal-fired power units in Zhejiang Province.[140]

Furthermore, due to the impact of the COVID-19 pandemic, some regions have also made provisions to reduce or exempt deviation charges. For example, on April 15, 2022, the Zhejiang Provincial Energy Bureau issued the "Notice on Reducing or Exempting the Deviation Settlement Charges of Medium- and Long-term Power Trading for March 2022." As per the notice, for wholesale market consumers in pandemic-affected areas, under certain conditions, the negative deviation settlement charges for the medium- and long-term power trading in March will be reduced or exempted. Similarly, for retail consumers in pandemic-affected areas, under certain conditions, the negative deviation settlement charges for the medium- and long-term power trading in March are recommended to be reduced or exempted. The deviation settlement mechanism aims to motivate users, power sellers, and other related entities to use electricity in a timely and appropriate manner as agreed upon. Failure to do so may result in the potential imposition of deviation settlement charges.

[140] Notice of the Zhejiang Provincial Development and Reform Commission, National Energy Administration Zhejiang Regulatory Office, and Zhejiang Provincial Energy Bureau on the Issuance of the "Zhejiang Province Medium- to Long-term Electricity Trading Rules (Revision 2021)" (Zhe Fa Gai Neng Yuan [2021] No. 427), Article 102, and Items (1) and (2) of Article 104.

Legal Risks in Market-Based Trading for Distributed Power Generation

Market-based trading for distributed power generation, also known as "direct local electricity trading," allows distributed energy projects to directly sell electricity to nearby energy consumers through the distribution grid. In this case, the grid company only charges "grid-connection fees" for the transmission and distribution services.[141] This means that the electricity generated by distributed projects can be traded with a diverse range of power users across a more extensive area, moving beyond the constraints of a single user. This mode effectively addresses the instability issues that project owners often face and the challenges associated with tariff collection under the "self-consumption with surplus electricity fed into the grid" model.[142] Compared to full feed-in projects, those engaging in market-based trading for distributed power generation can secure higher trading tariffs. The introduction of market-based trading for distributed power generation will further drive reforms toward market-based trading, expanding the sales channels for distributed projects. This shift will not only boost profitability but also diminish dependence on subsidies.

In 2017, NDRC and NEA jointly issued the "Notice on Launching a Pilot Market-based Trading for Distributed Power Generation" (Fa Gai Neng Yuan [2017] No. 1901), ushering in a new phase of market-based trading for distributed power generation in China. Firstly, the notice clarifies the scale limit of distributed power generation projects to ensure that the generated electricity can be consumed locally within the grid-connected voltage range. Specifically, the conditions for such projects are as follows: Stand-alone capacity should not exceed 20 megawatts, and the grid-connected voltage level should be at or below 35. For stand-alone projects with capacities exceeding 20 MW but not exceeding 50 mW, the grid-connected voltage level should not exceed 110 kW, and electricity should be consumed locally within this voltage range. The voltage limit is set at 110 kV primarily to prevent power from being fed back into the high-voltage grid of 220 kV. Secondly, the notice identifies three trading modes for distributed power generation: "direct trading," "entrusted trading," and "feed-in tariff purchase." Direct trading allows distributed generation project entities to engage in trading directly with power users, while grid companies charge the "grid-connection fees." This trading is typically confined to the power supply area of the transformer upstream from the connection point. In entrusted trading, distributed generation project entities entrust grid companies with the task of selling electricity on their behalf, with grid companies deducting the "grid-connection fees" from the comprehensive electricity tariffs. Feed-in tariff purchase refers to the purchase of electricity at the government-regulated feed-in tariff. Thirdly, the notice specifies that the "grid-connection fee" is tentatively determined based on the differential pricing for power transmission and distribution at different voltage levels. The standard "grid-connection fee" for distributed power generation is determined based

---

[141] See Li (2017).

[142] See Lin et al. (2021).

on the grid-connected voltage level and the classification of power transmission and consumption areas. But before the final determination, the fee is tentatively calculated by deducting the transmission and distribution price at the highest voltage level in the market-based trading for distributed power generation from the transmission and distribution price of the provincial grid's public network (including policy-based cross-subsidies) at the voltage level where the power user is connected.[143]

Since then, the pilot market-based trading for distributed power generation has gained additional momentum. On January 7, 2019, the National Development and Reform Commission and the National Energy Administration jointly issued the "Notice on Actively Promoting Subsidy-Free Grid Parity for Wind and Photovoltaic Power Generation" (Fa Gai Neng Yuan [2019] No. 19) In terms of pricing policy, this notice clarifies that "for the pilot market-based trading projects for distributed power generation included in the national pilot demonstrations, the traded electricity will only be subject to the transmission and distribution price of the distribution grid associated with the voltage level required for wind and PV power projects' grid connection and consumption. These projects are exempt from transmission fees for bypassed voltage levels. For renewable power for direct local trading that is included in the pilot, policy-based cross-subsidies will be reduced or exempted." In alignment with the national directive to encourage subsidy-free grid parity of PV and wind power generation,[144] the first batch of pilot regions for market-based trading for distributed power generation was launched in May 2019 ("First-batch Pilot Notice"). The "Notice of the General Office of the National Development and Reform Commission and the Comprehensive Affairs Department of the National Energy Administration on the Announcement of the First Batch of Pilot Grid Parity Projects for Wind and Photovoltaic Power Generation in 2019" (Fa Gai Ban Neng Yuan [2019] No. 594) was released on May 20, 2019, announcing the first batch of 26 pilot regions for market-based trading for distributed power generation, with a total capacity of 1.47 million kW.[145] In December 2019, Jiangsu Province, one of the pilot regions, took the lead in establishing local trading rules with the "Jiangsu Province Market-based Trading Rules for Distributed Power Generation" (collectively referred to as "Jiangsu Trading Pilot Policy" together with the "Jiangsu Pilot Notice"). In March 2020, the "Jiangsu Pilot Notice" was issued, specifying the scope, scale, and capacity in the pilot regions for market-based trading for distributed power generation in Jiangsu Province.

Since the end of 2021, the phrase "market-based trading for distributed power generation" has been increasingly prevalent in key national policy documents. On

[143] See Notice of the National Development and Reform Commission and the National Energy Administration on Launching a Pilot Market-based Trading for Distributed Power Generation (Fa Gai Neng Yuan [2017] No. 1901).

[144] See Chen et al. (2019).

[145] See Notice of the General Office of the National Development and Reform Commission and the Comprehensive Affairs Department of the National Energy Administration on the Announcement of the First Batch of Pilot Grid Parity Projects for Wind and Photovoltaic Power Generation in 2019 (Fa Gai Ban Neng Yuan [2019] No. 594).

December 22, 2021, the National Energy Administration released the "Implementation Opinions on Deepening the 'Streamlining Administration, Delegating Power and Strengthening Regulation and Improving Services' Reform to Improve the Business Environment in the Energy Sector" (Guo Neng Fa Fa Gai [2021] No. 63). It explicitly "supports the involvement of distributed generation in market-based trading." On December 29, 2021, the National Energy Administration, along with two other ministries and commissions, jointly issued the "Implementation Opinions on Accelerating Rural Energy Transformation and Development and Helping Rural Revitalisation" (Guo Neng Fa Gui Hua [2021] No. 66). This document proposes the "innovative development of new models such as direct supply of new energy and direct local electricity trading." This marks the first time the concept of "direct local electricity trading" has been introduced in national policies. On January 18, 2022, the National Development and Reform Commission and the National Energy Administration released the "Guiding Opinions on Accelerating the Construction of a National Unified Power Market System" (Guo Gai Ti Gai [2022] No. 118). This document advocates for "improving the market-based trading mechanism for distributed power generation; encouraging distributed PV and distributed wind power entities to directly trade with surrounding users." On January 29, 2022, NDRC and NEA issued the "14th Five-Year Plan for a Modern Energy System" (Fa Gai Neng Yuan [2022] No. 210), which calls for "the improvement of pricing policies and market rules that support market-based trading for distributed power generation."

However, the implementation of this market-based trading has run into considerable challenges.[146] In December 2019, only Jiangsu Province in the pilot projects took the initiative to issue the "Jiangsu Province Market-based Trading Rules for Distributed Power Generation." In March 2020, the "Jiangsu Pilot Notice" was issued, specifying the scope, scale, and capacity in the pilot regions for market-based trading for distributed power generation in Jiangsu Province. In December 2020, Zhenglu Industrial Park in Tianning District, Changzhou City, Jiangsu Province ushered in a milestone with the smooth grid connection of a 5 MW pilot market-based trading project for distributed power generation. This initiative stood as the first to become operational among all national pilot projects. Building on this progress, in 2021, Shandong and Zhejiang provinces released official guidelines to foster the local development and utilization of distributed renewable power by conducting market-based trading. Despite the initial successes, as of now, only a handful of the first batch of 26 pilot projects announced by China have been successfully commissioned. The underlying challenge hindering broader implementation lies in the existing structure of the power system. It proves difficult to reallocate "power, responsibilities, and interests" among grid companies and other stakeholders in the short term, when it comes to executing market-based trading for distributed power generation. Local power supply companies currently have fixed electricity sales targets, and the introduction of market-based trading for distributed power generation would necessitate them to cede a portion of their sales. Furthermore, the shift toward market-based trading places new demands on grid companies. They are required to facilitate

[146] See Policy Tailwinds Pick Up (2022).

the transmission and distribution of power, provide technical support, and manage the trading process itself. In cases where market-based trading contracts cannot be enforced, they must purchase the full electricity generated by the trading projects. All of these increase the operational costs for the grid companies.[147]

Acknowledging this challenge, the "Notice on Launching a Pilot Market-based Trading for Distributed Power Generation" stipulates that grid companies can charge "grid-connection fees" for market-based trading for distributed power generation. Therefore, the charging standard has become a critical factor in determining the smooth implementation of the pilot projects for market-based trading for distributed power generation. But the current standards for the grid-connection fees still fall short in a few areas.[148]

One issue is the imbalance of "power, responsibilities, and interests" in the current grid-connection fee structure. For entities and users involved in the market-based trading for distributed power generation, grid companies have an unlimited obligation to provide a failsafe power supply, while the distributed power generation entities and users do not fully bear the transmission and distribution costs. Distributed power sources, like wind and solar, offer intermittent supply and cannot guarantee stable, continuous power to users. This requires grid companies to handle transmission capacity reserves and ensure backup supply. On the one hand, market-based trading for distributed power generation demands technical support from grid companies for grid connection, transmission, distribution, and reliable supply to users, along with services like power balancing, metering, and billing. On the other hand, the large-scale connection of distributed power sources significantly impacts distribution network flow and operational boundaries, raising the bar for network upgrades, transformations, and operation control. However, the "Notice on Launching a Pilot Market-based Trading for Distributed Power Generation" proposes a grid-connection fee based on the differential pricing for power transmission and distribution at different voltage levels. This effectively prevents grid companies from recovering the capacity and reserve costs of the higher-level network, while reducing costs for the trading parties. Moreover, under current regulations, any discrepancies in the volume of electricity through market-based trading for distributed power generation are ultimately reconciled by the power dispatching organizations. The pricing mechanisms for ancillary services in place across most provinces are confined to the power generation sector, clearly neglecting the users' role as beneficiaries. This oversight disregards the principle of fair responsibility among participants in market-based trading.

The second issue pertains to the difficulty in recovering cross-subsidies from the grid-connection fee. The current electricity pricing system incorporates hidden cross-subsidies, making them difficult to delineate from the grid-connection fee for market-based trading for distributed power generation. The fee structure uses voltage levels as the only metric, but the cross-subsidies in the system are complex and layered, entangled across various voltage levels and user categories. As a result, the distribution

[147] See Hou and Lu (2020).

[148] See Fan and Wang (2022).

prices for voltages at or below 110 kV are undervalued, and the true costs of transmission and distribution across different user groups and voltage levels remain opaque. This complexity presents significant challenges in calculating the grid-connection fee for market-based trading for distributed power generation by merely adjusting for the transmission and distribution tariffs that vary by voltage level. As the trading pilot progresses, it is imperative to conduct a thorough assessment and provide clarity on the extent of policy-based cross-subsidies.

The third issue arises in reconciling the grid-connection fees for market-based trading for distributed power generation with national policies on energy conservation and emissions reduction. NDRC, the Ministry of Industry and Information Technology (MIIT), along with 11 other ministries and commissions, released the "Notice on the Issuance of Several Policies to Promote Steady Growth of the Industrial Economy." This notice advocates for the integration of various electricity pricing policies, including differential, tiered, and punitive pricing schemes. The aim is to establish a unified tiered pricing system specifically for industries with high-energy consumption. This initiative aims to motivate such companies to boost their investment in energy-saving and emission reduction technologies. It also seeks to decrease energy and carbon emissions on a per-unit basis and to use pricing as a tool to drive industrial transformation and upgrading, while preventing local authorities from introducing preferential electricity pricing due to a plethora of policy options.[149] If distributed generation projects participate in market-based trading to supply power directly to high-energy-consuming companies, this would contradict the national tiered pricing system for industries with high-energy consumption. Such a discrepancy is not aligned with the national "dual carbon" objectives and the agenda for energy conservation and emissions reduction. Additionally, it may lead to high-energy-consuming users engaged in market-based trading for distributed power generation projects obtaining electricity at preferential rates due to specific pricing policies. In contrast, high-energy-consuming companies not involved in market-based trading may face higher electricity costs. This disparity could be perceived as inequitable in the business environment.

Legal Risks of Price Fluctuations

Based on different operation modes of rooftop distributed photovoltaic power generation, there are two billing methods: "net metering" and "bidirectional metering with bidirectional settlement." The price of electricity generated by photovoltaic systems is subject to national policy influences, which introduces the legal risk of price fluctuations. This, in turn, may lead to disputes over electricity prices or subsidies.

[149] See National Development and Reform commission and Ministry of Industry and Information Technology, et al.. Notice on the Issuance of Several Policies to Promote Steady Growth of the Industrial Economy (Fa Gai Chan Ye [2022] No. 273).

China has implemented a price reduction policy for solar photovoltaic power generation to promote technological progress in this field, reduce costs and enhance market competitiveness.[150] On July 24, 2011, NDRC issued the "Notice on Improving the Feed-in Tariff Policy for Solar Photovoltaic Power Generation" (Fa Gai Jia Ge [2011] No. 1594), which proposed the establishment of a national unified benchmark feed-in tariff for solar photovoltaic power generation. The tariffs were set at CNY 1.15 and CNY 1 per kilowatt-hour.[151] On July 4, 2013, the State Council released the "Several Opinions on Promoting the Healthy Development of the Photovoltaic Industry" (Guo Fa [2013] No. 24), which refined relevant supportive policies. These include policies that strongly promote user-side photovoltaic applications (e.g., "self-generated electricity for self-consumption is not subject to tiered electricity pricing and is considered in the energy savings of local governments and users"), policies that enhance tariffs and subsidies (e.g., "Implement a policy of subsidizing distributed photovoltaic power generation according to electricity output"), policies that improve the management of subsidy funds (e.g., "For distributed photovoltaic power generation, establish a system where grid companies transfer subsidy funds on a monthly basis"), and policies that increase fiscal and taxation policy support (e.g., "Exempt government funds levied on electricity, such as renewable energy tariff surcharges, for the self-consumed electricity from distributed photovoltaic power generation"). On August 26, 2013, NDRC issued the "Notice on Utilizing Price Leverage to Promote the Healthy Development of the Photovoltaic Industry," setting standards for the pricing of distributed photovoltaic power generation. On one hand, a subsidy policy based on total electricity generated was implemented for distributed PV power generation, with a subsidy rate of CNY 0.42 per kilowatt-hour (tax-inclusive, same as below). This subsidy was funded by the Renewable Energy Development Fund and disbursed by grid companies. For surplus electricity fed into the grid from distributed PV systems, grid companies purchased it at the local benchmark feed-in tariff for coal-fired power units. On the other hand, self-consumed electricity from distributed PV systems was exempt from various funds and surcharges normally collected alongside the electricity tariff, as well as from system reserve capacity charges and other related grid-connection service fees.[152] According to the "Measures for Settlement of Electricity Charges Between Power Generators and Grid Companies" (Guo Neng Fa Jian Guan [2020] No. 79) issued by NEA on December 30, 2020, grid companies should comply with relevant settlement requirements. These include signing power purchase contracts as stipulated, clearly defining electricity settlement-related matters within these contracts, installing grid-fed electricity metering devices that conform to technical standards, strictly implementing national electricity pricing policies and market rules, promptly and fully transferring subsidies from the central government, among others, to renewable energy power generators within the national

[150] See Han et al. (2020).

[151] See Notice of the National Development and Reform Commission on Improving the Feed-in Tariff Policy for Solar Photovoltaic Power Generation (Fa Gai Jia Ge [2011] No. 1594).

[152] See Notice of the National Development and Reform Commission on Utilizing Price Leverage to Promote the Healthy Development of the Photovoltaic Industry (Fa Gai Jia Ge [2013] No. 1638).

subsidy scheme, making full and prompt payments of electricity charges based on the settlement statement confirmed by both parties, taking effective measures to collect electricity charges from users, and during the regulatory process, submitting reports on electricity settlement to energy regulatory authorities in accordance with the requirements for power company information submission.[153]

As PV power generation advances, China has been adjusting its subsidies for this sector, with a prevailing tendency to reduce subsidy levels and transition toward grid parity. The "Notice on Matters Related to Photovoltaic Power Generation in 2018" (Fa Gai Neng Yuan [2018] No. 823) issued by NDRC, the Ministry of Finance, and NEA on May 13, 2018, demanded the optimization of construction scale for new PV power generation capacity and called for an accelerated phase-out of PV subsidies and a reduction in subsidy intensity. For newly operational distributed PV power generation projects utilizing the "self-consumption with surplus electricity fed into the grid" model, the per-kWh subsidy for the total electricity generated was decreased by CNY 0.05, resulting in an adjusted subsidy rate of CNY 0.32 per kilowatt-hour (tax-inclusive). Distributed PV projects using the "full feed-in" model were subjected to the tariffs of PV power stations in their respective resource areas. Additionally, the notice reaffirmed that self-consumed electricity from distributed PV systems was exempt from various funds and surcharges normally collected alongside the electricity tariff, as well as from system reserve capacity charges and other related grid-connection service fees.[154] According to the "Notice on Actively Promoting Subsidy-Free Grid Parity for Wind and Photovoltaic Power Generation" (Fa Gai Neng Yuan [2019] No. 19) issued by NDRC and NEA on January 7, 2019, PV power generation in certain regions has essentially achieved grid parity with the benchmark feed-in tariff for coal-fired power units, eliminating the need for state subsidies. Therefore, the notice outlined strategies to advance subsidy-free grid parity for wind and PV power generation. These strategies include developing projects that achieve grid parity and pilot projects with tariffs below grid parity, enhancing the investment climate for such projects, ensuring priority generation and full guaranteed purchase of power, incentivizing reasonable returns for grid parity and below grid parity projects through green certificate trading, fostering the subsidy-free development of wind and PV power generation through power market-oriented trading, reducing the transmission and distribution tariffs and fees for direct local trading, steadfastly advancing the construction of locally consumed grid parity projects and below grid parity projects, furthering the establishment of subsidy-free wind and PV power generation projects in conjunction with the construction of interprovincial and interregional power transmission channels, as well as innovating financial support mechanisms, ensuring

[153] See National Energy Administration of China. Measures for Settlement of Electricity Charges Between Power Generators and Grid Companies (Guo Neng Fa Jian Guan [2020] No. 79).

[154] See Notice of the National Development and Reform Commission, the Ministry of Finance, and the National Energy Administration on Matters Related to Photovoltaic Power Generation in 2018 (Fa Gai Neng Yuan [2018] No. 823).

effective early warning management integration, and continually refining the evaluation support system for total energy consumption.[155] According to the "Notice on Improving the Feed-in Tariff Mechanism for Photovoltaic Power Generation" (Fa Gai Jia Ge [2019] No. 761) issued by the National Development and Reform Commission on April 28, 2019, the subsidy rate for newly added distributed PV power generation should be appropriately reduced. Specifically, the notice proposed that for industrial and commercial (namely, non-residential) distributed PV power generation projects included in the 2019 financial subsidy scope that adopted the "self-consumption with surplus electricity fed into the grid" model, the subsidy rate for the total electricity generated was adjusted to CNY 0.10 per kilowatt-hour; those adopting the "full feed-in" model were subjected to the guide price of centralized PV power stations in their respective resource areas. For industrial and commercial distributed projects allocated by the energy authorities through market competition, the price formed through market competition shall not exceed the guide price of the corresponding resource area, and the subsidy rate shall not exceed CNY 0.10 per kilowatt-hour. In addition, the subsidy rate for total electricity generated by residential distributed PV power generation projects included in the 2019 financial subsidy scope, whether using the "self-consumption with surplus electricity fed into the grid" or the "full feed-in" models, was adjusted to CNY 0.18 per kilowatt-hour. The notice also "encourages local governments to introduce targeted support policies to promote the development of the photovoltaic industry."[156] The "Notice of the National Energy Administration on Matters Related to the Construction of Wind and Photovoltaic Power Generation Projects in 2019" (Guo Neng Fa Xin Neng [2019] No. 49), issued on May 28, 2019, proposed to actively promote the construction of grid parity projects. The notice emphasized the need to assess and verify the feasibility of constructing grid parity projects in the specific regions. It stated that, after grid companies assessed and ensured the feasibility of power delivery and consumption for grid parity projects, priority should be given to the construction of such projects.[157]

On March 31, 2020, NDRC issued the "Notice on Matters Related to the Feed-in Tariff Policy for Photovoltaic Power Generation in 2020" (Fa Gai Jia Ge [2020] No. 511), which further reduced the subsidy rates for distributed PV power generation. Specifically, for industrial and commercial distributed PV power generation projects included in the 2020 financial subsidy scope that adopted the "self-consumption with surplus electricity fed into the grid" model, the subsidy rate for the total electricity generated was adjusted to CNY 0.05 per kilowatt-hour; those adopting the "full feed-in" model were subjected to the guide price of centralized PV power stations in their respective resource areas. For industrial and commercial distributed projects

[155] See Notice of the National Development and Reform Commission and the National Energy Administration on Actively Promoting Subsidy-Free Grid Parity for Wind and Photovoltaic Power Generation (Fa Gai Neng Yuan [2019] No. 19).

[156] See Notice of the National Development and Reform Commission on Improving the Feed-in Tariff Mechanism for Photovoltaic Power Generation (Fa Gai Jia Ge [2019] No. 761).

[157] See Notice of the National Energy Administration on Matters Related to the Construction of Wind and Photovoltaic Power Generation Projects in 2019 (Guo Neng Fa Xin Neng [2019] No. 49).

allocated by the energy authorities through market competition, the price formed through market competition shall not exceed the guide price of the corresponding resource area, and the subsidy rate shall not exceed CNY 0.05 per kilowatt-hour. In addition, the subsidy rate for total electricity generated by residential distributed PV power generation projects was adjusted to CNY 0.08 per kilowatt-hour.[158] The "Notice on Matters Related to the New Energy Feed-in Tariff Policy in 2021" (Fa Gai Jia Ge [2021] No. 833) issued by the National Development and Reform Commission on June 7, 2021, stated that starting from 2021, newly filed centralized PV power stations, industrial and commercial distributed PV projects, and newly approved onshore wind power projects (collectively referred to as "new projects") would no longer receive subsidies from the central government. Instead, grid parity would be implemented to guide investment rationally, promote the efficient use of resources, and promote the high-quality development of new energy industries such as PV power generation and wind power. The notice also called for the steady expansion of residential PV power generation projects, with the per-kWh subsidy rate to be determined in accordance with the relevant 2021 policies issued by the price authority of the State Council.[159] The "Letter on the Continuation of Grid Parity Policy for New Wind and Photovoltaic Power Generation Projects in 2022" issued by NDRC on April 8, 2022, stated that the grid parity policy would continue in 2022 for newly approved onshore wind power projects, newly filed centralized PV power stations, and industrial and commercial distributed PV projects (collectively referred to as "new projects"), and the feed-in tariff would be determined based on the local benchmark price for coal-fired power units. This shows that industrial and commercial distributed PV power generation projects have essentially entered the era of grid parity, while residential PV power generation projects continue to be supported by state financial subsidies.[160]

Taking Zhejiang as an example, in the initial development stage of distributed PV power generation, the government implemented substantial subsidy policies. The "Implementation Opinions on Accelerating the Application of Distributed Photovoltaic Power Generation to Promote the Healthy Development of the Industry" (Hang Zheng Han [2014] No. 29) issued on February 10, 2014, proposed the implementation of subsidies for the electricity generated by distributed PV systems. Projects that met certain criteria were eligible for an additional 0.1 CNY/kWh subsidy from the municipal budget on top of the national and provincial subsidies, based on their actual electricity output.[161] The "Supplementary Notice on Matters Concerning Financial Subsidies for Distributed Photovoltaic Power Generation Projects in Our City" (Hang Jing Xin Lian Gao Xin [2014] No. 463) issued on October 27, 2014,

[158] See Notice of the National Development and Reform Commission on Matters Related to the Feed-in Tariff Policy for Photovoltaic Power Generation in 2020 (Fa Gai Jia Ge [2020] No. 511).

[159] See Notice of the National Development and Reform Commission on Matters Related to the New Energy Feed-in Tariff Policy in 2021 (Fa Gai Jia Ge [2021] No. 833).

[160] See International Energy Network (2021).

[161] See Hangzhou Municipal Government. Implementation Opinions on Accelerating the Application of Distributed Photovoltaic Power Generation to Promote the Healthy Development of the Industry (Hang Zheng Han [2014] No. 29).

stated that "distributed PV power generation projects built and grid-connected within 2014 to 2015 will receive a continuous subsidy for five years (a full 60 months) starting from the month of grid connection." The "Notice on the Proper Execution of Distributed Photovoltaic Power Generation Project Policies" (Hang Jing Xin Lian Jie Xin [2015] No. 223) issued on August 5, 2015, made arrangements for the fulfillment of the aforementioned subsidy policies.[162] The "Several Opinions on Promoting the Healthy Development of Distributed Photovoltaic Power Generation" (Jia Zheng Fa [2013] No. 87), issued on December 13, 2013, proposed that "from 2013 to the end of 2015, city-level distributed PV power generation projects with a total capacity of 200 MW will receive a subsidy for the electricity they generate. The subsidy rate will be CNY 0.1 per kilowatt-hour, and it will be provided for three consecutive years." The "Implementation Opinions on Accelerating the Application of Distributed Photovoltaic Power Generation" (Shao Zheng Ban Fa [2014] No. 42) issued on March 20, 2014, proposed the provision of electricity subsidies. "For distributed PV power generation projects that are invested in by enterprises registered in Shaoxing and that are completed and connected to the grid before the end of 2015, the projects will receive a national subsidy of CNY 0.42/kWh and a provincial subsidy of CNY 0.1/kWh based on their actual power generation performance after completion. Additionally, the local government (or management committee) will provide an extra subsidy of CNY 0.2/kWh based on the actual power generation from the date of self-generation, for a period of five years." On October 30, 2015, the "Several Opinions on Supporting Distributed Photovoltaic Power Generation Projects in the Urban Areas of Taizhou" (Tai Zheng Ban Fa [2015] No. 82) were implemented, introducing electricity subsidies. "Distributed PV power generation projects that are connected to the grid and completed by the end of 2016 will receive a national subsidy of CNY 0.42/kWh and a provincial subsidy of CNY 0.1/kWh. Additionally, the local government will provide an extra subsidy of CNY 0.1/kWh based on the actual power generation from the date of grid connection. This additional subsidy will be granted continuously for a period of five years." The "Opinions of the Office of the People's Government of Ruian City on Comprehensively Promoting the Development of Clean Energy" (Rui Zheng Ban [2022] No. 39) proposed that for projects meeting the subsidy criteria, subsidies would be provided based on the type of entity involved. Commercial rooftop PV power generation projects would be granted a subsidy of CNY 0.3 per kilowatt-hour, effective from the date of passing the acceptance check and starting grid-connected power generation, for a continuous period of five years. Residential rooftop PV power generation projects would receive a subsidy of CNY 0.3 per kilowatt-hour, effective from the date of passing the acceptance check and starting grid-connected power generation, for a continuous period of five years. Rooftop owners would be awarded a subsidy of CNY 0.05 per kilowatt-hour based on their actual power generation, beginning from the date of project passing the acceptance check and starting grid-connected power generation,

[162] See Hangzhou Economy and Informatization Commission, Hangzhou Development and Reform Commission, and Hangzhou Finance Bureau. Notice on the Proper Execution of Distributed Photovoltaic Power Generation Project Policies (Hang Jing Xin Lian Jie Xin [2015] No. 223).

for a continuous period of five years as well. Public-owned projects and self-built models by enterprises (residents) were not eligible for subsidies.

According to information from chinapower.com.cn, the implementation of PV subsidies in Zhejiang in 2022 varied by region, with a general trend of decreasing subsidies.[163] In Yueqing City, the "Announcement on Adjusting Municipal Financial Subsidies for Residential Distributed Photovoltaic Power Generation Projects in the City," issued on April 8, 2021, outlined different municipal subsidy policies for distributed PV projects connected to the grid at various times. Residential distributed PV power generation projects connected after January 1, 2022, that met relevant regulations were eligible for a Yueqing municipal financial subsidy of CNY 0.1 per kilowatt-hour, valid until December 31, 2022. In Ningbo, the "Several Opinions on Vigorously Promoting the Application of Distributed Photovoltaic Power Generation Systems on Building Roofs" (Yong Jian Fa [2022] No. 15), released on February 14, 2022, supported subsidies for installing distributed PV power generation systems on existing residential buildings. The costs for foundational and roof renovations were included in the investment for the refurbishment of old residential communities. The municipal government provided subsidies according to the standards in document Yong Neng Yuan Dian Li [2021] No. 89 for power-generated post-grid connection. Lishui issued the "Implementation Opinions on Accelerating the Large-Scale Development of Distributed Photovoltaics" on November 16, 2021, which indicated that the city's finances, supplemented by national and provincial funds, would consolidate various policy resources to ensure support for municipal-level rooftop distributed PV development. Specific reward and subsidy measures were to be determined separately. For residential distributed PV projects connected to the grid in the urban area (including Liandu District and Lishui Development Zone) in 2022, 2023, and 2024, one-time construction subsidies would be provided at rates of CNY 0.60/watt, CNY 0.50/watt, and CNY 0.40/watt, respectively. The subsidy funds would be borne equally by the municipal finance and either Liandu District or Lishui Development Zone. In Wenzhou City, the "Notice on Issuing the Action Plan for Energy-saving Transformation of 1,000 Manufacturing Enterprises in Wenzhou" dated October 25, 2021, stated that while PV projects were encouraged to participate in electricity market transactions, distributed PV projects that had completed filing and were connected to the municipal-level distributed PV digital management platform, operating on a "self-consumption with surplus electricity fed into the grid" model, would receive a subsidy of CNY 0.1 per kilowatt-hour based on actual electricity generation. In addition, Pinghu City, Wuxing District of Huzhou, Keqiao District of Shaoxing, Taishun County, Ruian City, Jinhua City, Haiyan County, Hangzhou City, Taizhou City, Xianju County, Yuhuan City, Yongjia County, Jiashan County, Songyang County, and Quzhou City also provided PV subsidies.

In the context of PV subsidies and tariff changes, there is a risk of contract disputes arising from price fluctuations for both self-consumed and grid-fed electricity.

Firstly, with regard to self-consumed electricity, if the pricing is not stipulated or is ambiguously agreed upon, disputes may arise between project owners and users.

163 See China Power (2022).

According to Article 510 of the *Civil Code*, "After a contract becomes effective, where the parties have not agreed on such contents as the quality, price or remuneration, or the place of performance, and the like, or the relevant agreement is unclear, the parties may make a supplementary agreement; where the parties fail to reach a supplementary agreement, such contents shall be determined according to the relevant clauses of the contract or the course of dealing." Furthermore, Item (2) of Article 511 states that, where the price or remuneration is not clearly stipulated and cannot be determined through a supplementary agreement, relevant clauses of the contract, or the course of dealing, the contract shall be performed in accordance with the market price in the place of performance at the time the contract is concluded. Where a government-set or government-guided price shall be applied as required by law, the contract shall be performed at such a price.[164] It can be seen that in cases where the pricing of self-consumed electricity is not stipulated or is ambiguously agreed upon, the price can still be determined by entering into a supplementary agreement, following the relevant contract clauses or the course of dealing, or adhering to the market price in the place of performance at the time the contract is concluded, the government-set price or the government-guided price, during energy performance contracting. However, the price established by agreement or statutory method may not satisfy all parties involved in the energy performance contracting project and could lead to increased communication costs during the process. Therefore, it is essential to clearly define the self-consumed electricity price in advance to mitigate such risks.

Secondly, even with a pre-agreed self-consumed electricity price, there can be situations where it becomes challenging to adhere to the contractually agreed price due to tariff changes. In practice, there are two prevalent models for establishing electricity prices and relevant charges between project owners and users. The first model is a fixed electricity price, whereby both parties agree to a set price at the time of contract signing, and charges are calculated based on this fixed electricity price, which typically falls below the tariff offered by the State Grid Corporation or the power sellers. The second model involves a real-time electricity price discount, whereby charges are calculated based on the benchmark feed-in tariff for coal-fired power generation or the market-determined real-time price, factoring in a discount.

Under the fixed electricity price model, given that the project duration may extend up to 25 years, should the tariff set by the State Grid Corporation or the power sellers drop significantly below the fixed electricity price, this could lead users to favor the electricity supplied by the public grid. Such a shift in preference could impact the agreed-upon power consumption in the original contract and lead to disputes over PV power consumption. In the model featuring real-time electricity price discounts, contracts may be established with provisions for discounts calculated against the benchmark feed-in tariff for coal-fired power generation. According to the "Guiding Opinions on Deepening the Reform of the Feed-in Tariff Formation Mechanism for Coal-fired Power Generation" (Fa Gai Jia Ge Gui [2019] No. 1658) issued by the National Development and Reform Commission on October 21, 2019, "the benchmark feed-in tariff mechanism for coal-fired power generation is no longer suitable

[164] Civil Code of the People's Republic of China, Article 510 and Item (2) of Article 511.

for the evolving situation. It is particularly evident in its inability to effectively reflect changes in power market supply and demand, as well as cost variations of power companies. This is detrimental to the coordinated and sustainable development of the upstream and downstream power industries and hinders the market from playing a decisive role in the allocation of power resources." The guiding opinions suggested that "the current benchmark feed-in tariff mechanism for coal-fired power generation should be changed to a market-oriented pricing mechanism with a 'benchmark price with allowable fluctuations'" to gradually accomplish the objective of completely deregulating the feed-in tariff for coal-fired power generation.[165] According to the "Notice on Further Deepening the Market-oriented Reform of Feed-in Tariffs for Coal-fired Power Generation" (Fa Gai Jia Ge [2021] No. 1439), issued by the NDRC on October 11, 2021, "the electricity generated from coal-fired power units should, in principle, be entirely fed into the power market, where the feed-in tariff is determined within the range of 'benchmark price with allowable fluctuations' through market transactions. The current benchmark price for coal-fired power generation continues to serve as the reference point for the price formation of new energy generation and others." In addition, the "Notice on Matters Related to Adjusting the Catalog Sales Electricity Price in Our Province," issued by the Zhejiang Provincial Development and Reform Commission on October 21, 2021, also proposed the adjustment of the catalog sales electricity price in Zhejiang Province, the establishment of a purchasing agency mechanism for grid companies, and the orderly liberalization of the feed-in tariff for all coal-fired power generation.[166] The "Notice on Matters Related to the New Energy Feed-in Tariff Policy in 2021" (Fa Gai Jia Ge [2021] No. 833), issued by NDRCon June 7, 2021, stipulated that "the feed-in tariffs for new projects in 2021 should be set according to the local benchmark price for coal-fired power generation. New projects are allowed to participate in market-oriented trading to establish their feed-in tariffs, thereby better reflecting the value of green power from PV and wind power generation." It is evident that with the cancelation of the benchmark feed-in tariff for coal-fired power generation, project owners and users who previously relied on this standard to calculate the costs of PV power generation need to renegotiate. They have to recalculate discounts based on the tariffs set by the State Grid Corporation or the power sellers, or the market-determined real-time prices. From a contractual standpoint, both project owners and users require a standardized and transparent basis for settlement.[167] Without a reasonable agreement on electricity pricing, it could become challenging to maintain its long-term viability.

Thirdly, if some projects built earlier are terminated due to non-subjective factors such as demolition, and then the photovoltaics installed on the original property need to be relocated to a new construction site and new subsidy policies are applicable,

---

[165] See Guiding Opinions of the National Development and Reform Commission on Deepening the Reform of the Feed-in Tariff Formation Mechanism for Coal-fired Power Generation (Fa Gai Jia Ge Gui [2019] No. 1658).

[166] See Notice of the Zhejiang Provincial Development and Reform Commission on Matters Related to Adjusting the Catalog Sales Price Electricity in Our Province (Zhe Fa Gai Jia Ge [2021] No. 377).

[167] See CSG Energy (2024).

this could lead to disputes over electricity price subsidies. Given that the amounts of electricity price subsidies are progressively decreasing and the overall electricity price subsidy is being phased out, the subsidy benefits for newly established rooftop PV power generation projects are evidently less favorable than for those constructed earlier. The survey revealed that, owing to variations in subsidy policies, project owners and users impacted by demolition usually request the continuation of the original subsidy policy. However in practice, relocation often results in a change of the user account number, making it challenging to apply the original subsidy policy to the relocated PV system. Instead, the new subsidy policies must be adopted. Under these circumstances, stakeholders may only seek compensation for the lost power generation subsidies based on the standards of expropriation and compensation. According to Article 2 of the "Regulations on the Expropriation of Houses on State-owned Land and Compensation," "where a house of any entity or individual on state-owned land is expropriated for public interest, the owner of the expropriated house shall be fairly compensated." Paragraph 1 of Article 17 of the Regulations stipulates that municipal or county-level people's governments, when making decisions to expropriate houses, must provide compensation to the expropriated parties in three aspects: first, for the value of the expropriated houses; second, for relocation and temporary resettlement resulting from the expropriation of the houses; and third, for losses incurred due to the suspension of production or business caused by the expropriation. Article 23 of the Regulations states that "compensation for losses due to the suspension of production or business caused by the expropriation of houses is to be determined based on factors such as the profitability prior to the expropriation and the duration of the production or business suspension. Specific measures shall be formulated by the provinces, autonomous regions, and municipalities directly under the central government."[168] Existing regulatory documents do not explicitly state whether the original subsidy policy for rooftop distributed PV projects will continue after relocation or direct compensation will be provided through expropriation. Therefore, due to fluctuations in feed-in tariff subsidies, factors beyond the subjective control of project owners, such as demolition, may lead to disputes regarding the applicability of subsidy policies.

Clearly, the marketization trend is evident in the PV feed-in tariffs, with subsidies varying based on factors like regional differences and grid-connection timings. As a result, feed-in tariffs differ across various power generation points. Influenced by the market-oriented reforms of the electricity pricing mechanism, the absence of or an unclear agreement may lead to disputes over the price of self-consumed electricity between project owners and users, as well as additional communication costs. Whether a fixed electricity price or a real-time electricity price discount model is employed between project owners and users, there still exists a legal risk of pricing disputes over self-consumed electricity due to market price fluctuations, even with explicit agreements in place. In cases beyond the project owner's control, such as demolition, disputes may arise regarding whether to apply the electricity

[168] Regulations on the Expropriation of Houses on State-owned Land and Compensation, Article 2, paragraph 1 of Article 17 and Article 23.

price subsidy before or after demolition, and whether the difference in electricity price subsidies can be included in the demolition compensation.

Legal Risks of Equipment Damage or Loss

In energy performance contracting projects, there exists a separation of ownership and usage rights for energy-saving equipment, as well as the risk allocation that arises when the equipment is damaged or lost.[169] As per the reference contracts provided in the "Guidance on Energy Performance Contracting" from 2020, for both shared savings and guaranteed savings energy performance contracting projects, "after the project is delivered to Party A for operation and management, the possession and usage rights of the equipment are transferred to Party A." "Party B retains limited ownership of the equipment, which means that Party B holds the right to dispose of the equipment until Party A has fulfilled all payment obligations under the contract. In scenarios such as expropriation, demolition, or Party A's bankruptcy that require disposal of the equipment, Party A must not decide to dispose of the equipment without the consent of Party B, and any proceeds from such disposal shall belong to Party B." "The rights to benefits from the normal operation of the project shall be shared between Party A and Party B according to the proportions stipulated in this contract, with Party A being responsible for paying the energy-saving benefits (returns) to Party B."[170] After the project is delivered to the user for operation and management, the possession and usage rights of the equipment are transferred to the user, while the energy service company retains limited ownership of the equipment. The rights to benefits are distributed proportionally. This agreement on ownership and usufructuary rights clarifies the rights and obligations of each party involved in the construction and operation of the equipment. Moreover, since the ownership and usage rights of the energy-saving equipment do not transfer simultaneously, it is necessary to reasonably allocate the risk of damage or loss of the energy-saving equipment among the contractual parties to avoid potential disputes. The same principles apply to the construction of rooftop distributed PV projects. Unclear demarcation of property rights can lead to disputes over contractual rights and obligations and complicates the determination of responsibility for the risk of damage or loss to the rooftop distributed PV systems.

[169] See Yu (2016).

[170] See State Administration for Market Regulation, and Standardization Administration of China. Guidance on Energy Performance Contracting (GB/T 24915–2020).

Legal Risks of Tort Liability

Issues such as the detachment of photovoltaic equipment, electrical leakage, and roof leaks may lead to tort liability for damages.[171] According to Article 1253 of the *Civil Code*, where a building, structure, or another type of facility, or any object laid or hanged thereon, comes loose or falls down and thus causes damage to another person, the owner, manager, or user shall bear tort liability if it cannot be proven that he is not at fault. Where the damage is due to the fault of another responsible person, the owner, manager, or user who has paid compensation has the right to indemnification against the responsible person.[172] In the context of energy performance contracting projects, where photovoltaic equipment comes loose or falls down and thus causes damage to another person, the owner, manager, or user shall bear tort liability if it cannot be proven that he is not at fault. In terms of the electrical leakage risks, according to Article 1240 of the *Civil Code*, where damage is caused to another person by a person engaged in activities such as working at heights or in high-voltage environments, or conducting underground excavations, or by using high-speed rail transport vehicles, the operator shall bear tort liability, except that the operator does not assume any liability if it can be proven that the damage was intentionally caused by the victim or caused by force majeure. Where the infringed person is grossly negligent for the occurrence of the damage, the liability of the operator may be mitigated.[173] In energy performance contracting projects, where the photovoltaic equipment is considered high voltage and causes damage to another person, the operator shall bear tort liability if it cannot be proven that the damage was intentionally caused by the victim or caused by force majeure. For other tort risks such as roof leaks, according to paragraph 1 of Article 1165 of the *Civil Code*, an actor who through his fault infringes upon another person's civil rights and interests shall bear tort liability, and shall be liable for damages in accordance with Articles 1179–1187 of the *Civil Code*.[174]

References

Anli Law Firm (2022) Key points for due diligence and EMC Signing in the Development and Construction of Rooftop Distributed PV Power Stations. Retrieved March 14, 2024, from http://www.anlilaw.com/100031/1811

BJX (2018) Typical safety risks and countermeasures for rooftop distributed photovoltaics. Retrieved 14 March 2024, from https://guangfu.bjx.com.cn/news/20180328/888388.shtml

Beijing Power Exchange Center (2021) About 2.455 Billion Kilowatt-hours! the national market for excess renewable power consumption is launched for the first time! Retrieved 14 March 2024, from https://news.bjx.com.cn/html/20210209/1135730.shtml

---

[171] BJX (2018).

[172] Civil Code of the People's Republic of China, Article 1253.

[173] Civil Code of the People's Republic of China, Article 1240.

[174] Civil Code of the People's Republic of China, Articles 1165 and 1179–1187.

Chen M (2020) From game to coexistence: the scope and limitation of the protection of lease rights in the enforcement procedure—from the perspective of interest balancing under the principle of good faith enforcement. J Law Appl 2020(21):94–104

Chen P, Wu Y, Zou L (2019) Distributive PV trading market in China: a design of multi-agent-based model and its forecast analysis. Energy 185:423–436. https://doi.org/10.1016/j.energy.2019.07.070

China Power (2022) Summary of national photovoltaic subsidy policies in 2022. Retrieved 14 March 2024, from http://www.chinapower.com.cn/tynfd/hyyw/20220415/144303.html

Chongqing Blue Jay Electronic (2011). Energy management contract. Retrieved 14 March 2024, from https://www.energy-xprt.com/articles/energy-management-contract-250685

CSG Energy (2024) How is the electricity price determined in energy performance contracting projects? Retrieved 14 March 2024, from https://news.bjx.com.cn/html/20151125/685189-2.shtml

Energy Saver (2023) Grid-connected renewable energy systems. Retrieved 14 March 2024, from https://www.energy.gov/energysaver/grid-connected-renewable-energy-systems

Fan X, Wang Z (2022) The hurdles of mainstreaming "Direct local electricity trading"—Thoughts and Suggestions on "Direct Local Electricity Trading". Retrieved 14 March 2024, from http://ex.bjx.com.cn/html/20220427/40957.shtml

Fan N (2021) How to avoid risks caused by subleasing. Retrieved 14 March 2024, from https://www.spp.gov.cn/spp/llyj/202104/t20210421_516200.shtml

Guo J (2013) Beyond determination—the government must embrace efficiency. Retrieved 14 March 2024, from http://www.indaa.com.cn/zz/nypl/nyplellsdwqi/201305/t20130514_8046.html

Han Y, Lin S, Ye Y (2020) A review of photovoltaic power generation feed-in tariff policies. Retrieved 14 March 2024, from https://guangfu.bjx.com.cn/news/20201210/1121360.shtml

Hao L (2017) Analysis of the ten legal risks and related prevention countermeasures for rooftop leasing of distributed PV stations. Retrieved March 14, 2024, from http://www.tanpaifang.com/xinnengyuan/2017/0817/60316_8.html

Hao L (2018) Analysis of the ten legal risks and prevention countermeasures for rooftop leasing of distributed PV stations. Retrieved 14 March 2024, from https://guangfu.bjx.com.cn/news/20180313/885214.shtml

Hou B, Lu H (2020) Pilot market-based trading for distributed power generation: the game changer of "Direct Local Electricity Trading"? Retrieved 14 March 2024, from https://www.chinalawinsight.com/2020/07/articles/corporate-ma/%e5%88%86%e5%b8%83%e5%bc%8f%e5%8f%91%e7%94%b5%e5%b8%82%e5%9c%ba%e5%8c%96%e4%ba%a4%e6%98%93%e8%af%95%e7%82%b9%ef%bc%9a%e9%9a%94%e5%a2%99%e5%94%ae%e7%94%b5%e7%a0%b4%e5%b1%80%e8%80%85/

IEA (2019) Distributed solar PV, Renewable 2019 Analysis and forecast to 2024. Retrieved 14 March 2024, from https://www.iea.org/reports/renewables-2019/distributed-solar-pv

International Energy Network (2021) Breaking News! No more subsidies for photovoltaics; grid parity to be implemented! (See attached responses to reporters questions). Retrieved 14 March 2024, from http://www.chinapower.com.cn/xw/zyxw/20210611/80945.html

Jiang F, Lin Y (2021) Legal analysis of the relationships between parties in new rooftop distributed PV projects under energy performance contracting. Retrieved 14 March 2024, from http://www.360doc.com/content/21/1118/18/72475118_1004749434.shtml

Jingzhou District People's Court of Jingzhou City (2020) Protection of lessee's rights in the event of expropriation and demolition of leased property. Retrieved 14 March 2024, from https://www.thepaper.cn/newsDetail_forward_8166112

Juro. Understanding contract duration: how long should a contract last? Retrieved 14 March 2024, from https://juro.com/learn/contract-duration

Kang H, Qu W (2014) Discussing the impact of grid-connected new energy generation on power of power grid. Sci Technol Economy Market 8:51–52

Li X (2016) What is "Co-ownership"? Revisiting the distinction between co-ownership by shares and joint co-ownership. Oriental Law 2016(4):11–24. https://doi.org/10.3969/j.issn.1007-1466.2016.04.002

Li H (2012) Determination of the validity of a lease contract of an illegal building. Retrieved March 14, 2024, from https://www.chinacourt.org/article/detail/2012/10/id/668735.shtml

Li X (2017) Interpretation of the new and renewable energy department of the energy administration interpretation on the market-based trading for distributed power generation. Retrieved 14 March 2024, from http://www.nea.gov.cn/2017-12/27/c_136855153.htm

Lin Q, Liu L, Yuan M, Ge L, Wang Y, Zhang M (2021) Choice of the distributed photovoltaic power generation operating mode for a manufacturing enterprise: surrounding users vs a power grid. J Clean Prod 2021(293):126–199. https://doi.org/10.1016/j.jclepro.2021.126199

Liu Y (2020) Legal risks and prevention in contracts. Times Finance 2020(8):109–118

Liu B (2019) "Replacement" of quota system with consumption responsibility weights to strengthen power consumption guarantee mechanisms. Retrieved 14 March 2024, from https://www.huanbao-world.com/a/zhengce/2019/0516/103790.html

Lou X (2021) On the legal effect of rescission of executory contracts in bankruptcy. Arbitration Study 2021(2):34–35

Lu Y (2015) Discussion on applicable versions of engineering-related technical standards. Mach Ind Standard Qual 2015(9):22–23

Luoqima (2021) Characteristics of new power systems with new energy as the main body. Retrieved 14 March 2024, from http://www.chinapower.com.cn/xw/sdyd/20210706/85657.html

National Energy Administration (2022) The national energy administration holds a press conference to release the grid connection and operation of renewable energy in 2021 and answer related questions. Retrieved 14 March 2024, from http://www.gov.cn/xinwen/2022-01/29/content_5671076.htm

National Renewable Energy Laboratory (2021) Documenting a decade of cost declines for PV systems. Retrieved 14 March 2024, from https://www.nrel.gov/news/program/2021/documenting-a-decade-of-cost-declines-for-pv-systems.html

Policy Tailwinds Pick Up (2022) Is it time for the dormant "Direct Local Electricity Trading" to Make a Breakthrough? Retrieved 14 March 2024, from http://energylaw.chinalaw.org.cn/portal/article/index/id/3258.html

Qi E (2009) On the joint ownership of the buildings of the residence community: focusing on the roof and outer-wall of the building. Nankai J (philosophy, Literat Soc Sci Edition) 2009(6):102–111. https://doi.org/10.3969/j.issn.1001-4667.2009.06.020

Qiu Y, Pan J (2020) Strive to basically solve the problems of wasted hydro-, Wind- and Solar-power by 2020. Retrieved 14 March 2024, from http://www.gov.cn/xinwen/2019-07/04/content_5405844.htm

Supreme Court (2022) Protection should be provided to each individual rights holder when concomitantly disposing of real estate owned by different rights holders. Retrieved 14 March 2024, from http://www.jingqinglaw.com/h-nd-2522.html

Shao G (2020) Significant changes and practical guidelines of the civil code regarding the relationship between mortgage rights and lease rights. Retrieved 14 March 2024, from https://www.thepaper.cn/newsDetail_forward_8761000

Songming County People's Court of Yunnan Province. Unauthorized Lease of Rooftops in a Residential Complex? Owners File Lawsuit Against the Lessor. Retrieved 14 March 2024, from https://m.thepaper.cn/baijiahao_19889900

State Grid Corporation of China (2018) State grid accelerates the construction of first-class modern distribution grid. Retrieved 14 March 2024, from http://www.sasac.gov.cn/n2588025/n2588124/c9511383/content.html

The Economic Daily (2022) Boosting new energy consumption capacity. Retrieved 14 March 2024, from http://www.nea.gov.cn/2022-06/10/c_1310619664.htm

The First Civil Division of the People's Court (2021) Questions and answers on civil trial practice. Law Press China, pp 105–106

The Preventing Roof Collapse (2018) How to effectively assess rooftop load? Retrieved 14 March 2024, from https://news.solarbe.com/201801/10/123076.html
United States Agency for International Development (2020) Photovoltaic system standards. Retrieved 14 March 2024, from https://www.usaid.gov/energy/powering-health/technical-standards/photovoltaic-systems
Wu T (2021) Solutions to contract deadlocks with the enforcement of the civil code. Law Sci 2021(3):84–100
Xi J (2022) Hold high the great banner of socialism with Chinese characteristics and strive in unity to build a modern socialist country in all Respects. People's Daily, p 01
Xu D (2009) Executory contracts in bankruptcy. The Jurist, 2009(6):92–104 and 156
Yan H, Yan X (2012) On the legal relationships of energy performance contracting. J Nanjing Tech Univ (social Sci Edn) 2012(2):23–27. https://doi.org/10.3969/j.issn.1671-7287.2012.02.005
Yu Y (2016) On the system construction of risk allocation in contract law—Centered on risk bearing rules. Polit Sci Law 2016(4):77–85
Zhang X (2022) Issue 710 of [Jiannuo Daily Legal Review]: Lease Agreements for Unapproved Temporary Buildings Are Invalid. Retrieved March 14, 2024, from http://www.jiannuo-lawyer.com/view.php?id=930
Zhao J (2014) Legal policy issues in the development of solar photovoltaic power generation in China—From the perspective of optimization of policy tools. J Shanghai Jiao Tong Univ (philosophy and Soc Sci) 2014(6):26–34
Zhu Y, Hu Y, Xie J (2022) Interpretation of key points of preliminary development of distributed PV Projects. Retrieved 14 March 2024, from http://www.360doc.com/content/22/0621/13/62792725_1036867834.shtml

Chapter 7
Optimization of the Demand-Side Management System Under the Increasingly Stringent Requirements of Ensuring Supply

Power demand-side management (DSM) plays a crucial role in improving energy efficiency and alleviating the strain on power supply. The concept of power demand-side management encompasses a broad range of strategies, including load management, strategic energy conservation, and adjustments to the power market. This book focuses on two innovative models of power demand-side management: orderly power utilization and interruptible load management. It analyzes these models in conjunction with the legal challenges faced by grid companies when coordinating with the government during power outages and rationing. Orderly power utilization and interruptible load management fall within the realms of administrative directives and market regulations, respectively. The former is characterized by its compulsory nature, efficiency, and stratification, while the latter relies on civil contracts to incentivize users to voluntarily reduce their load.

Chinese academics generally agree that DSM involves strengthening the management of electricity consumption across society. This is achieved by comprehensively adopting reasonable and feasible technical and management measures to optimize the allocation of electricity resources. DSM aims to eliminate wasteful electricity use, reduce overall consumption, facilitate load shifting, encourage the use of renewable power, and decrease the emission of pollutants and greenhouse gases. Through these initiatives, DSM promotes electricity conservation, environmental protection, the use of green energy, the advancement of smart power solutions, and the orderly utilization of power.[1] DSM is a significant approach to energy conservation and emission reduction. Its objective is to utilize electrical energy effectively to achieve energy saving, environmental protection, and sustainable development of the economy and society. The orderly power utilization, which is the primary focus of this section, is one of the models of demand-side management.

[1] Hu and Han (2008).

H. Deng, *Green Energy Transition in China*, International Law in Asia,
https://doi.org/10.1007/978-981-97-2934-0_7

Carrying out demand-side management can not only bring direct economic benefits but also more prominent social benefits such as energy conservation and environmental protection. Specifically, DSM can improve electricity efficiency, reduce total electricity consumption, save primary energy, and cut pollutant emissions. Moreover, DSM can also lower the growth of peak loads, delay or reduce the need for building new power plants, decrease investment in power infrastructure, keep electricity prices stable, and enhance the utilization rate of social capital. All of these factors are of great significance for ensuring the sustainable development of China's economy and society. Especially during periods of tight power supply, DSM can help alleviate the contradiction between power supply and demand, stabilize the order of electricity usage in society, and ensure the smooth functioning of the social and economic systems.[2]

The implementation of DSM holds significant importance for power users, power supply companies, and power generators. "For power users, DSM can effectively reduce both power consumption and electricity expenses, thereby lowering production and operational costs, enhancing energy efficiency, and bolstering the competitiveness of their products. Power supply companies benefit from DSM as it alleviates the pressure of peak shaving and optimizes the load profile of the power grid, which in turn enhances the safety, stability, and cost-efficiency of the power system, as well as the reliability and quality of supply services. DSM is particularly crucial during times of tight power supply and demand, as it can significantly mitigate the need for rolling blackouts. For power generators, DSM contributes to higher utilization rates of power generation equipment, relieves stress on power generation units during peak times, reduces the frequency of unit start-ups and shut-downs, cuts down on coal consumption and operational costs, and strengthens their market competitiveness."[3]

History of Power Demand-Side Management System

In the twentieth century, China faced a long-term electricity shortage, which led to the implementation of the policy of "planned electricity usage, electricity conservation, and safe electricity usage." Government authorities, in conjunction with power bureaus, negotiated and signed power supply contracts with power users. These contracts specified the maximum electricity load and monthly electricity usage for major enterprises and included the installation of power limiters. Additionally, high-energy-consuming enterprises were required to comply with designated electricity usage times, controlled by the installation of timer switches to manage their power usage and load. These measures aimed to ensure the provision of electricity for essential sectors, enterprises, and people's daily lives while maintaining the secure operation of the power grid. In the 1960s, China saw the installation of more than 400,000 power limiters and timer switches, which led to significant improvements in

[2] See Zhang (2008).

[3] Jin (2005).

power usage efficiency. By the 1980s, to meet the needs of the country, China independently developed and applied a bidirectional wireless power load monitoring system, which was widely adopted by power companies across various provinces and cities. Local government authorities, in collaboration with power companies, negotiated and signed agreements with power-consuming enterprises. Under these agreements, enterprises installed bidirectional monitoring terminals and set their maximum power load limits, with provisions for power disconnection in cases of overload, which could be managed either remotely or locally. The disconnection and reconnection process was carried out in three to four cycles, based on the load values set for each cycle's tripping and closing. The system recorded the electricity consumption and charges by time of use and transmitted this information to the monitoring center. The monitoring center, situated within the local power company, was responsible for issuing power load control commands promptly to ensure a balance between power supply and demand. This initiative marked China's early implementation of demand-side management and power demand response within the framework of a planned economy. The approach not only promoted social harmony and stable economic growth but also delivered notable social and economic benefits.[4]

In the twenty-first century, with the ongoing deepening of the market economy, by the end of 2012, bidirectional power load monitoring devices had been installed for all power users with transformer capacities of 100 kVA or higher. The total number of these devices exceeded 2 million, monitoring over 70% of the national load and capable of controlling 10% of the load at any given time. Thanks to the sophisticated bidirectional power load monitoring system, instructions issued by the power demand side and the real-time responses from the demand side were recorded in real time at the monitoring center and on the user side. This shifted the situation from the past, where demand response was relatively passive and solely dependent on instructions from the management side, to an active demand response under a market economy approach.[5]

In 2006, the NDRC, MIIT, the State Grid Corporation of China, and the China Southern Power Grid began to focus on demand-side management. In 2011, six ministries and commissions including NDRC, the Ministry of Finance, and MIIT jointly issued the "Power Demand-Side Management Measures." Additionally, MIIT published the "Guiding Opinions on Implementing Power Demand-Side Management in the Industrial Sector," and the Ministry of Finance released a series of incentive policies to encourage demand-side management. These measures enabled the rapid and comprehensive implementation of demand-side management in China.[6]

In March 2011, NDRC issued the "Notice on Regulating Power Operations in 2011" (Fa Gai Yun Xing [2011] No. 662), which stated: "Reasonably control the total energy consumption, restrain the rapid growth of high-energy-consuming industries, and enhance energy efficiency. Given the tight power supply and demand situation in 2011, it is crucial to earnestly implement the 'Power Demand-Side Management

---

[4] Xiong and Zhou (2014).

[5] Same as above.

[6] Same as above.

Measures' to ensure a balance between power supply and demand." The notice also underscored the need for comprehensively strengthening demand-side management by focusing on five key areas: meticulous organization of orderly power utilization, commitment to a guaranteed but limited power supply, refinement of supporting policies, coordination of pilot demonstration projects, and vigorous promotion of education and training.[7]

On July 3, 2012, the Ministry of Finance and NDRC issued the "Notice on Carrying out Comprehensive Urban Pilot Projects for Power Demand-Side Management" (Cai Jian [2012] No. 368), initiating comprehensive urban pilot projects for demand-side management.[8] In addition, the "Interim Measures for the Management of Central Financial Incentive Funds for the Comprehensive Urban Pilot Projects for Power Demand-Side Management" (Cai Jian [2012] No. 367) was released to strengthen the management of financial funds and improve the efficiency of innovative fund utilization.[9]

According to the Interim Measures, the Ministry of Finance and NDRC would select some cities meeting specific criteria to carry out comprehensive pilot projects for demand-side management. These projects would be eligible for financial incentives. Such incentives covered various initiatives, including the development of power service management platforms, the implementation of efficiency power plants, the promotion of peak-load shifting technology, the execution of power demand response, and related scientific research, publicity, training, auditing and evaluation efforts. The financial incentives for sustained power load savings and peak-load shifts achieved through efficiency power plants and peak-load shifting technology were set at CNY 440 per kW in the eastern region and CNY 550 per kW in the central and western regions. For temporary peak power load reductions achieved through demand response initiatives, the incentive was CNY 100 per kW. Upon completion of the pilot projects, the Ministry of Finance, in conjunction with NDRC, would assess and verify the outcomes. If the actual power load savings, shifts, and reductions were less than 80% of the pilot project's target, the central finance would retract the pre-allocated incentive funds in full. Furthermore, for pilot projects that had already received other incentives or subsidies from the central government, such amounts would be deducted from the final settlement of the incentive funds.[10]

To support the implementation of the Interim Measures and ensure the successful execution of the comprehensive urban pilot projects for demand-side management, the Ministry of Finance and the NDRC also issued the "Guiding Opinions on

[7] See Notice of the National Development and Reform Commission on Regulating Power Operations in 2011 (Fa Gai Yun Xing [2011] No. 662).

[8] See Notice of the Ministry of Finance and the National Development and Reform Commission on Carrying out Comprehensive Urban Pilot Projects for Power Demand-Side Management (Cai Jian [2012] No. 368).

[9] See Ministry of Finance, and the National Development and Reform Commission. Interim Measures for the Management of Central Financial Incentive Funds for Comprehensive Urban Pilot Projects for Power Demand-Side Management (Cai Jian [2012] No. 367).

[10] Same as above.

Conducting Comprehensive Urban Pilot Projects for Power Demand-Side Management." The Guiding Opinions stated that, "The overarching goal of the comprehensive urban pilot projects for demand-side management is that, pilot cities should achieve a 4–6% reduction and shift in power load, compared with the base period, using consistent metrics. The five key tasks of pilot projects are the informatization of power management, namely the construction of a power service management platform with functions such as online monitoring, decision-making analysis, project management and statistics, orderly power utilization, and demand response; the scaling up of efficiency power plants, specifically large-scale implementation in key power-consuming industries and major power-consuming products; the intelligence of load management, which involves further promoting the construction of load management projects; the industrialization of power services, aimed at gradually establishing a standardized and orderly power service market to cultivate and expand the power service industry; and the ongoing development of capacity building, focusing on enhancing the foundation of talents, technologies, and institutions."[11] The five priorities highlighted the comprehensive nature of the urban pilot projects for demand-side management and their multifaceted role in promoting energy conservation, emission reduction, and the transformation of the economic development mode.

For the selection of pilot cities, the Guiding Opinions stipulated that four factors should be considered: "First, there should be significant potential for demand-side management and a relatively solid foundation already in place; second, there should be a pronounced imbalance between power supply and demand, along with substantial obligations for energy conservation, emissions reduction, and control over total energy consumption; third, the cities should serve as typical and demonstrative examples in terms of regional industries; fourth, the cities should fulfill the prerequisites regarding organizational structures and capacity building."[12] Moreover, the Guiding Opinions also set forth pertinent safeguarding measures and detailed requirements for the implementation of the pilot projects.

In light of China's national conditions and to expedite and enhance the implementation of power demand-side management and demand response initiatives, the Department of Economic Construction of the Ministry of Finance, and the Bureau of Economic Operations Adjustment of NDRC jointly issued the "Notice on Publicizing the List of the First Batch of Pilot Cities for Comprehensive Urban Pilot Projects for Power Demand-Side Management" in October 2012. This notice identified Beijing, Suzhou in Jiangsu Province, Tangshan in Hebei Province, and Foshan in Guangdong Province as the inaugural pilot cities. "Thanks to a year of dedicated efforts, these four cities have achieved promising starts. They have established innovative mechanisms, secured the necessary funding, and engaged businesses in actively participating in DSM activities. They have systematically developed city-level power service platforms and corporate-level power management systems, with

[11] Li (2012).

[12] Same as above.

the involvement of competent energy service companies, ensuring that the comprehensive urban pilot initiatives are advancing favorably according to plan." "The Ministry of Industry and Information Technology and the China Electricity Council have collaboratively established the China Industrial Power Demand-Side Management Promotion Center. This center is tasked with fostering DSM practices within the industrial sector. It has organized teams of experts to carry out DSM activities tailored to the industrial characteristics and categories within industrial parks located in Ningxia Hui Autonomous Region, Beijing, Guangdong Province, and Guangxi Zhuang Autonomous Region."[13]

In 2014, the General Office of NDRC issued the "Notice on the Construction and Application of the National Power Demand-Side Management Platform" (Fa Gai Ban Yun Xing [2014] No. 734). The notice emphasized that "to implement the State Council's directives on transforming government functions, leverage modern information technology to drive the advancement of demand-side management, and harness the positive role of demand-side management in ensuring power supply, improving power utilization efficiency, and strengthening economic operation monitoring and analysis, a national demand-side management platform has been developed in collaboration with relevant entities as per our commission's work plan, achieving significant initial results."[14] To accelerate the construction process, standardize construction standards, and prepare for the platform's application, the "National Power Demand-Side Management Platform Management Regulations (Trial 2014)" were released. The National Demand-Side Management Platform is a comprehensive, specialized, and open online application platform, organized and developed by the National Development and Reform Commission to deeply and broadly advance demand-side management efforts. It features capabilities such as information publishing, real-time monitoring, verification and certification, analysis of power supply and demand trends, orderly power utilization management, online training, economic analysis, and demand response. The platform aims to provide the most comprehensive and authoritative information on demand-side management to a diverse audience including power users, power service providers, grid companies, and relevant government departments.[15]

On April 7, 2015, NDRC and the Ministry of Finance issued the "Notice on Improving the Power Emergency Mechanism and Carrying out Comprehensive Urban Pilot Projects for Power Demand-Side Management" (Fa Gai Yun Xing [2015] No. 703). This notice stated that, to implement the "Several Opinions of the Central Committee of the CPC and the State Council on Further Deepening the Reform of the Electric Power System" (Zhong Fa [2015] No. 9), strengthen demand-side management, and improve the power emergency mechanism, relevant entities should build

[13] Xiong and Zhou (2014).

[14] Notice of the General Office of the National Development and Reform Commission on the Construction and Application of the National Power Demand-Side Management Platform (Fa Gai Ban Yun Xing [2014] No. 734).

[15] See Notice of the General Office of the National Development and Reform Commission on the Construction and Application of the National Power Demand-Side Management Platform (Fa Gai Ban Yun Xing [2014] No. 734), Annex 2.

upon the foundation of previous comprehensive urban pilot projects for demand-side management in Beijing, Suzhou, Tangshan, and Foshan, as well as the pilot demand response project in Shanghai. They should further enhance the distinctive features of these projects, establish long-term mechanisms, and better harness the leading and exemplary role of the pilots. Additionally, the notice proposed the following: Firstly, we should fully recognize the importance of demand-side management; secondly, we should strengthen mechanism innovation and implement demand response; thirdly, we should establish technical support and focus on capacity building; fourthly, we should strengthen experience exchange and mutual support and cooperation; fifthly, we should innovate the application of funds and establish long-term mechanisms; sixthly, we should clarify evaluation principles and prepare early.[16]

On August 23, 2016, the General Office of MIIT released the "Notice on Issuing the Special Action Plan for Power Demand-Side Management in the Industrial Sector (2016–2020)" (Gong Xin Ting Yun Xing Han [2016] No. 560). The notice set forth an overarching goal: "To engage 10,000 industrial enterprises nationwide in a special initiative over a five-year period. Of these, 1000 enterprises are expected to implement demand-side management guidelines, with the aim of establishing 100 exemplary demand-side management companies. These efforts are intended to enhance the distribution of electric power resources and boost the efficiency of industrial energy consumption. By 2020, the aim is for the participating industrial enterprises to realize an average reduction in electricity consumption per unit of added value by more than 10%." The notice also outlined five principal tasks: developing demand-side management guidelines for the industrial sector; constructing a demand-side management system platform; promoting the demonstration and wider application of demand-side management; supporting the technological innovation and industrial application of demand-side management; and expediting the growth of the power service industry.[17]

On September 27, 2023, NDRC, MIIT, the Ministry of Finance, MHURD, the State-owned Assets Supervision and Administration Commission of the State Council (SASAC), and the National Energy Administration, revised the existing "Power Demand-Side Management Measures" (Fa Gai Yun Xung Gui [2023] No. 1283) in response to new circumstances and tasks, releasing an updated version titled "Power Demand-Side Management Measures (Revised)." "During the implementation process, relevant entities should embrace the concept that 'the demand side of electricity represents the supply side of users' and should actively leverage the significant role of demand-side management to drive structural reforms on the supply side. The previous 'Power Demand-Side Management Measures' issued on

[16] See Notice of the National Development and Reform Commission and the Ministry of Finance on Improving the Power Emergency Mechanism and Carrying out Comprehensive Urban Pilot Projects for Power Demand-Side Management (Fa Gai Yun Xing [2015] No. 703).

[17] See General Office of the Ministry of Industry and Information Technology. Special Action Plan for Power Demand-Side Management in the Industrial Sector (2016–2020) (Gong Xin Ting Yun Xing Han [2016] No. 560).

September 20, 2017, have been concurrently repealed."[18] NDRC, aligning with the national "13th Five-Year Plan" goals for energy transformation and considering the construction of a market-oriented power system along with the changing landscape of power supply and demand, has stepped up its efforts in demand-side management. This includes the innovation of demand-side management mechanisms and domains, stringent assessments of grid companies' demand-side management performance, and the evaluation of comprehensive urban pilot projects for demand-side management, which have yielded notable successes.

Concepts Related to Demand-Side Management

Power demand-side management is an extensive concept that encompasses demand response, orderly power utilization, grid-overloaded power rationing, accident-induced power rationing, and interruptible load management. These elements represent specific business models or technical means for implementing power demand-side management. The following individually analyzes and clarifies these concepts.

Demand Response

According to the national standard "GB/T 32672-2016 General Technical Specification of Power Demand Response System," demand response refers to "a participatory behavior where power users react to price signals or incentive mechanisms issued by the implementing agency and change their patterns of power consumption."[19] In other words, demand response is a market-based response mechanism that encourages power users to temporarily adjust their power load within a designated time frame, effectively facilitating peak-load shifting, easing the imbalance between power supply and demand, and enhancing the capability for emergency power adjustments. To be precise, demand response is a business practice involving various stakeholders such as government regulatory authorities, service implementation organizations, power users, and agents. The peak-valley time-of-use electricity pricing, commonly recognized in our daily lives, is a classic example of a tariff-based demand response program. The expansion of demand response services in China still holds significant potential, influenced by factors such as the development of the power

[18] National Development and Reform commission, & Ministry of Industry, Information Technology, et al. Notice on Power Demand-Side Management under the Supply-Side Structural Reform (Fa Gai Yun Xing Gui [2017] No. 1690).

[19] General Administration of Quality Supervision, Inspection and Quarantine of the People's Republic of China, & Standardization Administration of China. General Technical Specification of Power Demand Response System (GB/T 32672–2016), Article 3.1.

market, the enforcement of demand response standards, public awareness, the structure of energy consumption, and the level of economic development. The growth of market entities like agents (also commonly referred to as "aggregators" in the technical standards for demand response) has been relatively slow. The implementation of services is primarily organized by provincial grid companies, whose marketing departments are tasked with organizing the business and aggregating resources from power users. The dispatching departments of the grid companies, based on the forecast results for the power grid balance, instruct the marketing departments to initiate the implementation of demand response services.

Demand response is primarily categorized into two types: peak shaving and valley filling.[20] Peak-shaving demand response can be further divided into four levels based on the advance notification time: day-ahead response, hour-level response, minute-level response, and (quasi-) second-level response. Each level of demand response has distinct operational processes, load adjustment methods, and subsidy standards. Local authorities dynamically issue demand response implementation plans in response to fluctuations in their power supply and demand situations. The allocation of demand response subsidy funds is governed by principles of transparency and openness. Following approval by the supervisory departments, power companies carry out these funds in line with the specific demand response plans for the current year.

The implementation of demand response services operates on the principle of user voluntariness. In the pilot phase, grid companies, as service implementation organizations, issue demand response event notifications to a targeted group of power users and aggregators. These notifications typically include the required reduction or increase of power load per unit capacity with corresponding incentive rates; the initiation time, duration, and allowed ramp-up period; and the deadline for responding to the demand response event. Power users, guided by the terms of the "Demand Response Agreement" they have signed with the implementation organizations, weigh their own production, operational, and daily electricity needs to decide whether to participate in the response. If they choose to participate, they will engage in additional interactions with the implementation organizations to ensure precise adherence to the issued demand response events. For those power users who have implemented upgrades to their automatic demand response capabilities, the aforementioned interactions can be managed by automated demand response terminals, saving users a substantial amount of time.

---

[20] Peak-shaving demand response occurs when there is a power shortfall; in this scenario, power management departments and power supply companies issue response invitations to eligible users through designated platforms, and users respond with their commitment to reduce power consumption based on the specified response time and capacity. Peak-shaving demand response includes day-ahead response, hour-level response, minute-level response, and (quasi-) second-level response. Valley filling demand response occurs when there is a surplus of power; in this scenario, power management departments and power supply companies extend response invitations to eligible users through designated platforms, and users respond with their commitment to increase power consumption based on the response time and capacity.

In the future, with the ongoing development of the power ancillary services market, the establishment of the spot market, and the progression of tariff reforms, the issuance of the "Regulations for the Management of Grid-Connected Operations of Grid Entities" and the "Management Measures for Power System Ancillary Services" ("Two Rules") will substantially boost the growth of demand response aggregators as key market players. The underlying reason for this is attributed to the latest revisions of the "Two Rules," which affirm the participation of demand-side resources and their aggregators in the ancillary services market for balancing and adjusting the power system. This essentially secures a stable source of profit for power users and demand response aggregators. Overall, the ancillary services provided by demand response are set to play a crucial role in the consumption of renewable energy and represent a focal point in the development of modern electric power systems.

Orderly Power Utilization

According to the "Power Load Management Measures (2023 Edition)" issued by NDRC and NEA in 2023, orderly power utilization is defined as "the practice of maintaining a stable equilibrium between power supply and demand by legally and systematically controlling certain power loads through administrative and technical means when the balance of power supply and demand is at risk due to anticipated shortages, and cannot be rectified through increasing power output, market adjustments, demand responses, and emergency dispatching."[21] Moreover, Article 36 of the "Zhejiang Province Electric Power Regulations" stipulates that in situations where power supply is anticipated to be insufficient and the balance of power supply and demand cannot be maintained through demand response, governments at the county level or above, their power management departments, and power supply companies are authorized to manage the power demand of certain users by implementing orderly power utilization measures. Power management departments are tasked with organizing the development of an annual scheme for orderly power utilization in accordance with relevant national regulations and projections of power supply and demand balance, submitting it to the government at the corresponding level for approval and then publishing it to the public. Power supply companies are required to create detailed implementation plans that adhere to the approved orderly power utilization scheme.[22]

It is evident that, unlike demand response initiatives that encourage users to voluntarily change their power consumption behavior through economic incentives, orderly power utilization initiatives are primarily enforced through administrative directives, underpinned by the "Electric Power Law" which carries legal weight.

[21] National Development and Reform commission, the National Energy Administration of China. Power Load Management Measures (2023 Edition) (Fa Gai Yun Xing Gui [2023] No. 1261), Article 13.

[22] Zhejiang Province Electric Power Regulations, Article 36.

Power users who are part of the orderly power utilization scheme and its detailed implementation plans are legally obligated to comply with grid companies in implementing peak-load shifting and peak-load avoidance measures. In some provinces and cities, power users who adhere to orderly power utilization protocols are entitled to discounts on interruptible tariffs and can receive financial compensation for the electricity used during off-peak times, which can range from several fen to several jiao per kilowatt-hour.

To ensure effective orderly power utilization, power operation authorities at all levels must collaborate with grid companies and other relevant entities annually to develop annual schemes for orderly power utilization. These schemes are then compiled by provincial power operation authorities and submitted to both the respective level government and NDRC for filing. When the dispatching department anticipates a power supply shortfall during the power grid operation, the marketing department will formulate an orderly power utilization execution plan for the next day based on the annual scheme and submit it to the competent government department for approval. Once approved, the plan is to be enacted by the designated power users. It is mandatory for all power users who are notified about the orderly power utilization execution plan to adhere to it without conditions.

Articles 4 and 5 of the "Power Load Management Measures (2023 Edition)" stipulate that the orderly power utilization scheme is initiated when a shortfall in power supply is anticipated and the balance of power supply and demand cannot be guaranteed through demand response. Power management departments of governments at the county level or above are responsible for overseeing orderly power utilization within their jurisdictions, and other relevant departments of the local governments are tasked with related duties within their areas of responsibility. Power supply companies are key actors in implementing orderly power utilization. Power users are expected to support and cooperate in the implementation of orderly power utilization. Provincial power management departments should establish annual regulatory targets for orderly power utilization based on forecasts for the annual power supply and demand balance as well as national policies, and allocate these targets to the power operation authorities of various cities. Power management departments of districted cities and counties (cities, districts) should develop regional orderly power utilization schemes in line with policies and the power supply and demand situation. Provincial power management departments should promptly compile and update the orderly power utilization schemes of various cities, prepare and optimize the provincial orderly power utilization schemes, and, after approval by the provincial people's government and filing with NDRC, make them public.[23]

[23] National Development and Reform commission, the National Energy Administration of China (2023). Power Load Management Measures (2023 Edition) (Fa Gai Yun Xing Gui [2023] No. 1261), Article 13.

Grid-Overloaded Power Rationing and Accident-Induced Power Rationing

Taking Zhejiang as an example, Article 38 of the "Zhejiang Province Electric Power Regulations" stipulates, "If orderly power utilization still cannot ensure the balance of power supply and demand for the day, the grid dispatching organization may implement power rationing according to the approved grid-overloaded power rationing order table. Power management departments should, in accordance with the principles for formulating orderly power utilization schemes, organize the creation of an annual grid-overloaded power rationing order table, and submit it to the people's government at the corresponding level for approval."[24] Grid-overloaded power rationing refers to compulsory power restriction measures that are implemented when, despite forecasting a power supply shortfall and executing demand response and orderly power utilization, the balance of power supply and demand for the day still cannot be ensured. The "2022 Zhejiang Orderly Power Utilization Plan" stipulates that if an emergency power supply gap arises due to uncontrollable factors such as unplanned unit outages and ultra-high voltage faults, the provincial power company should be able to act preemptively by initiating interruptible loads at the minute and second levels and by shutting down emergency mobile loads to ensure the safety and stability of the power grid. When the power supply gap exceeds the capacity of emergency mobile and interruptible loads, the provincial power company should strictly implement emergency measures such as the grid-overloaded power rationing order table and the accident-induced power rationing order table to ensure the safe operation of the power grid.

Article 39 of the "Zhejiang Province Electric Power Regulations" stipulates, "Power management departments should organize the compilation of an annual accident-induced power rationing order table and submit it to the people's government at the corresponding level for approval. In the event of a power supply accident, the grid dispatching organization may carry out power rationing according to the approved power rationing order table. If the amount of power rationing required due to a power supply accident exceeds the capacity specified in the accident-induced power rationing order table, the grid dispatching organization should handle the situation in accordance with relevant national regulations on safety and emergency management."[25] Accident-induced power rationing is a mandatory measure taken to ensure the safety of the power grid's operation by enforcing power rationing based on the approved accident-induced power rationing order table when a power supply accident occurs. Similar to grid-overloaded power rationing, accident-induced power rationing is both urgent and unplanned. Therefore, users do not need to be notified in advance. The entity responsible for implementing accident-induced power rationing is also the grid dispatching organization. The accident-induced power rationing order table refers to a prioritized list of power lines that the grid dispatching organization

[24] Zhejiang Province Electric Power Regulations, Article 38.

[25] Zhejiang Province Electric Power Regulations, Article 39.

may use for power rationing during a grid accident to ensure stable operation of the power grid and minimize accident-related losses. When a power supply accident occurs, the grid dispatching organization is authorized to initiate accident-induced power rationing according to this table. Power management departments at all levels are responsible for organizing the preparation of an annual accident-induced power rationing order table, which must be submitted for approval by the people's government at the corresponding level.

Interruptible Load

Using Zhejiang Province as an example, Article 40 of the "Zhejiang Province Electric Power Regulations" states, "In situations where orderly power utilization is implemented or power rationing occurs due to grid capacity constraints or power supply accidents, power supply companies are authorized to initiate interruptible loads following prescribed procedures. As defined in these Regulations, 'interruptible load' refers to a portion of the power load that can be directly disconnected by the power supply company using a power load control device, without causing personal injury or compromising the safety of the user's electrical equipment and facilities in the event of insufficient power supply."[26] Power supply companies are allowed to initiate interruptible loads following prescribed procedures in situations where orderly power utilization is implemented or power rationing occurs due to grid capacity constraints or power supply accidents. The "2022 Zhejiang Orderly Power Utilization Plan" stipulates that if an emergency power supply gap arises due to uncontrollable factors such as unplanned unit outages and ultra-high voltage faults, the provincial power company should be able to act preemptively by initiating interruptible loads at the minute and second levels and by shutting down emergency mobile loads to ensure the safety and stability of the power grid.

Interruptible load refers to the physical capability of a load to be interrupted. When a grid company assesses the interruptible load capacity of an industrial enterprise, it is not determined based on whether a certain piece of electrical equipment supports temporary shutdown or adjustment of power consumption. Instead, the grid company guides the industrial enterprise to determine this capacity by optimizing production and operational arrangements, such as temporarily shutting down a production line or a production unit, or reducing the number of machines in operation on a certain production line or unit. Therefore, in the context of orderly power utilization services, interruptible load is commonly referred to as "interruptible load capacity." The introduction of interruptible loads is aimed at satisfying the government's requirements for ensuring the safe and stable operation of the power grid. Taking Zhejiang Province as an example, the power supply company is responsible for constructing an interactive system between the power source, grid, and load that features a rapid response capability for interruptible loads on a second-level basis. In the event of a severe grid

[26] Zhejiang Province Electric Power Regulations, Article 40.

failure or a significant shortfall in the power supply capacity, the system can mitigate the impact on users by selectively disconnecting certain customer-side loads. This approach minimizes the damages from widespread outages that would otherwise result from the activation of the "Order Table for Accident-Induced Power Rationing," the "Emergency Shutdown List for 220 kV Substation Transformers in the Event of Accidents," and the "Order Table for Grid-Overloaded Power Rationing." While minimizing user losses, this system also ensures an orderly supply of electricity and contributes to social stability.

Legal Nature and System Optimization of Orderly Power Utilization and Interruptible Load Management

Legal Nature of Orderly Power Utilization and Interruptible Load Management

Referring to the "Zhejiang Province Electric Power Regulations," orderly power utilization is defined as an administrative directive, while interruptible load management is characterized as a market incentive.

The administrative directive method is an approach where administrative subjects leverage the authority of administrative organizations and utilize administrative means, including administrative orders, instructions, systems, regulations, ordinances, and regulatory systems, to carry out administrative management activities in accordance with the structure and hierarchy of administrative organizations. It is the most commonly employed method in actual administrative management processes and is also highly effective. Essentially, it involves management through the roles and responsibilities within administrative organizations.[27] Firstly, administrative directives are compulsory. This nature is demonstrated by the requirement for the administrative organizational system to conform to a centralized and unified will, both ideologically and disciplinarily. This means that the orders, regulations, ordinances, and other issuances from the administrative subject must be carried out with strict adherence. However, this differs from the compulsory nature of the universal binding force associated with legal methods; it is a specific directive for a specific context, allowing for adaptability in exceptional circumstances. Secondly, administrative directives are hierarchical. The method operates on a top-down, large-to-small basis, in accordance with the vertical structure of the administrative organization, with directives being passed down in a linear fashion through the levels. Thirdly, administrative directives are highly efficient. Since they represent the government's direct exercise of administrative power, they can swiftly facilitate the implementation of policies and the

[27] See Wu (2006).

alteration of actions.[28] Orderly power utilization is considered this type of administrative directive. "Power management departments of governments at the county level or above are responsible for overseeing orderly power utilization within their jurisdictions, and other relevant departments of the local governments are tasked with related duties within their areas of responsibility. Power supply companies are key actors in implementing orderly power utilization. Power users are expected to support and cooperate in the implementation of orderly power utilization."[29]

Interruptible load management is a way to encourage users to voluntarily reduce loads through incentives. Power grid companies enter into interruptible load contracts with users and decide whether to execute or forego the load interruption stipulated in the contracts based on actual conditions. Users can voluntarily choose to participate in interruptible load management. Specifically, users can proactively report to power supply companies and provide them with the interruptible switch number. Upon verifying that no critical loads, such as security loads that could jeopardize personal and equipment safety or cause significant economic loss, are present under these switches, power supply companies integrate the switch into the advanced power load management system via a load control terminal or a bus meter. This integration allows for remote monitoring and control by power supply companies. A formal "Interruptible Load Response Cooperation Agreement" is then signed between power supply companies and users. According to the agreement, power supply companies may interrupt users' designated switches when necessary. The agreement specifies the term, interruptible load capacity, duration of interruptible load, range of interruptible loads, advance notification time, and compensation fees, among other details.[30]

From a legal perspective, is the Interruptible Load Response Cooperation Agreement a civil contract or an administrative agreement? An administrative agreement, also known as an administrative contract, is an agreement with administrative legal rights and obligations negotiated and concluded by administrative agencies or units entrusted by them with citizens, legal persons, or other organizations to achieve administrative management or public service objectives.[31] Although there is still debate in the academic community about the concept of administrative agreements, the distinction from civil contracts has formed the mainstream view. Specifically, the administrative nature takes precedence over the contractual nature, and legality over contractuality. Unlike civil contracts, the establishment of administrative agreements may involve multiple steps due to explicit legal requirements, and administrative agencies typically need to perform corresponding administrative actions before concluding such agreements. Properly handling the relationship between precontractual administrative actions and the conclusion of administrative agreements has

[28] See Wei (2008).

[29] National Development and Reform commission. Measures for the Management of Orderly Power Utilization (Fa Gai Yun Xing [2011] No. 832), Paragraph 2 of Article 5 and Article 6.

[30] See Ling and Liu (2017).

[31] See Regulations of the Supreme People's Court on Several Issues Concerning the Trial of Administrative Agreement Cases (Fa Shi [2019] No. 17), Article 1.

a direct impact on the remedies for legitimate interests of the contracting parties, especially if the legality of precontractual administrative actions directly affects the legitimacy of the agreement.[32] Furthermore, administrative agencies possess the authority to unilaterally rescind or amend agreements according to legal provisions without statutory grounds for termination. This prerogative, often referred to as "administrative privilege," is one of the significant formal differences between administrative agreements and civil contracts. Therefore, administrative agreements usually have the following characteristics. First, one of the parties to an administrative contract must be an administrative entity, vested with administrative authority. An administrative contract is concluded by an administrative entity to achieve administrative management objectives, hence one of the parties must be an administrative entity. It is important to note that not all contracts involving administrative agencies are administrative contracts. Administrative agencies have dual identities, namely administrative entities and civil entities. When an administrative agency enters into a contract as a civil entity, such as purchasing office equipment from a factory, the contract is civil in nature. Only when the administrative agency acts as an administrative entity is the contract considered administrative. Second, the purpose of an administrative contract is to implement administrative management and safeguard the public interests, such as contracts for joint investment and construction of public facilities like roads, bridges, and airports between administrative entities and companies.[33] Third, administrative entities enjoy administrative privileges in the performance of administrative contracts. Unlike civil contract parties, which enter into contracts for their own interests, administrative entities conclude administrative contracts to achieve administrative management objectives and safeguard the public interests. Therefore, administrative entities possess administrative privileges distinct from those of civil contract parties, specifically the rights to supervise, direct, unilaterally modify, and terminate the contracts. Certainly, an administrative entity may exercise the right to unilaterally modify or terminate a contract only when, subsequent to the contract's formation, circumstances arise that necessitate such changes or dissolution due to the requirements of the public interest or significant adjustments in legal and policy frameworks. Where such actions result in damage to the legitimate rights and interests of the other party, compensation should be provided.[34] Fourth, disputes arising from the performance of an administrative contract between the parties are regulated by administrative law. According to relevant principles of administrative law, such disputes are resolved through administrative remedies.[35] The parties to Interruptible Load Response Cooperation Agreement are power supply companies and users, neither of which is an administrative entity vested with administrative authority. Moreover, in the event of disputes, such as the user arbitrarily operating the terminal equipment, the infringement or breach of contract should be determined according to the terms of the Interruptible Load Response Cooperation Agreement, rather than

[32] See Liu (2020).

[33] See Chen (2015).

[34] See Zhang (2022).

[35] See Sun and Wang (2022).

by administrative remedies. Therefore, the Interruptible Load Response Cooperation Agreement is a civil contract rather than an administrative agreement.

System Optimization of Orderly Power Utilization and Interruptible Load Management

System Optimization for Orderly Power Utilization

Refined Management of Orderly Power Utilization

First, the orderly power utilization system should adhere to the principle of proportionality. In an ideal state, the best outcome of orderly power utilization management is the optimal allocation of electrical resources and the minimization of comprehensive losses, thereby maximizing management benefits. In the actual management of orderly power utilization, effective methods should be employed to strive for a win–win situation for all parties involved in orderly power utilization, and to improve the overall benefits. Typically, the main objective of power companies' business activities is to ensure the safe and stable operation of the power grid, thereby increasing user satisfaction and ultimately achieving the company's sustainable development and the improvement of economic benefits. The purpose of power utilization for power users is to avoid circuit faults and maintain the smoothness of power utilization. Based on this, power companies and users need to communicate effectively. Power companies should fully understand and investigate the power usage and satisfaction of users and develop corresponding coordination mechanisms and systems according to the consumer psychology and expectations, thereby determining orderly power utilization plans with practical value.[36]

Second, the orderly power utilization system should be tailored to local conditions. When formulating an orderly power utilization plan, it should be tailored to local conditions, planning different electricity use strategies according to the different needs of various companies. For example, companies that are explicitly restricted by national regulations, such as the small-scale steel, coal mining, machinery, cement, and fertilizer companies and companies with high technology, high growth, and high added value, should be prioritized in orderly power utilization management, while general industrial companies and other ordinary electricity users should be determined based on the actual circumstances of the enterprise. Regarding the determination of management duration within the framework of orderly power utilization, it is imperative to specify the participation duration for each company involved in orderly power utilization, ensuring precise control over the management duration of orderly power utilization.[37]

---

[36] See Zhang (2016).

[37] Same as above.

Third, the orderly power utilization system should ensure a clear delineation of rights and responsibilities. In the actual management activities of orderly power utilization, it is necessary to refine each stage and management unit, thereby facilitating the implementation of supervision and assessment tasks. Additionally, the detailed classification of power users is essential for the timely grasp and analysis of each power user's demand for electricity, allowing for flexible adjustments and planning according to market dynamics and trends. Hence, market research holds significant practical value. Effective market research can scientifically capture the electricity consumption characteristics of users, thereby enhancing the scientific validity and feasibility of power utilization plans and improving the quality and efficiency of orderly power utilization management. In addition, power companies should also focus on the division of rights and responsibilities, clarifying the duties and authorities of each department and employee to facilitate the implementation of subsequent performance assessments.[38]

Fourth, the orderly power utilization system should be strictly enforced. In the actual management process of orderly power utilization, relevant management personnel must identify the focal points and challenges of their management objects, conduct thorough inspections on focal points, and engage in repeated practices for challenges. To avoid unlawful activities in practical work, managers need to be vigilant, strictly supervising and controlling the execution process of power utilization plans. In addition, managers should establish a clear and comprehensive performance assessment system, using reward and punishment mechanisms to urge staff to work strictly in accordance with relevant requirements, thus promoting the normal progress of refined management work in orderly power utilization.[39]

Orderly Power Utilization Management Should Be Based on Accurate Load Forecasting

Accurate load forecasting is an indispensable foundation for formulating orderly power utilization plans. Only by understanding the future load demand of a region can targeted measures be taken to change the temporal distribution of power demand, thereby reducing the system's electricity requirements during mid-peak periods and shifting them to off-peak periods.[40]

Moreover, the establishment of reasonable orderly power utilization measures must be founded on the analysis of user load data and load characteristics. Typically, before formulating orderly power utilization plans, local grid companies first analyze user load data using their marketing system data and load control system

---

[38] Same as above.

[39] Same as above.

[40] Hu et al. (2015).

data, grasp the electricity consumption patterns of various types of enterprises, establish a database covering the power utilization of each critical user, and ensure regular updates.[41]

Of course, grid companies need to consider the individual requirements of users when investigating user load characteristics:

(1) Ascertain the capacity of the user's distribution transformers, the capacity of electrical equipment, the actual load of the electrical equipment, equipment utilization rates, the installation location of the electrical equipment, the nature of electricity usage, as well as the role of the equipment in the production line and the ownership of the production line;
(2) Ascertain the impact of sudden power outages on users and even each piece of electrical equipment, as well as the impact of equipment downtime on workers;
(3) Ascertain the equipment that users can use intermittently, including the name, capacity, and interval time;
(4) Ascertain the relationship between the user's electricity production load and other factors (such as temperature);
(5) Ascertain the actual load of users during different periods.[42]

Social Responsibility of Grid Companies Under Orderly Power Utilization Management

In accordance with the principle of government leadership and power supply companies as the main implementation entities, grid companies should strictly implement the orderly power utilization plan approved by the government. They must keep real-time track of the power supply and demand levels in their regions and conduct accurate power load forecasting.

First of all, grid companies should improve their internal management level for orderly power utilization. First, all employees should be trained on orderly power utilization, and orderly power utilization drills should be carried out with customers, including the preparation of orderly power utilization plans, notification of peak-shifting requirements, load control, monitoring of customer load levels, assessment of the effects of orderly power utilization, and publicity and reporting. Secondly, companies should fully utilize dispatch load monitoring systems and marketing systems to analyze the effectiveness of orderly power utilization, study the implementation status, evaluate the authenticity and participation level of customers, and timely report relevant information to the government. Data during the period of orderly power utilization should be promptly compiled and archived to serve as a basis for the next orderly power utilization.[43]

Secondly, the effects of the implementation of orderly power utilization should be monitored. First, orderly power utilization users and user loads should be properly

---

[41] See Li (2005).

[42] See Cai (2004).

[43] See Shi (2021).

managed to ensure the effectiveness of peak-shifting and load control measures; second, the user load control feature test of the power information collection system should be done well, especially the batch setting value feature testing, to ensure system functionality. User groups and metering profiles for orderly power utilization should be properly set up in the electricity collection system, with close attention paid to load conditions. In addition, close attention should be paid to the form of electricity supply, and the load setpoints of key accounts should be closely monitored at all times. Finally, power users are required to reasonably adjust their production plans, strictly control their electricity loads in accordance with the issued power setpoints, cooperate with orderly power utilization efforts, and develop power outage emergency plans and non-electrical safety measures. For electricity customers who do not follow the orderly power utilization plan or use electricity beyond the plan, they will be punished in strict accordance with the "Business Rules for Electricity Supply and Consumption" and the "Regulations on Grid Dispatch Management" and will be punished for breach of contract or violation of grid dispatching disciplines, and any losses or issues arising from such actions will be borne by the customers themselves.[44]

Finally, it is necessary to strengthen communication and exchange with the news media, power users, and all sectors of society, to clearly explain the reasons for electricity shortages, and to impart knowledge about energy conservation, electrical safety, and orderly power utilization, seeking societal understanding and support for orderly power utilization efforts. Taking the experience of Changsha as an example, the Changsha Power Supply Company established a visiting team led by the leaders of the municipal power supply company's secondary units to conduct interviews with major industrial customers, large commercial complexes, large hotels and guesthouses, large residential communities, and infrastructure and charging station sites to understand the electricity demands under orderly power utilization and to timely revise the orderly power utilization plan. They also strengthened the management of power utilization in designated areas, with power service stations and substations delving into their jurisdictions to ensure timely responses to customer demands and the effective execution of orderly power utilization. At the same time, they ensured the safety of power supply and consumption during the winter peak to prevent accidents such as fires. During the period of orderly power utilization, complaint handling and power outage control were intensified, with improvements and rectifications being made to exposed issues and lines or substations with concentrated outages, along with regular monitoring of online public opinion to prevent risks related to service public sentiment.[45]

[44] Same as above.

[45] Same as above.

Risk Prediction and Response Strategies for Interruptible Load Management

Risk Prediction of Interruptible Load Response Cooperation Agreement

First, there is a risk that customers will not cooperate in the installation, commissioning, and maintenance of terminals. Customers may fail to adequately assess their own equipment conditions and production processes, leading to the possibility that the branch switches connected to the system may include loads that endanger personal and equipment safety, causing significant economic losses. Alternatively, customers may not have developed corresponding internal emergency plans, resulting in significant safety incidents and economic losses after the branch switches are tripped. Article 655 of the *Civil Code* stipulates, "A consumer shall use the electricity in a safe, economical and planned manner in accordance with the relevant regulations of the State and the agreement between the parties. Where a consumer fails to use the electricity in accordance with the relevant regulations of the State or the agreement between the parties, and thus causes losses to the supplier, the consumer shall bear the liability for compensation."[46]

Second, there is a risk that customers will dismantle or disable power load control devices without the permission of the power supply company. Article 30 of the "Regulations on Supply and Consumption of Electric Power" stipulates, "Users may not commit the following acts that threaten the safety of electricity supply and utilization and disrupt the normal order of electricity supply and utilization:…(5) without authorization, remove, change or operate the electricity metering apparatus, load control facilities or supply facilities of the power supply company or the user's electricity receipt equipment which shall be managed by the power supply company as agreed." Article 40 stipulates, "If anyone illegally use electricity in violation of the provisions of Article 30 of these Regulations, the power supply company may, according to the violation facts and the consequences, demand the electricity fee and, pursuant to relevant regulations of the administrative department of electric power of the State Council, charge extra electricity fees and other fees stipulated by the state. When the circumstances are serious, the power supply company may cease to supply electricity according to the procedures stipulated by the state."[47]

Third, disputes over interruptible load compensation may arise. Interruptible load compensation is a mechanism within the electricity market that involves system operators requesting certain users to reduce their electricity load during system overloads to ensure the stable operation of the power system, while providing these users with certain compensation fees. Disputes may arise during the implementation of interruptible load compensation, such as disputes over compensation fees, which may arise due to the lack of clear and specific compensation standards and calculation methods, resulting in unreasonable and unfair compensation, and thus leading to disputes.

---

[46] Civil Code of the People's Republic of China, Article 655.

[47] Regulations on Supply and Consumption of Electric Power, Item 5 of Article 30 and Article 40.

Fourth, there are other contractual risks. These include, but are not limited to, the failure of users to fulfill payment obligations in accordance with the contract's stipulated time and method; the use of electricity not in the manner and under the conditions agreed upon in the contract; failure to provide load data as required by the contract or the provision of false data; and violations of laws, regulations, or relevant provisions that impede the power company's ability to dispatch electricity or operate safely.

Risk Prevention of Interruptible Load Management

First, grid companies should ensure proper installation, commissioning, and maintenance of terminals, conduct regular inspections and trip tests to guarantee that the terminals are always capable of remote disconnection.

Second, grid companies should fulfill their notification obligations. When grid companies need to activate the interruptible system for emergency handling, they should notify users in advance through voice calls, text messages, etc., and the time limit for advance notification should be clearly stated in the interruptible load agreement. Article 652 of the *Civil Code* stipulates, "Where a supplier of electricity needs to cut off electricity supply due to scheduled or unscheduled overhauls of the electricity supply facilities, restriction on electricity consumption in accordance with law, or consumer's illegal consumption of the electricity, and the like, he shall notify the consumer in advance in accordance with the relevant regulations of the State. Where a supplier cuts off the electricity supply without notifying the consumer in advance, thus causing losses to the consumer, the supplier shall bear the liability for compensation."[48]

Third, the contract should clearly specify terms such as the duration of the interruption, conditions for load recovery, and the basis for subsidy distribution. For example, it can be agreed that "each interruption should not exceed one hour in principle" and "Party A may organize Party B to participate in the electricity demand response work and distribute response subsidies in accordance with the regulations issued by the Provincial Development and Reform Commission and the Provincial Energy Administration for the current year."

[48] Civil Code of the People's Republic of China, Article 652.

Legal Risks and Countermeasures for Grid Companies Cooperating with Government Power Outages and Rationing

Legal Nature of Grid Companies Cooperating with Government Power Outages and Rationing

Legal Nature of Government Power Outages and Rationing

Grid companies cooperating with the government to implement power outage and rationing measures on specific power users is an act with legal basis. Certain laws, regulations, normative documents, and local regulations have provisions on this, and the "Measures for the Supervision of Electricity Supply" also clearly state that "power supply companies shall strictly implement the power outage and rationing decisions made by the relevant government departments to eliminated, closed, or environmentally non-compliant companies."[49] Therefore, cooperating with the government in implementing power outages is one of the obligations of grid companies. Generally, the governments power outage and rationing actions fall into the following three categories.

First, administrative compulsory measures. Administrative compulsory measures refer to the temporary restriction of the personal freedom of citizens or temporary control of the property of citizens, legal persons, or other organizations according to law by administrative organs in the process of administration for such purposes as stopping illegal acts, preventing destruction of evidence, avoiding damage and containing expansion of danger.[50] Article 9 of "Administrative Compulsion Law" specifies five categories of administrative compulsory measures, with power outage measures falling under the fifth category as a catch-all provision that can only be established by laws and regulations.[51] Paragraph 1 of Article 70 of the "Work Safety Law" stipulates that "For any organization where significant accident hazards are identified, the authority responsible for supervising and managing production safety may, in accordance with applicable laws or regulations, order the organization to suspend operation, production or construction, or to stop using related facilities or equipment. Such organization must fulfill the orders and promptly rectify the accident hazards. If the organization refuses to fulfill such orders and there is an imminent danger of a production safety accident, the authority supervising and managing production safety, with the approval of the persons in charge and provided that safety is ensured, may take action such as notifying the organization that its power supply or the supply of civil explosives will be cut off to compel the organization to fulfill the orders."[52] This provision can be understood as establishing the administrative

[49] Measures for the Supervision of Electricity Supply, Paragraph 3 of Article 24.

[50] Administrative Compulsion Law, Paragraph 2 of Article 2.

[51] See Administrative Compulsion Law, Article 9.

[52] Work Safety Law, Paragraph 1 of Article 70.

compulsory measure of power outage at the legal level. Administrative compulsory measures may arise due to administrative decisions or as remedy measures to meet the needs of the public interest. Depending on the urgency of the situation, administrative compulsory measures can be divided into immediate compulsory measures and general compulsory measures. The "Administrative Compulsion Law" mainly stipulates the procedures for general compulsory measures, but Article 19 provides for the remedy procedure of "going through the approval formalities" for immediate compulsory measures.[53] Administrative compulsory measures are statutory acts of authority and must be explicitly authorized by laws, regulations, etc.; they must be implemented strictly in accordance with the procedures stipulated by law. Otherwise, they may be deemed illegal by the court.

[Case study]

Intermediate People's Court of Huzhou's First-Instance Administrative Judgment on the Case between Zhang Yuncheng and the People's Government of Anji County on Administrative Compulsion (Zhe Hu Xing Chu Zi [2015] No. 40).[54]

The defendant People's Government of Anji County notified the Anji County Power Supply Bureau on June 12, 2015, to stop supplying electricity to the plaintiff Zhang Yuncheng's precast yard, which is associated with the electric meter number 3712308694. The plaintiff disagreed with the defendant's request for the power supply bureau to stop supplying electricity and filed a lawsuit with this court on June 25.

The defendant provided the following evidence within the statutory period: 1. Individual industrial and commercial business license, to prove that the illegal construction used by the plaintiff is the Anji County Xiaofeng Yuncheng Precast Yard run by the plaintiff. 2. "Low-Voltage Power Supply and Consumption Contract," to prove that the precast yard run by the plaintiff uses the electricity of the original Xiaofeng Village precast yard. 3. Case filing approval form, "Administrative Penalty Decision" (An Cheng Guan Fa Zi [2015] No. 006) and proof of service of Anji County Urban Management and Law Enforcement Bureau, "Administrative Penalty Notice" (An Cheng Guan Gao Zi [2015] No. 009) and proof of service of Anji County Urban Management and Law Enforcement Bureau, "1985–2000 Anji County Xiaofeng Town Master Plan," and "1995–2010 Anji County Master Plan Revision." This set of evidence was used to prove that the buildings used by the Anji County Xiaofeng Yuncheng Precast Yard run by the plaintiff, located on Yinsha Road, Xiaofeng Town, covering 602.3 square meters, belongs to the Xiaofeng Town urban planning area, and the buildings have been identified as illegal buildings by the Anji County Urban Management and Law Enforcement Bureau. 4. "Anji County Construction Land Planning Approval Application Form" and "Anji County Temporary Land Use Report Form." This set of evidence is used to prove that the temporary construction land

[53] See Administrative Compulsion Law, Article 19.

[54] See Judicial case. The first-instance administrative judgment between Zhang Yuncheng and People's Government of Anji County on planning administrative compulsion, Huzhou Intermediate People's Court ([2015] Zhe Hu Xing Chu Zi No. 40), Nonmember 11, 2015.

use period for the original Xiaofeng Village precast yard was approved for three years, while the temporary land use period was for two years. 5. The inspection records, on-site inspection drawings, and photos produced by Anji County Urban Management and Law Enforcement Bureau on April 10, 2015, to prove that the Anji County Xiaofeng Yuncheng Precast Yard operated by the plaintiff in this case used the illegal buildings covering 602.3 square meters located on Yinsha Road, Xiaofeng Town. 6. "Letter Regarding Inquiry on Whether Corrective Measures Can Be Taken for Suspected Illegal Buildings within Anji County Xiaofeng Yuncheng Precast Yard on Yinsha Road, Xiaofeng Town" of Anji County Urban Management and Law Enforcement Bureau (An Zhi Han Zi [2015] No. 049), the reply letter from Anji County Bureau of Planning regarding this letter, and three pieces of circumstantial evidence attached to the inquiry letter: investigation records of Chen Rengen, Shen Huojin, and Sun Zhengming by the staff of Anji County Urban Management and Law Enforcement Bureau. 7. "Administrative Penalty Decision on Land Violation Cases" issued by the People's Government of Xiaofeng Town, Anji County (Xiao Tu Zi [96] No. 2), a special receipt for township finance collection in Anji County dated May 30, 1996, a fact sheet issued by Xiaofeng Community Residents' Committee of Xiaofeng Town on March 30, 2015, investigation records of Wang Xiaobao and Wang Baihong by Anji County Urban Management and Law Enforcement Bureau, "Letter from Anji County Urban Management and Law Enforcement Bureau Requesting Copies of Relevant Investigation Materials for Zhang Yuncheng's Administrative Reconsideration Case" (An Zhi Xie Han Zi [2015] No. 1) issued by the Anji County Urban Management and Law Enforcement Bureau, and inquiry records of Zhang Yuncheng, Zhao Ximin, Huang Shengqi, Zhou Liangmin, and Sun Mingli produced by Huzhou Urban Management and Law Enforcement Bureau. This set of evidence was used to prove that the Anji County Xiaofeng Yuncheng Precast Yard operated by the plaintiff had not been previously investigated as illegal buildings before the Anji County Urban Management and Law Enforcement Bureau issued the "Administrative Penalty Decision" (An Cheng Guan Fa Zi [2015] No. 006). 8. "Administrative Reconsideration Decision" (Hu Zhi Fu Jue Zi [2015] No. 1) issued by the Huzhou Urban Management and Law Enforcement Bureau and "Administrative Penalty Decision" (An Zhi Fa Zi [2014] No. 228) revoked by the "Administrative Reconsideration Decision" and proof of service, "Administrative Penalty Notification" (An Zhi Gao Zi [2014] No. 390) produced by the Anji County Urban Management and Law Enforcement Bureau in the process of making the "Administrative Penalty Decision" and the proof of service, "Administrative Penalty Decision Approval Form," case investigation closure report, inquiry notice, on-site inspection transcript, on-site inspection diagram, on-site photos produced by Anji County Urban Management and Law Enforcement Bureau on October 16, 2014, investigation records of Zhang Yuncheng, Zhang Yuncheng's identity card, "Letter Regarding Inquiry on Whether Corrective Measures Can Be Taken for Suspected Illegal Buildings within Anji County Xiaofeng Yuncheng Precast Yard on Yinsha Road, Xiaofeng Town" (An Zhi Zi Han (2014) No. 390), and the "Reply Letter from Xiaofeng Town People's Government Regarding the Suspected Illegal Construction Issues within Anji County Xiaofeng Yuncheng Precast Yard on Yinsha Road, Xiaofeng Town."

This set of evidence was presented to prove that the buildings used by the plaintiff for the businesses of Anji County Xiaofeng Yuncheng Precast Yard, located on Yinsha Road, Xiaofeng Town covering 602.3 square meters, are illegal buildings. The defendant presented the following evidence to prove the legality of the procedure of the contested administrative action: 9. Internal Review Form for Power Outage, to prove the internal process review procedure for the defendant's administrative action. 10. Power outage application issued by Xiaofeng Town People's Government. 11. Fact sheet issued by Xiaofeng Town People's Government. 12. "Administrative Penalty Decision" (An Cheng Guan Fa Zi [2015] No. 006). 13. Notice to stop power supply issued to Anji County Power Supply Bureau. The defendant provided the following legal basis for the contested administrative action: 14. Paragraph 1 of Article 107 of the Constitution of the People's Republic of China; 15. Article 59 of Organic Law of the Local People's Congress and Local People's Governments of the PRC; 16. Article 5 of the "Regulations on the Disposal of Illegal Buildings in Zhejiang Province"; 17. Item 5 of Paragraph 1 of Article 5 of the "Implementation Opinions on Dealing with Illegal Buildings in the 'Renovations of Old Residential Areas, Old Factory Areas, and Urban Villages and Demolition of Illegal Buildings' Action in Zhejiang," to prove that the defendant has the statutory authority to carry out the contested administrative action. 18. Article 33 of the "City Planning Law of the People's Republic of China." 19. Article 35 of the "Measures of Zhejiang Province for the Implementation of the City Planning Law of the People's Republic of China." 20. Article 44 of the "Law of the People's Republic of China on Urban and Rural Planning." 21. Item 3 of Paragraph 1 of Article 2 of the "Implementation Opinions on Dealing with Illegal Buildings in the 'Renovations of Old Residential Areas, Old Factory Areas, and Urban Villages and Demolition of Illegal Buildings' Action in Zhejiang." 22. Item 3 of Article 3 of the "Measures for the Identification and Disposal of Illegal Buildings in Anji County," to prove the basis for identifying the plaintiff's buildings involved in the case as illegal buildings.

The plaintiff Zhang Yuncheng claimed that on June 15, 2015, demolition personnel forcibly stopped the electricity supply at the plaintiff's location, and it was only when the plaintiff demanded evidence for the power outage that he learned of the document jointly issued by the Office of the Leading Group for Comprehensive Environmental Remediation in Anji County and the Office of the Anji County People's Government, requesting the Anji County Power Supply Bureau to stop supplying electricity to the plaintiff. The Office of the Leading Group for Comprehensive Environmental Remediation in Anji County and the Office of the Anji County People's Government do not have the authority to request the Anji County Power Supply Bureau to stop supplying electricity to the plaintiff, and their actions constitute an overreach of authority, making the specific administrative action illegal. Therefore, to protect his lawful rights and interests, the plaintiff submitted the following claims to the court: 1. To legally confirm that the defendant's action on June 12, 2015, requesting to stop supplying electricity is illegal; 2. the costs of this case are to be borne by the defendant.

The plaintiff provided the following evidence to the court: 1. Power outage notice, to prove that the defendant carried out the contested administrative action;

2. Individual industrial and commercial business license, to prove the legality of the plaintiff's identity in filing the lawsuit.

The defendant, People's Government of Anji County, argued that I. The plaintiff's subject is incorrect. Anji County Xiaofeng Yuncheng Precast Yard was an individual industrial and commercial household invested and established by the plaintiff. Therefore, according to legal provisions, the case should have the Anji County Xiaofeng Yuncheng Precast Yard as the plaintiff, not an individual. II. The buildings used by Anji County Xiaofeng Yuncheng Precast Yard are illegal buildings. Anji County Xiaofeng Yuncheng Precast Yard operates on Yinsha Road, Xiaofeng Town, Anji County. The area of illegal buildings within the operating site is 602.3 square meters. These illegal buildings are used by the Anji County Xiaofeng Yuncheng Precast Yard. When the Anji County Xiaofeng Yuncheng Precast Yard uses electricity for daily operations, it utilizes production electricity, which was registered under the original Xiaofeng Village Precast Yard in Xiaofeng Town, Anji County, with the account number 3712308694. After receiving the notice, Anji County Power Supply Bureau stopped the electricity supply that was registered under the original Xiaofeng Village Precast Yard, not the electricity consumption of the plaintiff's separate account. III. The defendant has sufficient legal basis for notifying the Anji County Power Supply Bureau to stop supplying electricity to the plaintiff's precast yard. Item 3 of Paragraph 1 of Article 2 of the "Implementation Opinions on Dealing with Illegal Buildings in the 'Renovations of Old Residential Areas, Old Factory Areas, and Urban Villages and Demolition of Illegal Buildings' Action in Zhejiang" stipulates that "buildings on temporary land exceeding the approved period or buildings exceeding the approved period of temporary construction project planning permits" should be identified as illegal buildings. Moreover, provisions such as Article 33 of the "City Planning Law of the People's Republic of China" explicitly state that temporary constructions within the urban planning area should be demolished within the approved period of use. Item 5 of Paragraph 1 of Article 5 of the "Implementation Opinions on Dealing with Illegal Buildings in the 'Renovations of Old Residential Areas, Old Factory Areas, and Urban Villages and Demolition of Illegal Buildings' Action in Zhejiang" stipulates that "Power supply, water supply, gas supply, communication, and other services shall not be provided to illegal buildings. Power supply, water supply, gas supply, communication, and other service organizations shall not provide relevant services to buildings that do not possess property ownership certificates or relevant planning permits." In conclusion, the defendant's action on June 12, 2015, in issuing a notice to the Anji County Power Supply Bureau to stop supplying electricity to the plaintiff's precast yard is lawful. The plaintiff's claims lack factual and legal basis, and the defendant requests the court to dismiss the plaintiff's lawsuit in accordance with the law.

During the cross-examination at trial, the plaintiff objected to Evidence 1 provided by the defendant, arguing that Evidence 1 could prove that Zhang Yuncheng is an appropriate plaintiff for this case. The plaintiff raised objections to the authenticity, legality, and relevance of Evidence 2. The plaintiff also disputed the legality and relevance of the third set of evidence, arguing that it did not prove the legality of the defendant's notification to the power supply bureau to stop supplying electricity to the plaintiff. The plaintiff considered Evidences 4–8 to be irrelevant to the case. The plaintiff objected to Evidences 9–13, arguing that these five pieces of evidence could not prove the procedural legality of the contested administrative action taken by the defendant. The plaintiff believed that the legal and normative documents provided by the defendant could not serve as the legal basis for the defendant's contested administrative action.

The defendant contended that Evidence 1 and Evidence 2 provided by the plaintiff could prove that the plaintiff is not an appropriate plaintiff for this case.

Upon review, the court believed that the evidence provided by the plaintiff could prove the contested administrative action taken by the defendant, and that the plaintiff, Zhang Yuncheng, is the operator of Anji County Xiaofeng Yuncheng Precast Yard.

The court's determination of the evidence provided by the defendant is as follows: Evidence 1 is consistent with Evidence 2 provided by the plaintiff and is not subject to duplicate determination. Evidence 2 can prove the fact that Xiaofeng Village Precast Yard signed a "Low-Voltage Power Supply and Consumption Contract" with State Grid Anji County Power Supply Company. The court did not accept the claim that Evidences 3–8 lack relevance to the case. Evidence 9 can prove the fact that the contested administrative action underwent internal approval by the administrative authority. Evidences 10 and 11 can prove the fact that the People's Government of Xiaofeng Town, Anji County issued a "Fact Sheet" and "Application for Power Outage to Illegal Buildings at No. 23 Nanxi Road, Xiaofeng Town" to the defendant's internal organs. Evidence 12 can prove the fact that the Anji County Urban Management and Law Enforcement Bureau issued the "Administrative Penalty Decision" (An Cheng Guan Fa Zi [2015] No. 006). Evidence 13 is consistent with Evidence 1 provided by the plaintiff and is not subject to duplicate determination.

After trial, it was found that the Anji County Xiaofeng Yuncheng Precast Yard operated by the plaintiff Zhang Yuncheng is located on Yinsha Road, Xiaofeng Town, Anji County. Anji County Urban Management and Law Enforcement Bureau issued the "Administrative Penalty Decision" (An Cheng Guan Fa Zi [2015] No. 006) on June 12, 2015, identifying three buildings totaling 602.3 square meters within the Anji County Xiaofeng Yuncheng Precast Yard as illegal buildings and ordering their demolition within fifteen days from the date of delivery of the decision. On the same day, the Office of the Anji County People's Government and the Leading Group for Comprehensive Environmental Remediation in Anji County notified the Anji County Power Supply Bureau to stop supplying power to the buildings involved at 10:30 a.m. on June 15, 2015. On the 15th of the same month, the power supply to the precast yard operated by the plaintiff was stopped. On the 25th of the same month, the plaintiff filed an administrative lawsuit with the court.

This court believes that, in accordance with Article 25 of the "Administrative Procedure Law of the People's Republic of China," "A person subjected to an administrative action or any other person which is a citizen, a legal person, or any other organization with an interest in the administrative action shall have the right to file a complaint against the administrative action." In this case, the internal organs of the defendant, the People's Government of Anji County, required the Anji County Power Supply Bureau to stop supplying electricity to the precast yard operated by the plaintiff, Zhang Yuncheng, which bears a direct interest relationship with the plaintiff. Thus, the plaintiff Zhang Yuncheng has the right to bring a lawsuit against the said administrative action.

According to Paragraph 2 of Article 20 of the "Interpretations of the Supreme People's Court on Several Issues Concerning the Execution of the 'Administrative Procedure Law of the People's Republic of China'," if an internal organ or local agency of an administrative authority, without the authorization of laws, regulations or rules, enacts a specific administrative action in its own name, and the party concerned brings a lawsuit against it, the administrative authority shall be the defendant. The Office of the Anji County People's Government and the Leading Group for Comprehensive Environmental Remediation in Anji County, as internal organs of the defendant, the People's Government of Anji County, issued a notice requiring the Anji County Power Supply Bureau to stop supplying electricity to the precast yard operated by the plaintiff Zhang Yuncheng. In the administrative litigation initiated by the plaintiff against this administrative action, the People's Government of Anji County is the appropriate defendant.

The administrative action taken by the defendant, the People's Government of Anji County, on June 12, 2015, which required the power supply bureau to stop supplying electricity to the precast yard operated by the plaintiff Zhang Yuncheng, is legally characterized as an administrative compulsory measure. According to Article 18 of the "Administrative Compulsion Law of the People's Republic of China," in implementing administrative compulsory measures, an administrative organ shall comply with the following provisions: (1) Before implementation, a report on implementation shall be submitted to the person in charge of the administrative organ and an approval of implementation shall be obtained. (2) An administrative compulsory measure shall be implemented by two or more law enforcement personnel of the administrative organ. (3) Law enforcement identity certificates shall be produced. (4) The party concerned shall be notified to be present. (5) The party concerned shall be notified on the spot of the reasons and basis for taking the administrative compulsory measure and the rights of and remedies available to the party concerned according to law. (6) The statements and arguments of the party concerned shall be heard. (7) On-site transcripts shall be made. (8) The on-site transcripts shall be signed or sealed by the party concerned and the law enforcement personnel of the administrative organ, and if the party concerned refuses to do so, it shall be noted in the transcripts. (9) If the party concerned is not present, witnesses shall be invited to be present, and the witnesses and the law enforcement personnel of the administrative organ shall sign or seal the on-site transcripts. (10) Other procedures as prescribed by laws and regulations. In this case, there is no evidence to indicate that the defendant legally informed the plaintiff of the reasons for taking the measure to stop the supply of electricity, the basis thereof, and the rights and remedies available to the plaintiff, nor is there evidence to suggest that the defendant ensured the plaintiff's right to make statements and defenses. Therefore, the administrative action of the defendant requesting the Anji County Power Supply Bureau to stop supplying electricity to the plaintiff's premises was not implemented in accordance with the prescribed procedures of the "Administrative Compulsion Law of the People's Republic of China," constituting a procedural violation.

In conclusion, the defendant's contested administrative action violates the legal procedures. The court renders a judgment as follows in accordance with Item 1 of Paragraph 2 of Article 74 of the "Administrative Procedure Law of the People's Republic of China":

The Court confirms that the administrative action taken by the defendant, the People's Government of Anji County, on June 12, 2015, which issued a notice to the Anji County Power Supply Bureau to stop the supply of electricity to the promises of the plaintiff, Zhang Yuncheng, is unlawful.

The case acceptance fee of CNY 50 shall be borne by the defendant, the People's Government of Anji County.

If the verdict is not accepted, it may, within 15 days from the date of service of the judgment, submit the petition for appeal to the court and provide its copies whose number is as per that the counterparts, and appeal to the High People's Court of Zhejiang Province.

Second, administrative enforcement. Administrative enforcement refers to the enforcement by an administrative organ with the power of administrative enforcement according to the provisions of the "Administrative Compulsion Law" when a party does not fulfill its obligations within the period determined by the administrative organ after a legal administrative decision has been made. Administrative enforcement is established by law. Article 12 of the "Administrative Compulsion Law" lists five common manners of enforcement, with the Item 6 "Other manners of enforcement" serving as a catch-all provision. Although the "Administrative Compulsion Law" does not explicitly stipulate that stopping power supply is one of the enforcement manners, Paragraph 2 of Article 43 prohibits forced power outages for residents' daily use and also indirectly clarifies that stopping the supply of electricity to non-residential users is one of the manners of administrative enforcement. At the same time, the "Administrative Compulsion Law" does not stipulate that the enforcement manner must be stipulated by law. Therefore, the power outage, which is often found in various regulations, normative documents, and local regulations, is mostly considered a manner of administrative enforcement. In practice, the manner of administrative enforcement through power outage is used by many administrative organs. The court generally reviews the legality of the administrative enforcement from aspects such as the legal basis of the administrative decision and the enforcement procedures, thereby determining the legality of the power outage.

[Case study]

Intermediate People's Court of Shaoxing's First-Instance Administrative Judgment on the Case Between Shengzhou Pinhao Silk Apparel Co., Ltd. and the Shengzhou Municipal People's Government (Zhe Shao Xing Chu Zi [2015] No. 7).[55]

---

[55] See Judicial case. The Intermediate People's Court of Shaoxing's administrative judgment on the administrative forced demolition case between Shengzhou Pinhao Silk Apparel Co., Ltd. and the

The administrative action disputed by the plaintiff: On June 18, 2013, the defendant Shengzhou Municipal People's Government organized urban management and other departments to forcibly demolish the plaintiff's plant. The plaintiff, Shengzhou Pinhao Silk Apparel Co., Ltd., claimed that the plaintiff had a plant on Huancheng Road, Shangyang Village, Shengzhou Economic Development Zone, which was used for knitted textile fabric processing and other business operations. The relevant expropriation implementation unit carried out demolition and reconstruction of the plaintiff's plant under the guise of "Renovations of Old Residential Areas, Old Factory Areas, and Urban Villages and Demolition of Illegal Buildings," which is actually an act of government expropriation and real estate commercial development. The plaintiff did not reach a compensation and resettlement agreement with the expropriation implementation unit, and the government did not follow the legal procedures for expropriation. On June 17, 2013, the Shengzhou Municipal Urban Management and Law Enforcement Bureau issued "Decision on Ordering Demolition (Rectification) within a Specified Period" (Sheng Cheng Guan [2013] Ze Gai Zi No. 00154). The next day, the defendant Shengzhou Municipal People's Government organized urban management and other departments to forcibly demolish the plaintiff's plant, during which a large number of valuable items were damaged. The plaintiff believed that the forced demolition carried out by the defendant violated the legal procedures stipulated by laws such as the "Administrative Compulsion Law," applied the law incorrectly, and constituted an illegal administrative action. After applying for administrative reconsideration to the Shaoxing Municipal People's Government, the plaintiff received "Administrative Reconsideration Decision" (Shao Shi Fu Fu Jue Zi [2013] No. 43) issued by the Shaoxing Municipal People's Government on October 21, 2013, which upheld the specific administrative action carried out by the defendant. Now, the plaintiff has filed a lawsuit in court according to the provisions of the "Administrative Procedure Law," requesting the court to legally confirm that the administrative forced demolition carried out by the defendant on the plaintiff's plant is illegal, and that the defendant should bear the costs of this lawsuit.

To substantiate its claims, the plaintiff submitted the following evidence to the court: Evidence 1. Copies of the Business License for an Enterprise as a Legal Person, Organization Code Certificate, and Tax Registration Certificate, proving that the plaintiff is a legally established business entity; Evidence 2. A set of 48 pages of electronic tax payment vouchers (copies), proving that the plaintiff is a legally business entity that pays various taxes and fees in accordance with the law; Evidence 3. Three site lease contracts; Evidence 4. A certificate jointly issued by the Shangyang Village Committee of Shengzhou Economic Development Zone and the Shengzhou Economic Development Zone Management Committee; Evidence 5. Two attached pictures (copies); Evidence 6. An application for building a house submitted by Yang Chuanliang to the local village committee. Evidences 3–6 prove the legality of the construction of the plaintiff's plant and the source of the site; Evidence 7. Two pictures, proving that the "renovations of old residential areas, old factory areas,

---

Shengzhou Municipal People's Government (Zhe Shao Xing Chu Zi [2015] No. 7), October 26, 2015.

and urban villages and demolition of illegal buildings" carried out in the involved area are essentially commercial development actions after government expropriation; Evidence 8. Copies of the "Decision on Ordering Demolition (Rectification) within a Specified Period" (Sheng Cheng Guan [2013] Ze Gai Zi No. 00154) and "Administrative Reconsideration Decision" (Shao Shi Xing Zhi Fu Jue Zi [2013] No. 1) issued by the Shengzhou Municipal Urban Management and Law Enforcement Bureau, proving that the plaintiff had applied for administrative reconsideration for the "Decision on Ordering Demolition (Rectification) within a Specified Period" (Sheng Cheng Guan [2013] Ze Gai Zi No. 00154); Evidence 9. Two copies of the administrative complaint and one EMS express mail receipt (sender's copy) with the number 1028262158202, proving that the plaintiff filed administrative lawsuits with the Shengzhou Municipal People's Court and the Shaoxing Municipal People's Court respectively due to the "Decision on Ordering Demolition (Rectification) within a Specified Period" (Sheng Cheng Guan [2013] Ze Gai Zi No. 00154); Evidence 10. One CD and a set of three images (screenshots from the CD), proving that the defendant organized and implemented the forced demolition of the plaintiff's plant; Evidence 11. One list of property damage and a set of two photos, demonstrating the damage to the plaintiff's machinery and equipment and other items, caused by the defendant's forced demolition; Evidence 12. "Administrative Reconsideration Decision" (Shao Shi Fu Fu Jue Zi [2013] No. 43) issued by the Shaoxing Municipal People's Government, proving that the plaintiff had initiated an administrative reconsideration procedure against the involved forced demolition.

The defendant Shengzhou Municipal People's Government argued that 1. Shengzhou Pinhao Silk Apparel Co., Ltd. is not an appropriate plaintiff in this case. The lessee of the site lease contract involved in the case is Yang Chuanliang, and the owner of the illegal plant buildings involved in the case is also Yang Chuanliang. Therefore, the counterparty in the case of forced demolition is Yang Chuanliang, not Shengzhou Pinhao Silk Apparel Co., Ltd. 2. Even if Shengzhou Pinhao Silk Apparel Co., Ltd. were an appropriate subject, this case has exceeded the time limit for prosecution. Shengzhou Pinhao Silk Apparel Co., Ltd. applied to the Shaoxing Municipal People's Government for administrative reconsideration on August 9, 2013, regarding the forced demolition carried out by the respondent. On October 18 of the same year, the Shaoxing Municipal People's Government issued the "Administrative Reconsideration Decision" (Shao Shi Fu Fu Jue Zi [2013] No. 43), deciding to uphold the defendant's approval action. According to Paragraph 2 of Article 38 of the "Administrative Procedure Law of the People's Republic of China" prior to its amendment, "Anyone who refuses to accept the reconsideration decision may bring a suit before a people's court within 15 days from the day of the receipt of the reconsideration decision." The respondent did not receive the relevant materials for the lawsuit until February 2015, which clearly exceeds the time limit for filing an administrative lawsuit stipulated by the above-mentioned law. Therefore, the lawsuit filed by Shengzhou Pinhao Silk Apparel Co., Ltd. should be rejected. 3. The respondent has clear facts, conclusive evidence, and sufficient legal basis for determining that the plant buildings constructed by Yang Chuanliang are illegal buildings. Firstly, according to the "Site Lease Contract" involved, Shangyang Village of Shengzhou

Economic Development Zone leased 4.3 mu of land to Yang Chuanliang, who was supposed to build temporary facilities on the leased site only after obtaining written approval from the Shengzhou Economic Development Zone and after complying with the relevant department's regulations and procedures. However, in reality, Yang Chuanliang built temporary facilities without obtaining written consent from the lessor, Shangyang Village of Shengzhou Economic Development Zone, nor did he follow the corresponding required procedures. Secondly, according to Paragraph 1 of Article 40 of the "Law of the People's Republic of China on Urban and Rural Planning," Article 39 of "Urban and Rural Planning Regulations of Zhejiang Province," and Section 4 of the "Implementation Opinions on Dealing with Illegal Buildings in the 'Renovations of Old Residential Areas, Old Factory Areas, and Urban Villages and Demolition of Illegal Buildings' Action in Zhejiang," both units and individuals must obtain a construction land planning permit when constructing plants. In this case, According to the "Letter" and the "Approval Form for Forced Demolition of Illegal Buildings" sent from the Shengzhou Planning Bureau to the Office of the Leading Group for Controlling and Demolishing Illegal Buildings in Shengzhou City on June 13, 2013, and the conversation with Yang Chuanliang by the Shengzhou "Renovations of Old Residential Areas, Old Factory Areas, and Urban Villages and Demolition of Illegal Buildings" Command on April 23, 2013, it can be proven that the plant buildings involved in the case have never been approved for planning. The respondent therefore determined that the plant buildings constructed by Yang Chuanliang without planning approval were illegal buildings, and the facts were clear, the evidence was conclusive, and the legal basis was sufficient. Thirdly, this case does not involve the expropriation of land, houses, etc. Since the plant buildings involved are illegal buildings, according to Section 4 of the "Implementation Opinions on Dealing with Illegal Buildings in the 'Renovations of Old Residential Areas, Old Factory Areas, and Urban Villages and Demolition of Illegal Buildings' Action in Zhejiang," "Demolition of illegal buildings should generally not be compensated in any form, and all economic losses and civil liabilities related to the illegal buildings shall be borne by the parties themselves." Now, Shengzhou Pinhao Silk Apparel Co., Ltd.'s request for land expropriation compensation is inconsistent with the law. 4. The respondent's action of forcibly demolishing Yang Chuanliang's illegally constructed plant was done in accordance with due process. Based on the above facts and laws, the Shengzhou Economic Development Zone Management Committee, the Shengzhou Municipal Urban Management and Law Enforcement Bureau, and the Shengzhou Land and Resources Bureau jointly issued a notice on May 10, 2013, "Notice on the Joint Law Enforcement of the Sections in the Economic Development Zone that Meet the Conditions Specified in the 'Renovations of Old Residential Areas, Old Factory Areas, and Urban Villages and Demolition of Illegal Buildings' Policy," deciding to conduct comprehensive rectification and joint enforcement in the Shangyang Village and Xiemu Village areas targeted for rectification. All household owners involved in the rectification area were required to immediately terminate the lease with the lessees upon receiving the notice, and to urge the lessees to clear all equipment and related items and vacate the premises by June 10. From June 11, 2013, the relevant departments would take measures such as cutting off electricity and water on a selected date and carry out joint enforcement. On June 17, 2013, the Shengzhou Municipal Urban Management and Law Enforcement Bureau issued "Decision on Ordering Demolition (Rectification) within a Specified Period" (Sheng Cheng Guan [2013] Ze Gai Zi No. 00154), ordering Yang Chuanliang to demolish the illegally constructed buildings by himself before 24:00 on the same day. However, Yang Chuanliang did not demolish it on his own, so the respondent approved and agreed to take forced demolition measures against Yang Chuanliang's illegal buildings according to the law on June 18, 2013. On the same day, the Shengzhou Economic Development Zone Management Committee took the lead, together with the Urban Management and Law Enforcement Bureau, the Public Security Bureau and other relevant departments, to carry out the forced demolition measures against Yang Chuanliang's illegal buildings. In summary, the respondent's administrative action of approving and agreeing to forcibly demolish Yang Chuanliang's illegal buildings according to the law has clear facts, sufficient evidence, and legal procedures. The court is requested to reject the lawsuit filed by Shengzhou Pinhao Silk Apparel Co., Ltd. or reject its litigation request.

The defendant, Shengzhou Municipal People's Government, has submitted the following evidence and grounds to this court: Evidence 13. A record of the conversation held on April 23, 2013, between the Shengzhou "Renovations of Old Residential Areas, Old Factory Areas, and Urban Villages and Demolition of Illegal Buildings" Command and Yang Chuanliang; Evidence 14. A copy of the "Notice on the Joint Law Enforcement of the Sections in the Economic Development Zone that Meet the Conditions Specified in the 'Renovations of Old Residential Areas, Old Factory Areas, and Urban Villages and Demolition of Illegal Buildings' Policy" issued by the Shengzhou Economic Development Zone Management Committee, Shengzhou Municipal Urban Management and Law Enforcement Bureau, and Shengzhou Land and Resources Bureau on May 10, 2013; Evidence 15. A copy of the "Letter" sent from the Shengzhou Planning Bureau to the Office of the Leading Group for Controlling and Demolishing Illegal Buildings in Shengzhou City on June 13, 2013. The aforementioned Evidences 13–15 prove that the plant buildings rented by the plaintiff are illegal buildings. Evidence 16. A copy of "Decision on Ordering Demolition (Rectification) within a Specified Period" (Sheng Cheng Guan [2013] Ze Gai Zi No. 00154) issued by the Shengzhou Municipal Urban Management and Law Enforcement Bureau on June 17, 2013; Evidence 17. A copy of the "Approval Form for Forced Demolition of Illegal Buildings" approved and consented to by the Shengzhou Municipal People's Government on June 18, 2013.

The aforementioned Evidences 16–17 prove that the demolition procedure is legal.

The defendant clarifies that Paragraph 1 of Article 40 and Article 64 of the "Law of the People's Republic of China on Urban and Rural Planning," Article 39 and Article 69 of "Urban and Rural Planning Regulations of Zhejiang Province," Sections 1 and 2 and 4 of "Implementation Opinions on Dealing with Illegal Buildings in the 'Renovations of Old Residential Areas, Old Factory Areas, and Urban Villages and Demolition of Illegal Buildings' Action in Zhejiang," Paragraph 2 of Article 38 of the "Administrative Procedure Law of the People's Republic of China" before amendment and other regulations are the legal bases for its approval and agreement to forcibly demolish Yang Chuanliang's illegal buildings according to the law.

During the cross-examination at trial, the parties' opinions on the evidence are as follows: Regarding Evidences 1–12, the defendant contended that for Evidence 1, there was no objection to authenticity but there was an objection to relevance, as the rights holder of the illegal buildings involved should be Yang Chuanliang, which is unrelated to the plaintiff; for Evidence 2, there are objections to both authenticity and relevance, as it was unilaterally created by the plaintiff and the administrative authority's penalties and demolition of the illegal buildings are directed at Yang Chuanliang, unrelated to the plaintiff; for Evidence 3, there is no objection to authenticity, but the legality of the contract itself and whether Shangyang Village Committee can lease the involved plot need to be examined, and the three contracts' counterparty is Yang Chuanliang, which can prove that the plaintiff is not the appropriate subject in this case; for Evidence 4, there is no objection to authenticity, but there is no signature from the handler or testimony in court, which does not meet the formal requirements of evidence, and further confirms that the plaintiff is not the appropriate subject in this case, according to the defendant's understanding, the certificate was issued by the relevant department at the request of Yang Chuanliang when handling the business registration procedures for Shengzhou Pinhao Silk Apparel Co., Ltd.; for Evidence 5, there are objections to both authenticity and relevance, even if it is authentic, it cannot replace the corresponding land use and planning approval, nor can it demonstrate that the buildings involved are legal; for Evidence 6, there is no objection to authenticity, but there is an objection to the purpose of proof, as temporary buildings still require planning approval; for Evidence 7, there is no objection to authenticity but there is an objection to relevance, as it cannot prove that this case involves administrative expropriation; for Evidence 8, there are no objections to the authenticity, legality, and relevance; for Evidence 9, there is an objection, as the defendant has never received the relevant administrative litigation response documents; for Evidence 10, there is an objection, as it cannot be confirmed whether it is the demolition site of the involved plant buildings, but the fact that the plant buildings have been forcibly demolished is acknowledged; for Evidence 11, there are objections to the authenticity, legality, and relevance, as it was unilaterally created by the plaintiff, and according to the defendant's understanding, Yang Chuanliang had already moved all items from the plant buildings before the demolition, so the photos cannot reflect the demolition site of the involved plant; for Evidence 12, there are no objections to the authenticity, legality, and relevance, and the decision to uphold by the reconsideration authority confirms the legality of the demolition action.

Regarding Evidences 13–17, the plaintiff contended that for Evidence 13, there is no objection to authenticity, as it indeed represents Yang Chuanliang's statement and signature, but there is an objection to the purpose of proof, as it is believed that it cannot prove that the involved plant buildings are illegal; for Evidence 14, there is no objection to authenticity, but there is an objection to the purpose of proof, as the plaintiff has never received this notice, and the defendant is accused of expropriating under the guise of demolition, with the aim of commercial development, which is illegal; for Evidence 15, there is no objection to authenticity, but it is believed that the absence of the signature of the legal representative of the Shengzhou Planning Bureau lacks the formal requirements of evidence, and the content regarding the buildings involved not having planning approval is inconsistent with the facts; for Evidence 16, there is no objection to authenticity, but it is believed that the decision itself has issues with unclear fact-finding, erroneous application of law, and illegal procedures; for Evidence 17, the plaintiff was not aware of the approval form and believed that the approval action and the demolition action occurring on the same day can prove procedural illegality, and that the defendant's approval and agreement to demolish contains serious errors in fact-finding and application of law.

The court's authentication of the aforementioned evidence is as follows: Evidence 1 can prove the basic information of the plaintiff's company and is thus confirmed; Evidence 2 lacks relevance to this case and is not confirmed; Evidence 3, the defendant does not dispute the formal authenticity and can prove the fact that Yang Chuanliang once signed a site lease contract with the Shangyang Village Committee, which is confirmed; Evidence 4, the defendant has no objection to the authenticity, but it does not meet the plaintiff's purpose of proof, and the court confirms the authenticity of the evidence; Evidence 5, the authenticity cannot be verified, and it formally differs from the corresponding land use approval and planning approval, and is not confirmed; Evidence 6 can reflect the situation where Yang Chuanliang applied to the Shangyang Village Committee for the construction of temporary buildings and is confirmed; Evidence 7 lacks relevance to this case and cannot achieve the plaintiff's purpose of proof and is not confirmed; Evidence 8 can prove that Yang Chuanliang applied for administrative reconsideration regarding the "Decision on Ordering Demolition (Rectification) within a Specified Period" (Sheng Cheng Guan [2013] Ze Gai Zi No. 00154) issued by the Shengzhou Municipal Urban Management and Law Enforcement Bureau, and later the Shaoxing Municipal Urban Management and Law Enforcement Bureau decided to maintain the fact with the "Administrative Reconsideration Decision" (Shao Shi Xing Zhi Fu Jue Zi [2013] No. 1), which is confirmed; Evidence 9 lacks relevance to the contested administrative organ and action in this case and is not confirmed; Evidence 10, the fact that the involved plant has been forcibly demolished is confirmed by the court; Evidence 11 is unilaterally created by the plaintiff, its authenticity cannot be verified, and it does not fall within the scope of examination in this case and is not confirmed; Evidence 12 can prove that the plaintiff applied for administrative reconsideration on the grounds that the administrative forced demolition action carried out by the defendant on its plant was illegal, and later the Shaoxing Municipal People's Government decided to uphold the defendant's demolition approval action with the "Administrative Reconsideration Decision" (Shao Shi Fu Fu Jue Zi [2013] No. 43), which is confirmed.

Evidence 13 can reflect the fact that the "Renovations of Old Residential Areas, Old Factory Areas, and Urban Villages and Demolition of Illegal Buildings" Command of the Shengzhou Economic Development Zone had conversations with Yang Chuanliang regarding the leased plot of land, which is confirmed; Evidence 14 can prove the fact that the Shengzhou Economic Development Zone Management Committee, Shengzhou Municipal Urban Management and Law Enforcement

Bureau, and Shengzhou Land and Resources Bureau issued a joint law enforcement notice, which is confirmed; Evidence 15 can prove the fact that the Shengzhou Planning Bureau sent a letter to the Office of the Leading Group for Controlling and Demolishing Illegal Buildings in Shengzhou City on June 13, 2013, which is confirmed; Evidence 16 is already included in Evidence 8 and will not be authenticated again; Evidence 17, in conjunction with Evidence 12, can prove the fact that the defendant approved and agreed to the lawful demolition on June 18, 2013, which is confirmed.

Through the trial, it has been ascertained that Yang Chuanliang is a resident of Shangyang Village in the Shengzhou Economic Development Zone. On January 25 and January 30, 2001, Yang Chuanliang signed two "Site Lease Contracts" with the Shangyang Village Committee, agreeing to lease a part of the vacant site in Shangyang Village to Yang Chuanliang for a period of ten years, from February 1, 2001, to January 31, 2011. On January 30, 2011, the parties renewed a "Site Lease Contract," making corresponding adjustments to the location, boundaries, area, lease term, rent, and payment method of the leased site. After the contract was signed, Yang Chuanliang built temporary buildings on the leased site for factories, warehouses, dormitories, etc.

On April 23, 2013, the "Renovations of Old Residential Areas, Old Factory Areas, and Urban Villages and Demolition of Illegal Buildings" Command of the Shengzhou Economic Development Zone investigated the situation of Yang Chuanliang's leased site and the construction of buildings. On May 10 of the same year, the Shengzhou Economic Development Zone Management Committee, the Shengzhou Municipal Urban Management and Law Enforcement Bureau, and the Shengzhou Land and Resources Bureau jointly issued the "Notice on the Joint Law Enforcement of the Sections in the Economic Development Zone that Meet the Conditions Specified in the 'Renovations of Old Residential Areas, Old Factory Areas, and Urban Villages and Demolition of Illegal Buildings' Policy," deciding to conduct comprehensive rectification and joint enforcement in the Shangyang Village and Xiemu Village areas targeted for rectification. All household owners involved in the rectification area were required to immediately terminate the lease with the lessees upon receiving the notice, and to urge the lessees to clear all equipment and related items and vacate the premises by June 10, 2013. From June 11, 2013, the relevant departments would take measures such as cutting off electricity and water on a selected date and carry out joint enforcement. On June 13, 2013, the Shengzhou Planning Bureau sent a letter to the Office of the Leading Group for Controlling and Demolishing Illegal Buildings in Shengzhou City, clarifying that the buildings on Yang Chuanliang's leased plot had not been approved for planning. On June 17 of the same year, the Shengzhou Municipal Urban Management and Law Enforcement Bureau issued "Decision on Ordering Demolition (Rectification) within a Specified Period" (Sheng Cheng Guan [2013] Ze Gai Zi No. 00154), determining that the buildings on Yang Chuanliang's leased plot violated the provisions of Paragraph 1 of Article 40 of the "Law of the People's Republic of China on Urban and Rural Planning" and Article 36 of "Urban and Rural Planning Regulations of Zhejiang Province," and ordered Yang Chuanliang to demolish them by himself before 24:00 on the same day. The next day, the

Shengzhou Municipal Urban Management and Law Enforcement Bureau submitted the "Approval Form for Forced Demolition of Illegal Buildings" to the defendant Shengzhou Municipal People's Government, proposing forced demolition of the buildings on Yang Chuanliang's leased plot. The defendant approved and agreed to "demolish according to the law" on the same day. On the same day, the Shengzhou Economic Development Zone Management Committee took the lead, together with the Shengzhou Municipal Urban Management and Law Enforcement Bureau, the Shengzhou Municipal Public Security Bureau, and other relevant departments, to carry out the forced demolition of the aforementioned buildings.

It has also been ascertained that the plaintiff, Shengzhou Pinhao Silk Apparel Co., Ltd., was established on December 19, 2011, by Yang Chuanliang and his wife as investors, and used part of the temporary buildings built by Yang Chuanliang on the leased plot as the company's domicile. Furthermore, it has been ascertained that the plaintiff applied for administrative reconsideration to the Shaoxing Municipal People's Government on the grounds that the administrative forced demolition carried out by the defendant on its plant buildings was illegal. The Shaoxing Municipal People's Government issued "Administrative Reconsideration Decision" (Shao Shi Fu Fu Jue Zi [2013] No. 43) on October 18, 2013, deciding to uphold the specific administrative action of forcibly demolishing Yang Chuanliang's illegal buildings as approved and consented to by the Shengzhou City People's Government on June 18, 2013. On October 28, 2013, the plaintiff mailed the indictment and related materials for this case to this court via EMS (tracking number: EY311796362CS).

The court holds the following: I. Regarding the subject qualification of the plaintiff and defendant in this case. Firstly, in accordance with Article 25 of the "Administrative Procedure Law of the People's Republic of China," "A person subjected to an administrative action or any other person which is a citizen, a legal person, or any other organization with an interest in the administrative action shall have the right to file a complaint against the administrative action." In this case, combined with the valid evidence and the court statements of both parties, it was found that although the plant buildings involved were built by Yang Chuanliang, they were actually managed and disposed of by the plaintiff Shengzhou Pinhao Silk Apparel Co., Ltd., and Yang Chuanliang did not raise any objection or claim for rights during the trial. At the same time, taking into account the cost of litigation and reducing the litigation burden on the parties, the court confirmed the plaintiff's qualification to sue. Secondly, the defendant Shengzhou Municipal People's Government admitted that it approved the forced demolition of the buildings involved on June 18, 2013, and that the Shengzhou Economic Development Zone Management Committee took the lead in the implementation, and the Shengzhou Economic Development Zone Management Committee was a local agency of the defendant. Therefore, the defendant Shengzhou Municipal People's Government is an appropriate defendant in this case.

II. Regarding the issue of time limit for prosecution. Upon examination of the EMS and receipt records, the plaintiff mailed the indictment and related materials for this case on October 28, 2013. Therefore, the court does not accept the defendant's argument that the lawsuit has exceeded the time limit for prosecution.

III. Regarding issues such as the legality of the contested administrative action. Firstly, Paragraph 1 of Article 40 of the "Law of the People's Republic of China on Urban and Rural Planning" stipulates that, "for the construction of buildings, structures, roads, pipelines and other projects in an area covered by the plan of a city or town, the developing unit or individual shall apply for a permit for a planned construction project to the department in charge of urban and rural planning under the people's government of the city or county concerned or to the township people's government designated by the people's government of the province, autonomous region, or municipality directly under the Central Government." In this case, the "Letter" sent from the Shengzhou Planning Bureau to the Office of the Leading Group for Controlling and Demolishing Illegal Buildings in Shengzhou City has determined that the plant buildings involved were not approved for planning. The evidence submitted by the plaintiff also failed to effectively prove that the land use and construction of the plant buildings involved had been approved by the relevant functional departments. Therefore, the court does not support the plaintiff's claim that the land use and construction of the plant buildings involved are legal. Secondly, Article 35, Article 36, Article 37, Article 38, and Article 44 of the "Administrative Compulsion Law of the People's Republic of China" explicitly stipulates that if an administrative authority deems a building, structure, facility, etc., to be illegal and in need of forced demolition, it should first make an administrative penalty decision. If the party concerned neither applies for reconsideration nor initiates litigation within the statutory period nor does not comply with the administrative penalty decision, the administrative authority should issue a written notice urging the party to fulfill its obligations. The party has the right to make statements and defenses after receiving the notice. After the notice, if the party still fails to comply with the administrative decision within the deadline without justifiable reasons, the administrative authority may make a decision for forced execution. After the forced execution decision is delivered to the party, the administrative authority should announce it publicly, setting a deadline for the party to demolish the property by themselves. If the party does not apply for administrative reconsideration or initiate administrative litigation within the statutory period and does not carry out the demolition, the administrative authority may forcibly demolish it according to law. In this case, the defendant did not carry out an effective notice procedure before demolishing the involved plant buildings, nor did it make an administrative enforcement decision or inform the plaintiff of the available remedies and deadlines. The administrative forced demolition was carried out the day after the "Decision on Ordering Demolition (Rectification) within a Specified Period" was served, which violates legal provisions. Given that the action no longer has content that can be revoked, the plaintiff's lawsuit requesting the court to confirm that the defendant's forced demolition of the involved plant buildings is illegal is well-founded, and the court supports it.

In conclusion, in accordance with Item 1 of Paragraph 2 of Article 74 of the "Administrative Procedure Law of the People's Republic of China," the judgment is as follows: It is confirmed that the administrative action of the defendant, Shengzhou Municipal People's Government, in forcibly demolishing the plant buildings of the plaintiff, Shengzhou Pinhao Silk Apparel Co., Ltd., located in Shangyang Village of the Shengzhou Economic Development Zone on June 18, 2013, is illegal. The case acceptance fee of CNY 50 shall be borne by the defendant, Shengzhou Municipal People's Government. If the verdict is not accepted, it may, within 15 days from the date of service of the judgment, submit the petition for appeal to the court and provide its copies whose number is as per that the counterparts, and appeal to the High People's Court of Zhejiang Province.

Third, internal administrative actions. Internal administrative actions refer to those carried out by an administrative entity within the internal administrative management process, which only have internal effects and do not directly produce external effects. This is primarily manifested in working relationships, such as the relationship between leaders and subordinates. Whether internal administrative actions are litigable is a matter of dispute in judicial practice. Those who argue that internal administrative actions should be litigable are based on the provisions of Item 6 of Article 1 of "Interpretations of the Supreme People's Court on Several Issues Concerning the Execution of the 'Administrative Procedure Law of the People's Republic of China'," which states "Acts that do not have an actual impact on the rights and obligations of citizens, legal persons, or other organizations are not within the scope of administrative litigation." It is presumed that as long as the act has an actual impact on the rights and obligations of citizens, legal persons, or other organizations, it should be included in the scope of administrative litigation. Once internal administrative actions are included in the scope of administrative litigation, if the legal procedures for administrative enforcement or administrative compulsory measures are not followed, the relevant administrative authorities often face adverse legal consequences. In practice, internal administrative actions are rarely used as the basis for requiring power supply companies to cooperate with power outages. Administrative authorities generally base their requests for power supply companies to implement power outages on the need for administrative compulsory measures or administrative enforcement.

[Case study]

The Second-Instance Administrative Ruling of the High People's Court of Zhejiang Province on the Administrative Approval of Shengzhou Tianzhang Silk Weaving and Finishing Factory and Shengzhou People's Government ([2014] Zhe Xing Zhong Zi No. 76).[56]

The first-instance court, after examination, confirmed that on December 28, 2007, the plaintiff entered into a "Land Lease Contract" with Shangyang Village Committee and Economic Cooperative of Shengzhou Economic Development Zone, leasing 9.302 mu of land on Miaoshan in Shangyang Village of Shengzhou Economic Development Zone for factory site usage. On May 10, 2013, the Shengzhou Economic Development Zone Management Committee, Shengzhou Urban Management and Law Enforcement Bureau, and Shengzhou Land and Resources Bureau jointly issued

[56] See Judicial case. The approval appeal case of the Shengzhou People's Government and Shengzhou Tianzhang Silk Weaving and Finishing Factory, Administrative Ruling of the High People's Court of Zhejiang Province (Zhe Xing Zhong Zi No. 76), June 11, 2014.

the "Notice on the Joint Law Enforcement of the Sections in the Economic Development Zone that Meet the Conditions Specified in the 'Renovations of Old Residential Areas, Old Factory Areas, and Urban Villages and Demolition of Illegal Buildings' Policy. The notice informed the relevant house owners that all house owners within the area of renovation should immediately terminate their lease contracts with the lessees upon receiving this notice. Starting from June 11, 2013, the relevant departments would, on a selected date, implement measures to stop water and electricity supply in the designated area and carry out joint law enforcement. On June 13, the Shengzhou Planning Bureau wrote a letter to the Office of the Leading Group for Controlling and Demolishing Illegal Buildings in Shengzhou City, stating that no planning permits were found for the Miaoshan plot leased by Zhao Zhiyan (the legal representative of the plaintiff), and the building in that area was not approved. On June 16, the Shengzhou Economic Development Zone Management Committee submitted the "Request for Power Disconnection for Shengzhou Tianzhang Silk Weaving and Finishing Factory" to the defendant. On the same day, the defendant issued the "Reply of Shengzhou People's Government on Agreeing to Implement Power Disconnection Measures for Shengzhou Tianzhang Silk Weaving and Finishing Factory" (Sheng Zheng Pi [2013] No. 24) and approved the implementation of power disconnection measures for Shengzhou Tianzhang Silk Weaving and Finishing Factory, starting from June 17, 2013, at 00:00. The reply was also forwarded to Shengzhou Power Supply Bureau. Later, the Shengzhou Power Supply Bureau used this as a basis to cut off the power supply to the plaintiff. The plaintiff disagreed with this decision and filed an administrative reconsideration with the Shaoxing People's Government. The Shaoxing People's Government made an administrative reconsideration decision (Shao Shi Fu Fu Jue Zi [2013] No. 39) and upheld the specific administrative action taken by the defendant on June 16, 2013, as stated in the "Reply of Shengzhou People's Government on Agreeing to Implement Power Disconnection Measures for Shengzhou Tianzhang Silk Weaving and Finishing Factory" (Sheng Zheng Pi [2013] No. 24). The plaintiff was still dissatisfied and filed a lawsuit with the court.

The first-instance court considered that there were two key points of dispute in this case. First, whether the defendant's action of issuing the "Reply of Shengzhou People's Government on Agreeing to Implement Power Disconnection Measures for Shengzhou Tianzhang Silk Weaving and Finishing Factory" was justiciable. Second, whether the defendant's action in issuing the aforementioned reply was correct.

1. The Defendant's Reply in the Case Is Justiciable

The reply in this case is the defendant, Shengzhou People's Government's response to the request from the Shengzhou Economic Development Zone Management Committee. In terms of its form, it is a document related to the internal handling of administrative affairs within the administrative authority. However, when determining whether an action is an internal or external act, it is important to analyze the characteristics of the content of the action, rather than solely considering its form. Internal administrative actions should refer to the directives, supervision, coordination, and other actions taken by an administrative authority that do not directly affect the rights and interests of the administrative counterpart. The target and content of such actions should be internal to the administrative authority. Although the reply in this case has the form of an internal administrative document, its target is the power supply contract between the plaintiff and the power supply company, which involves civil legal relationships. The content of the reply specifies the object and duration of the power supply disconnection. The reply is clearly directed at specific subjects and specific matters, granting administrative enforceability, and it was communicated to the plaintiff by the power supply company. Although the defendant stated in the reply: "You (Shengzhou Economic Development Zone Management Committee) should make timely coordination with relevant departments," the defendant did not provide evidence of the alleged subsequent coordination within the statutory deadline to this court. After the reply was sent to Shengzhou Power Supply Bureau, it had the objective effect of causing the power supply company to stop providing power supply to the plaintiff. Therefore, the defendant's contention that the content of the reply does not directly have legal effect on the plaintiff is not accepted by this court. The defendant's act of issuing the reply has exceeded the boundaries of internal administrative actions and has had a substantial impact on the rights and obligations of the plaintiff. According to Article 1 of the "Interpretations of the Supreme People's Court on Several Issues Concerning the Execution of the 'Administrative Procedure Law of the People's Republic of China'," the defendant's act of issuing the reply falls within the scope of administrative litigation accepted by the people's court.

2. The Reply Issued by the Defendant Has No Legal Basis

According to Article 52 and Article 53 of the "Administrative Procedure Law of the People's Republic of China," in handling administrative cases, the people's courts shall take the law, administrative rules and regulations, and local regulations as the criteria. The defendant approved the implementation of power disconnection measures against the plaintiff based on the claim that the plaintiff's factory was an illegal building. However, laws and regulations relating to the handling of illegal buildings, such as the "Urban and Rural Planning Law of the People's Republic of China" and the "Urban and Rural Planning Regulations of Zhejiang Province," only grant the local government's planning authority at the county level or above the right to impose administrative penalties on administrative counterparts through legal procedures. The defendant does not have the legal authority granted by relevant laws and regulations to make decisions regarding power disconnection measures for illegal buildings. According to the principle of statutory authority, the defendant's approval of implementing power disconnection measures against the plaintiff without legal authorization or basis is considered illegal.

In addition, the defendant's reply in the case also violates the requirements of due process. A key aspect of due process is the necessity of hearing the opinions of the parties involved before making administrative decisions that may have negative consequences on them. This ensures that the administrative counterpart has the right to be informed and the right to participate. Disconnecting the power supply to an operating enterprise will directly affect the normal operation of the enterprise. Before the defendant issued the reply to approve the power disconnection, they solely relied on the request from the Shengzhou Economic Development Zone Management Committee without hearing the plaintiff's statement or defense. By directly granting the approval, they also violated the principles of due process. This should be rectified.

The plaintiff claimed in the lawsuit that the defendant failed to fulfill the statutory procedures for expropriation and that their "demolition instead of expropriation" action was illegal. This court finds that the aforementioned facts are not relevant to the disputed facts of the present case and fall outside the scope of the examination for this case.

In conclusion, the court finds that the defendant's "Reply of Shengzhou People's Government on Agreeing to Implement Power Disconnection Measures for Shengzhou Tianzhang Silk Weaving and Finishing Factory" (Sheng Zheng Pi [2013] No. 24) lacks legal basis and should be revoked according to the law. In accordance with Item (2) b of Article 54 of the "Administrative Procedure Law of the People's Republic of China," this court hereby rules to revoke the "Reply of Shengzhou People's Government on Agreeing to Implement Power Disconnection Measures for Shengzhou Tianzhang Silk Weaving and Finishing Factory" (Sheng Zheng Pi [2013] No. 24) issued by the defendant, Shengzhou People's Government.

The Shengzhou People's Government appealed and stated that I. The "Reply of Shengzhou People's Government on Agreeing to Implement Power Disconnection Measures for Shengzhou Tianzhang Silk Weaving and Finishing Factory" (Sheng Zheng Pi [2013] No. 24) is not justiciable. 1. The authority that issued the reply is not an appropriate defendant. The reply in the case was issued by a higher-level authority in response to a request from a lower-level authority. The lower-level authority was the entity responsible for performing specific administrative actions toward the administrative counterpart. According to Article 19 of the "Interpretation of the Supreme People's Court on Several Issues Concerning the Execution of 'Administrative Procedure Law of the People's Republic of China'," "if a party disagrees with a specific administrative action approved by a higher-level administrative authority and files a lawsuit with the people's court, the defendant shall be the authority whose name is indicated on the document that is legally effective to external parties." 2. The reply issued by the administrative authority does not have legal effect externally. The reply in the case is an internal document between higher-level and lower-level authorities for internal instructions. The content of the reply does not directly have legal effect on the administrative counterpart. It is the specific administrative action of the lower-level authority, not the reply itself that directly affects the rights and obligations of the respondent in the appeal. II. The fact that the respondent's factory building is illegal is evident, supported by solid evidence, and has sufficient legal basis. According to the "Letter" sent from the Shengzhou Planning Bureau to the Office of the Leading Group for Controlling and Demolishing Illegal Buildings in Shengzhou City, the factory building constructed by the respondent in Shangyang Village, Shengzhou Economic Development Zone was not approved. Based on the "Approval Form for Forced Demolition of Illegal Buildings" issued by the relevant functional departments and the transcript in which the legal representative of the respondent, Zhao Zhiyan, admitted that the building was illegal, the factory building constructed by the respondent is considered illegal. III. The fact that the reply issued by the appellant is clear, supported by sufficient evidence, and follows lawful procedures. Based on the aforementioned facts and the request of the Development Zone Management Committee, the appellant issued the reply in accordance with Article 5 of the "Implementation Opinions on Dealing with Illegal Buildings in the 'Renovations of Old Residential Areas, Old Factory Areas, and Urban Villages and Demolition of Illegal Buildings' Action in Zhejiang," which states that "power supply, water supply, gas supply, communications, and other services shall not be provided to illegal buildings. Power supply, water supply, gas supply, communications, and other service organizations shall not provide relevant services to buildings that do not possess property ownership certificates or relevant planning permits." IV. The first-instance judgment in this case failed to consider the current situation of the province's ongoing "renovations of old residential areas, old factory areas, and urban villages and demolition of illegal buildings" work and lacked objectivity. The province is actively carrying out the "renovations of old residential areas, old factory areas, and urban villages and demolition of illegal buildings" work, which is different in terms of scale and intensity compared to previous efforts. The societal consensus now supports a "zero tolerance" approach towards illegal buildings. Power supply, water supply, gas supply, communications, and other service organizations shall not provide relevant services to organizations and individuals that use illegal buildings for production or business purposes. On July 26, 2013, the Fourth Meeting of the Standing Committee of the Twelfth People's Congress of Zhejiang passed the "Regulations on the Disposal of Illegal Buildings in Zhejiang," reaffirming its importance. Furthermore, the first-instance judgment in this case has a significant negative impact from a legal perspective. The judgment will undoubtedly contribute to fostering a sense of impunity among those engaging in illegal construction, thus resulting in a substantial negative impact on the "renovations of old residential areas, old factory areas, and urban villages and demolition of illegal buildings" work in Shengzhou City. In light of the above, we request the revocation of the first-instance judgment and the dismissal of the respondent's lawsuit.

Shengzhou Tianzhang Silk Weaving and Finishing Factory failed to submit a defense statement within the statutory period. During the second-instance court hearing, the defense argued that the first-instance judgment accurately established the facts, correctly applied the law, and demonstrated judicial fairness. Therefore, it should be upheld.

During the second-instance court hearing, this court focused on examining key issues such as whether the appellant's (Shengzhou People's Government) document, "Reply of Shengzhou People's Government on Agreeing to Implement Power Disconnection Measures for Shengzhou Tianzhang Silk Weaving and Finishing Factory" (Sheng Zheng Pi [2013] No. 24), falls within the scope of administrative litigation.

After hearing, this court endorsed the facts found by the first-instance court.

This court holds that the factory building of Shengzhou Tianzhang Silk Weaving and Finishing Factory (the respondent) is included in the rectification area for "renovations of old residential areas, old factory areas, and urban villages and demolition of illegal buildings" due to the lack of legal building approval documents. The Shengzhou Economic Development Zone Management Committee submitted the "Request for Power Disconnection for Shengzhou Tianzhang Silk Weaving and Finishing Factory" to the appellant, Shengzhou People's Government. The request states, "According to the overall arrangement of the 'renovations of old residential areas, old factory areas, and urban villages and demolition of illegal buildings' work in the development zone, we request to initiate a power supply disconnection for Shengzhou Tianzhang Silk Weaving and Finishing Factory starting from June 17. Please provide your approval." In response, the Shengzhou People's Government issued the "Reply on Agreeing to Implement Power Disconnection Measures for Shengzhou Tianzhang Silk Weaving and Finishing Factory" to the Development Zone Management Committee. The reply states, "we agree to implement power disconnection measures for Shengzhou Tianzhang Silk Weaving and Finishing Factory starting from June 17, 2013, at 00:00. You should make timely coordination with relevant departments." Subsequently, the Shengzhou Economic Development Zone Management Committee sent the reply to the Shengzhou Power Supply Bureau. The Power Supply Bureau then proceeded to disconnect the power supply to Shengzhou Tianzhang Silk Weaving and Finishing Factory in accordance with the reply. Since the aforementioned reply is an internal approval made by the Shengzhou People's Government in response to the request from its subordinate, the Shengzhou Economic Development Zone Management Committee, it does not directly affect the rights and obligations of Shengzhou Tianzhang Silk Weaving and Finishing Factory. The respondent's lawsuit against the reply action does not fall within the scope of administrative litigation and should be dismissed according to the law. The Shengzhou People's Government argues that there are no justifiable reasons to file a lawsuit against the reply, and this court accepts the argument. The first-instance court determined that the reply fell within the jurisdiction of the people's court for administrative litigation and conducted an improper substantive review of the case, which should be corrected according to the law. According to Item (2) of Article 61 of the "Administrative Procedure Law of the People's Republic of China," the ruling is as follows:

1. The administrative judgment, (2013) Zhe Shao Xing Chu Zi No. 15, issued by Shaoxing Intermediate People's Court, is revoked.
2. The lawsuit filed by Shengzhou Tianzhang Silk Weaving and Finishing Factory is dismissed.

This ruling is final.

Legal Nature of Grid Companies Cooperating with Government Power Outages and Rationing

There are also two different views on the legal nature of grid companies' cooperation with the government in implementing power outages and rationing. One view argues that the grid company's cooperation with the government in implementing power outages and rationing falls under the legally authorized administrative action specified in Article 70 of the "Administrative Compulsion Law of the People's Republic of China" ("Administrative Compulsion Law"). Article 29 of the "Electric Power Law of the People's Republic of China" ("Electric Power Law") clearly grants power supply companies the right to implement power rationing in accordance with the law. Article 28 of the "Regulations on Supply and Consumption of Electric Power" also stipulates that power supply companies can restrict or disconnect power supply in accordance with predetermined power restriction orders without the need for additional administrative procedures. Article 6 of the "Measures for the Management of Orderly Power Utilization" specifies that power supply companies are the implementers of specific administrative actions by the authority responsible for orderly power utilization management. Therefore, this view argues that power supply companies have the authority to carry out power disconnection in accordance with predetermined power restriction orders in the management of orderly power utilization. Another view argues that grid companies, in the management of orderly power utilization, act as the executors of administrative orders.[57] The government and power administrative management departments possess the authority for orderly power utilization management. The specific administrative actions of grid companies in cooperating with the government to implement power supply outages and rationing can only be carried out by the government and power administrative management departments. Therefore, power supply companies' action to dispatch personnel to disconnect power supply on-site, in accordance with the government's request and in coordination with law enforcement officers, is considered an auxiliary implementation action. Power supply companies perform this action to fulfill their legal obligations and assist the government and relevant government departments in carrying out specific administrative actions.[58]

Based on the relevant court precedents in China, the cooperation of grid companies with the government in implementing power outages should be classified as auxiliary implementation actions rather than authorized administrative actions. The reasons are as follows. Firstly, there is no legal or administrative regulatory authorization for grid companies to cooperate with the government in implementing power outages and rationing. Article 70 of the "Administrative Compulsion Law" requires authorization from laws and administrative regulations for authorized administrative actions. The basis for grid companies to cooperate with power outages and rationing is the "Measures for the Supervision of Electric Power," which are departmental regulations rather than laws and administrative regulations. Secondly, the cooperation of grid

[57] Shan (2018).

[58] Same as above.

companies with the government in implementing power outages and rationing aligns with the specific characteristics of auxiliary implementation actions. The cooperation of grid companies with the government in implementing power outages and rationing has the following characteristics: First, the grid companies' cooperation with the government in implementing power outages and rationing is based on government decisions and not on the companies' own discretion. Second, grid companies cannot refuse the government's request for cooperation in implementing power outages and rationing without sufficient justification. Third, the implementation of power outages and rationing by grid companies in cooperation with the government must strictly adhere to the procedures required by the "Administrative Compulsion Law," rather than the relevant regulatory provisions for power supply companies. Fourth, when personnel dispatched by grid companies implement power outages, they do not need to indicate the identity of the company and only need to provide technical support. Fifth, disputes arising from grid companies' cooperation with the government in power outages and rationing are generally resolved through administrative litigation.

Therefore, the cooperation of grid companies with the government in implementing power outages and rationing is an action carried out in response to government requests. The legal responsibilities arising from power outages and rationing and other administrative coercion actions should be borne by the government. As a result, grid companies do not have a direct legal relationship of rights and obligations with users for their cooperation with the government in power outages and rationing. Specifically, grid companies should not bear the following civil legal responsibilities when cooperating with the government in implementing power outages and rationing. First, grid companies should not bear the legal responsibility for breaching the power supply agreement. According to the provisions of the "Electric Power Law," "the power supply company shall supply electricity continuously without shut-off under normal operation of the power-generating and supplying systems."[59] Power supply companies enter into power supply contracts with users, based on which they provide power supply and collect fees. They cannot terminate the power supply without justifiable reasons. However, when power supply companies cooperate with the government in implementing power outages and rationing in accordance with the law, it is not a civil action undertaken by the companies based on their own will. Instead, it is an entrusted act to fulfill public authority, which constitutes an appropriate intervention of public authority into private rights. The responsibility for the government's power outage and rationing actions lies with the administrative authorities rather than the power supply companies. If power users have objections to the government's power outage actions, they should seek to protect their legitimate rights and interests through administrative reconsideration or administrative litigation. Second, grid companies are not liable for damages suffered by users due to tort. The cooperation of grid companies with the government in implementing power outages and rationing often occurs under the premise that users' operations have lost legal basis and the benefits generated are not considered legitimate rights. Therefore, power supply companies

[59] Electric Power Law, Paragraph 1 of Article 29.

are not required to bear the losses incurred by users due to power outages resulting from illegal operations.

[Case study]

The plaintiff, Zhu XXX, built a steel shed factory and set up a processing workshop in the factory. The defendant, a power supply company, had been supplying power to the processing workshop. On April 22, 2016, the local Urban Management and Law Enforcement Bureau sent a "Decision on Ordering Demolition (Rectification) within a Specified Period" to the processing workshop. The decision stated that the steel shed factory had not obtained legal approval and ordered the factory owner to rectify the situation within a specified period. However, the factory was not rectified and demolished within the specified time period. As a result, the Urban Management Law Enforcement Bureau in that area made a written request to the power supply company to implement power disconnection measures on the factory. The defendant, the power supply company, then dispatched technical personnel to disconnect the power supply to the factory. On December 19, 2016, the plaintiff filed a lawsuit against the defendant, seeking compensation for the losses incurred due to the power disconnection. The plaintiff argued that as an independent corporate entity, the power supply company had no legal subordination or affiliation with the law enforcement bureau, which issued the order or instruction to disconnect the power supply. There were no factual or legal grounds for the power supply company to carry out the power disconnection measures against the plaintiff. According to the provisions of the "Contract Law," the defendant should bear civil liability for breach of contract due to their power disconnection actions.

The court considered that the notification from the law enforcement authority to the defendant to disconnect the power supply was a preparatory measure before demolishing the illegal building. Therefore, the power disconnection measure implemented by the power supply company, the defendant in this case, was a step involved in the process of demolishing the illegal building. The power supply company was only the operator in this scenario. Even if there were economic losses incurred after the power disconnection of the processing workshop, those losses were a result of the demolition of the illegal building and should not be borne by the specific operator. The demolition of the illegal building was an administrative action carried out by the administrative authority, and any losses resulting from this specific administrative action should be resolved within the framework of administrative litigation. The compensation claim made by the plaintiff did not fall within the scope of civil compensation. The ruling was made to dismiss the plaintiff's lawsuit.[60]

Power supply companies' action to disconnect power supply in cooperating with the government is essentially an auxiliary implementation action of the government's administrative action. The legality of power disconnections carried out by power supply companies depends on the legality of the administrative actions taken by the government to order those power disconnections. From the perspective of cooperating with law enforcement agencies to implement power disconnections,

---

[60] See Qiu (2018).

the motivation behind them stems from relevant administrative documents issued by government agencies, rather than contractual agreements between power supply companies and power users. In addition, the purpose of the power disconnection is to achieve specific administrative objectives. Power supply companies cannot refuse the government's request for cooperation in implementing power disconnections without sufficient justification.[61] The act of cooperating with law enforcement for power disconnections reflects the intentions of the administrative authorities, rather than being driven by the interests of the power supply company. Therefore, power supply companies' cooperation with law enforcement for power disconnections is an auxiliary implementation action of the government's administrative action. The implementation of power disconnections by power supply companies in accordance with the requirements of law enforcement agencies is part of administrative actions and does not fall within the scope of civil legal relationships.[62]

The grid company's cooperation with law enforcement agencies to implement power disconnections is an auxiliary implementation action and a part of a specific administrative action and is not an independent civil action. Therefore, the corresponding legal responsibility should be borne by the administrative authority that carries out the administrative action, rather than the grid company. Power supply companies do not establish legal rights and obligations directly with users as a result of cooperating with government for power disconnections.[63] Specifically, power supply companies should not bear any civil legal responsibility for cooperating with government-ordered power disconnections in accordance with the law. First, power supply companies enter into "Power Supply Contracts" with users, and they shall provide continuous power supply to users. They cannot terminate the power supply without justifiable reasons. However, when power supply companies cooperate with the government in implementing power disconnections in accordance with the law, it is not a civil action undertaken by the companies based on their own will. Instead, it is an entrusted act to fulfill public authority, which constitutes an appropriate intervention of public authority into private rights. The responsibility for the government's power disconnection actions lies with the administrative authorities rather than the power supply companies. If power users have objections to the government's power outage actions, they should seek to protect their legitimate rights and interests through administrative reconsideration or administrative litigation. Second, power supply companies are not liable for compensating users for damages due to tort. The cooperation with the government in implementing power disconnections often occurs under the premise that users' operations have lost legal basis and the benefits generated are not considered legitimate rights. Therefore, power supply companies are not required to bear the losses incurred by users due to power outages resulting from illegal operations.

[61] Same as above.

[62] See Wang and Gao (2021).

[63] Same as above.

Legal Risks for Grid Companies Cooperating with Government Power Outages and Rationing

For example, for orderly power utilization management, if power outages and rationing are necessary due to insufficient power supply, the local power industry authorities shall act in accordance with the requirements of "orderly power utilization management." According to regulations, the development of orderly power utilization plans in different regions is guided by the power authorities. The grid companies formulate these plans based on the annual indicators determined by the provincial power authorities. In practical implementation, after the grid companies in each city (city divided by districts) complete such plans, they are submitted to the local power authorities for approval and issuing. For example, the Guangzhou Municipal Industrial and Information Technology Bureau issued the "2021 Guangzhou Orderly Power Utilization Plan" on May 10, 2021. Following the principles of classification management, optimal power supply, ensuring key areas, and emphasizing efficiency, the plan arranges the balance of power supply and demand in a sequential order of voluntary load shifting, reducing usage during peak hours, power rationing, and forced load shifting at the line level. The plan prioritizes ensuring power supply for public utilities and other essential services, employs centralized control measures, and arranges users to shift peak load and reduce usage during peak hours. The plan is valid for 1 year and takes effect from the date of issuance. Once the power or electricity deficit reaches the specified threshold, a warning (divided into four levels) will be issued, and the orderly power utilization plan will be initiated. Upon receiving the warning, grid companies in different regions are legally obligated to provide advance notice to users through means such as public announcements, phone calls, faxes, and SMS messages. The length of time in advance is not specified in relevant laws and regulations, and is usually specified in the local "plans." For example, the "2021 Guangzhou Orderly Power Utilization Plan" stipulates that the control center, based on power supply and grid operation conditions, shall issue load shifting warnings for different areas in Guangzhou for the next day or a specific period in the future. Upon receiving the load shifting warnings issued by the control center, the power supply bureaus in each district shall provide advance notice to their users one day in advance, informing them about the load shifting warnings for the next day or a specific period in the future and related information.[64] In practice, the following legal risks are associated with power outages and rationing due to orderly power utilization.

Firstly, the content and issuance of the order table for power outages and rationing may not comply with the required procedures. Fault-induced power outages are typically unpredictable and occur suddenly, making it difficult to provide advance notice to power users. This can lead to unexpected consequences or losses. For fault-induced power outages, both the "Regulations on Supply and Consumption of Electric Power" and the "Power Supply Business Rules" require power supply companies to carry

[64] See Guangzhou Municipal Industry and Information Technology Bureau. Reply on the 2021 Guangzhou Orderly Power Utilization Plan, released on May 11, 2024.

out power outages or rationing according to the predetermined order.[65] Therefore, power supply companies must create the "Order Table for Accident-Induced Power Rationing" in advance to establish the order for fault-induced power outages and rationing and periodically update it. Similarly, the orderly power utilization plan and the accident emergency response plan for orderly power utilization need to be approved and issued by the people's government. Article 13 of the "Measures for the Supervision of Electricity Supply" stipulates, "in the event of power outages or rationing due to grid failures or power shortage, power supply companies shall act in accordance with the orderly power utilization plan or accident emergency response plan approved by the local people's government."[66]

Secondly, the order table for power outages and rationing may not be announced as required. The information regarding power outages and rationing falls within the scope of proactive disclosure by power supply companies. Article 68 of the "Power Supply Business Rules" states that "when power supply system failures occur, resulting in the need for power outages or rationing, or planned power rationing or outages occur, power supply companies shall carry out power outages or rationing according to the determined power restriction order. The power restriction order shall be announced in advance to power users."[67] If a power supply company fails to announce the order table for power outages and rationing as required, it may be subject to relevant administrative penalties. Furthermore, the provisions in laws and regulations regarding the announcement of the order table for power outages and rationing are often vaguely defined, and power supply companies often choose to announce it through traditional local media. However, this type of announcement is usually overlooked by power users, which leads to numerous disputes. Orderly power utilization is led and promoted by various levels of government and relevant government departments. The orderly power utilization plan includes the "Order Table for Grid Overload Measures." The "Order Table for Grid Overload Measures" is formulated and approved by the relevant government departments to ensure the balance of power supply and demand and the safe and stable operation of the power grid, particularly during periods of high power demand. It aims to prevent grid accidents and potential safety issues caused by excessive power consumption by users beyond the planned capacity. The power supply companies are responsible for acting in accordance with this order table. The "Order Table for Grid Overload Measures" is included in the orderly power utilization plan. The local economic and information departments at various levels are responsible for preparing the annual orderly power utilization plan for their respective regions and making it publicly available.

---

[65] See Regulations on Supply and Consumption of Electric Power, Article 28; Power Supply Business Rules (Order No. 8 of the Ministry of Electric Power Industry of the People's Republic of China), Article 68.

[66] Measures for the Supervision of Electricity Supply, Item (3) of paragraph 2 of Article 13.

[67] Power Supply Business Rules" Order No. 8 of the Ministry of Electric Power Industry of the People's Republic of China, Item 3 of Article 68.

Thirdly, the order table for power outages and rationing may not be followed. Once the "Order Table for Accident-Induced Power Rationing" and the "Order Table for Grid Overload Measures" are issued, they immediately gain credibility. In the event of grid failures, power shortage, or unexpected incidents, power supply companies must adhere to the specified power outage or rationing range as defined in the "Order Table for Accident-Induced Power Rationing" and the "Order Table for Grid Overload Measures." Failure to do so will result in legal liability for compensation related to illegal power outages or rationing.

Fourthly, the administrative authority may not be qualified. In cases where other grid companies cooperate with the government in implementing power outages or rationing, a common legal risk is associated with whether the administrative authority possesses the corresponding administrative powers. Administrative actions taken by the administrative authority beyond its jurisdiction are considered ultra-vires and lack legal effect. If an administrative entity that lacks qualification demands power supply companies to cooperate with power outages, it will bear the legal consequences of losing the lawsuit. In recent years, with the progress of land expropriation and demolition by government agencies, as well as actions to address illegal buildings, government departments frequently resort to power outages or rationing as a means of enforcement. It has been observed on multiple occasions that the administrative authorities making decisions to require power outages or rationing are not the competent authorities responsible for implementing such actions, or they exceed their own jurisdiction in making such decisions. Additionally, there are instances where the administrative authorities fail to adopt other appropriate measures and instead demand the administrative counterpart to comply with administrative decisions through power outages or rationing. There have also been cases where administrative authorities violate statutory procedures in making power outage or rationing decisions. For example, county-level people's governments establish offices such as the "Renovations of Old Residential Areas, Old Factory Areas, and Urban Villages and Demolition of Illegal Buildings" Office and the Water Pollution Management Office to perform administrative functions related to demolition and control of illegal buildings, as well as water pollution management. There is ongoing controversy regarding whether these organizations are qualified administrative entities. Power supply companies often find themselves in a defensive position in legal disputes when they comply with power outage requests based on the requirements of these organizations.

Fifthly, there may be insufficient basis for power outages and rationing. As a third party outside of the power supply contract, government departments do not have the authority to unilaterally suspend or terminate the performance of the power supply contract in the absence of legal grounds. The legal basis for power supply companies to cooperate with government (judicial) agencies in implementing power outages or rationing is scattered across various laws, regulations, and rules. Moreover, there are relatively few direct provisions in these laws and regulations that explicitly allow for power outages or rationing. In practice, government agencies usually rely on normative government documents as the basis to demand power supply companies to cooperate with power outages. While these normative documents have certain administrative effectiveness when they do not violate laws, regulations, or in cases where laws and regulations do not provide specific provisions, there is controversy in legal practice regarding whether power outage or rationing measures, which have significant impacts on power users, fall within the regulatory scope of the normative documents. Thus, using them as a basis for power outages and rationing carries significant legal risks.

Sixthly, power outage procedures may be violated. In the process of cooperating with the government in implementing power outages or rationing, even though the entity making the power outage decision is not the power supply company, it still needs to comply with the provisions regarding power outage procedures in laws and regulations. However, in practice, the process of cooperating with power outages or rationing usually involves temporary and sudden actions. Power supply companies often overlook the relevant procedural requirements, such as failing to follow the power outage approval process and notification obligations stipulated in Article 66 of the "Power Supply Business Rules." In the process of cooperating with the government in power outages, power supply companies only provide technical assistance and support. Therefore, some scholars argue that power outage notifications should be prepared and delivered by government agencies. There is also controversy in practice regarding whether administrative agencies fulfilling the notification obligation can exempt power supply companies from their obligation.

Seventhly, civil litigation may occur. Power supply companies' cooperation with government agencies in implementing power outages or rationing is an auxiliary action to support administrative enforcement or assist judicial execution, and power supply companies are not the main actors in power outages or rationing. However, due to the existence of power supply contracts between power supply companies and power users, users often file separate civil lawsuits against power supply companies, alleging a breach of the power supply contract and seeking power restoration and compensation for damages.

Eighthly, there are legal risks associated with power outages and rationing for residents. Article 43 of the "Administrative Compulsion Law" stipulates, "administrative authorities shall not use means such as stopping water supply, power supply, heating supply, or gas supply to force individuals to comply with administrative decisions."[68] In practice, administrative authorities often make decisions to stop or limit power supply for residents. If power supply companies cooperate and implement power outages or rationing for residents, such action is often considered a legally prohibited action, resulting in a series of adverse consequences.

[68] Administrative Compulsion Law, Paragraph 2 of Article 43.

References

Cai H (2004) Remote controllable client load management system and orderly power utilization. Power Demand-Side Manage 2004(3):28–31. https://doi.org/10.3969/j.issn.1009-1831.2004.03.011

Chen W (2015) Litigation of administrative agreements: current status and prospects. Tsinghua Law J 2015(4):94–108. https://doi.org/10.3969/j.issn.1673-9280.2015.04.006

Hu Z, Han X (2008) Integrated resource strategic planning and demand-side management—theories, methods and practice. China Electric Power Press

Hu Z, Han X, Wen Q, Zheng Y (2015) Comprehensive resource strategic planning and power demand-side management. China Electric Power Press, p 30

Jin W (2005) Anticipation of five major measures for power demand-side management. Guangxi Electric Power 2005(10):55–56

Li L (2012) Comprehensive urban pilot projects for power demand-side management officially launched. Power Demand Side Manage 2012(5):3

Li Y (2005) Decision management system for orderly power utilization. Master's Dissertation, Southeast University

Ling J, Liu T (2017) Research on interruptible loads in electricity demand-side management. Enterp Reform Manage 2017(16):201

Liu H (2020) Distinguishing and handling administrative contracts and civil contracts—reflections triggered by two judgments of the Z City intermediate people's court. J West 2020(19):77–80

Qiu C (2018) Considerations for power supply companies in cooperating with law enforcement agencies to implement power outages. Popular Utilization of Electricity 2018(1):10–11

Shan Y (2018) The legal nature and regulations of power supply companies implementing administrative power disconnection. Master's Dissertation, Southeast University

Shi Z (2021) Social responsibility of power supply companies for orderly power utilization. Electric Power Equipment Manage 2021(7):155–157

Sun H, Wang X (2022) Relief dilemmas and resolution paths of administrative agreements. Public Adm Law 2022(9):112–119

Wang S, Gao W (2021) Analysis of the nature of administrative agency's "cooperation in power outage letter." Popular Utilization Electricity 2021(1):13–14

Wei W (2008) Research on the legalization of crisis management in China. Doctor's Dissertation, East China Normal University

Wu Y (2006) Integration of incentives and constraints for civil servants. Bridge Century 2006(2):43–45

Xiong M, Zhou Z (2014) Development of power demand-side management and demand response. Distrib Utilization 2014(3):18–20. https://doi.org/10.3969/j.issn.1006-6357.2014.03.004

Zhang X (2016) Research on refined management of orderly power utilization and its implementation measures. New Technol New Prod China 2016(22):157–158

Zhang Q (2022) Criteria and specification of the content of administrative agreements. Nanjing Univ Law J 2022(5):137–149

Zhang X (2008) Research on the theory and countermeasures of the coordinated development of China's electric power industry and national economy. Doctor's Dissertation, Donghua University

Chapter 8
Legal Issues on the Construction of Energy Storage Projects for New Power Systems

On September 22, 2020, China made a commitment to the world to "peak carbon dioxide emissions before 2030 and achieve carbon neutrality before 2060."[1] One essential pillar supporting China's efforts to achieve these goals is the construction of new power systems with new energy as the main energy source.[2] In report of the 20th NCCPC on behalf of the 19th Central Committee, President Xi Jinping proposed: "We will work actively and prudently toward the goals of reaching peak carbon emissions and carbon neutrality. Based on China's energy and resource endowment, we will advance initiatives to reach peak carbon emissions in a well-planned and phased way in line with the principle of building the new before discarding the old. We will thoroughly advance the energy revolution. Coal will be used in a cleaner and more efficient way. We will speed up the planning and development of a system for new energy sources, and get actively involved in global governance in response to climate change."[3] In light of the broader objectives of "peaking CO_2 emissions by 2030 and achieving carbon neutrality by 2060," the consensus is to prioritize renewable energy in the dual-carbon economy strategy. Photovoltaic and wind power systems, being well-established clean energy technologies, have witnessed a continuous increase in their installed capacities. However, their output is affected by unpredictable weather patterns and fluctuations in electricity demand, resulting in an unstable power supply. Furthermore, the mismatch between power generation and consumption poses challenges, and traditional thermal power generation cannot meet the short-term, high-power regulation needs. To address these issues, various rapid energy storage methods have emerged as ancillary services, enabling the storage of energy, relieving the pressure on integrating renewable energy sources, and managing peak shaving and frequency regulation in the power grid.

[1] See Xinhua News Agency (2020).

[2] Xinhua News Agency (2021).

[3] Xi (2022).

H. Deng, *Green Energy Transition in China*, International Law in Asia,
https://doi.org/10.1007/978-981-97-2934-0_8

To facilitate the progress of energy storage projects, national and local governments have introduced a range of incentive policies. For example, the "Action Plan for Standardization Enhancement of Energy Carbon Emission Peak and Carbon Neutrality" issued by the NEA on September 20, 2022, emphasizes the acceleration of the improvement of new energy storage standards and technologies.[4] In 2017, the NDRC, NEA, and three other authorities jointly issued the "Guiding Opinions on Promoting the Development of Energy Storage Technology and Industry," which call for the exploration of several replicable business models, the cultivation of a number of competitive market entities, and the promotion of the energy storage industry to the initial commercialization stage.[5] In 2021, the NDRC and NEA issued the "Guiding Opinions on Accelerating the Development of New Energy Storage," which state the objective of transitioning new energy storage from the initial commercialization stage to large-scale development by 2025, with an installed capacity of over 30 million kilowatts. By 2030, we aim to achieve comprehensive market-oriented development of new energy storage, with an installed capacity that can largely meet the demands of the new power system, becoming a key support for carbon emission peak and carbon neutrality in the energy field.[6] To further promote the development of energy storage projects at the local level, for example, in Zhejiang Province, the Zhejiang Provincial Development and Reform Commission and the Zhejiang Provincial Energy Bureau have issued the "Implementation Opinions on Accelerating the Demonstration and Application of New Energy Storage in Zhejiang Province." These opinions propose accelerating technological innovation in new energy storage, establishing and improving supporting mechanisms, and achieving high-quality development of new energy storage.[7] Energy storage projects are experiencing rapid growth.

With energy storage playing a fundamental role in China's high-quality development of green energy, this book relies on scholarly research to delve into the subject of energy storage projects and their classifications. It differentiates between business models based on business scenarios and load aggregation scenarios, while also forecasting the practical challenges that energy storage projects may encounter in relevant business contexts. Building upon this foundation, the report suggests that future regulations for electrochemical energy storage projects will exhibit four key characteristics in their development. These include a fundamental standard system as the underlying regulation, specific regulations tailored for emerging projects, authority management regulations based on grid companies, and market-oriented promotion

[4] See National Energy Administration of China. Action Plan for Standardization Enhancement of Energy Carbon Emission Peak and Carbon Neutrality, released on October 9, 2022.

[5] See National Development and Reform Commission, the National Energy Administration of China et al. Guiding Opinions on Promoting the Development of Energy Storage Technology and Industry (Fa Gai Neng Yuan [2017] No. 1701).

[6] See National Development and Reform Commission, and National Energy Administration of China. Guiding Opinions on Accelerating the Development of New Energy Storage (Fa Gai Neng Yuan Gui [2021] No. 1051).

[7] See Zhejiang Provincial Development and Reform Commission, & Zhejiang Provincial Energy Bureau. Implementation Opinions on Accelerating the Demonstration and Application of New Energy Storage in Zhejiang Province (Zhe Fa Gai Neng Yuan [2021] No. 393).

regulations. In light of the above, the report conducts a specialized investigation into the cost management challenges faced by pumped-storage power stations and the market positioning of new energy storage systems, with a particular focus on electrochemical energy storage, within the development of new power systems. It examines the legal risks associated with pumped-storage power stations, including site selection and planning, development rights, resettlement of affected communities, and compliance management. Additionally, it addresses the legal risks associated with electrochemical energy storage projects, such as product quality and safety, ecological and environmental risks, and the absence of industry standards.

Energy Storage Technologies and Their Business Models

Energy storage technologies can be divided into physical energy storage and chemical energy storage. Physical energy storage technologies include electrical storage (such as pumped storage, compressed air energy storage, flywheel energy storage, and superconducting magnetic energy storage) and thermal storage (such as sensible heat storage and latent heat storage). Chemical energy storage technologies include electrical storage (such as lithium-ion batteries, sodium-sulfur batteries, flow batteries, fuel cells, supercapacitors, and hydrogen storage) and thermal storage (thermochemical heat storage).[8] Among different energy storage technologies, pumped storage stands out as a mature option. Its characteristics include a long operational lifespan, high power and storage capacity, and cost-effective operation, which contribute to its extensive utilization. On the other hand, electrochemical energy storage technologies, represented by lithium-ion batteries, are less influenced by geographical constraints and can be rapidly deployed. This flexibility enables their application across different segments of the power system and various other scenarios.[9] The promising future of electrochemical energy storage is being shaped by continuous cost reductions and the increasing maturity of commercial applications. Various business models have emerged, including energy storage integrated with new energy sources, energy storage integrated with microgrids, and energy storage in ancillary services.[10]

---

[8] See Zhang et al. (2008).

[9] See Xu et al. (2013).

[10] See Wang et al. (2013).

Energy Storage Business Model Based on Business Scenarios

Business Operation Model of Energy Storage Integrated with New Energy Sources

New energy sources such as solar and wind power are characterized by their randomness, intermittency, and rapid variability in power generation. The direct grid integration of an extremely large number of these new energy generating units could potentially trigger safety incidents.[11] Therefore, with increasing demand for new energy sources to be integrated into the grid, there is a growing necessity for adjusting energy storage devices in real time.

The United States has consistently been at the forefront of the new energy storage field. Taking the solar industry as an example, the United States has been actively promoting the application of residential solar PV storage products through three primary business models. First, the equipment purchase model, where users make a one-time purchase of solar PV storage equipment, utilizing and maintaining it for their own consumption. Second, the PV leasing model, where users pay a monthly rental fee to the solar PV storage company based on a predetermined rate without the need to purchase the equipment. Third, the power purchase agreement model, where the solar PV storage system provider signs a third-party agreement with the user and the power company. The system provider is responsible for the construction and maintenance of the system and sells the electricity to the power company; the power company resells it to the user; the user provides their rooftop for power generation and pays a lower electricity price.[12]

Germany also has a significant number of residential PV installations. In terms of distributed solar PV storage, there are two main business models in Germany. First, ownership model of PV plus storage, where users purchase a solar storage system and consume the electricity generated by their rooftop PV stations. The energy storage company retains control over the storage system. In addition to earning equipment fees, the company can also generate revenue by integrating user-side energy storage systems to provide load balancing and other ancillary services. The second one is the community sharing model. In this model, distributed PV, energy storage, combined heat and power (CHP) systems, and other devices are connected to the system. The model leverages the complementarity between the community's power generation capacity and electricity demand to create a "current account" where energy revenue can offset expenditures and generate economic gains.[13]

Currently, the energy storage systems in China that are associated with new energy sources are primarily demonstration projects. "These projects are mainly undertaken by grid companies or power generators. The project funding typically comes from the company's own capital, technology project funds, bank financing, and cost recovery through electricity sales." "Examples of these projects include the

[11] See Liu et al. (2011).

[12] See Li et al. (2020).

[13] Same as above.

'Zhangbei Wind and Solar Storage and Transmission Demonstration Project' that adopts the user investment model, and the "Wuxi Singapore Industrial Park Intelligent Distribution Network Energy Storage System" that adopts the energy performance contracting model. In the future, it is necessary to establish electricity pricing policies, preferential tax policies, subsidy policies, and other policies to provide a favorable policy environment for the development of "energy storage + new energy" in China. It is also important to explore the various benefits of energy storage, establish a sound revenue model, and utilize various financial instruments to monetize future returns and generate positive cash flow is crucial."[14] For example, in Zhejiang, China, Quzhou introduced supportive policies for "new energy + energy storage" at the beginning of 2021. These policies explicitly stated that new energy enterprises should prioritize the use of energy storage through leasing or purchasing services to maximize the shared usage of energy storage stations. In September, Haining City in Jiaxing issued guidelines encouraging newly constructed new energy projects to allocate 10–20% of their capacity to energy storage, with a minimum storage duration of 2 h.

Business Operation Model of Frequency Regulation and Peak-Shaving Ancillary Services

(1) Operational model where microgrid operators develop into electricity sellers

The liberalization of the electricity selling market is a key focus of the power market reform. In this context, grid-connected microgrid operators can establish themselves as electricity sellers and participate in the competitive electricity selling market. By constructing and operating microgrid infrastructure and offering diversified energy services, they can optimize energy consumption patterns, improve energy efficiency, and provide customized energy solutions to customers. Through bidirectional information exchange with users, these operators can better understand users' energy consumption habits and provide tailored energy solutions.

By integrating energy storage into microgrids, it provides support for distributed energy resources and demand-side management within the microgrid and has a significant impact on the economic viability of the microgrid. The economics of a microgrid are highly sensitive to the price difference between electricity purchase and sale. In the long term, as electricity prices increase and the cost of energy storage continues to decrease, microgrid electricity sellers with energy storage systems will see an increase in the sale of self-generated electricity. They can also profit by purchasing the shortfall of electricity within the microgrid from the main grid at a lower price and selling the electricity, thus improving their internal financial returns and achieving profitability.[15]

(2) Operational model where microgrid operators become virtual power plants

---

[14] Same as above.

[15] See Zhao et al. (2020).

Microgrids are localized power systems that supplement the main power grid and can generate power. By aggregating the power resources within the microgrids, they can function as virtual power plants and participate in the wholesale electricity market to supply electricity and earn revenue through bidding. For example, the Swedish power company Vattenfall uses wireless communication technology to aggregate multiple microgrid resources, including multiple wind farms in Berlin, thermal storage power plants, combined cooling, heat and power (CCHP) systems, and electrical facilities. They form a virtual power plant that participates in the power market and ancillary services market.

Compared to the model where microgrid operators develop into electricity sellers, this virtual power plant model has higher technological requirements and involves significant technology costs. Currently, it can complement and expand the electricity seller model, and represents a future trend in the development of microgrid operation models.[16]

Business Operation Model of Energy Storage in Ancillary Services

(1) Business model of pumped storage in ancillary services

Pumped-storage power stations play a crucial role in ensuring the safe, stable, and cost-effective operation of the power system. They are responsible for tasks such as providing system backup, load shifting, frequency regulation, and peak shaving.

In China, pumped-storage power stations are divided into two main types: stations wholly owned by grid companies and stations where grid companies hold a controlling interest. Since the service target of pumped-storage power stations is the power grid, grid companies have the responsibility and obligation to coordinate the planning of pumped-storage power stations, regardless of whether it is before or after the power system reform. However, the heavy capital requirements of pumped-storage power stations often limit the ability of grid companies to independently invest and construct these stations, and the development of stations wholly owned by grid companies is often difficult. By establishing a reasonable electricity pricing mechanism, clarifying the functional benefits of pumped-storage power stations, specifying a fair distribution system for relevant beneficiaries, and determining a reasonable return on investment, we can help attract investment from power generators and local governments on the construction of pumped-storage power stations.[17]

(2) Business model of electrochemical energy storage in ancillary services

The involvement of electrochemical energy storage in the ancillary services market is not a new thing outside China. Additionally, there are favorable policies in place. For example, in 2011, the Federal Energy Regulatory Commission (FERC) issued the "Frequency Regulation Compensation in the Organized Wholesale Power Markets,"

---

[16] See Li et al. (2020).

[17] Same as above.

introducing a two-part compensation methodology that emphasizes the effectiveness of frequency regulation. This provides a favorable policy environment for high-quality frequency regulation resources such as energy storage.[18]

China is also exploring the involvement of energy storage in ancillary services. In June 2016, the NEA issued the "Notice on Promoting the Participation of Electrical Energy Storage in the Compensation (Market) Mechanism Pilot Work for Electricity Ancillary Services in the 'Three North' Regions." The notice identifies the market entities that can participate in peak shaving and frequency regulation ancillary services markets using energy storage. It does not impose restrictions on the identity of energy storage and allows the following entities to participate: Power generators, including new energy power plants with integrated energy storage, and companies with generation and selling who can improve power quality through energy storage; Grid companies, where energy storage systems can replace or be combined with traditional units in ancillary services; Power sellers who can improve power quality and enhance core competitiveness through energy storage; Users who are provided with resources centrally to gain benefits.[19]

Business Model Based on Load Aggregation

Demand response is one of the core technologies of smart grids. By applying demand response technology, the resources on the demand side can be fully utilized, and comprehensive optimization and allocation of resources can be achieved. However, there is still room for further exploration of load adjustment capacity and a need to increase the level of user response systems. A new type of specialized demand response provider called a load aggregator has emerged outside China.[20]

Definition of Load Aggregator

A load aggregator (LA) is an independent organization that integrates user demand response and provides it to market buyers. It not only allows small and medium-sized loads to participate in market regulation but also uses specialized technical methods to fully utilize load resources and provide the necessary ancillary service products for the market.[21] Currently, LAs have transformed from their original role as power procurers to demand response resource integrators that offer a range of technologies and services. A load aggregator can serve as a business model to integrate demand

---

[18] Same as above.

[19] See Notice on Promoting the Participation of Electrical Energy Storage in the Compensation (Market) Mechanism Pilot Work for Electricity Ancillary Services in the "Three North" Regions (Guo Neng Jian Guan [2016] No. 164).

[20] See Zhu (2018).

[21] See Qiu et al. (2021).

response resources and allow unused small and medium-sized loads with regulation capabilities to participate in the market. According to IKAHEIMO's definition, an aggregator is a company who acts as intermediator between electricity end-users, who provide distributed energy resources, and those power system participants who wish to exploit these services, to allow users to access the power market in an effective way and provide more flexible services and technologies.[22] California Independent System Operator (CAISO) defines it as "a municipality or other governmental entity, an energy services provider, a scheduling coordinator, a utility distribution company, or any other entity representing single or multiple loads for the purpose of providing demand reduction service to the independent system operator (ISO)."[23] Some scholars define a load aggregator as any entity that combines loads into a "block" that can be controlled in response to requests by the ISO.[24] According to the previous definitions, it is evident that an LA is an integrator of demand response resources. It assesses the demand response potential of users through specialized technical evaluations and consolidates demand response resources to participate in power system operations. From the perspective of system operators, an LA is viewed as a large-scale power generator (similar to a VPP) or a load resource that provides scheduled generation capacity or ancillary services.[25]

Role of Load Aggregator

(1) From the perspective of system operation, an LA provides the system with more options for acquiring ancillary service products such as active power regulation, voltage control, and balancing mechanisms. This reduces the operational costs of the system. As the load demand increases, it poses greater challenges to the operation of the power system. The difficulty of meeting the growing load demand through the construction of new power networks is increasing. The demand response integration services provided by an LA can help defer investments in power generation and transmission/distribution infrastructure, thus reducing generation costs and improving the efficiency of the power market.[26]
(2) From the perspective of the load, the role of an LA can be divided into two aspects.

On one hand, it provides an opportunity for small and medium-sized loads to participate in market regulation, establishing a connection between demand response suppliers and buyers, which enhances the effectiveness of demand response. If small

---

[22] Ikaheimo et al. (2010).

[23] California Independent System Operator. (2008). Process for participating load program (ancillary services/supplemental energy).

[24] Sandia National Laboratories. (2010). *Energy storage for the electricity grid: Benefits and market potential assessment guide* (SAND2010-0815). A Study for the DOE Energy Storage Systems Program.

[25] See Gao et al. (2013).

[26] Faria et al. (2011).

and medium-sized power users with demand response resources individually engage with demand response buyers, it would result in numerous bilateral transactions, and the load elasticity of these users may not meet the minimum level required for participating in demand response. It becomes challenging for them to find an entry point into power trading. Furthermore, demand response buyers, such as transmission system operators, may not be interested in managing small and medium-sized loads. Therefore, as an intermediary entity, an LA can integrate user demand response resources and introduce them into market transactions, enabling unused load resources to be utilized effectively. At the same time, it brings benefits to other participants in the power system.

On the other hand, an LA unlocks the demand response potential of loads through specialized technical means. Demand response capability is a crucial resource for load regulation. Among small and medium-sized power users, there are a significant number of untapped potential demand response resources. These users often lack real-time information of price fluctuations in the wholesale market, and some price-based demand response approaches are not effective in guiding user responses to system control requests. Small and medium-sized power users may not have the capability to uncover their own demand response potential. However, with the assistance of an LA, they can adopt a scientifically informed approach for power usage and improve the power efficiency of their devices.[27]

Classification of Load Aggregator Control Resources

With the development of the power system and power market, demand response resources have become increasingly diverse. The following are common types of demand response resources that an LA integrates for market participation.[28]

(1) Controllable load

The load adjustment capability of power users is an important control resource for LAs. Controllable loads refer to users' loads that can be temporarily shifted, reduced, or increased based solely on the characteristics of the load, without relying on backup power sources or energy storage units for short-term power assistance. Traditionally, loads have been seen as passive and controlled physical endpoints.[29] However, many loads have a certain degree of elasticity. Some of the loads of users' electrical devices can be transferred or reduced. When aggregated, the quantity of these loads can be substantial, and their scheduling can be flexible. This presents a significant potential for participation in demand response programs. Through appropriate load control strategies, an LA aggregates controllable loads. In addition to providing controllable generation capacity to the system, similar to traditional power generators, LAs can also offer various ancillary services (such as frequency control, voltage control, and

[27] See Gao et al. (2013).

[28] Same as above.

[29] See Xue et al. (2007).

reserve capacity), participate in demand response programs, bid for increasing or decreasing power in the balancing market, and alleviate transmission and distribution congestion.[30]

(2) Energy storage device

Energy storage devices enable convenient temporal and spatial transfer of loads and are essential components for the operation of future power systems. They are also expected to become one of the ideal control resources for LAs. Energy storage devices can be classified into fixed energy storage devices and mobile energy storage devices based on their spatial portability. For example, sodium-sulfur batteries installed at substations are fixed energy storage devices, while electric vehicles (EVs) equipped with vehicle-to-grid (V2G) capabilities are mobile energy storage devices.

The rapid development of the EV industry has led to an increasing amount of research on utilizing EVs for demand response resources through their charging and discharging control. LAs, as an intermediary between system operators and EVs, can leverage the V2G technology of EVs to facilitate interaction between EVs and the power system. LAs can achieve load shifting through effective control strategies or utilize the energy storage capacity of EV batteries to provide ancillary services.[31]

(3) Distributed power source

The widespread integration of distributed power sources into the grid has increased the availability of variable generation capacity. Some of these distributed power sources can be adjusted and are valuable control resources for LAs. Distributed power sources are installed close to the user and come in various forms, each with different adjustment capabilities. Depending on the user group and intended use, these sources can serve as backup power supplies or help in peak shaving. LAs can utilize distributed power sources that have excellent scheduling and peak-shaving capabilities to provide services to power system operators, and offer security and reliability services to larger power systems.[32]

In response to the needs of controllable loads in the construction of new power systems, China has been actively promoting the participation of load aggregators in the power market. On November 22, 2022, the General Administration Department of the National Energy Administration issued the "Basic Rules for Electricity Spot Market (Draft for Comment)." The document explicitly states that load aggregators and other entities are allowed to participate in electricity spot trading. It also encourages more new energy generation projects to engage in the electricity spot

[30] See Zhang et al. (2009).

[31] Sortomme and El-Sharkawi (2012).

[32] See Liu et al. (2007).

market.[33] According to Article 2 of the "Regulations for the Management of Grid-Connected Operations" (Guo Neng Fa Jian Guan Gui [2021] No. 60), "load-side grid-connected entities with traditional high-energy-consuming industrial loads, ... and other controllable loads that can respond to power scheduling instructions (including those aggregated through load aggregators, virtual power plants, etc.), as well as grid-connected entities within the jurisdiction of provincial-level and lower-level power scheduling agencies shall be subject to the provisions of these regulations based on their impact on the operation of the power system."[34] At present, exploratory practices of energy storage power stations participating in electricity spot trading have been initiated in some regions of China. For example, in Shandong, by the end of February and early March 2022, four energy storage power stations, Liuge Guotou Energy Storage Power Station, Tengyuan Huadian Energy Storage Power Station, Guanjia Sanxia Energy Storage Power Station, and Quanfu Huaneng Energy Storage Power Station, were registered and publicly announced by the Shandong Power Trading Center. They became trading participants in the electricity spot market in Shandong province. These four power stations were the first batch of independent energy storage power stations to participate in electricity spot market trading in China.

In addition, in May 2021, a grid company conducted the first special market transaction for load response in Lishui, Zhejiang. In this special transaction, a total of 25 power users participated or entrusted power sales companies to participate in the trial operation of load response. The total volume of response transactions reached 110,000 kWh. At the same time, relevant companies participated in this demand response for the first time in the role of load aggregators. They acted as agents for 16 users and successfully bid for a power load of 12,200 kW. According to the agency agreement, they received a service fee equal to 1/10 of the compensation price. To fully unlock the regulation potential of demand-side flexible resources, the grid company has also conducted a trial operation of high-elasticity grid load response in Lishui. This trial explores market-based bidding and government financial compensation mechanisms for demand-side market response, aiming to encourage eligible demand response participants to engage in ancillary service transactions. It has laid the foundation for a power supply guarantee system that is "primarily based on demand response, supplemented by orderly power utilization and interruptible loads." This development represents the initial establishment of a new scenario where multiple integrated high-elasticity grid-supporting market mechanisms are applied.[35]

[33] See Notice of the General Administration Department of the National Energy Administration on Soliciting Public Opinions on the "Regulations for the Management of Grid-Connected Operations of Grid Entities (Draft for Comment)" and "Management Measures for Power System Ancillary Services (Draft for Comment)", released on August 30, 2021.

[34] National Energy Administration of China. Regulations for the Management of Grid-Connected Operations (Guo Neng Fa Jian Guan Gui [2021] No. 60).

[35] Chen et al. (2021).

Development Challenges of Energy Storage Projects

New Energy and Energy Storage

The business model of grid-side energy storage relied on incorporating the costs into users' transmission and distribution pricing. However, this model was discontinued due to regulatory restrictions after the introduction of the "Measures for Supervision and Review of Power Transmission and Distribution Pricing Costs" in 2019 and the "Provincial-Level Grid Transmission and Distribution Pricing Measures" in 2020. Both of these regulations explicitly state that the costs of electrochemical energy storage systems shall not be included in the transmission and distribution costs.[36]

Subsequently, the development approach for energy storage has shifted toward a quota-based system. Energy regulatory authorities or power companies in several provinces have required new energy companies, such as those investing in and owning wind and solar projects, to allocate a certain percentage of energy storage capacity. Rough calculations suggest that if a PV power station is required to allocate energy storage capacity equivalent to 20% of its power output for a duration of 2 h, considering depreciation, maintenance, and capital costs, the cost of solar electricity will increase by CNY 0.09-0.1 per kilowatt-hour. During the early stage of achieving cost parity for new energy, this poses a heavy burden on the relevant companies.

It is controversial to simply transfer the cost of energy storage development to new energy companies through grid-connection requirements. While it may seem reasonable for new energy companies to bear the costs of energy storage development based on the principle of "beneficiary pays," there are certain factors to consider. On one hand, the carbon reduction benefits of new energy development are shared by the whole society. In the absence of a well-functioning carbon market, requiring new energy companies to bear the peak-shaving costs may not align with the objective of encouraging the development of green energy. On the other hand, the mandatory allocation of energy storage capacity and duration lacks sufficient basis. If new energy companies are required to bear the costs of peak shaving, they should have the right to choose alternative options. The simplest option would be to curtail electricity generation during specific periods. In fact, using energy storage capacity quotas as a requirement for grid connection in new energy projects does not guarantee the construction quality of energy storage projects. It becomes even more difficult to effectively monitor and supervise its operation. Consequently, the desired peak-shaving effect may not be achieved.

---

[36] See National Development and Reform Commission, and National Energy Administration of China. Measures for Supervision and Review of Power Transmission and Distribution Pricing Costs (Fa Gai Jia Ge Gui [2019] No. 897); National Development and Reform Commission of China. Provincial-Level Grid Transmission and Distribution Pricing Measures (Fa Gai Jia Ge Gui [2020] No. 101).

Independent Frequency Regulation Power Station

Frequency regulation services are a successful application of electrochemical energy storage. In general, compensation for regional frequency regulation ancillary services is provided according to the "Two Rules" issued by the State Electricity Regulatory Commission (SERC). With the progress of power market reform, some provinces have started adopting market-based approaches for pricing and cost allocation of frequency regulation ancillary services. Currently, the frequency regulation markets in provinces such as Shandong, Shanxi, Fujian, and Guangdong have entered the operational or trial operation stage.

By installing electrochemical energy storage devices in thermal power plants, the overall regulation performance indicator Kp (which measures the rate, time, and accuracy of regulation) can be significantly improved. This allows the units to be assigned with more frequency regulation tasks. For example, in Shanxi, in order to encourage power plants to participate in frequency regulation services, the fixed frequency regulation price in Shanxi was CNY 15 per megawatt (MW) before 2018. This means the frequency regulation compensation was calculated as the frequency regulation task power multiplied by Kp and multiplied by CNY 15. Based on the actual situation, after installing energy storage systems, the average value of Kp for thermal power units increased from around 2.8 to 4.6. Additionally, participating in frequency regulation services only requires a quick and short-term response in terms of power. Generally, the required duration of participation is around 0.5 h. This reduces the investment in electrochemical energy storage and allows early entrants of the frequency regulation sector to recover their costs in approximately two years.

Electrochemical energy storage is currently economically viable for frequency regulation, but future profits are subject to significant uncertainty. In China's current ancillary services market, based on the "Two Rules," compensation for ancillary services is primarily funded through cost-sharing among power generators. In this arrangement, there is a zero-sum game regarding the allocation of these costs. Historical data suggest that the annual size of the ancillary services market hovers around CNY 15 billion, with AGC frequency regulation representing about 30%, or roughly CNY 4.5 billion. As the frequency regulation market gains more attention and additional participants enter, it is expected to become saturated quickly, leading to a sharp decline in compensation rates. Reflecting these concerns, in October 2017, the Shanxi Energy Regulatory Office issued the "Operational Rules for the Shanxi Electric Power Frequency Regulation Ancillary Services Market." In 2018, Shanxi's frequency regulation market adopted competitive bidding rules. The bid prices for frequency regulation services started at CNY 12-20/MW in 2018, but by the year's end, the range had been adjusted to CNY 5-10/MW, indicating a significant reduction in revenue from frequency regulation services. Similarly, Guangdong Province implemented new policies in 2020, with the frequency regulation mileage subsidy standard decreasing by more than 40% in 2021 and over 50% in 2022.[37]

---

[37] See Shanxi Energy Regulatory Office. Operational Rules for the Shanxi Electric Power Frequency Regulation Ancillary Services Market (Jin Jian Neng Shi Chang [2017] No. 143).

The market capacity for energy storage frequency regulation is limited. With the increasing share of renewable energy, it is commonly believed that as the demand for frequency regulation grows, so too will the opportunities for providing these services. Deviations in the power grid frequency are the result of imbalances between power generation and load. Both frequency regulation and peak-shaving services aim to correct active power deviations, and their directions of adjustment are aligned. The allocation of market shares for these services is determined through specific calculation methods, and they have the potential to be integrated. Consequently, the market share for frequency regulation services in the Northeast and Southern power grids of China is quite small. Given the overarching goal of controlling electricity price hikes in China, it is improbable that the costs of frequency regulation services will be transferred to users. Unless there is a breakthrough from the "Two Rules" framework, which currently dictates a "zero-sum game" among power generators, the scope for these services will remain confined to slicing shares within the existing electricity pricing structure, without a noticeable increase in the overall societal electricity cost. Moreover, it is more logical to categorize the grid disturbances caused by renewable energy generation under peak shaving, which also makes it easier to integrate peak-shaving services with the spot market. Thus, the future prospects for the frequency regulation market may not be very optimistic.

Taking into account these factors, new entrants to the energy storage frequency regulation market will face significant risks. In a saturated market, power stations that have already recouped their investments may be inclined to offer lower prices, potentially leading to a downward price spiral and making it challenging for investments in new power stations to be recovered.

Peak-Valley Spread Arbitrage

Peak-shaving services are the most extensive application of energy storage. However, since the value of peak-shaving services is only recognized on the user side through the differentiation of peak and valley electricity pricing, only provinces that have introduced specific peak-shaving tariffs can profit from participating in these services. More commonly, users engage in arbitrage by exploiting the price differences between peak and off-peak periods.

For example, considering user-side peak-valley arbitrage, using lithium iron phosphate batteries under the current investment costs and technical conditions, and operating with a twice-daily charge and discharge cycle over an 8-year lifespan, profitability is limited even with a peak-valley plus peak-off-peak price differential of CNY 1.3-1.4. With the ongoing reduction in general industrial and commercial electricity rates, only users in a few developed regions such as Beijing are currently able to undertake energy storage arbitrage. The growth of this business hinges on the reduction in costs and enhancement in the performance of electrochemical energy storage systems.

Laws, Regulations, and Regulatory Policies for Energy Storage Projects

Pumped Storage Projects

Given that pumped-storage projects entail substantial investments, extended construction timelines, and significant impacts on both the natural geographical landscape and local community life, it is essential to thoroughly understand the potential legal risks of the projects and establish a comprehensive compliance system. As of July 2022, the effective laws, regulations and policies for the pumped-storage industry mainly include: "Pumped Storage Medium and Long-term Development Plan (2021–2035)," "Opinions of the National Development and Reform Commission on Further Improving the Price Formation Mechanism for Pumped Storage" (Fa Gai Jia Ge [2021] No. 633), "Notice of the National Development and Reform Commission and the National Energy Administration on Issuing the 'Measures for Supervision and Review of Power Transmission and Distribution Pricing Costs'" (Fa Gai Jia Ge Gui [2019] No. 897), "Reply Letter from the National Energy Administration on Matters Related to the Adjustment of Site Selection Planning for Pumped-Storage Power Stations in Zhejiang" (Guo Neng Han Xin Neng [2018] No. 116), "Notice from the General Administration Department of the National Energy Administration on Implementing Ecological and Environmental Protection Requirements in the Planning and Construction of Pumped-Storage Power Stations" (Guo Neng Zong Fa Xin Neng [2017] No. 3), "Regulations on the Compensation for Land Acquisition and Relocation for Construction of Large and Medium-sized Hydraulic and Hydroelectric Projects (Revised in 2017)," "Management Measures for the Water Project Construction Planning Consent System (Trial) (Revised in 2017)," "Water Drawing Licensing Management Measures (Revised in 2017)," "Opinions of the National Development and Reform Commission on Promoting the Healthy and Orderly Development of Pumped-Storage Power Stations" (Fa Gai Neng Yuan [2014] No. 2482), "Notice of the National Development and Reform Commission on Improving the Price Formation Mechanism for Pumped-Storage Power Stations" (Fa Gai Jia Ge [2014] No. 1763), "Notice of the National Energy Administration on Strengthening the Operation and Management of Pumped-Storage Power Stations" (Guo Neng Xin Neng [2013] No. 243), and "Notice of the National Energy Administration on Further Improving the Construction of Pumped-Storage Power Stations" (Guo Neng Xin Neng [2011] No. 242).

Encouraging Policies for Pumped-Storage Projects

In August 2021, the NEA released the "Pumped Storage Medium and Long-term Development Plan (2021–2035)," which sets forth the following targets: by 2025, the total operational capacity of pumped storage will exceed 62 gigawatts; by 2030, the operational capacity will reach approximately 120 gigawatts; and by 2035, the industry will be capable of satisfying the demand for large-scale development with a high proportion of new energy sources.[38] "The Outline of the 14th Five-Year Plan for Economic and Social Development and Long-Range Objectives Through the Year 2035 of the People's Republic of China" issued in March 2021 proposes to advance the energy revolution and build a clean, low-carbon, safe, and efficient energy system to enhance the capacity for energy supply security. It calls for accelerating the intelligent transformation of power grid infrastructure and the construction of smart microgrids, and enhancing the power system's ability for complementary operation and intelligent regulation. It emphasizes the need to strengthen the integration of energy generation, grid, load, and storage, thereby improving the consumption and storage capabilities for clean energy. The goal is also to enhance the power transmission and distribution to remote areas, promote the flexible retrofitting of coal-fired power plants, and expedite the construction of pumped-storage power stations along with the large-scale deployment of novel energy storage technologies.[39] The "Notice on Issuing a Package of Policies and Measures to Firmly Stabilize the Economy," published on May 24, 2022, emphasizes the importance of strategically deploying a series of pumped-storage power stations in the effort to ensure energy security. These stations should not only play a crucial role in safeguarding the stability of the power system but also significantly boost the large-scale expansion of new energy sources while offering comparatively superior economic performance. The notice also urges the expedited construction initiation for ready-to-proceed projects.[40] The "Implementation Plan for Promoting the High-Quality Development of New Energy in the New Era," issued on May 14, 2022, puts forth measures to comprehensively enhance the regulation capacity and flexibility of the power system. The plan focuses on refining the compensation mechanism for peak-shaving and frequency-regulating power sources, ramping up the construction of pumped-storage projects, accelerating the advancement of innovative energy storage technologies, and exploring mechanisms for the recovery of energy storage costs.[41] The "Action Plan for Carbon Dioxide Peaking before 2030," released by the State Council in October 2021, proposes to speed up the construction of the new power system, formulate a new round of mid- and long-term development plans for pumped-storage power stations, and refine policies and mechanisms for spurring the development of this type of energy storage. The plan also aims to accelerate the broad demonstration and application of new types of energy storage. By 2025, the installed capacity of new types of energy storage is expected to exceed 30 gigawatts. By 2030, the installed capacity of pumped-storage power stations is expected to reach approximately 120 gigawatts, and provincial-level

[38] See the National Energy Administration of China. Pumped Storage Medium and Long-term Development Plan (2021–2035).

[39] See Xinhua News Agency (2021).

[40] See Notice of the State Council on Issuing a Package of Policies and Measures to Firmly Stabilize the Economy (Guo Fa [2022] No. 12).

[41] See forwarded by the General Office of the State Council. Implementation Plan of the National Development and Reform Commission and the National Energy Administration for Promoting the High-Quality Development of New Energy in the New Era (Guo Ban Han [2022] No. 39).

power grids will be equipped with peak-load response capacity of 5% or more.[42] The NDRC issued the "Opinions on Further Improving the Price Formation Mechanism for Pumped Storage" in April 2021, which advocate for the continuation of the two-part tariff policy as the core approach to further refine the price formation mechanism for pumped storage. The policy aims to establish the energy tariff competitively and incorporate the capacity tariff into the recovery of transmission and distribution costs. Additionally, it emphasizes strengthening the integration with the construction and development of the power market, progressively encouraging the participation of pumped-storage power stations in the market. The focus is on enhancing the scientific basis, practicability, and effectiveness of the electricity price formation mechanism, fully leveraging the role of price signals to motivate the engagement of all stakeholders. The first initiative is to determine the energy tariff competitively. The energy tariff reflects the value of peak-shaving services provided by pumped-storage power stations, which recover the operational costs of water pumping and power generation through the energy tariff. The second initiative is to refine the capacity tariff verification mechanism. Pumped-storage power stations recover costs, other than the operational costs of water pumping and power generation, through the capacity tariff and obtain reasonable returns.[43]

Regulatory Policies for Pumped-Storage Projects

The "Water Law of the People's Republic of China (Revised in 2016)" (Water Law (2016)) clearly stipulates: "The construction of water projects must adhere to the comprehensive planning of river basins. For the construction of water projects on the key rivers and lakes defined as such by the State or on rivers and lakes crossing provinces, autonomous regions, and municipalities directly under the Central Government, the construction entity shall not commence work without obtaining a planning consent signed by the relevant river basin management agency to show that the water project meets the requirements of comprehensive river basin planning. For the construction of water projects on other rivers and lakes, the construction entity shall not commence work without obtaining a planning consent signed by the water administration department of the local people's government at the county level or above, in accordance with the administration authority, to show that the water project meets the requirements of comprehensive river basin planning. If the construction of a water project involves flood control, the relevant provisions of the Flood Control Law shall be observed. If other regions and industries are involved, the construction entity shall solicit comments from the relevant regions and departments in advance." "In the case of inter-basin water transfer, comprehensive planning, and scientific assessment are required to ensure that the water needs of both the donor

[42] See State Council. Action Plan for Carbon Dioxide Peaking before 2030 (Guo Fa [2021] No. 23).

[43] See Opinions of the National Development and Reform Commission on Further Improving the Price Formation Mechanism for Pumped Storage (Fa Gai Jia Ge [2021] No. 633).

and recipient basins are adequately considered. It is essential to balance these needs to prevent damage to the ecological environment." "In constructing hydropower stations, it is essential to protect the ecological environment while also addressing the needs for flood control, water supply, irrigation, navigation, as well as the transport of bamboo and logs, and fisheries." "When constructing permanent dam or sluice structures across rivers that serve as migration pathways for aquatic life, or are used for navigation or the transport of bamboo and logs, the responsible construction entities must also build fish passage, vessel navigation, and log rafting facilities concurrently. Alternatively, they may implement other remedial actions with the approval of departments authorized by the State Council. In addition, these entities are responsible for ensuring the protection of aquatic life, the maintenance of navigation, and the continuation of bamboo and log transport during the construction and water storage phases. All associated costs must be borne by the construction entities." "The State applies a development-oriented approach to resettlement for the construction of water projects, adhering to a principle that combines initial compensation and subsidies with subsequent support, to properly arrange for the production and living needs of the displaced inhabitants, safeguarding their legitimate rights and interests. The resettlement shall proceed in tandem with the project construction. Construction entities shall tailor the resettlement plans to the environmental capacity and the principles of sustainable development of the receiving areas. These plans, once legally approved, shall be executed by the relevant local people's governments. The financial requirements for the resettlement of inhabitants must be factored into the overall investment budget for the construction of the project." "Any organization or individual that directly extracts water resources from rivers, lakes, or underground sources shall, in accordance with the regulations of the water drawing licensing system and the compensated use of water resources system, apply to the water administration department or the river basin authority for a water drawing license and pay a water resource fee to obtain the legal right to extract water."[44]

According to the "Flood Control Law of the People's Republic of China (Revised in 2016)" (Flood Control Law (2016)), "The construction of flood control projects, as well as other water projects and hydropower stations on rivers and lakes must comply with the requirements of flood control planning. Reservoirs must maintain a flood storage capacity that meets flood control planning requirements. Construction entities are not permitted to commence construction of the aforementioned flood control projects, other water projects or hydropower stations without obtaining a planning consent document signed by the water administration department concerned that confirms the project's compliance with flood control planning requirements." "The construction of bridges, docks, roads, ferries, pipelines, cables, water drawing, and drainage facilities that cross over or pass through rivers, levees, or are situated near rivers, must comply with flood control standards, shoreline planning, navigation requirements, and other technical specifications. Such structures must not compromise the integrity of levees, affect the stability of the river regime, or obstruct the

[44] Water Law, Article 19, Article 22, paragraph 2 of Article 26, paragraph 1 of Article 27, Article 29, and paragraph 1 of Article 48.

free flow of floodwaters. Construction projects cannot commence without their plans being reviewed and approved by the relevant water administration department in accordance with the aforementioned flood control requirements. For projects and facilities that require the use of land within the management boundaries of rivers or lakes, span the airspace above them, or traverse riverbeds, the construction entity must obtain approval from the relevant water administration department regarding the positions and boundaries of the construction. Only after receiving such approval can the entity legally proceed with the commencement formalities. Construction must then be conducted according to the positions and boundaries authorized by the water administration department." "For construction projects not related to flood control within floodplains or flood storage and detention basins, an assessment must be conducted regarding the potential impact of floods on the construction project and the potential impact of the project on flood control measures. A flood impact assessment report must be compiled, outlining the necessary preventative actions. The construction may not commence until the flood impact assessment report has been reviewed and approved by the relevant water administration department. The flood impact assessment report for construction projects such as oil fields, railways, highways, mines, power plants, telecommunications facilities, and pipelines within flood storage and detention basins shall include flood control and avoidance plans developed by the construction entity itself. Before a construction project enters into production or use, its flood control structures and facilities must undergo acceptance checks by the water administration department. The flat-roof structure shall be adopted for the houses built in flood storage and detention basins."[45]

The "Pumped Storage Medium and Long-term Development Plan (2021–2035)" issued by the National Energy Administration in August 2021 sets forth the developmental tasks for pumped-storage projects. The first task is the protection of resource sites. The second is to actively advance the construction of ongoing projects by enhancing construction management, promoting intelligent construction techniques, and ensuring proper environmental protection and resettlement efforts. The third is to expedite the initiation and construction of new projects through improved project layout optimization, intensified research efforts, and accelerated construction timelines. The fourth task involves bolstering the reserve and management of planned sites. The fifth is to develop small- and medium-sized pumped-storage facilities in accordance with local conditions. The sixth is to explore and advance the integrated retrofitting for hydropower cascades. The seventh is to reinforce innovation in technology and equipment. Lastly, the eighth task is to establish a monitoring system for the industry.[46] The "Opinions on Further Improving the Price Formation Mechanism for Pumped Storage" issued by the National Development and Reform Commission in April 2021 emphasizes the need to enhance the construction and management of pumped-storage power stations. The construction of these stations should take into account the requirements of the power system, the conditions of

[45] Flood Control Law, Articles 17, 27 and 33.

[46] See the National Energy Administration of China. Pumped Storage Medium and Long-term Development Plan (2021–2035).

the site resources, the economic viability of the project, and the local electricity pricing affordability. It is essential to engage in unified planning, rational layout, and orderly construction. Projects not included in the relevant construction plans are not allowed to be built. There is also a need to strengthen the operational management of pumped-storage power stations. Grid companies and pumped-storage power stations must prioritize ensuring a stable power supply, maintaining grid security, and facilitating the consumption of new energy sources. They should plan the operation of pumped-storage stations effectively, sign annual dispatch and operation agreements, and disclose these agreements to the public, maximizing the comprehensive benefits of pumped-storage stations. The National Energy Administration and its branches are tasked with intensifying the monitoring and evaluation of the use of pumped-storage power stations. If a station is not performing adequately, it should be directed to rectify the issue promptly and be subject to legal actions if necessary. Local governments should also bolster the operational management of these facilities. Moreover, the stable operation of pumped-storage power stations invested in by non-grid entities must be ensured. Grid companies are required to enter into formal mid- to long-term power purchase and sale agreements with pumped-storage stations built by non-grid investors. They should dispatch these stations impartially and transparently, adhering to the principles of fairness and justice. It is imperative to strictly apply the capacity tariffs approved by NDRC and the energy tariffs established by these opinions. Payments for electricity should be settled monthly to safeguard the interests of non-grid investors.[47] In November 2017, NEA issued the "Notice on Implementing Ecological and Environmental Protection Requirements in the Planning and Construction of Pumped-Storage Power Stations." The notice underscores the imperative of prioritizing ecological considerations and upholding environmental standards throughout the planning and construction phases of pumped-storage power stations. It emphasizes the need to diligently enforce environmental protection measures in compliance with the ecological constraints mandated by legal and regulatory frameworks. All projects within the planned scope must advance strictly in accordance with legal procedures. Provincial energy authorities and relevant local governments in the regions where planned pumped-storage sites are located are responsible for the diligent protection of these resources. They must develop and execute various measures to guarantee the orderly realization of the approved pumped-storage site selection plans (including recommended and alternative site locations, the same below), as well as the planned site resources specified in "The 13th Five-Year Plan for Hydropower Development." Provincial energy authorities and planning entities should strengthen the integration of pumped-storage planning with the delineation of ecological conservation redlines and related planning efforts. It is important to ensure that the planning and construction of pumped-storage power stations are well-coordinated with national key functional zone planning, urban and rural construction planning, general land use planning, ecological function zoning, comprehensive water resource planning, environmental protection planning, and the

[47] See Opinions of the National Development and Reform Commission on Further Improving the Price Formation Mechanism for Pumped Storage (Fa Gai Jia Ge [2021] No. 633).

various types and levels of protected areas. Environmental assessments must be conducted for the planned sites to confirm the absence of ecological and environmental constraints. Should there be significant alterations to the construction conditions of a planned site, or the presence of major environmentally sensitive constraints that could profoundly impact the project's viability, the planning entity must spearhead a re-evaluation and validation process.[48] The "Management Measures for the Water Project Construction Planning Consent System (Trial)" issued in December 2017 state: "Construction entities are not permitted to commence construction of water projects without obtaining the water project construction planning consent, which must be reviewed and signed by either the river basin authority or the water administration department of the local people's government at the county level or above, according to their administration authority. The content of the water project construction planning consent includes the review and signature of opinions on whether the water project construction complies with the comprehensive river basin planning and flood control planning." "If a construction entity undertakes a water project without the required water project construction planning consent, or if it constructs a water project in violation of the stipulations of the consent, penalties shall be imposed in accordance with the relevant provisions of the 'Water Law of the People's Republic of China' and the 'Flood Control Law of the People's Republic of China'."[49] The "Regulations on the Compensation for Land Acquisition and Relocation for Construction of Large and Medium-sized Hydraulic and Hydroelectric Projects (Revised in 2017)" specifically stipulate the resettlement provisions for the construction of pumped-storage power stations. The "Opinions on Promoting the Healthy and Orderly Development of Pumped-Storage Power Stations" released by the National Development and Reform Commission in 2014 set forth guidelines for project site selection planning: "The construction of pumped-storage power stations must be reinforced with enhanced planning efforts. The national energy regulatory authority shall systematically organize the site selection planning, which should encompass considerations of regional power grid peak-shaving resources, systemic demands, and site resource conditions. The planning should involve an analysis of the construction scale and distribution of pumped-storage power stations, and the determination of recommended sites, construction timelines, and service areas should be made judiciously. This site selection planning is to be the essential foundation for the planning and construction of pumped-storage power stations in all regions. Investment and construction entities for pumped-storage power stations are required to develop implementation strategies based on this planning, to define the scope of services of the station, and to ascertain its primary roles and strategic positioning within the operation of the power grid."[50] In addition, the "Notice on

---

[48] See Notice from the General Administration Department of the National Energy Administration on Implementing Ecological and Environmental Protection Requirements in the Planning and Construction of Pumped-Storage Power Stations (Guo Neng Zong Fa Xin Neng [2017] No. 3).

[49] Management Measures for the Water Project Construction Planning Consent System (Trial) (Revised in 2017) (Ministry of Water Resources Order No. 49), Articles 4 and 16.

[50] Opinions of the National Development and Reform Commission on Promoting the Healthy and Orderly Development of Pumped-Storage Power Stations (Fa Gai Neng Yuan [2014] No. 2482).

Strengthening the Operation and Management of Pumped-Storage Power Stations," "Management Measures for the Acceptance of Hydropower Projects," and "Notice on Further Improving the Construction of Pumped-Storage Power Stations" issued by the National Energy Administration further clarify the standards for the construction acceptance and operational management of pumped-storage power stations.

Electrochemical Energy Storage Projects

Electrochemical energy storage, as one of the most promising directions in the market for energy storage, has seen encouraging or regulatory policies issued by both central and local authorities in recent years. These policies have created a favorable environment for the development of the electrochemical energy storage industry, promoting the acceleration of market-oriented regulation and deployment of electrochemical energy storage.

Encouraging Policies for Electrochemical Energy Storage

On February 18, 2019, the Office of the State Grid Corporation of China issued the "Guiding Opinions on Promoting the Healthy and Orderly Development of Electrochemical Energy Storage," which put forward development suggestions for electrochemical energy storage projects from the perspective of power source, power grid, and users. On the power source side, it supports the configuration of energy storage with new energy generation and the configuration of energy storage with conventional thermal power. From the grid perspective, energy storage is to be incorporated into the overall power grid planning with ongoing adjustments, recognizing grid-side energy storage as a crucial electrical component and a viable technical option, which should be subjected to comprehensive selection and demonstration. On the user side, electrochemical energy storage systems are encouraged to participate in grid demand response, energy balancing, and the improvement of load characteristics. Priority for investment and construction is given to regions where grid regulation is challenging, and where the costs of retrofitting and upgrading are prohibitively high.[51] The "Guiding Opinions on Accelerating the Development of New Energy Storage" issued by the National Development and Reform Commission and the National Energy Administration in July 2021 propose that by 2025, new energy storage should transition from the initial stage of commercialization to large-scale deployment. With an installed capacity exceeding 30 gigawatts, new energy storage technologies are playing a significant role in advancing the energy sector toward carbon peaking and carbon neutrality. By 2030, new energy storage is anticipated

[51] See Office of the State Grid Corporation of China. Guiding Opinions on Promoting the Healthy and Orderly Development of Electrochemical Energy Storage (Guo Jia Dian Wang Ban [2019] No. 176).

to be fully integrated into the market. It is poised to become a critical pillar in supporting the energy sector's goals of carbon peaking and carbon neutrality. The guidelines highlight the necessity of advancing energy storage project construction on the power source side, strategically deploying energy storage on the grid side, and fostering diverse development of energy storage on the user side. Additionally, they assert the independent market status of new energy storage entities, call for the improvement of the pricing mechanism for new energy storage, and advocate for strengthened incentive mechanisms for "new energy + energy storage" projects.[52] The "Notice on Issuing the Action Plan for Carbon Dioxide Peaking before 2030," issued by the State Council in November 2021, further proposes accelerating the construction of innovative electric power systems. The plan actively promotes the development of "new energy + energy storage," the integration of power source, grid, load, and storage, and the synergy of various energy sources. It supports the strategic placement of energy storage systems alongside distributed new energy installations. In addition, the plan mandates the creation of a new series of medium- and long-term development strategies for pumped-storage power stations and the refinement of policy mechanisms to facilitate the growth of pumped storage. The plan also aims to accelerate the broad demonstration and application of new types of energy storage. By 2025, the installed capacity of new types of energy storage is expected to exceed 30 gigawatts. By 2030, the installed capacity of pumped-storage power stations is expected to reach approximately 120 gigawatts, and provincial-level power grids will be equipped with peak-load response capacity of 5% or more.[53] The National Development and Reform Commission and the National Energy Administration released the "Implementation Plan for New Type Energy Storage Development in the '14th Five-Year Plan'" in January 2022. According to the plan, by 2025, new energy storage will move from the initial stage of commercialization to large-scale development, ready for widespread commercial use. The innovation capabilities for new energy storage technologies will be significantly enhanced, with substantial improvements in the autonomy and control of core technologies and equipment. The framework of standards will be essentially complete, the industrial system will be increasingly comprehensive, and the market environment and business models will be fundamentally mature. Specifically, the performance of electrochemical energy storage technology will see further improvements, with system costs reduced by over 30%. New energy storage technologies that rely on conventional power sources, such as steam extraction storage for thermal and nuclear power plants, and 100-megawatt-level compressed air energy storage technology, will be applied on an engineering scale. Megawatt-level flywheel energy storage and other mechanical storage technologies will gradually mature. Significant advancements will be made in long-duration energy storage technologies such as hydrogen storage and thermal (cold)

---

[52] See National Development and Reform Commission, & the National Energy Administration of China. Guiding Opinions on Accelerating the Development of New Energy Storage (Fa Gai Neng Yuan Gui [2021] No. 1051).

[53] See State Council. Notice on Issuing the Action Plan for Carbon Dioxide Peaking before 2030 (Guo Fa [2021] No. 23).

storage. By 2030, new energy storage is anticipated to be fully integrated into the market.[54] The General Office of the National Development and Reform Commission and the General Administration Department of the National Energy Administration issued the "Notice on Promoting the Participation of New Energy Storage in the Power Market and Scheduling" in May 2022. This notice clarifies the market status of electrochemical energy storage projects: "New energy storage projects that meet the relevant criteria can be converted into independent energy storage systems, participating in the power market as independent entities. We encourage the joint participation of co-located new energy storage and its associated power sources in the power market, accelerate the involvement of independent energy storage in assisting with grid peak shaving, fully leverage the technical advantages of independent energy storage to provide ancillary services,[55] maintain a predominantly market-oriented approach to optimize energy storage dispatch and operation, and further support the development of user-side energy storage. At the same time, we are investigating the establishment of a capacity tariff mechanism for grid-side independent energy storage stations to progressively encourage their participation in the power market. We are also exploring the inclusion of the cost–benefit of grid-alternative energy storage facilities into the recovery of transmission and distribution tariffs."[56]

Turning to Zhejiang Province, we'll explore its policies on electrochemical energy storage. The "Zhejiang Province's Action Plan for Carbon Peaking and Carbon Neutrality through Science and Technology Innovation" released in June 2021 proposes: "We should focus on research into mechanisms and methods in the fields of renewable energy and energy storage, particularly electrochemical energy storage. Centered around key technologies such as large-scale energy storage, we aim to advance the construction of an integrated power system that seamlessly incorporates 'source, grid, load, and storage' with a substantial proportion of renewable energy access. The target set for 2025 is to achieve the application of electrochemical energy storage technology at the hundred-megawatt scale." The "Implementation Opinions on Accelerating the Demonstration and Application of New Energy Storage in Zhejiang Province," issued in November 2021, outline that, "From 2021 to 2023, the province aims to complete the construction of new energy storage demonstration projects with a grid-connected capacity of 1 million kilowatts. By the end of the '14th Five-Year Plan', the goal is to reach approximately 2 million kilowatts for new energy storage demonstration projects. In alignment with the evolution of new power

---

[54] See National Development and Reform Commission, and National Energy Administration of China. Implementation Plan for New Type Energy Storage Development in the "14th Five-Year Plan" (Fa Gai Neng Yuan [2022] No. 209).

[55] The costs for ancillary services should be allocated according to the relevant provisions of the "Management Measures for Power Ancillary Services", following the principle of "those who provide benefit and those who benefit bear the costs", and should be reasonably shared by the relevant grid-connected entities on the generation side and power users.

[56] See Notice of the General Office of the National Development and Reform Commission and the General Administration Department of the National Energy Administration on Promoting the Participation of New Energy Storage in the Power Market and Scheduling (Fa Gai Ban Yun Xing [2022] No. 475).

systems, the focus will be on supporting the construction of large-scale centralized energy storage projects (with a capacity of no less than 50,000 kW) and distributed platform aggregated projects (with a capacity of no less than 10,000 kW), providing capacity support and peak-shaving capabilities for the power systems. We encourage the exploration, research, and demonstration of innovative energy storage technologies such as hydrogen storage and molten salt energy storage. It is essential to systematically advance the construction of energy storage on the power source side, the grid side, and the user side and promote the construction of independent energy storage."[57] The "14th Five-Year Plan for Energy Development in Zhejiang Province," issued in May 2022, sets forth objectives to "enhance the flexibility and reliability of the power system. We should actively explore the development of new energy storage facilities, pilot the construction of hydrogen energy storage and cold and thermal energy storage projects, and build a number of electrochemical energy storage projects on the power source side, the grid side, and the user side. By promoting the integration of power source, grid, load, and storage, as well as the synergy of multiple energy sources, and by advancing the construction of virtual power plants, we aim to facilitate the consumption of renewable energy. Furthermore, we should implement power demand-side response measures. By 2025, the precise load response capacity for power is expected to increase to tens of millions of kilowatts, with demand-side peak-shaving capabilities accounting for 5% of the peak societal load."[58]

Regulatory Policies for Electrochemical Energy Storage

In September 2021, the NEA issued the "Specification for the Management of New Energy Storage Projects (Interim)," which delineates the division of responsibilities, management procedures, and planning requirements for the governance of new energy storage projects. During the planning and layout phase, the energy authority of the State Council is tasked with developing a national plan for new energy storage advancement; provincial energy authorities are to conduct research on the scale and distribution of new energy storage development within their regions, providing scientifically sound guidance for the construction of new energy storage projects. In the project filing phase, local energy authorities are responsible for managing the filing of new energy storage projects according to relevant investment laws, regulations, and systems, and must forward these filings to the branches of the National Energy Administration. The filings for new energy storage projects should encompass: basic information about the project entity, project name, construction location, construction scale, construction details (including technical approaches, application scenarios, main functions, technical standards, as well as environmental and safety

[57] Zhejiang Provincial Development and Reform Commission, & Zhejiang Provincial Energy Bureau. Implementation Opinions on Accelerating the Demonstration and Application of New Energy Storage in Zhejiang Province (Zhe Fa Gai Neng Yuan [2021] No. 393).

[58] General Office of the People's Government of Zhejiang Province. 14th Five-Year Plan for Energy Development in Zhejiang Province (Zhe Zheng Ban Fa [2022] No. 29).

considerations), total investment, and a declaration of compliance with industrial policies. In the construction phase, entities in charge of project design, consultation, construction, and supervision must possess the necessary qualifications as prescribed by the state; major equipment must conform to relevant standards and specifications, be certified by accredited institutions, and network-related equipment must meet the technical requirements for the safe operation of the electrical grid; management procedures for project safety, fire protection, and environmental protection should be strictly implemented. During the grid-connection phase, associated power grid projects should be coordinated in tandem with the construction of new energy storage projects. Grid companies are expected to offer fair and non-discriminatory grid-connection services to new energy storage projects. Prior to grid commissioning, new energy storage projects must complete all relevant procedures in accordance with national regulations on quality, environmental, and fire safety standards. In the dispatching and operation phase, entities managing new energy storage projects should be equipped with the necessary communication and information systems to upload operational data to the power grid dispatching authorities as per established procedures, and to comply with dispatching orders. These entities must also conduct effective operational status monitoring of the energy storage projects and undertake timely corrective actions when necessary. If, after remediation, the project still does not meet the required standards, the managing entity should promptly implement decommissioning measures. In the monitoring and supervision phase, the energy authority of the State Council is responsible for building a national new energy storage management platform to facilitate information management of new energy storage projects across the country. Local authorities should bolster the development of monitoring and management systems for new energy storage projects and regularly publish research reports on the development scale, construction layout, and operational dispatch of new energy storage.[59]

In December 2021, NEA released the "Management Measures for Power Ancillary Services," which outline regulations regarding the provision, utilization, assessment, compensation, settlement, and supervision of power ancillary services (including new energy storage technologies like electrochemical, compressed air, and flywheel systems) within the jurisdiction of provincial-level and higher-level power dispatching agencies. Provision and utilization: Services should be selected and utilized in accordance with relevant national and industry standards or regulations. Compensation and allocation: Differentiated compensation or allocation standards should be established based on the type and performance of power ancillary services. Sharing mechanism: A gradual establishment of a sharing mechanism for power ancillary services that involve power users is encouraged, with participation either independently or through delegated representation. Information disclosure: The power dispatching agency must promptly push information regarding assessment, compensation, and allocation to the power trading agency, which in turn must disclose this information to all market participants before the 10th of the following

[59] See National Energy Administration of China. Specification for the Management of New Energy Storage Projects (Interim) (Guo Neng Fa Ke Ji Gui [2021] No. 47).

month. Supervision and management: These responsibilities fall under NEA and its local branches.[60]

In December 2021, NEA issued the "Regulations for the Management of Grid-Connected Operations," aimed at refining the management framework for grid connections in terms of scope of application, operational management, and division of responsibilities. The scope of application is clarified: It is specifically applicable to entities on the generation side and new types of energy storage that are directly dispatched by provincial-level or higher power dispatching agencies, as well as to entities on the load side and those within the jurisdiction of power dispatching agencies below the provincial level. Operational management is standardized: The requirement for grid-connected entities to comply with operational modes and power generation dispatch plans determined by market clearing is added. Specific measures and indicators for frequency and voltage regulation by generation-side entities are defined. The importance of assessing unplanned outages or grid disconnections is emphasized. Black-start plans must be implemented promptly and reliably for black start power sources. The regulations also detail the technical guidance and management for secondary frequency regulation, voltage regulation, new energy stations, new types of energy storage, and user-side adjustable loads. The division of responsibilities is clarified: The responsibilities of energy regulatory authorities, grid companies, power dispatching agencies, and power trading agencies in the operation of grid connections are specified.[61]

To further enhance the safety management of electrochemical energy storage stations, NEA issued the "Notice on Strengthening the Safety Management of Electrochemical Energy Storage Stations" in April 2022. The notice outlines comprehensive safety management planning for electrochemical energy storage stations, covering aspects such as planning and design, equipment selection, completion acceptance, grid-connection acceptance, operational maintenance, emergency response, and firefighting. Key points include: prioritizing the safety management of electrochemical energy storage stations (elevating awareness and implementing primary responsibilities); strengthening the safety management in the planning and design phase (enhanced risk assessment and rigorous design review); ensuring proper equipment selection (strict quality control and intensified spot-checking upon delivery); enforcing strict construction completion acceptance (improving construction management and rigorous acceptance checks); implementing rigorous grid-connection acceptance (ensuring readiness for grid integration and strengthening acceptance checks); enhancing the safety management of operational maintenance (clarifying delegated responsibilities, strengthening daily management, standardizing information submission, intensifying staff training, and managing equipment retirement); improving emergency firefighting capabilities (fulfilling

[60] See National Energy Administration of China. Management Measures for Power Ancillary Services (Guo Neng Fa Jian Guan Gui [2021] No. 61).

[61] See National Energy Administration of China (2021). Regulations for the Management of Grid-Connected Operations (Guo Neng Fa Jian Guan Gui [2021] No. 60).

firefighting responsibilities, conducting emergency drills, and establishing linkage mechanisms).[62]

As required in the "Interim Measures for the Safety Management of Electrochemical Energy Storage Stations (Draft for Comments)" released by the National Development and Reform Commission and the General Administration Department of the National Energy Administration in August 2021, safety management for electrochemical energy storage stations must adhere to the principles of "safety first, prevention-oriented, and comprehensive governance," and a management mechanism that involves "corporate responsibility, industry self-regulation, government oversight, and public supervision" should be established. Safety management encompasses various aspects, including project approval, production and quality control, design consultation, construction and acceptance, grid connection and dispatch, operation and maintenance, decommissioning, emergency response, and accident handling. Construction entities of energy storage stations, as the primary responsible units for safety, must comply with laws, regulations, and standards related to production safety. They should integrate energy storage safety into their corporate safety management systems, enhance the systems for ensuring and supervising production safety, and enforce a comprehensive safety production accountability system for all employees. These entities should establish a graded safety risk management and control system, as well as a mechanism for the identification and rectification of potential hazards, to strengthen safety oversight and control throughout the entire process, including design, construction, operation, and decommissioning. Additionally, construction entities are required to create a robust safety risk assessment and validation mechanism. They should engage a qualified engineering consulting organization to develop the project's feasibility study report. This ensures prudent determination of the energy storage station's siting, layout, and safety facility construction. The project must be duly filed in accordance with the relevant requirements. It is essential to prioritize safety investment, ensuring that safety facilities are designed, constructed, and commissioned concurrently with the main project. If there are changes to the implementation plan of the energy storage station during planning, design, construction, or operation phases, which affect the main facilities, equipment, or technical approaches, the construction entity shall refile the changes. Manufacturers of energy storage-related products and systems must transfer relevant safety management documentation to the construction entity, which should clearly include descriptions of hazard sources, hazard prevention measures, safety protection, and emergency response measures. Energy storage products and systems must meet national (industry) standards and undergo testing before they can be released onto the market.[63]

---

[62] See Notice of the General Administration Department of the National Energy Administration on Strengthening the Safety Management of Electrochemical Energy Storage Stations (Guo Neng Zong Tong An Quan [2022] No. 37).

[63] See National Energy Administration of China. Announcement on the Public Solicitation of Comments on the "Interim Measures for the Safety Management of Electrochemical Energy Storage Stations (Draft for Comments)", released on August 24, 2021.

Policy Analysis of Energy Storage Development

Pumped storage is the most prevalent and emblematic form of energy storage, and China's pumped-storage projects are characterized by the highest market share, critical importance, grand development plans, extensive industrial distribution, and intricate regulatory requirements. Notably, some Chinese provinces are deficient in energy and mineral resources but possess abundant hydro resources. For instance, in Zhejiang Province, the majority of the main rivers' upper and middle reaches run through hilly and mountainous areas with steep gradients, harboring immense hydrokinetic potential. The rivers in the southwestern mountainous areas are particularly suited for constructing pumped-storage power stations due to their advantageous topography, which includes high water heads, short water conveyance distances, and minimal flooding losses. Beyond catering to the provincial power grid's needs, these stations also undertake crucial tasks in peak shaving, valley filling, and energy storage for the East China power grid, making Zhejiang the province with the most pumped-storage projects in the nation. Currently, Zhejiang houses 5 operational pumped-storage power stations with a total installed capacity of 6.68 gigawatts, and 6 more large-scale pumped-storage power stations under construction, which will add 8.5 gigawatts to the capacity. Additionally, 33 pumped-storage power stations are incorporated into the national medium and long-term plan, aiming for a collective installed capacity of 36.5 gigawatts. Pumped storage is a crucial component in ensuring the secure, stable, and green low-carbon development of energy supply at affordable prices in Zhejiang Province. To facilitate the secure, orderly, and market-driven expansion of new energy, while also meeting the peak-shaving demands of the East China power grid, the advancement of pumped storage should be guided by grid requirements. Coordinated planning between the two is essential to ensure a logical arrangement and adequate capacity of pumped-storage facilities, preventing the wastage of resources due to disorganized investment. This approach has become a significant focus in the establishment of Zhejiang's provincial demonstration zones for an innovative power system.[64]

An analysis of the existing normative documents reveals that, given the realities of China's vast power grid and the essential role of pumped-storage power stations in adjusting grid load, the marketization of pumped storage currently remains quite limited. Consequently, there is no pressing need to formulate specialized administrative regulations. Regulatory authorities typically address issues that are phased, specific, and urgent through administrative orders and notices. Government regulation always keeps pace with market development: (1) Since the inception of pumped storage in 2004, the national authorities have confined it within the domain of grid companies, explicitly mandating that construction and management be primarily undertaken by grid operators. The costs for construction and operation were to be included in the unified settlement of power grid operating expenses, essentially eliminating the market characteristics of pumped-storage power stations; (2) In 2014,

[64] See Interpretation Review of "Zhejiang Province Electric Power Regulations" (Second Draft), released on February 17, 2023.

the National Development and Reform Commission's "Opinions on Promoting the Healthy and Orderly Development of Pumped-storage Power Stations" suggested "gradually establishing a diversified, market-oriented investment system that incorporates social capital. In regions where conditions permit, it is encouraged to determine the project owners of pumped-storage power stations through methods such as bidding and market-based pricing, who should independently invest in and construct these stations in accordance with national strategies and policy requirements."[65] Despite a slight relaxation instance, the market is still largely confined to grid companies and central state-owned enterprises in the electricity sector; (3) The "Pumped Storage Medium and Long-term Development Plan (2021–2035)" issued on September 17, 2021, adopts a more open approach. It calls for "the further refinement of related policies and the careful advancement of selecting investment entities for pumped-storage power station projects through methods such as bidding and market-based pricing… as well as encouraging social capital to invest in the construction of pumped-storage facilities."[66] Anticipating future regulatory trends for pumped-storage projects, it can be reasonably deduced that once power market reforms yield incremental and definitive outcomes, a dedicated government ordinance for the oversight of pumped-storage power station projects is likely to be established.

Compared with traditional pumped storage, electrochemical energy storage boasts advantages such as lower geographic constraints and reduced initial investment costs. Therefore, electrochemical energy storage can be flexibly utilized across the three key segments of the power system: generation, transmission, and consumption, offering favorable conditions for commercial expansion. With the cost of electrochemical energy storage steadily decreasing in recent years and its commercial applications becoming more widespread and mature, the benefits of this technology are increasingly evident. However, from a practical standpoint, the rapid expansion of electrochemical energy storage projects in 2022 has surpassed the regulatory foresight. The inherent limitations of subsidies, scalability, and other control measures available in the government's toolkit have made regulatory bodies more cautious. From the standpoint of regulations and policies, the current management norms are insufficient to fully support compliant project implementation, and future norms will need to adapt to the evolution of the power market reform. As a result, the market exhibits certain "disorderly" characteristics, while the regulatory framework appears "inactive and ineffective." By analyzing regulatory policies and the development trends of electrochemical energy storage projects, we can deduce that future regulatory trends for such projects will exhibit the following four characteristics:

Firstly, basic standard systems as the foundational norms. On February 22, 2023, the Standardization Administration of China and NEA issued the "Guidelines for the Construction of New Energy Storage Standard Systems." This document outlines a

---

[65] See Opinions of the National Development and Reform Commission on Promoting the Healthy and Orderly Development of Pumped-Storage Power Stations (Fa Gai Neng Yuan [2014] No. 2482).

[66] See National Energy Administration of China. Pumped Storage Medium and Long-term Development Plan (2021–2035).

comprehensive framework for 205 new energy storage standards, developed in accordance with the construction logic of electrochemical energy storage stations and the requirements of new power system construction. It covers eight key areas: foundational general standards, planning and design, equipment testing, construction acceptance, grid-connection operations, maintenance and monitoring, operational maintenance, and safety emergency procedures. These standards aim to provide normative guidance for a variety of new energy storage projects and to offer benchmarks for the enforcement activities of government regulatory agencies.[67]

Secondly, special norms for emerging projects. While lithium-ion battery energy storage currently holds a predominant share of the market, a variety of other energy storage technologies including compressed air energy storage, flow battery energy storage, lead-acid battery energy storage, as well as flywheels and gravity-based systems, are progressively making their way into the market. Notably, projects involving flow batteries are showing a robust expansion trend. It is anticipated that regulatory authorities will consider the tension between macro-planning and micro-market dynamics to derive value orientations, and present compliance management requirements in flexible forms (such as notices and guidelines) to indirectly steer the market. In addition, in response to specific incidents, regulatory authorities will likely enact targeted safety regulations for particular categories of energy storage technology to establish standards, correct misconceptions, and quell fears.

Thirdly, regulatory norms are based on the authorization management by grid companies. For electrochemical energy storage projects, whether they are supplementary storage or stand-alone storage, the prerequisite for their effective operation is integration into the power grid and inclusion in the power market, both of which are under the purview of grid companies. The "Specification for the Management of New Energy Storage Projects (Interim)" imposes legal obligations on grid companies, including coordinating the planning and construction of associated power grids, providing non-discriminatory and fair grid-connection services, defining procedures for grid-connection testing and acceptance, and prioritizing the utilization efficiency of new energy storage. However, it does not grant corresponding examination and management authority to grid companies, resulting in a situation where the enthusiasm of grid companies is hindered in practice.[68] Therefore, it is reasonable for regulatory authorities to incorporate the management standards pertaining to grid connection and power market access set by grid companies through an approval process. For example, NDRC and NEA officially approved the "Inter-Provincial Electricity Spot Trading Rules (Trial)" in November 2021 and approved the "Work Plan for the Southern China Regional Power Market" on January 27, 2022.

Fourthly, promotive norms are based on the principles of marketization. The "Guiding Opinions on Accelerating the Development of New Energy Storage" have

---

[67] See Standardization Administration of China, & National Energy Administration of China. Guidelines for the Construction of New Energy Storage Standard Systems (Guo Biao Wei Lian [2023] No. 6).

[68] See National Energy Administration of China. Specification for the Management of New Energy Storage Projects (Interim) (Guo Neng Fa Ke Ji Gui [2021] No. 47).

set forth development goals for new types of energy storage, including electrochemical energy storage. These goals state that "by 2025, new energy storage should transition from the initial stage of commercialization to large-scale development; by 2030, new energy storage is anticipated to be fully integrated into the market."[69] The "Implementation Plan for New Type Energy Storage Development in the '14th Five-Year Plan'" also calls for an "acceleration of the marketization pace of new energy storage."[70] Furthermore, the "Notice on Promoting the Participation of New Energy Storage in the Power Market and Scheduling" specifies the market role of electrochemical energy storage, encouraging it to participate in the power market as an independent energy storage entity. It aims to motivate more participants to involve themselves in the construction and operation of electrochemical energy storage projects through the use of market pricing and adjustment mechanisms.[71]

Research on Key Legal Issues of Energy Storage Projects Within New Power Systems

Research on Cost Transfer Mechanism of Pumped-Storage Power Stations

In pursuit of the "dual carbon goals," China is advancing the development of new power systems dominated by renewable energy. To counteract the considerable variability of renewable energy sources within these systems, it is imperative to maximize the role of energy storage projects in maintaining the grid's security and stability. Pumped-storage projects, in particular, boast the longest history, greatest technological maturity, and best economic efficiency among energy storage options in power systems.[72] However, the operating costs of pumped-storage power stations are subject to a variety of factors, such as operational lifespan, installed capacity, natural conditions, and technological standards of equipment. These factors create technical complexities in establishing reasonable capacity tariffs for pumped-storage stations. These complexities have led to practical challenges, including difficulties in cost recovery, dominance of single investors, and subdued enthusiasm among

---

[69] See National Development and Reform Commission, and National Energy Administration of China. Guiding Opinions on Accelerating the Development of New Energy Storage (Fa Gai Neng Yuan Gui [2021] No. 1051).

[70] See National Development and Reform Commission, the National Energy Administration of China (2022): Implementation Plan for New Type Energy Storage Development in the "14th Five-Year Plan" (Fa Gai Neng Yuan [2022] No. 209).

[71] See Notice of the General Office of the National Development and Reform Commission and the General Administration Department of the National Energy Administration on Promoting the Participation of New Energy Storage in the Power Market and Scheduling (Fa Gai Ban Yun Xing [2022] No. 475).

[72] See Huang et al. (2022).

social capital investors, all of which obstruct the pumped-storage projects from fully functioning as "stabilizers" in new power systems.

Development History and Business Model Evolution of Pumped-Storage Projects

Before the reform of China's electric power system, pumped-storage power stations were operated uniformly by grid companies. These power stations were invested in, constructed, operated, and managed by grid companies, with costs being recouped through the sale of electricity. Following the power system reform, the business model for pumped-storage power stations transitioned to a grid leasing phase. Business operations of pumped storage were separated from power transmission and distribution services. Grid companies primarily used a leasing model, paying leasing fees (capacity tariffs) to pumped-storage stations.[73] This leasing model originated in Europe, as seen with the pumped-storage power stations owned by Chluch-seewerk in southern Germany and SEO in Luxembourg, which both utilize this business method. Independent power plants (companies) with large-scale nuclear, coal, or combined cycle units, which are either technically unsuitable for adjustment (such as nuclear power) or opt not to adjust for economic reasons, participate in leasing the capacity of pumped-storage power stations, with grid companies ensuring their safe and stable operation.[74] However, this model has a drawback: when the power grid and power plants are operated by different stakeholders, the electricity losses incurred from the operation of pumped-storage power stations are entirely borne by grid companies. This has led to a decrease in grid companies' motivation to invest in and operate pumped-storage power stations.[75] During the advancement of market-oriented reforms in the power sector, the pricing and cost policies for pumped storage were not effectively aligned, and the associated costs were not included in the pricing for power transmission and distribution. Consequently, the electricity fees for pumped storage could not be recouped from market-oriented users through transmission and distribution tariffs, leading to a temporary obstruction in cost allocation. As the reform toward a market-oriented power system progressively unfolds, the pricing mechanism for pumped storage has been steadily refined. In May 2021, NDRC issued the "Opinions on Further Improving the Price Formation Mechanism for Pumped Storage" (Fa Gai Jia Ge [2021] No. 633), which specifies that pumped-storage power stations will adopt a two-part tariff system, incorporating the capacity tariff into the transmission and distribution pricing for recovery. The capacity tariff, established by NDRC, reflects the value of ancillary services provided by pumped-storage power stations, such as reserve capacity, peak shaving, frequency regulation, phase modulation, and black-start capabilities. Settlements for the capacity tariff are made between provincial grid companies and pumped-storage power stations, with

[73] Same as above.

[74] See Hua (2019).

[75] Same as above.

the capacity fees included in the unified accounting of local provincial grid operating costs. The energy tariff primarily compensates for variable costs such as pumping and generation losses incurred by pumped-storage power stations. The energy tariff level is based on the local benchmark feed-in tariff for coal-fired power units (which includes environmental protection charges such as desulfurization, denitrification, and dust removal, with the same conditions applying below). For the pumped energy provided by the grid company to the pumped-storage power station, the price is set at 75% of the benchmark feed-in tariff for coal-fired power units.[76]

Development History and Business Model of Foreign Pumped-Storage Projects

This section outlines the development history of pumped-storage power stations abroad. The world's first pumped-storage power station was built in Switzerland in 1882, over 140 years ago. In the first half of the twentieth century, the growth of pumped-storage power stations was modest, primarily serving as energy storage for hydropower stations and providing regulation during low water periods. The golden age for the construction and development of these stations spanned from the 1960s to the 1980s, driven by developed countries and regions such as the United States, Western Europe, and Japan, to support nuclear power peak shaving. Entering a mature phase from the 1990s to the early twenty-first century, the expansion of pumped-storage power stations slowed down due to the economic deceleration in developed countries and the swift rise of power stations with strong regulatory capacities, such as those using liquefied natural gas (LNG) and liquefied petroleum gas (LPG), which lessened the reliance on pumped-storage facilities. Since the dawn of the twenty-first century, the rapid advancement of renewable energy sources has reignited interest in pumped-storage power stations among major nations. The International Renewable Energy Agency (IRENA) predicts in "Electricity Storage and Renewables: Costs and Markets to 2030" that by 2030, the global installed capacity for pumped storage will have increased by approximately 40%–50% compared to 2017.[77]

The following describes some operation examples of pumped-storage power stations in the United States, the United Kingdom, France, and Japan. Japan initiated power market reforms in the early 1990s. Since 1995, the power market has been open to independent power producers. However, the top ten traditional power companies remain the main power suppliers and operators of transmission and distribution networks in their respective operating regions. Moreover, these companies own the majority of pumped-storage power stations. As assets of the power companies, pumped-storage power stations recover costs through electricity sales and operate under unified grid management. For the few pumped-storage power stations invested in and constructed by independent power producers, all are operated through grid leasing. The United States revised the "Energy Policy Act" in 1992 and implemented

[76] Zhang et al. (2018).

[77] See Huang et al. (2022).

market-oriented reforms in power generation. Most pumped-storage power stations are constructed and operated by grid companies, while a minority are developed by independent companies. The majority of the stations run by grid companies are subject to unified grid dispatch, and their operational costs are included in the grid company's electricity pricing. This allows for the recovery of costs through electricity sales, ensuring cohesive grid management. The few pumped-storage power stations built by non-grid companies are operated through grid leasing. Additionally, California boasts a well-established power trading market that features both a power energy market and an ancillary services market. Pumped-storage power stations operate on a market-based model, freely choosing to trade within either or both markets. For instance, the Helms Pumped Storage Plant participates in both California's power energy market and ancillary services market, with income from ancillary services comprising 60% of its total revenue. In 1990, the United Kingdom initiated reforms to privatize power generation while maintaining public ownership of the power grid, leading to the establishment of a relatively mature power trading market and an ancillary services market. Pumped-storage power stations operate under a market-oriented model, allowing them to freely participate in market competition. Their revenue consists of two parts: annual lease transaction income, which accounts for 70–80% of the power station's total annual revenue, and electricity sales income from competitive bidding, which makes up only 20%–30%. However, the market-oriented reforms and pricing mechanisms in the UK have not provided sufficient investment incentives for pumped-storage power stations. Due to the uncertainty of long-term potential income, no new pumped-storage power stations have been built in the UK since the 1990s. Research reports indicate that due to intense market competition and product designs that do not fully capitalize on the technical advantages of pumped-storage power stations, these facilities have not been successful in the market. During the market-oriented reforms of the French power system, following years of domestic debate, pumped-storage power stations began to participate in market competition as independent competitive power plants in 2000. However, due to the inability to compensate for their costs under market operations, Électricité de France (EDF) considered halting all pumped-storage power stations between 2000 and 2004. It was only after 2004, when pumped-storage power stations were reintegrated as regulatory power sources and operated uniformly by the power grid, that they were able to resume normal operations.[78]

Through the analysis of operation examples of pumped-storage power stations in major developed countries and regions including Europe, the United States, and Japan, three primary business models and pricing mechanisms have been identified. The first is the unified operation by the power grid (integrated model). In countries or enterprises that maintain an integrated management system for power generation, transmission, and distribution post-power market reforms, pumped-storage power stations built solely by grid companies are operated uniformly by the grid. The operation and maintenance costs, as well as revenues of pumped storage, are incorporated into the power company's electricity sales price for recovery. The second is power

[78] Same as above.

grid leasing (leasing model). In countries and enterprises where power generation and transmission are separate post-reform, pumped-storage power stations are generally operated through leasing agreements by grid companies, which pay leasing fees to the stations. The third model is grid bidding (market-oriented model). In countries or regions with a mature power market and an established ancillary services market, pumped-storage power stations provide services to the grid but do not passively accept grid dispatch. They operate independently as third parties and can earn income through competitive bidding in the ancillary services market. Additionally, in countries or regions with advanced power trading markets, pumped-storage power stations can profit through competitive bidding among peak-load units within the power market.[79] About 85% of the world's 150 million kW pumped-storage power stations adopt the integrated model or the leasing model, as seen in countries like France and Japan, and in some states of the United States. Under these models, the pumped-storage power station either operates as a component of the power grid or is a third-party-invested facility leased by the power grid. The related costs are incorporated into the power grid's unified accounting and are offset through the electricity sales price.[80] Approximately 15% of the world's pumped-storage power stations generate income by competing in the power market, with notable examples being the United Kingdom and areas covered by Regional Transmission Organizations (RTOs)/ISOs in the United States. In this model, pumped-storage power stations are typically financed and built by independent power producers (IPPs) or utility companies that handle both generation and distribution (sales). They earn revenue by participating in the energy market and ancillary services market. However, the revenue from the market only covers about 20% to 30% of their costs. To address the return on investment issue, these stations must also sign medium to long-term contracts with dispatch trading institutions to sell services such as black start and reactive power, ensuring a stable income.[81]

Through the study of operation examples of foreign pumped-storage projects, it can be preliminarily summarized that the main reasons why global pumped-storage power stations rarely address the income return problem through market competition mechanisms are as follows: First, the income is difficult to ascertain. The ancillary services such as emergency backup and black start provided by pumped-storage power stations play a significant role in ensuring the safe and stable operation of the power system. However, since the beneficiaries are widespread and difficult to quantify, it becomes challenging to establish compensation standards. Second, there is a high market risk. Given the risks associated with fluctuations in electricity prices, investors generally prefer to invest in projects with lower risk. Over the past decade, with the rapid development of renewable energy sources such as wind and solar, there has been a significant increase in demand for pumped storage. Yet, foreign countries also face the issue of low investment enthusiasm in pumped-storage power stations due to market risks. The third issue is historical inertia. The majority of

[79] Same as above.

[80] Luo et al. (2013), Barbour et al. (2016).

[81] Zhang et al. (2018).

pumped-storage power stations built in the twentieth century are owned by vertically integrated monopoly power companies, which continue to use the existing income return model that incorporates costs into the electricity sales price.[82]

Realistic Dilemmas in the Pricing Mechanism of Pumped-Storage Power Stations

Pumped-storage power stations are significantly influenced by policy factors and currently possess a relatively singular profit model. Amidst the uncertain market environment and policy mechanisms, their development continues to encounter numerous challenges.

Firstly, there is an absence of an investment recovery mechanism for new pumped-storage power stations. Capacity tariffs or leasing fees represent the primary means for these power stations to achieve cost recovery and economic benefits. The "Measures for Supervision and Review of Power Transmission and Distribution Pricing Costs" issued in 2019 stipulates that pumped-storage power stations cannot be included in the transmission and distribution pricing costs. This makes it challenging for the costs of new pumped-storage power stations to be transferred to the power users through transmission and distribution prices or other electricity pricing channels.[83] Moreover, regarding development entities, the National Energy Administration has emphasized that pumped-storage power stations are generally developed and operated by grid companies. This limits the participation of social capital in this sector and hinders the introduction of competition and cost reduction during the construction phase of the power stations.

Secondly, pumped-storage power stations receive relatively low economic compensation from ancillary services. The "Two Rules" in the East China region[84] indicate that pumped-storage power stations can earn economic compensation by providing ancillary services such as peak shaving and frequency regulation. However, the compensation these stations receive in actual operation is low and does not align with their investment, operation, and maintenance costs. Looking at mature foreign power markets, market-oriented power trading significantly widens the peak-to-valley price difference, enhancing the value of pumped-storage power stations

[82] Same as above.

[83] Jin et al. (2021).

[84] At the end of 2021, following the National Energy Administration's release of the new versions of the "Regulations for the Management of Grid-Connected Operations" and the "Management Measures for Power Ancillary Services", regional energy regulatory bureaus began to successively issue the official drafts or drafts for solicitation of comments for the "Two Rules". The East China region released a draft of the "Two Rules" for public comments in May. After several months of collecting feedback, the East China Energy Regulatory Bureau of National Energy Administration issued the "Implementation Rules for the Management of Power Ancillary Services in East China (Simulated Operation Draft)" and the "Implementation Rules for Grid-Connected Power Operation and Management in East China (Simulated Operation Draft)" ("Two Rules") on August 29, 2022.

through participation in both the power and ancillary services markets, leading to better market price feedback.[85]

Thirdly, there is the challenge of balancing site selection planning for pumped-storage power stations with ecological protection. The reports to the 19th and 20th NCCPC put forward a series of new ideas, goals, requirements, and strategies for building an ecological civilization. In response, national and local governments at all levels have developed and implemented numerous policies and regulations concerning ecological and environmental protection. Ecological protection redlines and control areas have been established across various regions. The planning and construction of pumped-storage projects are required to adhere to the principles of ecological civilization construction and the new development concept, ensuring effective ecological and environmental protection efforts. However, the planning and siting of pumped-storage power stations often take place in high mountain areas and near rivers or ravines, which happen to be within ecological protection barriers. As a result, the development of sites with favorable technical and economic conditions for pumped-storage stations faces significant restrictions. Some projects that have already been included in the planning phase are progressing slowly in their initial stages. Moving forward, effectively managing the coordination between pumped-storage reserve sites and environmental constraints, such as ecological protection redlines, is crucial. It is essential to harmonize these aspects with national land space, ecological redlines, and environmental protection, and to swiftly adjust them to be included in the priority implementation project portfolio. Additionally, ensuring the effective planning of pumped-storage projects and the protection of site resources presents challenges to project owners and local governments.[86]

Policy Recommendations for the Development of Pumped-Storage Projects

According to the arrangements for China's power market reform, a power energy spot market and an ancillary services market will be gradually built in the future. Assuming that pumped-storage power stations participate in the power market competition as required by the government, they can profit from participating in the power energy and ancillary services markets, such as AGC and conventional reserves. However, according to international experience, the price of power ancillary services is very low and its market size is limited. For example, in both the Australian power market and various US power markets, the proportion of ancillary service fees to the total power costs is within 2%.[87] In addition, as the difficulty of site resource development

---

[85] Jin et al. (2021).

[86] Gao (2021).

[87] Zhao et al. (2011); Mandal et al. (2007); Zhou et al. (2016). *Survey of U.S. ancillary services markets* (ANL/ESD-16/1). Argonne National Laboratory. https://doi.org/10.2172/1236451; Australian Energy Market Operator. (2023). *Guide to ancillary services in the national electricity market*. Retrieved March 15, 2024, from https://www.aemo.com.au/-/media/files/electricity/nem/security_and_reliability/ancillary_services/guide-to-ancillary-services-in-the-national-electricity-market.pdf.

increases, the investment cost of pumped-storage power stations is likely to rise in the future, further increasing the investment risks of pumped-storage power stations due to the uncertainty of long-term market revenue expectations.[88]

It should be recognized that pumped-storage power stations differ from other power sources in that their main purpose is not power generation, but rather they serve as an important device to ensure the safety and stability of the system through pumping operations. The "commodity attributes" of certain services provided by pumped-storage power stations are not pronounced. Ancillary services such as black start and emergency backup, due to the limited number of providers and significant uncertainty, face challenges in forming efficient transaction channels in practice, making it difficult to manifest their commodity attributes. Additionally, the services provided by pumped-storage power stations are universal, cross-cutting, and difficult to quantify, and vary in functional positioning across in different regions: ① The frequency regulation, emergency backup, and black-start functions of pumped-storage power stations benefit the entire power system, with universally applicable benefits. Under the current policy landscape, it is impossible to accurately identify the beneficiaries. ② The ancillary services offered by pumped storage are multifaceted, enabling them to concurrently provide services such as peak shaving, new energy consumption, and support for UHV development. ③ The direct economic benefits of pumped storage are relatively clear in operational scenarios such as peak shaving and valley filling. However, quantifying the benefits of other types of ancillary services is challenging. For services aimed at ensuring system safety, stable operation, and timely recovery post-accidents, such as emergency backup and black start, quantifying benefits is particularly difficult; ④ Pumped-storage power stations in different regions may focus on different functions and play varied roles. Therefore, in the process of deepening the reform of the power system, especially in terms of cost recovery, it is imperative not to equate pumped storage entirely with conventional power sources. There is a need to develop policy mechanisms that align with its unique characteristics.[89]

Based on the above analysis and research, the following policy recommendations are proposed:

Add provisions in the pricing policy for pumped-storage power stations within the framework of power market reform. This should involve a dual-pricing mechanism that combines market revenue with regulated revenue, ensuring a guaranteed minimum regulated revenue. In the context of power market reform, the determination of permissible revenue for pumped-storage power stations should still follow the principle of permissible costs plus reasonable revenue. This revenue should be divided into two parts: regulated revenue and market revenue. Regulated revenue is intended to compensate for the functions of pumped-storage power stations that cannot be reflected through market competition and to address the insufficient revenue within the market system. It should be reflected through a capacity tariff

[88] Zhang et al. (2018).

[89] Same as above.

mechanism, where the capacity tariff equals the regulated revenue (or the capacity of the pumped-storage power station). Market revenue reflects the revenue generated by pumped-storage power stations through various services, such as participating in peak-valley arbitrage and multiple ancillary services markets. The market revenue is calculated based on the market price system. Then, the regulated revenue is determined by subtracting the market revenue from the permissible revenue. The combination of the market price system and capacity tariff forms the pricing mechanism and policy for pumped-storage power stations in the context of power market reform. Calculations from a pumped-storage power station indicate that the current market revenue for pumped-storage power stations mainly consists of revenue from power energy market arbitrage and ancillary services markets. However, this is insufficient to compensate for the costs and reasonable returns of pumped-storage power stations. The dual-pricing mechanism is reasonable and effective. The regulated revenue guarantee mechanism is beneficial for promoting the sustainable development of pumped-storage power stations, while the market system provides an internal incentive and constraint mechanism for these stations.[90]

List the capacity tariff or cost within the regulated revenue of pumped-storage power stations separately. This should be explicitly included in the permissible costs provision of the Provincial-Level Grid Transmission and Distribution Pricing Measures.[91] Pumped-storage power stations are social public goods that serve various user groups who are difficult to classify. Therefore, the capacity tariff and pumping losses should be shared by all users to ensure fairness in their distribution. In practice, it can be implemented by collecting these costs together with the transmission and distribution charges. The pricing methods for regional grid transmission and distribution charges should explicitly state that the regional grid's permissible costs include the "ancillary service" fees (including capacity tariffs) paid by grid companies to pumped-storage power stations and the costs associated with pumping losses. Issues related to the coordination with the pricing cycle and the scope of cost-sharing should also be addressed. Firstly, the existing and upcoming pumped-storage power station projects should be determined within the pricing cycle of transmission and distribution charges. This ensures that once these projects are put into operation, they can operate smoothly. Due to the long construction period of pumped-storage power stations, their commissioning time may not align with the pricing cycle. Therefore, the commissioning time of pumped-storage power stations should be considered in the pricing scheme. Before the start of each pricing cycle, the capacity tariffs of the existing operational pumped-storage power stations and the expected new stations within that pricing cycle should be included in the pricing scheme. This ensures an adequate source of capacity tariffs for pumped-storage power stations. Secondly, the scope of cost-sharing for capacity tariffs of pumped-storage power stations should be expanded gradually. The costs should be shared based on the relationship of scheduling operations and the actual beneficiary regions. Currently, most pumped-storage power stations in China are scheduled by regional grids, and the beneficiaries

[90] Ye et al. (2020).

[91] Same as above.

extend beyond the province where the power station is located. The beneficiary scope includes other provinces within the region. In order to reflect the principle of "beneficiary pays" and to reduce the cost-sharing burden on provinces with a large number of pumped-storage power stations, the scope of capacity tariff sharing should be spread to all beneficiary provinces within the region. In practical terms, the capacity tariffs can be included in the regional grid transmission and distribution costs. Based on the principle of "beneficiary pays," the relevant provincial-level grids within the regional grid should share the costs, and the revenue can be recovered through provincial-level grid transmission and distribution charges. The pumped-storage power stations settle electricity fees with provincial grid companies based on price standards approved by the government's pricing authority.[92]

Enhance and refine the mechanism for selecting sites and planning for pumped-storage power stations. While promoting the accelerated development of pumped-storage power stations, site selection and planning for pumped-storage stations should be carried out in stages and in accordance with demand. Furthermore, strengthening the legal effect of the Chinese government's approval opinions on-site selection and planning is fundamental to the orderly development of pumped-storage power stations. Conducting preliminary work within the site selection and planning sites and obtaining project approvals should be considered as mandatory requirements. The state governments control the planning process, while provincial governments are responsible for approval, development rights permits, and project acceptance, which represents the new norm in the management of pumped-storage power station investments. At the same time, it is important to maintain the mature technical management system that has been established over time. This includes conducting thorough preliminary assessments and ensuring adherence to standards and specifications, as well as guaranteeing the quality of the projects in the later stages. In response to the rapid development of new power systems and emerging business models, it is necessary to promptly initiate a new round of site selection and planning for pumped-storage power stations. According to China's development direction and structural adjustments, significant changes are expected in China's power structure, especially after 2030. The proportion of new and renewable energy sources such as wind energy, solar energy, and nuclear power will increase substantially. To ensure the secure and stable operation of the power system and promote the development and utilization of new energy sources, it is necessary to allocate a reasonable number of pumped-storage power stations that are flexible in terms of start-up and shutdown, capable of rapid response, and clean and low-carbon in nature. To meet the development, construction, and operational needs of pumped-storage power stations in China, and considering the reasonable construction duration of these power stations, it is necessary to organize a new round of site selection and planning. It is recommended that the NEA organize the China Renewable Energy Engineering Institute to start preparing for a new round of site selection and planning and to start site selection and planning at an appropriate time.[93] The grid company in Zhejiang can

---

[92] Zhang et al. (2018).

[93] See Jia (2015).

conduct systematic resurveying, re-evaluation, and reselection of potential resource sites within the province, especially for medium and small-scale pumped-storage power station resources. They can utilize information technology and digital tools to explore the development potential of pumped storage within the province. Every effort should be made to identify projects with suitable conditions and promptly report them to the NEA.

Introduce detailed rules for bidding methods and determine project owners. It is defined that the bidding methods are used to determine project owners. To facilitate the participation of private capital in the development of pumped-storage power stations, bidding management procedures and implementation guidelines should be established and some projects should be selected as pilot programs for promotion.[94]

Legal Status of New Energy Storage Projects

On August 30, 2021, the NEA issued the "Regulations for the Management of Grid-Connected Operations of Grid Entities (Draft for Comment)." The regulations clearly specify that the regulations apply to grid entities, including thermal power, hydropower, nuclear power, wind power, solar PV power, pumped storage, and new energy storage projects that are directly scheduled by power dispatching agencies at or above provincial level, as well as controllable loads (including controllable loads aggregated through aggregators, virtual power plants, etc.) and self-supplied power plants that can respond to instructions from power dispatching agencies at or above provincial level, and grid entities with participation conditions that can be indirectly scheduled by power dispatching agencies at or below municipal level (collectively referred to as grid entities). The draft proposes the establishment of a filing system for grid connection and dispatching agreements and power purchase contracts. The parties involved in the contract (agreement) should regularly sign grid connection and dispatching agreements and power purchase contracts and file them with the relevant authorities of the NEA within ten business days after the contract (agreement) is signed. If the agreement is signed with the State Grid Corporation of China or China Southern Power Grid, both parties should directly file with the NEA.[95] On December 21, 2021, the NEA issued revised versions of the "Regulations for the Management of Grid-Connected Operations" and the "Management Measures for Power Ancillary Services." These documents expand the scope of entities providing ancillary services. In addition to grid-connected power generation entities, it also includes new energy storage power stations (such as electrochemical storage, compressed air energy storage, and flywheel energy storage stations) and controllable loads capable

[94] Same as above.

[95] See Notice of the General Administration Department of the National Energy Administration on Soliciting Public Opinions on the "Regulations for the Management of Grid-Connected Operations of Grid Entities (Draft for Comment)" and "Management Measures for Power System Ancillary Services (Draft for Comment)", released on August 30, 2021.

of promptly responding to power dispatching instructions. This further establishes the independent market entity status of new energy storage power stations, to meet the needs of large proportions of new energy sources and large proportions of power electronic devices integrated into the system. It also promotes the consumption of new energy, enhances the reliability and power quality of the power system, and better guarantees energy security while driving green and low-carbon development.[96] In May 2022, the General Office of the NDRC and the General Administration Department of the NEA issued the "Notice on Promoting the Participation of New Energy Storage in the Power Market and Scheduling." The notice specifies that we shall establish and improve market mechanisms for the participation of energy storage systems, encourage new energy storage to autonomously choose to participate in the power market, and adhere to market-oriented pricing. The notice also proposes to continuously improve dispatching and operation mechanisms, leverage the advantages of energy storage technology, and enhance the overall utilization level of energy storage to ensure reasonable returns on energy storage investments and promote the healthy development of the industry. The notice further clarifies the market position of new energy storage systems from four aspects: First, encouraging independent participation of new energy storage systems in the power market; second, encouraging joint participation of new energy generation stations and co-located energy storage systems in the power market; third, accelerating the integration of independent energy storage systems in power market operations for peak shaving; fourth, leveraging the technical advantages of independent energy storage systems for providing ancillary services. The "Notice" consists of 12 detailed provisions, and after outlining the general requirements, the "Notice" specifies four consecutive provisions that are related to "independent energy storage." Firstly, the "Notice" proposes that new energy storage systems can participate in the power market as independent energy storage systems. Regarding new energy storage projects that are co-located with other types of power sources, the "Notice" specifies that the power market participation of these projects with the power sources as a unified entity is encouraged. In the past two years, independent energy storage has experienced rapid development in China. The swift growth of the independent energy storage model may be seen as a response to address the implementation of mandatory or competitive energy storage requirements in proportion to new energy sources. The participation of independent energy storage in the power market is aimed at resolving the cost-related issues faced by independent energy storage systems through market mechanisms. The clarification of the role of independent energy storage lays the foundation for promoting the participation of new energy storage in market operations.[97]

[96] See National Energy Administration of China. Regulations for the Management of Grid-Connected Operations (Guo Neng Fa Jian Guan Gui [2021] No. 60); National Energy Administration of China. Management Measures for Power Ancillary Services (Guo Neng Fa Jian Guan Gui [2021] No. 61).

[97] See Notice of the General Office of the National Development and Reform Commission and the General Administration Department of the National Energy Administration on Promoting the Participation of New Energy Storage in the Power Market and Scheduling (Fa Gai Ban Yun Xing [2022] No. 475).

The above document issued by the NDRC and NEA clarifies the market position of new energy storage and effectively removes barriers to its independent participation in the power market. This establishes a policy foundation for further leveraging new energy storage for power generation, grid, and users. In addition, the "Zhejiang Province Electric Power Regulations," which came into effect in 2023, include various participating entities and cover different aspects of power generation, construction, and safe operation. The regulations have significant implications for promoting the development of renewable energy, establishing a new power system that integrates source, grid, load, and storage, and achieving the "dual carbon" goals. According to the provisions of the Regulations, "the development of energy storage shall align with the requirements of enhancing the power system's regulation capabilities. Regional resource advantages shall be considered to strategically plan pumped-storage power stations and various types of new energy storage projects to guide the secure, orderly, and market-oriented development of energy storage."[98] The Regulations also propose specific provisions regarding energy storage grid-connection services, stating that "if power supply, energy storage, and other projects meet the national grid-connection conditions and standards, the power supply companies shall provide grid-connection services within the specified time limit and shall not, without authorization, change the grid-connection standards. Power supply companies shall sign grid-connection agreements with project owners of power source, energy storage, and other projects to clarify the rights and obligations of both parties. In cases where the parties cannot reach an agreement, the provincial power management department shall coordinate and make a decision. If there are separate regulations from the state-level authorities regarding the coordination and decision-making responsibilities, those regulations shall apply. Project owners of power source, energy storage, and other projects shall ensure the security of the power grid in accordance with relevant national technical standards and specifications and shall not, without authorization, connect to the grid."[99] The "Zhejiang Province Electric Power Regulations" clearly state that grid entities and grid companies shall sign grid connection and dispatching agreements and power purchase contracts in a timely manner, following the principles of ensuring the safe operation of the power system. These agreements and contracts should be based on the sample agreements provided by relevant departments in China, such as the "Grid Connection and Dispatching Agreement" and "Power Purchase Contract." In addition, all types of grid entities shall adhere to Chinese laws and regulations, industry standards, and grid stability requirements during the planning, design, construction, and operation of their projects.[100]

---

[98] Zhejiang Province Electric Power Regulations, Article 16.

[99] Zhejiang Province Electric Power Regulations, Article 28.

[100] See Interpretation Review of "Zhejiang Province Electric Power Regulations" (Second Draft), released on February 17, 2023.

Legal Risk Analysis and Prevention for Energy Storage Projects

Legal Risks and Prevention for Pumped-Storage Projects

The early development process of pumped-storage power stations shares similarities with hydropower projects, but it also has its own unique characteristics. The investors should focus on these unique aspects.

Site Selection and Planning for Pumped-Storage Power Stations

In accordance with the provisions of the "Notice of the General Office of the National Energy Administration on Implementing Site Selection and Planning for Pumped-Storage Power Stations and Further Improving the Planning and Construction of pumped-storage power stations" (Guo Neng Zong Xin Neng [2014] No. 699) and the "Opinions of the National Development and Reform Commission on Promoting the Healthy and Orderly Development of Pumped-Storage Power Stations" (Fa Gai Neng Yuan [2014] No. 2482), the approved site selection and planning scheme for pumped-storage power stations by the NEA serves as the fundamental basis for provinces and municipalities to formulate relevant development plans, carry out preliminary project work, and approve construction. Projects that are not included in the site selection and planning scheme are not allowed to be included in the energy development plans of provinces and municipalities, and the determination of project owners, preliminary project work, and approval of construction shall not be performed. During the project approval process, the conformity of the site selection and planning should be assessed. In order to proceed with subsequent preliminary work, pumped-storage power stations must first be included in the site selection and planning for pumped-storage power station construction.

Development Rights of Pumped-Storage Power Stations

- Determination of investors

The investors of pumped-storage power stations have experienced a shift. Grid companies used to solely construct these stations, and now social capital investment is encouraged to participate.

On July 31, 2011, the NEA issued the "Notice on Further Improving the Construction of Pumped-Storage Power Stations" (Guo Neng Xin Neng [2011] No. 242), which explicitly stipulated that, in principle, pumped-storage power stations shall be orderly developed and solely constructed by grid operating companies. The construction and operation costs shall be incorporated into the operating expenses of the power grid.[101]

Later, the "Opinions on Promoting the Healthy and Orderly Development of Pumped-Storage Power Stations" (Fa Gai Neng Yuan [2014] No. 2482) and "Guiding Opinions on Encouraging Social Capital to Invest in Hydropower Stations" (Guo Neng Xin Neng [2015] No. 8) and other documents were issued in China to start encouraging social capital investment in the sector.

On September 17, 2021, the NEA issued the "Pumped Storage Medium- and Long-term Development Plan (2021–2035)," which emphasizes the importance of steadily promoting the determination of investors for pumped-storage power station projects through methods such as bidding and market-based pricing. In addition, the development of new business models such as integrated nuclear and pumped-storage systems, as well as bases that consist of hybrid wind and solar energy with pumped storage shall be supported to encourage social capital to invest in the construction of pumped-storage power stations and accelerate the establishment of an independent market entity status for pumped-storage power stations.[102]

- Revocation of development rights

The acquisition of development rights for pumped-storage projects by investors through bidding, tendering, and market-based pricing does not imply a permanent acquisition of these rights. The development rights may be revoked. Based on practical experience, some cooperative development agreements signed between local governments and project investors also include explicit provisions that grant the government regulatory authorities the right to unconditionally revoke the project's development rights if the project is not constructed according to the agreed development schedule.

Therefore, before investing in a pumped-storage project, investors should understand the local policies and regulations related to the investment, development, and construction of pumped-storage projects, and create a well-defined development schedule in advance.

Resettlement Associated with the Construction of Pumped-Storage Power Stations

The "resettlement before construction" policy is an important principle in the development of pumped-storage power stations. After the resettlement plan is completed, it is reviewed by the immigration administration authorities of the provincial,

---

[101] See Notice of the National Energy Administration on Further Improving the Construction of Pumped-Storage Power Stations (Guo Neng Xin Neng [2011] No. 242).

[102] See National Energy Administration of China. Pumped Storage Medium and Long-term Development Plan (2021–2035).

autonomous regional, or municipal people's governments. The owner of the pumped-storage project must obtain the approval of the resettlement plan to proceed with subsequent procedures to obtain project approvals and land use documents.

According to the "Notice of the National Archives Administration of China, Ministry of Water Resources of the People's Republic of China, and the National Energy Administration on Issuing the Management Measures for Archives of Resettlement in Hydraulic and Hydroelectric Projects" (Dang Fa [2012] No. 4) and the "Regulations on the Compensation for Land Acquisition and Relocation for Construction of Large and Medium-sized Hydraulic and Hydroelectric Projects" (State Council Order No. 679), the main workflow for pumped-storage power station projects before the approval for the resettlement plan is obtained is as follows.

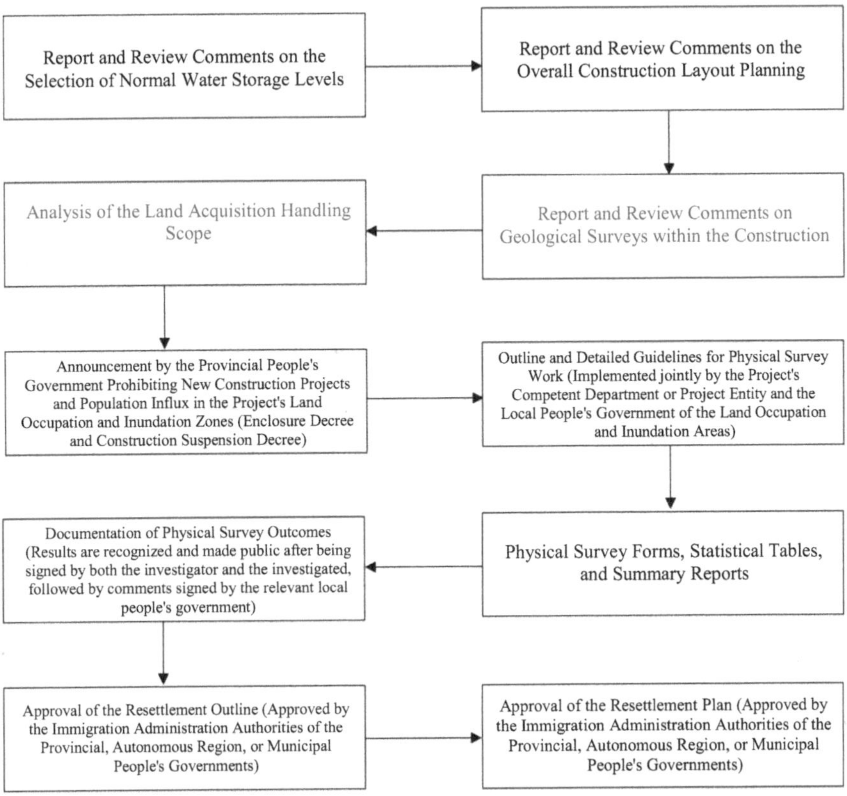

Approval of Pumped-Storage Projects

- Approval authority and required documents

The "Catalogue of Investment Projects Subject to the Approval of the Government (2016)" stipulates that pumped-storage power stations shall be approved by provincial governments in accordance with relevant plans formulated by the state. Based on the required documents for the approval of pumped-storage power stations in various provinces and cities in practice, the documents that need to be obtained before the approval of a pumped-storage power station usually include the site selection plan, pre-approval and site selection opinion for land for construction projects, soil and water conservation plan approval document, social stability and risk assessment report, and approval of resettlement plan.[103]

- Issues associated with change of investor after project approval

According to the provisions of the "Administrative Regulations on the Approval and Record-filing of Enterprise Investment Projects" and the "Administrative Measures for Approval and Record-filing of Enterprise Investment Projects," if there are significant changes in the approved project construction or other major circumstances that require adjustments to the content specified in the project approval documents, the project entity shall promptly submit a written application for changes to the original project approval authority.[104] In some provinces such as Jiangsu, Zhejiang, and Guangdong, their relevant policy documents on the administration of approval and filing of enterprise investment projects further specify that if there is a change in the corporate shareholder or investor of the project, an application for change shall be submitted to the original project approval authority.

Therefore, before investing in the construction of a pumped-storage power station, the investors should communicate in advance with the local investment regulatory department of the project to verify whether the investors can be changed after project approval. This allows for early planning and preparation of subsequent investment arrangements.

Land Use Models of Pumped-Storage Power Stations

According to the "Specification on Land Acquisition and Resettlement Design for Construction of Water Resources and Hydropower Project" (SL 290-2009), the land occupied by a pumped-storage power station is divided into two parts based on the land area and nature of use. These two parts are the reservoir inundation zone of the hydraulic complex and the construction area of the hydraulic complex and other hydraulic projects.[105]

---

[103] See State Council. Catalogue of Investment Projects Subject to the Approval of the Government (Guo Fa [2016] No. 72).

[104] See Administrative Regulations on the Approval and Record-filing of Enterprise Investment Projects (State Council Order No. 673); Administrative Measures for Approval and Record-filing of Enterprise Investment Projects (NDRC Order No. 1).

[105] See Ministry of Water Resources. Specification on Land Acquisition and Resettlement Design for Construction of Water Resources and Hydropower Project (SL 290–2009).

- Reservoir inundation zone of the hydraulic complex

The reservoir inundation zone of the hydraulic complex involves land acquisition for reservoir inundation. The reservoir inundation zone includes the areas that are regularly submerged below the normal water level of the reservoir and the areas that experience temporary flooding above the normal water level of the reservoir due to factors such as backwater from reservoir floods, waves, and ship-generated waves. According to the provisions of the "Opinions on Increasing Policy Support to Promote the Construction of Large and Medium-sized Hydraulic and Hydroelectric Projects" (Guo Tu Zi Gui [2016] No. 1) issued by the Ministry of Land and Resources, National Development and Reform Commission, Ministry of Water Resources, and National Energy Administration, differentiated management is implemented for land in the reservoir inundation zone of pumped-storage projects. The project owner shall submit a land application to the competent land resources department of the city or county where the land is located. During the land approval process, the approval for land for construction shall be used for the conversion of agricultural land and land acquisition documents for the reservoir water area. However, since the reservoir inundation zone does not change the nature of land use, if it involves the conversion of agricultural land, it does not occupy the overall scale of construction land determined by the land use plan and the annual land use plan indicators. However, if it involves the occupation of arable land and basic farmland, the project owner shall fulfill the obligation of arable land replacement and the local government shall allocate an equivalent area of basic farmland in compensation.[106]

- Construction area of the hydraulic complex and other hydraulic projects

The construction area of the hydraulic complex and other hydraulic projects is composed of permanent land acquisition areas and temporary land use areas. The permanent land acquisition areas generally include the construction zone of permanent buildings or structures, land for external transportation purposes, and management zones. The temporary land use areas typically include material storage areas, waste disposal areas, operation sites, temporary roads, construction camps, other temporary facility sites, and areas affected by construction blasting.

For land for the construction area of the hydraulic complex and other hydraulic projects, the project owner shall submit a land use application to the competent land and resources department of the city or county where the land is located. For the permanent land acquisition part, the approval for the conversion of land for construction purposes is required. For the temporary land use part, the land and resources department of the county-level or higher-level government shall grant approval and corresponding compensation shall be provided to the land rights holders for their losses. If the temporary land use results in land damage, the project owner shall

---

[106] See Opinions of the Ministry of Land and Resources, & National Development and Reform Commission, Ministry of Water Resources and National Energy Administration on Increasing Policy Support to Promote the Construction of Large and Medium-sized Hydraulic and Hydroelectric Projects (Guo Tu Zi Gui [2016] No. 1).

comply with the relevant provisions of the "Regulations on Land Reclamation" and fulfill the land reclamation obligations.

Environmental Requirements for Pumped-Storage Power Stations

In response to the environmental protection issues of pumped-storage power stations, the General Administration Department of the NEA issued the "Notice on Implementing Ecological and Environmental Protection Requirements in the Planning and Construction of Pumped-Storage Power Stations" (Guo Neng Zong Fa Xin Neng [2017] No. 3) on November 30, 2017. The notice states that during the planning and construction processes of pumped-storage power stations, ecological considerations should be prioritized and a minimum level of environmental protection should be ensured. Relevant requirements regarding ecological and environmental constraints set forth by environmental protection laws and regulations should be implemented.[107] The "Pumped Storage Medium- and Long-term Development Plan (2021–2035)" further specifies that the strictest environmental protection measures should be implemented for pumped-storage power stations. The plan states that project construction should not encroach upon environmental constraints such as protected natural areas or environmental bottom lines. The aim is to ensure the harmonious development of pumped storage and environmental preservation.[108]

- Preparation and approval of environmental impact report

According to the "Management Catalogue for the Classification of the Environmental Impact Assessment of Construction Projects" (2021 Edition), environmental impact reports are required for pumped-storage power stations.[109] In accordance with Article 21 of the "Law of the People's Republic of China on Environment Impact Assessment," for construction projects that require an environmental impact report, "the construction entity shall hold a feasibility meeting, public hearing, or use other methods to solicit opinions from relevant organizations, experts, and the public before submitting the environment impact report for approval."[110]

After the project owner completes the environmental impact report, they shall submit it to the environmental protection department with approval authority designated by the province or city and obtain the environmental impact assessment approval.

---

[107] See Notice from the General Administration Department of the National Energy Administration on Implementing Ecological and Environmental Protection Requirements in the Planning and Construction of Pumped-Storage Power Stations (Guo Neng Zong Fa Xin Neng [2017] No. 3).

[108] See the National Energy Administration of China (2021): Pumped Storage Medium and Long-term Development Plan (2021–2035).

[109] See Management Catalogue for the Classification of the Environmental Impact Assessment of Construction Projects (2021 Edition), Article 2.

[110] Law of the People's Republic of China on Environment Impact Assessment, Paragraph 1 of Article 21.

- Environmental constraints

According to the "Notice of the Ministry of Environmental Protection and the National Energy Administration on Deepening the Implementation of Ecological and Environmental Protection Measures for Hydropower Development" (Huan Fa [2014] No. 65), the environmental constraints for pumped-storage power stations can be categorized into two categories.

First, determination of environmentally sensitive areas and protection scope. This involves identifying and avoiding environmentally sensitive areas, such as nature reserves, scenic spots, and areas with concentrated distribution of rare species to minimize the loss of watershed biodiversity and important ecological functions. It also involves coordinating and formulating environmental protection measures for each stage of the project.

Second, environmental protection measures for resettlement. Based on the local natural resources, ecological environment, and social conditions, as well as urbanization planning and requirements, the environmental suitability of resettlement methods is analyzed. The environmental protection work related to resettlement should be considered as an important component of the environmental protection acceptance upon the completion of pumped-storage power stations.[111]

Water-Related Preliminary Compliance Procedures for Pumped-Storage Power Stations

Since pumped-storage power stations are classified as water hydraulic and hydroelectric projects, water-related preliminary compliance procedures are required. The following approval procedures may be involved:

- Water resource assessment and water drawing license application

According to the regulations outlined in the "Water Drawing Licensing Management Measures," "Administrative Measures for the Assessment of Water Resources for Construction Projects," and "Regulation on the Administration of the License for Water Drawing and the Levy of Water Resource Fees," the project owner of a pumped-storage project shall prepare or engage another entity to prepare a water resource assessment report for the construction project. The report must then be reviewed by the water administration department at or above the county level or the river basin authority with the participation of relevant experts. After completing the water resource assessment, the project owner shall submit a water drawing license application to the water administration department of the provincial, autonomous regional, or municipal people's government. Only after obtaining the water drawing

[111] See Ministry of Environmental Protection, and National Energy Administration of China. Notice on Deepening the Implementation of Ecological and Environmental Protection Measures for Hydropower Development (Huan Fa [2014] No. 65).

approval document issued by the water approval authority, the project owner can proceed with the construction of the pumped-storage project.[112]

- Flood impact assessment report

According to the provisions of the "Flood Control Law of the People's Republic of China," for pumped-storage projects not related to flood control within floodplains or flood storage and detention basins, an assessment must be conducted regarding the potential impact of floods on the project and the potential impact of the project on flood control measures. A flood impact assessment report must be compiled, outlining the necessary preventative actions. The construction may not commence until the flood impact assessment report has been reviewed and approved by the relevant water administration department.[113]

- Consent for water project construction planning

According to the provisions of the "Management Measures for the Water Project Construction Planning Consent System (Trial)," the project owner of a pumped-storage project shall submit an application for the consent for water project construction planning to the river basin authority or the water administration department of the local people's government at or above the county level, which has the authority to review and sign the consent document. Once the reviewing and signing authority accepts the application, they shall evaluate the project based on the legal requirements and make a decision to grant approval, and sign the consent for water project construction planning. The construction may not commence until the consent for water project construction planning has been obtained.[114]

- Review by river authority

According to the provisions of the "Regulations on the Management of Construction Projects within the Scope of River Management," for pumped-storage power stations constructed within the management scope of rivers (including riverbanks, lakes, reservoirs, artificial waterways, floodways, flood retention basins, and flood detention basins), the project owner must submit an application to the river management authority in accordance with their jurisdiction. After reviewing the application, if the river management authority approves the construction, they shall issue a review approval document. The construction may not commence until the approval from the river authority is obtained.[115]

---

[112] See Water Drawing Licensing Management Measures, Article 5, paragraph 1 of Article 8 and Article 9; Administrative Measures for the Assessment of Water Resources for Construction Projects, Article 2, Article 5, and paragraph 1 of Article 8; Regulation on the Administration of the License for Water Drawing and the Levy of Water Resource Fees, paragraph 2 of Article 11.

[113] See Flood Control Law of the People's Republic of China, paragraph 1 of Article 33.

[114] See Management Measures for the Water Project Construction Planning Consent System (Trial), paragraph 1 of Article 4 and Article 6.

[115] See Regulations on the Management of Construction Projects within the Scope of River Management, paragraph 1 of Article 3.

- Review of the impact assessment of navigational conditions on waterways

According to the provisions of the "Management Measures for the Review of the Impact Assessment of Navigational Conditions on Waterways," if the construction of a pumped-storage power station involves waterways, the project owner shall prepare an impact assessment report on the navigational conditions of the waterways in accordance with the relevant regulations and technical standards set by the Ministry of Transport of China. The project owner must then submit an application for the review of the impact assessment of navigational conditions to the competent transportation department or waterway management authority authorized to conduct the review. If the review department approves the assessment, they shall provide an opinion stating that it has passed the review. The construction may not commence until the review opinion of the impact assessment of navigational conditions on waterways is obtained.[116]

Legal Risks and Prevention for User-Side Electrochemical Energy Storage Projects

Business and Investment Risks

In China, the main business models for energy storage power stations are new energy + energy storage, independent frequency regulation power stations, and peak-valley arbitrage. The new energy + energy storage model features a grid-side electrochemical energy storage system, whose costs cannot be included in the transmission and distribution costs. It is an alternative model required by local power regulatory authorities. Strictly speaking, it is not a market-based business model but rather a cost transfer where new energy storage costs are borne by new energy companies due to grid-connection requirements.

For independent frequency regulation power stations, given the overarching goal of controlling electricity price hikes in China, it is improbable that the costs of frequency regulation services will be transferred to users. Unless there is a breakthrough from the "Two Rules" framework, which currently dictates a "zero-sum game" among power generators, the scope for these services will remain confined to slicing shares within the existing electricity pricing structure, without a noticeable increase in the overall societal electricity cost. Thus, the future prospects for the frequency regulation market may not be very optimistic. In addition, new entrants to the energy storage frequency regulation market will face significant risks. In a saturated market, power stations that have already recouped their investments may be inclined to offer lower prices, potentially leading to a downward price spiral and making it challenging for investments in new power stations to be recovered.

---

116 See Management Measures for the Review of the Impact Assessment of Navigational Conditions on Waterways, Articles 5 and 10.

For the peak-valley arbitrage model, if lithium iron phosphate batteries are used under the current investment costs and technical conditions, with a twice-daily charge and discharge cycle over an 8-year lifespan, profitability is limited even with a peak-valley plus peak-off-peak price differential of CNY 1.3-1.4. With the ongoing reduction in general industrial and commercial electricity rates, only users in a few developed regions such as Beijing are currently able to undertake energy storage arbitrage. The growth of this business hinges on the reduction in costs and enhancement in the performance of electrochemical energy storage systems.

Due to the immaturity of business models for electrochemical energy storage, energy storage system providers tend to focus on pursuing low prices and reducing costs and often neglect the safety and quality of the storage systems. This has resulted in a "bad money drives out good" situation, where providers who focus on technical quality for their advantage are unable to obtain their deserved market share. Thus, the growth of electrochemical energy storage is stalled, and mechanical pumped storage is still the predominant method in the energy storage sector.

Product Quality and Safety Risks

Energy storage projects have specific technical features that make their quality and safety risks different from those of traditional new energy stations. Managing these risks, especially during the operational phase, is crucial. Recent tragic incidents in the energy storage sector have caused substantial loss of life and property, raising concerns about the investment and development approaches and the need for proper regulation of chemical energy storage projects.

On April 16, 2021, a fire broke out in the south area of the Beijing Guoxuan Fuweisi Energy Storage Power Station. Two firefighters were killed, one injured (in stable condition), and one employee was missing. The incident caused a direct financial loss of CNY 16.6081 million. Based on the on-site inspections from the fire and rescue agency, testing, analysis, simulation, and expert evaluations, an investigation team determined that the direct cause of the fire in the south building was an internal short circuit in a lithium iron phosphate battery located in the west battery room of the project, which led to thermal runaway and ignition of the battery. The direct cause of the explosion in the north building was traced back to an internal short circuit in an individual lithium iron phosphate battery in the south building's battery room. This fault led to thermal runaway of the battery and battery modules, causing a fire to spread. Flammable and explosive components generated by the accident entered the energy storage room of the north building through the cable trench and spread, mixing with air to form an explosive gas mixture, which ignited upon encountering an electrical spark, causing the explosion.[117]

Based on the findings and analyses of the expert group, there are four primary reasons for the fire incident at the energy storage station: first, battery system defects; second, incomplete protection systems for electrical malfunctions; third,

[117] See Hu et al. (2022).

poor management of the operating environment; and fourth, deficiencies in the overall management of the energy storage system. Battery system defects may be one of the main factors that could lead to fire. The core issue for energy storage safety lies in the battery itself. The sources that may trigger safety incidents include flaws in the battery manufacturing process and degradation in the safety of the energy storage system due to battery aging.[118] Energy storage systems are widely recognized within the industry as an important solution for the secondary utilization of power batteries. Available data suggests that a number of upstream and downstream companies in the power battery industry, including BYD, CATL, Guoxuan High-Tech, Soundon New Energy, CLOU Electronics, and Shanshan, have all implemented strategies for battery recycling and reuse. Some experts believe the energy storage station involved in the 416 incident used retired lithium iron phosphate batteries repurposed for energy storage. The most significant challenge for energy storage at present is ensuring that all components of power batteries, from cells to system integration, fulfill the needs of energy storage applications. This is to prevent system reliability and safety issues that can occur with combined systems.

The safety of energy storage power stations includes multiple aspects such as electrical safety, fire safety, chemical safety, and mechanical safety. Different forms of energy storage have different safety risks. For example, lithium-ion battery energy storage, sodium-sulfur battery energy storage, and hydrogen storage require special attention to fire safety. Flow battery energy storage requires a focus on chemical safety. Flywheel energy storage requires a focus on mechanical safety.[119]

The battery pack that forms the energy storage power station is a high-voltage, high-energy system. As the specific energy and power of batteries increase, the risk of accidents also increases. Fire and explosion after a fire are two main types of disasters that pose a threat to the safety of energy storage power stations. According to statistics, there have been over 30 fire incidents in energy storage power stations worldwide in the past year. Currently, China does not have national standards for the fire protection of electrochemical energy storage stations. There is a lack of specialized training and knowledge for station constructors, operators, maintenance personnel, and professional firefighting agencies regarding the safety and fire protection of electrochemical energy storage stations. The existing fire protection facilities and fire control methods cannot meet the site requirements. The fire suppression systems used in these projects are not supported by standards, and the effectiveness of fire extinguishing agents and measures has not been validated. As a result, energy storage power stations face significant fire safety risks during construction, operation, and maintenance.

According to the "Science Knowledge of Fire Safety in Electrochemical Energy Storage Stations" issued by the Tianjin Fire Science and Technology Research Institute of the Ministry of Emergency Management of China (MEM), battery packs in electrochemical energy storage stations are highly concentrated. Under the influence of internal and external factors such as overcharging, over-discharging, overheating,

[118] See Qin (2020).

[119] See Han (2021).

and mechanical impact, the battery packs are prone to membrane collapse and internal short circuits. These issues can lead to thermal runaway. If thermal runaway occurs and spreads within the battery module, it can lead to fire incidents in the system. The electrolyte used in batteries often consists of flammable and combustible organic solvents, which also increases the probability of fire incidents. The characteristics of energy storage power stations, such as frequent battery charging and discharging cycles and battery reuse, also contribute to an increased fire risk.[120]

In addition, system design flaws, improper operational management, and inadequate fire protection are significant factors that impact safety. Traditional fire suppression measures are often ineffective in suppressing thermal runaway of batteries, which can result in the initial fire spreading and eventually escalating into a large-scale fire. The generation of toxic and flammable gases during the fire also poses challenges for fire suppression and may lead to explosions. As the service life of energy storage power stations increases, some energy storage systems will approach their designed number of charge–discharge cycles, and lithium battery packs will reach their end of life. This will gradually reveal fire safety issues. In the design specifications for electrochemical energy storage stations, no targeted fire protection design requirements are specified. The design is usually based on general industrial building standards. Moreover, the performance indicators for batteries in energy storage system standards are vague, and the requirements for emergency response and rescue measures are not sufficient. These factors can lead to regulatory oversights. As a major concern for fire safety worldwide, lithium battery fire management calls for enhanced research into energy storage station safety, targeting fire control, early warning systems, and emergency response.

Ecological and Environmental Risks

During the production process of lithium batteries, lithium cobalt oxide or lithium iron phosphate is used, and fluorides and organic solvents are used as electrolytes and dispersants. In the event of a fire or explosion, the pollutants from lithium batteries can spread into the environment. In an incident, lithium cobalt oxide, which is used as the positive electrode material in lithium batteries, can disperse into the air in the form of dust particles. Cobalt dust can cause hard metal lung diseases and result in symptoms such as allergic asthma, respiratory distress, dry cough, occasional chemical pneumonia (interstitial pneumonia), and pulmonary edema. This can lead to environmental pollution.

Fluorides, as part of the electrolyte in batteries, can form hydrogen fluoride in the event of an incident. Hydrogen fluoride is an inorganic acid with the formula HF. Under normal conditions, it is a colorless, strongly irritating, and toxic gas. It has a high affinity for moisture, and upon contact with air, it produces white fumes. It dissolves easily in water to form hydrofluoric acid.[121]

---

[120] See Wang (2020).

[121] Feng et al. (2022).

NMP (N-Methyl-2-pyrrolidone, an organic solvent), as a dispersant for the positive electrode in batteries, is a hazardous chemical with irritant and reproductive toxicity properties. It is also flammable with a flash point of 86 °C. In an incident, it can generate harmful vapors.

The United States has classified lithium-ion batteries as a type of battery that encompasses ignitability, leaching toxicity, corrosivity, and reactivity. They are considered to be the most toxic batteries among various types of batteries. The metals such as cobalt, nickel, lithium, manganese, as well as inorganic and organic compounds present in lithium-ion batteries, can pose a pollution hazard to the atmosphere, water, and soil.[122]

Lack of Clarity in Documents and Requirements in the Investment, Construction, and Operation Phases

According to current regulatory environments, energy storage projects, as a type of construction project, need to adhere to the basic investment process of general construction projects and obtain various documents and licenses throughout the investment, construction, and operation phases. Additionally, procedures and requirements related to project planning and land use need to be completed, taking into account the unique characteristics of different types of energy storage projects (such as station-based storage or container-based storage). However, due to the specific nature of energy storage projects, requirements for certain documents and licenses are not clearly defined at the legal and regulatory levels. These documents include:

1. Investment approval. Currently, there are no unified regulations at the national level in China to standardize the investment and development process of energy storage projects. Based on our research and previous project experiences, we have observed that investment and development processes for grid-side, user-side, and power generation-side projects in different regions have both similarities and differences. Depending on the differences in investors and funding sources, energy storage projects should comply with the existing approval, authorization, and filing systems under the current investment framework. In some regions, user-side energy storage projects need to be included in the regional power grid plan or provincial-level power grid plan (or distribution grid plan) based on their rated power.
2. Environmental impact assessment and safety equipment documents. Environmental impact assessments and relevant document are required for construction projects in accordance with the law. However, energy storage projects are not included in the "Catalogue of Classified Management of Discharge Permits for Stationary Pollution Sources" (2021). The specific form of environmental impact assessment for energy storage projects is not clearly defined in regulations, and some regions even believe that it is not necessary to conduct an environmental impact assessment. Regarding safety equipment issues, based on the "Measures

[122] Sun et al. (2015).

for the Supervision and Administration of 'Three Simultaneities' for the Safety Equipment of Construction Projects," a separate safety condition review is not required for energy storage projects, and there is no explicit requirement for independent safety equipment design review and approval for energy storage power stations or projects. Considering the technical characteristics of energy storage projects, safety equipment plays a crucial role in risk control. Adding requirements in the regulatory and supervision process can help enhance risk control measures. Furthermore, considering the importance of energy storage system design in ensuring project safety, we believe that the industry should explore how to enhance regulatory oversight through various stages such as project investment approval, investment filing, and design review.

3. Grid-connection requirements. Regarding the question of whether it is mandatory for energy storage projects to be connected to the grid, or whether the grid has an obligation to accept energy storage projects on fair terms, the current laws and regulations do not have a clear answer. There may be different practices in various locations based on the rated power of the project and the specific requirements of the local power grid. The grid connection of energy storage projects is closely related to aspects such as grid supply–demand balance, safety management, and energy storage business models. It is recommended that the state establish unified requirements and standards for the grid-connection requirements of energy storage projects.
4. Electric power business license. Is an electric power business license required for energy storage projects? According to current regulations, a power generation business license is not required for independent generation-side energy storage projects that are not jointly invested and constructed with new energy power stations. For user-side projects, it is explicitly stated that a power generation business license is not required. However, we believe that these requirements may change with the development of the energy storage industry, particularly for user-side energy storage projects.

Based on the above analysis, the requirements for energy storage projects in certain regulatory aspects are not clear and may not fully align with the requirements for safe operation and risk control during the operational phase of energy storage projects. At the same time, with the development of the energy storage industry and the evolution of smart grids and intelligent energy systems, including "virtual power plants," traditional regulatory models may face challenges. Regulatory laws and policies need to be adjusted to accommodate the development of the industry.

Risks Associated with Lack of Standards

Currently, the Chinese national standards in the energy storage industry mainly include the "Design Code for Electrochemical Energy Storage Station" (GB 51048-2014), "General Technical Requirements for Electrochemical Energy Storage System in Power System" (GB/T 36558-2018), and "Lithium Ion Battery for Electrical

Energy Storage" (GB/T36276-2018). In recent years, certain regional technical alliances have also organized relevant companies to develop group standards based on practical project experiences, which are intended for industry-wide promotion and use.

In January 2020, the NEA, MEM, and SAMR jointly issued the "Implementation Plan for Strengthening Energy Storage Standardization." According to the plan, by 2021, a government-guided and multi-party mechanism for energy storage standardization shall be established. Efforts shall be made to develop a relatively comprehensive energy storage standard system, strengthen the revision of key technical standards for energy storage, and promote the internationalization of energy storage standards.[123] However, based on our discussions and exchanges with industry experts, as of today, the progress in developing a comprehensive standard system has been slow. Many standards and assessment systems are still based on the content of the electric vehicle battery industry. The application scenarios and technological requirements of energy storage differ significantly from those of electric vehicle batteries, and using these standards in the energy storage sector lead to various issues. Furthermore, electric vehicle batteries generally have a smaller capacity compared to energy storage power stations. Therefore, stricter standards should be applied in various aspects such as construction design, fire safety, and acceptance procedures for energy storage power stations.[124] Recently, authorities in some regions have issued mandatory energy storage policies, which promote industry development and heighten the need for enhanced project safety management. It is urgent to develop an energy storage standard system to address the above concerns.

Legal Liability Risks

Criminal liability risks

Paragraph 1 of Article 134 of the "Criminal Law of the People's Republic of China" (Criminal Law) stipulates the crime of major liability incidents, "if anyone violates safety management rules and regulations, thereby causing an accident involving heavy casualties or causing other serious consequences, the individual shall be sentenced to fixed-term imprisonment of not more than three years or criminal detention; if the circumstances are especially flagrant, the individual shall be sentenced to fixed-term imprisonment of not less than three years but not more than seven years."[125]

Article 1 of the "Interpretation of the Supreme People's Court and the Supreme People's Procuratorate on Several Issues Concerning the Application of Law in the

[123] See General Administration Department of the NEA, & General Office of MEM, General Office of the SAMR. Implementation Plan for Strengthening Energy Storage Standardization (Guo Neng Zong Tong Ke Ji [2020] No. 3).

[124] See Lu (2021).

[125] Criminal Law the People's Republic of China, Paragraph 1 of Article 134.

Handling of Criminal Cases Involving Crimes Endangering Production Safety" stipulates: "The subjects of crime provided in paragraph 1 of Article 134 of the Criminal Law include the persons in charge, managerial personnel, actual controllers, investors, and other persons responsible for organizing, commanding, or managing production or operations as well as persons directly engaging in production or operations."

Article 6 stipulates: "Where any person commits the acts as prescribed in Article 132, paragraph 1 of Article 134, Article 135, Article 135 (I), Article 136, and Article 139 of the Criminal Law, thus causing the occurrence of a production safety accident, and the accident falls under any of the following circumstances, it shall be determined that such acts 'cause serious consequences' or 'extraordinarily serious accidents with casualties or other serious consequences' and the relevant responsible person shall be sentenced to fixed-term imprisonment of not more than three years or criminal detention:

(1) Causing the death of more than one person or any serious injury to more than three persons;
(2) Causing direct economic losses of more than CNY 1 million; or
(3) Any other circumstance of causing serious consequences or extraordinarily serious production safety accidents."

Article 7 stipulates: "Where any person commits the acts as prescribed in Article 132, paragraph 1 of Article 134, Article 135, Article 135 (I), Article 136, and Article 139 of the Criminal Law, thus causing the occurrence of a safety accident, and the accident falls under any of the following circumstances, the relevant responsible person shall be sentenced to fixed-term imprisonment of not less than three years and not more than seven years:

(1) Causing the death of more than three persons or any serious injury to more than ten persons as the primary person responsible for the accident;
(2) Causing direct economic losses of more than CNY 5 million as the primary person responsible for the accident; or
(3) Any other circumstance of causing serious consequences or extraordinarily serious accidents."

Article 12 stipulates: "Where any person commits the acts as prescribed in Article 132, Articles 134 to 139 (I) of the Criminal Law and the act falls under any of the following circumstances, the person shall receive heavy punishment:

(1) Engaging in production or business activities without obtaining the required safety permits in accordance with the law or engaging in such activities with expired, suspended, revoked, or canceled safety permits;
(2) Shutting down or damaging necessary safety monitoring and alarm equipment;
(3) Failing to take measures after the discovery of accident hazards reported by relevant departments or individuals;
(4) Having received administrative or criminal penalties within one year for violating laws or committing crimes related to endangering production safety;

(5) Employing deceptive or corrupt practices to deliberately evade or obstruct supervision and inspection by departments responsible for safety supervision and management;
(6) Transferring assets with the intention of evading liability after a safety accident occurs;
(7) Other circumstances warranting heavy punishment.

If the act specified in Item 5 also constitutes a crime as defined in Article 389 of the Criminal Law, the person shall be punished according to the provision of cumulative punishment for multiple crimes."

Article 13 stipulates: "Where any person commits the acts as prescribed in Article 132, Articles 134 to 139 (I) of the Criminal Law but actively organizes or participates in rescue operations after a safety accident occurs, or actively cooperates in investigations and voluntarily compensates for losses, the person may receive lighter punishment at the discretion of the authorities."[126]

Administrative liability risks

Article 3 of the "Regulations on the Reporting, Investigation and Disposition of Work Safety Accidents" stipulates: "By the casualty or direct economic losses caused in a production safety accident (hereafter 'accident'), the accidents shall be generally graded as follows:

(1) Especially serious accident refers to an accident that has caused the deaths of at least 30 persons, serious injuries to at least 100 persons (including acute industrial poisoning), or direct economic losses of at least CNY 100 million;
(2) Serious accident refers to an accident that has caused the deaths of at least 10 but less than 30 persons, serious injuries to at least 50 but less than 100 persons, or direct economic losses of at least CNY 50 million but less than CNY 100 million;
(3) Large accident refers to an accident that has caused the deaths of at least 3 but less than 10 persons, serious injuries to at least 10 but less than 50 persons, or direct economic losses of at least CNY 10 million but less than CNY 50 million; and
(4) Ordinary accident refers to an accident that has caused the deaths of less than 3 persons, serious injuries to less than 10 persons, or direct economic losses of less than CNY 10 million."

Article 37 stipulates: "Where the organization responsible for an accident is found to be at fault for the occurrence of the accident, fines shall be imposed in accordance with the following provisions:

(1) For an ordinary accident, a fine of more than CNY 100,000 and less than CNY 200,000 shall be imposed;

---

[126] Interpretation of the Supreme People's Court and the Supreme People's Procuratorate on Several Issues Concerning the Application of Law in the Handling of Criminal Cases Involving Crimes Endangering Production Safety(Fa Shi [2015] No. 22), Article 1, paragraph 1 of Article 6, paragraph 1 of Article 7, and Article 12–13.

(2) For a large accident, a fine of more than CNY 200,000 and less than CNY 500,000 shall be imposed;
(3) For a serious accident, a fine of more than CNY 500,000 and less than CNY 2 million shall be imposed;
(4) For an especially serious accident, a fine of more than CNY 2 million and less than CNY 5 million shall be imposed."

Article 38 stipulates: "If the principal responsible person of the organization where an accident occurs fails to fulfill the safety production management responsibilities as required by law, resulting in the occurrence of the accident, the following fines shall be imposed. If the person is a state functionary, the person shall be punished in accordance with the law, and if a crime is constituted, the person shall be subject to criminal liabilities in accordance with the law:

(1) For an ordinary accident, a fine shall be imposed equivalent to 30% of the annual income of the previous year;
(2) For a large accident, a fine shall be imposed equivalent to 40% of the annual income of the previous year;
(3) For a serious accident, a fine shall be imposed equivalent to 60% of the annual income of the previous year;
(4) For an especially serious accident, a fine shall be imposed equivalent to 80% of the annual income of the previous year."[127]

Civil liability risks

Civil torts and liability for damages

Paragraph 1 of Article 1165 of the *Civil Code* stipulates: "An actor who through his fault infringes upon another person's civil-law rights and interests shall bear tort liability.

In the event of an accident that causes personal injury or property damage to a third party, the party at fault shall bear the corresponding tort liability."

Article 1179 of the *Civil Code* stipulates: "Where a person suffers personal injury as a result of an infringement by another person, compensation shall be made for medical expenses, nursing expenses, transportation expenses, nutrition expenses, food allowances for hospitalization, and other reasonable expenses for treatment and rehabilitation, as well as lost earnings due to missed work. Where a person is disabled as a result of an infringement by another person, compensation shall also include the costs of auxiliary equipment and disability compensation. Where a person dies as a result of an infringement by another person, compensation shall also include his funeral expenses and death compensation."

Article 1184 of the *Civil Code* stipulates: "In case of an infringement upon another person's property, property damage shall be calculated according to the market price at the time the damage occurs or by other reasonable methods."

---

[127] Regulations on the Reporting, Investigation and Disposition of Work Safety Accidents, Paragraph 1 of Article 3 and Article 37–38.

Environmental pollution and ecological damage liability

Article 1229 of the *Civil Code* stipulates: "A tortfeasor who has polluted the environment or harmed the ecological system and thus causes damage to others shall bear tort liability."[128]

In cases where an accident causes environmental pollution and ecological damage, the entities responsible shall be held liable for the resulting environmental pollution and ecological damage.

The main forms of civil liability for environmental infringements include: (1) cessation of the infringement; (2) removal of the nuisance; (3) elimination of the danger; (4) restoration; (5) compensation for losses; (6) apologies. The forms of civil liability provided above may be applied separately or concurrently.[129]

Risk Prevention of Electrochemical Energy Storage Projects

Compared to new energy power stations, energy storage projects, especially user-side projects, may have significant safety hazards if there are issues with the quality of raw materials, inadequate or poorly implemented fire safety measures, or improper operation. In the event of a serious safety accident, the project owner, especially the owner of a user-side energy storage project, may not only fail to recover the investment cost but also face substantial compensation claims. In extreme cases, the company may face bankruptcy and liquidation, and the involved parties may even be subject to criminal liability according to the law.

On one hand, unclear business models lead to unclear financing and investment returns. On the other hand, technical characteristics and associated accident hazards result in significant risks and liabilities. The mismatch between risks and returns can potentially hinder the healthy development of the industry. We believe that, in addition to the aforementioned strengthening of the national standard system and regulatory oversight in relevant aspects, it is also crucial to consider appropriate risk balancing and diversification in project transaction schemes and documents to promote investment in the energy storage sector. For example, in user-side projects that adopt the energy performance contracting model, the allocation and distribution of rights and obligations between the energy storage project developer/operator and the user can be discussed in relevant contracts to appropriately mitigate the risks for the project owner. More suitable insurance products can be used to diversify project risks, with the insurance costs shared by the project owner and the user. Additionally, standards and provisions with more requirements can be specified in the contracts for aspects such as safety design, project design, completion acceptance, operational guidelines, and supporting conditions based on relevant technical requirements.

---

[128] Civil Code of the People's Republic of China, Articles 1165, 1179, 1184 and 1229.

[129] See Environmental Protection Law of the People's Republic of China, Article 64; Civil Code of the People's Republic of China, Article 179.

References

Australian Energy Market Operator (2023) Guide to ancillary services in the national electricity market. Retrieved March 15, 2024, from https://www.aemo.com.au/-/media/files/electricity/nem/security_and_reliability/ancillary_services/guide-to-ancillary-services-in-the-national-electricity-market.pdf

Barbour E, Wilson IA, Radcliffe J, Ding Y, Li Y (2016) A review of pumped hydro energy storage development in significant international electricity markets. Renew Sustain Energy Rev 2016(61):421–432

Chen Y, Hong Y, Huang L (2021) State grid zhejiang electric power conducts first special market transaction for load response. Retrieved March 15, 2024, from https://zjnews.zjol.com.cn/gdxw2021/202105/t20210527_22589485.shtml

Faria P, Vale Z, Soares J, Ferreira J (2011) Demand response management in power systems using a particle swarm optimization approach. IEEE Intell Syst 28(4):43–51. https://doi.org/10.1109/MIS.2011.35

Feng J, Xia Y, Peng X, Cai X (2022) Comparative study on determination of gaseous fluorine in waste gas of fixed pollution source by ion chromatography and ion selective electrode. J Green Sci Technol 2022(16):211–213 and 218. https://doi.org/10.16663/j.cnki.lskj.2022.16.015

Gao B (2021) Opportunities and challenges for pumped storage development in Jiangsu under the "dual carbon" goals. Ind Innovation 2021(24):64–66

Gao C, Li Q, Li H, Zhai H, Zhang L (2013) Methodology and operation mechanism of demand response resources integration based on load aggregator. Autom Electr Power Syst 2013(17):78–86

Han Y (2021) Three issues to be resolved for integrated equipment in large-scale energy storage power stations. China Energy News 09

Hu Q, Qiao X, Liu F, Pei B, Wang Y (2022) Study on thermal runaway hazard and prevention countermeasures of marine lithium batteries. Mar Electr Electron Eng 2022(6):28–31. https://doi.org/10.13632/j.meee.2022.06.015

Hua P (2019) Development and prospect of pumped-storage power stations. Inner Mongolia Electric Power 2019(6):5–9

Huang H, Zhao, Hong, Zhai D (2022) Research on pumped storage cost compensation mechanism and cost influencing factors. Price: Theory Pract 2022(2):12–19. https://doi.org/10.19851/j.cnki.cn11-1010/f.2022.02.069

Ikaheimo J, Evens C, Karkkainen S (2010) DER aggregator business: the finish case (Research Report VTT-R-O6961-O9). VTT Technical Research Centre of Finland. Retrieved March 15, 2024, from https://citeseerx.ist.psu.edu/document?repid=rep1&type=pdf&doi=a040f91a2afc8a6b8548def8e0fcfd6549d77101

Jia K (2015) Why is pumped-storage power station development so slow?—Interview with Peng Cheng, Secretary of the Party Committee and Deputy Director of the China Renewable Energy Engineering Institute. China Energy News 02

Jin L, Liu W, Ji D (2021) Design of trading mechanism for pumped-storage power stations under the background of power market. Sci Technol Eng 2021(27):11632–11641. https://doi.org/10.3969/j.issn.1671-1815.2021.27.023

Li D, Shi Y, Li Y (2020) Research on the business model of energy storage systems in the energy internet. Power Demand Side Manage 2020(2):7–82. https://doi.org/10.3969/j.issn.1009-1831.2020.02.014

Liu J, Li R, Yang W, Liu G (2007) An overview of the current status and application prospects of distributed generation technologies. Paper presented at the meeting of the 23rd Annual Academic Conference of Chinese Society of Universities—Electric Power System and Automation, Hefei, China

Liu Y, Lu Z, Lei J, Li Y (2011) Application of battery energy storage systems in smart grids. Paper presented at the meeting of the Development and Application of Large-Scale Energy Storage Technologies, Tianjin, China

Lu Q (2021) Critical security vulnerabilities in the energy storage sector. China Energy News 01
Luo S, Liu Y, Liu G, Nie J (2013) Pumped-storage power station development in foreign countries and inspiration for China. Sino-Glob Energy 2013(11):26–29. https://doi.org/10.3969/j.issn.1673-579X.2013.11.005
Mandal P, Senjyu T, Urasakin, Funabashi T, Srivastava AK (2007) A novel approach to forecast electricity price for PJM using neural network and similar days method. IEEE Trans Power Syst 22(4):2058–2065. https://doi.org/10.1109/TPWRS.2007.907386
Qin Z (2020) What should be done to eliminate energy storage safety hazards. China Sci Daily 03
Qiu C, Qu D, Fan J, Liu Q, Liu X, Tang Q (2021) Distribution network energy optimization based on the participation of electric vehicle aggregators in demand response. Mech Electr Eng Technol 2021(5):72–75. https://doi.org/10.3969/j.issn.1009-9492.2021.05.019
Sandia National Laboratories (2010) Energy storage for the electricity grid: benefits and market potential assessment guide (SAND2010-0815). A Study for the DOE Energy Storage Systems Program
Sortomme E, El-Sharkawi MA (2012) Optimal scheduling of vehicle-to-grid energy and ancillary services. IEEE Trans on Smart Grid 3(1):351–359. https://doi.org/10.1109/TSG.2011.2164099
Sun J, Li J, Dang S, Tang N, Zhou T, Li J, Wei S, Yang K, Gao F (2015) Research of toxic productions from thermal runaway processes of li-ion battery and materials. Energy Storage Sci Technol 2015(6):609–615
Wang J (2020) Research on the present situation and prospect of lithium battery energy storage. Electron Test 2020(6):118–119 and 108. https://doi.org/10.16520/j.cnki.1000-8519.2020.06.048
Wang S, Lai X, Cheng S (2013) An analysis of prospects for application of large-scale energy storage technology in power systems. Autom Electr Power Syst 2013(1):3–8 and 30. https://doi.org/10.7500/AEPS201209150
Xi J (2022) Hold high the great banner of socialism with Chinese characteristics and strive in unity to build a modern socialist Country in all respects. People's Daily, p 01
Xinhua News Agency (2020) Xi Jinping's speech at the general debate of the 75th session of the United Nations General Assembly. Retrieved March 15, 2024, from http://www.xinhuanet.com/politics/leaders/2020-09/22/c_1126527652.htm
Xinhua News Agency (2021) The outline of the 14th five-year plan for economic and social development and long-range objectives through the year 2035 of the People's Republic of China. Retrieved March 15, 2024, from https://www.gov.cn/xinwen/2021-03/13/content_5592681.htm
Xu F, Chen L, Jin H, Liu Z (2013) Modeling and application analysis of optimal joint operation of pumped-storage power station and wind power. Autom Electr Power Syst 2013(1):149–154. https://doi.org/10.7500/AEPS201209256
Xue Y, Luo Y, Li B, Luo J, Dong Z, Ledwich G (2007) A review of interruptible load participating in system reserve. Autom Electr Power Syst 10:1–6. https://doi.org/10.3321/j.issn:1000-1026.2007.10.001
Ye Z, Huang S, Wang Y (2020) Research on electricity price mechanism of pumped-storage power station under the background of electricity market reform. Price Theory Pract 2020(11):26–29 and 40
Zhang W, Qiu M, Lai X (2008) Application of energy storage technologies in power grids. Power System Technology 2008(7):1–9
Zhang W, Liu Z, Wang M, Yang X (2009) Research status and development trend of smart grid. Power Syst Technol 2009(13):1–11
Zhang F, Liu C, Jiang J, Yang L, Jiao B, Xu Z, Feng J (2018) Study on pricing mechanism of pumped hydro energy storage (PHES) Under China's electricity tariff reform. Water Power 2018(4):100–104. https://doi.org/10.3969/j.issn.0559-9342.2018.04.024
Zhao X, Liu X, Liu P, Feng T (2011) The mechanism and policy on the electricity price of renewable energy in China. Renew Sustain Energy Rev 15(9):4302–4309. https://doi.org/10.1016/j.rser.2011.07.120

Zhao W, Wang W, Gao D (2020) Research on the business model of energy storage systems in the energy internet. Green Environ Prot Build Mater 2020(8):22–23
Zhou Z, Levin T, Conzelmann G (2016) Survey of U.S. ancillary services markets (ANL/ESD-16/1). Argonne National Laboratory. https://doi.org/10.2172/1236451
Zhu X (2018) Research and application of home appliance load aggregation control strategy based on cyber-physical integration. Master's Dissertation, North China Electric Power University

Uncited References

Chen Y, Chen W (2006) Host Nations' governing system of M & A by Foreign Capital & Home Nations' legal countermeasures. Wuhan Univ J (PhilosSoc Sci) 59(6):852–856. https://doi.org/10.3969/j.issn.1672-7320.2006.06.022
Deng H, Farah PD (2020) China's energy policies and strategies for climate change and energy security. Soc Sci Electron Publishing 13(2):141–156. https://doi.org/10.1093/jwelb/jwaa018
Xinhua News Agency (2020) Statement by H.E. Xi Jinping President of the People's Republic of China at the General Debate of the 75th Session of the United Nations General Assembly. Retrieved January 5, 2024, from http://www.cppcc.gov.cn/zxww/2020/09/23/ARTI1600819264410115.shtml
Xinhua News Agency (2021) Xi Jinping Presides Over the Ninth Meeting of the Central Financial and Economic Affairs Commission. Retrieved January 5, 2024, from https://www.gov.cn/xinwen/2021-03/15/content_5593154.htm

FSC
www.fsc.org
MIX
Papier | Fördert gute Waldnutzung
FSC® C083411

Kolibri 360 GmbH
Ferdinand-Jühlke-Straße 7
99095 Erfurt, Deutschland
produktsicherheit@kolibri360.de